STUDIES IN EVANGELICAL HISTORY

Reinventing English Evangelicalism, 1966-2001

A Theological and Sociological Study

STUDIES IN EVANGELICAL HISTORY AND THOUGHT

STUDIES IN EVANGELICAL HISTORY AND THOUGHT

Reinventing English Evangelicalism, 1966-2001

A Theological and Sociological Study

Rob Warner

Foreword by David Bebbington

MILTON KEYNES · COLORADO SPRINGS · HYDERABAD

Copyright © Rob Warner 2007

First published 2007 by Paternoster

Paternoster is an imprint of Authentic Media
9 Holdom Avenue, Bletchley, Milton Keynes, Bucks, MK1 1QR
1820 Jet Stream Drive, Colorado Springs, CO 80921, USA
OM Authentic Media, Medchal Road, Jeedimetla Village,
Secunderabad 500 055, A.P., India
www.authenticmedia.co.uk
Authentic Media is a division of IBS-STL UK, a company limited by guarantee
(registered charity no. 270162)

13 12 11 10 09 08 07 7 6 5 4 3 2 1

British Library Cataloguing in Publication Data
A catalogue record for this book is available from the British Library

ISBN 978–1–84227–570–2

Typeset by R.E. Warner
Printed and bound in Great Britain
for Paternoster
by Nottingham Alpha Graphics

Studies in Evangelical History and Thought

Series Preface

The Evangelical movement has been marked by its union of four emphases: on the Bible, on the cross of Christ, on conversion as the entry to the Christian life and on the responsibility of the believer to be active. The present series is designed to publish scholarly studies of any aspect of this movement in Britain or overseas. Its volumes include social analysis as well as exploration of Evangelical ideas. The books in the series consider aspects of the movement shaped by the Evangelical Revival of the eighteenth century, when the impetus to mission began to turn the popular Protestantism of the British Isles and North America into a global phenomenon. The series aims to reap some of the rich harvest of academic research about those who, over the centuries, have believed that they had a gospel to tell to the nations.

Series Editors

For Claire, James and Tom

Contents

Chapter 11

List of Tables

FOREWORD

And what makes us thankful it is for to know
The Saints do love oneness and God loves it so.
These artless lines are taken from a collection of hymns used by an unusual Evangelical congregation meeting at Loxwood in Sussex in the nineteenth and twentieth centuries. Belonging to the tiny body officially called the Society of Dependants but popularly known as the Cokelers, the congregation consisted largely of agricultural labourers. They composed their hymns themselves, passing the words down the generations in manuscript form, and so expressed some of their deepest convictions in song. Among their strongest distinctive beliefs was that the oneness celebrated in this hymn is good and that its opposite, 'twoness', is bad. Twoness was any preference for some particular person over the whole community. It expressed itself in courtship and marriage, which the community therefore disapproved. For that reason the denomination soon dwindled and is now extinct. Notwithstanding the dire consequences of their encouragement of celibacy, the Cokelers insisted on twoness being the worse choice:

No twoness we among them see
But all in one they will agree.[1]

This Evangelical group saw a stark contrast between singleness and duality. The same antithesis, Rob Warner explains in this book, is the key to understanding the trajectory of recent Evangelicalism in Britain.

Taking the period 1966 to 2001 for investigation, the author portrays a unitary movement that gradually polarised. At the beginning, though diverse, Evangelicalism was self-consciously a single coalition, but two contrasting tendencies soon began to gather force. One, described here as 'entrepreneurial' and drawing largely on a charismatic constituency, placed particular emphasis on the conversionist and activist traits so fundamental to Evangelical identity. The other was more theologically minded, largely Calvinist and stressed the biblicist and crucicentric dimensions of Evangelicalism. The first tended to adopt populist and even anti-intellectual stances that the second group deplored. Because Rob Warner was a participant observer in many of the developments on the entrepreneurial side,

---

[1] Peter Jerrome, *John Sirgood's Way: The story of the Loxwood Dependants* (Petworth, West Sussex: Window Press, 1998), p. 228.

he possesses special insight into its world. Led by Clive Calver, general secretary of the Evangelical Alliance in the 1980s and early 1990s, the entrepreneurs built up the Alliance and the associated Spring Harvest conferences with energy and flair - what the author calls 'hyper-Calverism'. Although the Alpha evangelistic programme sustained much of the same approach into the twenty-first century, the project began to run out of steam in the mid-1990s. Christian periodicals were losing sales drastically and the foundation of personal spirituality in the devotional quiet time was falling into neglect. Members of the more theologically orientated side took up some of the running, adapting Alpha to create their own Christianity Explored programme of evangelism in 2001. By then the divergence was well established.

This process of polarisation, which has a strong bearing on the future prospects of Christianity in Britain and in other parts of the world, is illuminated in this book as never before. It includes lively commentary, carefully garnered statistics and thorough analysis of statements of faith. The whole study is placed in the context of the relevant sociological literature. Rob Warner reveals how a sense of oneness turned into twoness. The Cokelers would not have been pleased.

David Bebbington
University of Stirling

Acknowledgements

My warm appreciation is expressed to my supervisor, Professor Andrew Walker. His synthesis of sociological and theological appraisal of the British house church networks was an inspiring model for this study of broader trends in contemporary evangelicalism. My thanks also go to the postgraduate seminar in Theology, Religion and Culture at King's College, London, where the discussion and debate were rewardingly exploratory and rigorous. Various papers related to the themes of this book were given at King's College, London, to postgraduate seminars at the universities of Durham, Lancaster, York St John and the University of Wales, Lampeter, and to the Study Group on the Sociology of Religion of the British Sociological Association. I am indebted to the many constructive comments which have refined my thinking. I am grateful to Professor Martyn Percy and Dr Nigel Wright for their instructive critiques. I am also grateful to Professor David Bebbington and Professor Linda Woodhead, who each took the trouble to encourage me to research, publish and supervise in this field. My senior colleagues at Lampeter also deserve thanks, particularly Frances, Tom, Nigel and D.P. for promoting a highly congenial department of Theology and Religious Studies, in which the research culture is exemplary.

My thanks are also due to those who made themselves available for interview, who willingly opened their organisational archives for research, and who supplied statistical data that proved invaluable in reconstructing the real stories of contemporary evangelicalism, beyond the hype of entrepreneurialism and the dogma of secularism. In the secular university in recent years, the sociology of Christianity in general and evangelical and charismatic studies in particular have received less attention than they deserve. In a period of sustained church decline and yet determined resilience, there is much that can be the subject of rewarding study, both for the Academy and the Church.

Because this study focuses upon the development of trans-denominational evangelical identities, it does not explore in detail the current ferment of rival understandings of evangelicalism within specific denominations. In May 2007, the intensifying rivalry among Anglicans made headlines in both the national and religious press, with reports of mass resignations from the staff of a theological college as the new principal was claimed to be moving the institution determinedly to the Right. This study provides insight into these traumas from the wider context, in which progressive evangelicals committed to a generous orthodoxy are discovering increasing prospects of mutual exclusivity with the expansive certainties and oppositional mindset of calvinistic-exclusivism. This study argues that, for the Right, moderate and progressive evangelicals have become the 'enemy within' who must be purged. As for the Left, they may tire of being tarnished with the excesses of extremism, and abandon the name of 'evangelical', perhaps with some relief. Conversely, if the Left choose to retain identification and continuity with the longstanding, broad and self-critical evangelical tradition, they will surely need to disown the extremism of the Right, who have become Evangelicalism's Militant Tendency, the sectarians whom the Labour Party needed to marginalise before public credibility could be restored. Calvinistic-exclusivism is a mutation of the authentic, broad and self-critical tradition of evangelicalism, and is more accurately designated, by its exponents and critics alike, as nothing less than unreconstructed fundamentalism. Further research is required, both on the bifurcation of the evangelical tradition, particularly within Anglicanism, and upon the convictions, power-base and durability of British neo-fundamentalism.

My thanks above all go to my dear wife, Claire, my inspiration and my sustainer.

Rob Warner
University of Wales, Lampeter
June 2007

Abbreviations

ACE	Alliance of Confessing Evangelicals
ACUTE	The Alliance Commission on Unity and Truth among Evangelicals
BEC	British Evangelical Council
BUGB	Baptist Union of Great Britain
CARE	Christian Action Research and Education
CICCU	Cambridge Inter Collegiate Christian Union
EA. EAUK	Evangelical Alliance of the United Kingdom
EE	Evangelism Explosion
EEA	European Evangelical Alliance
EMA	Evangelical Missionary Alliance (from 1 January 2000 known as Global Connections)
EMW	Evangelical Movement of Wales
FIEC	Fellowship of Independent Evangelical Churches
GNDYS	Good News Down Your Street
HTB	Holy Trinity Brompton, the church where *Alpha* began
IVF	Inter Varsity Fellowship
IVCF	Inter Varsity Christian Fellowship (USA)
IVP	Inter Varsity Press
JL	Just Looking
NAE	National Association of Evangelicals (USA)
NEAC	National Evangelical Anglican Congress
NFI	New Frontiers International
PP	Person to Person
SH	Spring Harvest
SU	Scripture Union
SUIC	Scripture Union International Council
UCCF	Universities and Colleges Christian Fellowship (previously IVF)
WEF	World Evangelical Fellowship
YFC	Youth for Christ
YWAM	Youth with a Mission

INTRODUCTION

A Resurgent, Contested Tradition

A Tradition in Self-perceived Resurgence

In the UK, for the first time in 1986, over 50% of Anglican ordinands in residential colleges were identified as evangelical.[1] By 1989, Spring Harvest, the leading annual gathering of evangelicals, was claiming an attendance of 80,000 each year. By the mid nineties TEAR Fund,[2] which originated within EAUK in the late 1960s as *The Evangelical Alliance Relief Fund*, had grown to become the twenty-fifth largest British charity. The global context indicates a burgeoning movement to a much greater degree. In South America, for example, there were 50,000 evangelicals in 1900, but 130,000,000 by the mid 1990s when the global total was estimated at 300,000,000.[3]

In the United States, 1976, the year of Jimmy Carter's "born again" Presidential election, was designated by *Newsweek* "The American Year of the Evangelical". A Gallup poll at that time revealed that the percentage of Americans willing to describe themselves as *born again* was 34%, rising by 1984 to 40%.[4] The proportion also willing to accept a literal view of the Bible and engage in personal evangelism was significantly lower but still substantial: 18% in 1976 and 22% in 1984. By the turn of the millennium, a billion dollars was spent annually on evangelical publications in the United States. As Kent Hughes observed, unconsciously echoing Weber's pioneering study of American Protestant sects:

> Being 'born again' can be profitable. Jesus saves, but Jesus also sells. Evangelicalism is big business.[5]

With one in five Americans a conservative evangelical, two in five professing to be born again, and a thriving commercial sub-culture, American evangelicals warrant the growing number of sociological and historical studies.[6] However,

---

[1] Saward, 1987: 34; Bebbington, 1989: 270, citing *Baptist Times*, 31 December 1989: 7.
[2] Organizational abbreviations are defined in the appended list.
[3] Barratt, George and Johnson, 1982, 2001.
[4] Gallup, 1996: 38.
[5] Hughes, 1995: 16; Weber, 1948: 302-322.
[6] Kelley, 1972; Hunter 1983, 1987; Marsden, 1980, 1984, 1987, 1990, 1991; Wuthnow, 1988; Ammerman, 1990; Noll, Bebbington and Rawlyk, 1994; Noll, 1994, 2000, 2004; Smith 1998, 2000; Roof, 1999; Bramadat, 2000; Tamney, 2002; Penning and Smidt, 2002.

although evangelicals inhabit a substantial American sub-culture numerically and economically, their influence upon the wider culture, particularly in the arts and non-specialist media, appears to be minimal. This begs the question whether evangelicalism may have become a quasi-established, structurally differentiated religion, baptizing materialism and the American Way. It also raises questions about primary and secondary allegiances, or "professed" and "operative religion" in Herberg's categories.[7] Notwithstanding the high proportion of Americans professing evangelical beliefs, these may not be the primary or dominant convictions in the personal lives and socio-political convictions of American churchgoers.

Senior evangelical commentators have been queuing up to announce an evangelical resurgence, not only claiming that evangelicalism stands alongside Roman Catholicism and Islam as a global faith[8] but even claiming a British evangelical renaissance.[9] David Bebbington ended his magisterial study of two hundred of fifty years of British Evangelicals with the claim:

> Moulded and remoulded by its environment, Evangelical religion has been a vital force in modern Britain.[10]

To this he added a confident aspiration -

> ...growth was intended and expected. The movement was likely to occupy a more salient position within British Christianity in the twenty-first century than in the twentieth.[11]

Alister McGrath, when Principal of Wycliffe Hall, expressed a more moderated optimism:

> The Christian vision of the future now seems increasingly to belong to evangelicalism, which is coming more and more to constitute the mainstream of American Protestant Christianity... The future seems to beckon to evangelicalism, inviting it to advance and mature still further.[12]

Derek Tidball, the sociologist-theologian Principal of the London School of Theology (known in the twentieth century as London Bible College), identified two measures of the tradition's late twentieth century perceived success - the number of evangelicals and their socio-political influence:

---

[7] Herberg (1955) argued that, irrespective of religious profession as Protestant, Catholic or Jew, the dominant operative religion was the "American Way of Life". Marsden (2001: 225) summarized the values of this operative religion as democracy, individualism, optimism, idealism, humanitarianism, nationalism and tolerance of other Americans.

[8] Lewis, 2004.

[9] Not so Martin, 2005.

[10] Bebbington, 1989: 276.

[11] Bebbington, 1989: 270.

[12] McGrath, 1993: 1-2.

The Evangelical Alliance has become a movement to be reckoned with. Justifiably claiming to represent one million evangelicals, it has adopted a pro-active stance and is now widely consulted by the Government and even more widely by the media in a way previously unknown, at least in its recent history. Intervention has borne fruit in the area of Sunday trading, commercial advertising, religious TV, issues of religious liberty and a host of others.[13]

Clive Calver, General Director of the Evangelical Alliance through the period of dramatic growth we examine in chapter two and co-founder of Spring Harvest, was characteristically assertive:

...evangelicalism which was threatened with extinction just decades ago, but is now marked by evangelistic success and a growing intellectual presence.[14]

This pervasive, newly assertive evangelical optimism was echoed in the early 1990s by a Sunday Times journalist who claimed, "The future belongs to them." [15] Writing in 1944, Max Warren, General Secretary of the Church Missionary Society 1942-1963, described an entirely different climate for his generation of evangelicals. His words indicate a subsequent and monumental turnaround in evangelical fortunes:

...all too commonly today, an Evangelical in the Church of England is a person labouring under a sense of frustration and discouragement often so deep as to engender...an inferiority complex.[16]

In the new millennium, evangelical claims of a growing impact in politics, media and society look more like pious optimism than demonstrable and lasting achievements. To revisit some putative successes cited by Tidball: residual restrictions on Sunday trading have come under increasingly assertive commercial pressure; British laws reflecting traditional Christian ethics were rescinded in equalising the age of consent for homosexuals and legalising therapeutic cloning; religious coverage in the secular media appears increasingly marginal. Far from shaping society at the dawn of the twenty-first century, British evangelicals, in common with all Christians, increasingly need to fight a rearguard action to preserve some semblance of their own moral legitimacy. The emergent moral framework within a post-Christian and emphatically pluralistic context entails an instinctive sense of *moral superiority* to the conventional morality of the church, which appears repressive and authoritarian, anti-women and anti-gay.[17] Little more than a decade

---

[13] Tidball, 1994: 8. This new assertiveness from evangelicals reflects a general and global trend in which religions reject the model of rigorous privatization and reassert their claim to a legitimate place in the public sphere (Casanova, 1994; see also Martin, 2005).

[14] Calver and Warner, 1996: 135.

[15] Calver and Warner, 1996: 135.

[16] Warren, 1944: 7.

[17] Harries, 2002. See also Pullman's trilogy, *His Dark Materials*, (1995, 1997, 2000),

after Tidball made his claims, which at the time reflected the common currency among evangelicals of a self-perceived resurgence, his optimistic description of evangelical impact upon politics, media and society looks increasingly unfounded.

Nor can the unalloyed enthusiasm of many evangelical commentators evade the underlying religious trends in Britain. While there has been an undoubted - but difficult to quantify - upsurge of interest in new spiritualities,[18] affiliation to traditional religious groupings continues to nose-dive. In December 2000, the National Centre for Social Research revealed that 59% of those aged 25-34 do not follow any religion. Of those aged 18-24 the figure rose to 66%.[19] We shall explore trends in church attendance later, but the massive levels of indifference to organised religion among young adults suggests that evangelicals may have enjoyed a brief flurry of prominence in the residual remains of the churches in England before the entire edifice of organised and institutional Christianity sinks into an accelerating or even terminal decline. A similar perspective was voiced in the American context by Donald Bloesch, in blunt riposte to the characteristic triumphalism of those who count the rising tide of the born again and postulate an inevitable spiritual and moral transformation:

> The striking resurgence of evangelicalism in America may be an Indian summer before the total collapse of organized religion in this country.[20]

A Contested Tradition[21]

The last two decades of the twentieth century saw a sustained, even alarmist critique of the state of American evangelicalism from within. In some ways this is a sign of health, since religious movements that fail to be self-critical are likely to have become complacent, superficial and conformist, or entrenched in sterile dogmatism. But the level of internal critique is acute. The examination in this book of English evangelicalism in this period, while recognising many differences in cultural context, needs to take full account of such analyses, which, at the very least, are symptomatic of a changing evangelical climate. In an era when English evangelicals became more self-confident, and when numerical growth and strength were often paraded, English evangelicalism may have been drinking heartily and uncritically

---

conceived as a Blakean antidote to *Narnia* for a post-Christian era.
[18] Bruce argues for the failure of the new age to disrupt the secularization paradigm (2002:75-105); Heelas and Seel (in Davie, Heelas and Woodhead 2003: 229-247) argue for an ageing new age movement, with similar implications. Heelas and Woodhead (2005) fail to make the case for a "spiritual revolution" since their empirical data more plausibly indicates that participation in alternative spiritualities is indicative merely of a spiritual residue (contra Croft, Frost et al, 2005).
[19] *Baptist Times*, 7 December, 2000.
[20] Bloesch, 1984: 91.
[21] The phrase "essentially contested" was first used of the evangelical tradition by William Abraham, 1984: 10.

from the operative religion of success in the American way. This could be all the more precarious at a time when leading north American evangelical theologians, conservative and progressive, have argued that their movement is suffering from a profound and potentially self-destructive cultural captivity - anti-intellectual, theologically anaemic, consumerist, hyper-individualist and deluded by its own rhetoric of success.

Mark Noll produced a devastatingly damning catalogue of the blight of anti-intellectualism in the history of fundamentalism, which he condemns as an "intellectual disaster":[22]

...the major indictment of the fundamentalist movement...was its intellectual sterility.[23]

He laid a similarly trenchant charge against the subsequent development of the broader evangelical community:

The scandal of the evangelical mind is that there is not much of an evangelical mind.[24]

A movement that believes it is guarding the gospel by preserving its own integrity is bound to engage in polemical self-definition. The aim will often be not merely to define the characteristic theological convictions, but also to safeguard evangelical "soundness" against the latest enemy, sometimes external, as has tended to happen with the formulation of quasi-creedal statements, but also, and perhaps increasingly often, against "the enemy within". David Wells has charged that evangelicalism has become "descriptively anaemic". In a provocatively non-irenic metaphor, Wells likens contemporary sub-categories within evangelicalism to parasites that finally destroy their unsuspecting victim.

To say that someone is an evangelical says little about what they are likely to believe (although it says more if they are older and less if they are younger). And so the term is forced to compensate for its theological weakness by borrowing meaning from adjectives the very presence of which signals the fragmentation and disintegration of the movement. What is now primary is not what is evangelical, but what is adjectivally distinctive, whether Catholic, liberationist, feminist, ecumenist, young, orthodox, radical, liberal, or charismatic. It is, I think, the dark prelude to death, when parasites have finally succeeded in bringing down their host.[25]

We note that "reformed", "calvinistic", "conservative" and "inerrantist" are not included among the adjectival sub-groups Wells sought to marginalise. While his analysis acknowledged an increasing diversification within the evangelical coalition, his approach is unambiguously partisan.

R. Kent Hughes, warmly commended by evangelical gurus Packer and

---

[22] Noll, 1994: Chapter 5 is trenchantly entitled *The Intellectual Disaster of Fundamentalism*.
[23] Noll, 1994: 137.
[24] Noll, 1994: 3.
[25] Wells, 1993: 134.

MacArthur, provides an ostensibly inclusive summary of evangelical convictions that typifies the tendency to insert a polemical and exclusive twist:

> The classical definition of evangelical is: one who believes the Bible is divinely inspired and infallible and who subscribes to doctrinal formulations that teach the depravity of man, the substitutionary death and atonement of Christ, salvation by unmerited grace though personal faith in Christ (not good works), the necessity of a transformed life, the existence of a literal heaven and hell, and the visible, personal return of Jesus Christ to set up his Kingdom of righteousness...[26]

While the use of "infallible" is surprising by a conservative in the American context, where the preferred adjective is usually "inerrant", and the term used to describe human sinfulness is distinctly calvinistic, the most telling phrase is "literal heaven and hell". Like many unreconstructed conservatives, Hughes insists that a literalistic conception of eternal torment is as much a non-negotiable doctrine as salvation by unmerited grace, and thus tacitly acknowledges this former evangelical consensus is now questioned.[27]

D. A. Carson, doyen of the old school conservatives, exemplifies the internal evangelical tension between inclusivity and keeping the traditional boundaries of evangelicalism adequately defined and guarded. When Carson summarises evangelical convictions, he provides a considered and comprehensive summary of the doctrinal emphases found within traditional evangelical creedal statements:

> We insist that salvation is gained exclusively through personal faith in the finished cross-work of Jesus Christ, who is both God and man. His atoning death, planned and brought about by his heavenly Father, expiates our sin, vanquishes Satan, propitiates the Father, and inaugurates the promised kingdom. In the ministry, death, resurrection, and exaltation of Jesus, God himself is supremely revealed, such that rejection of Jesus, or denials of what the Scriptures tell us about Jesus, constitute nothing less than rejection of God himself. In consequence of his triumphant cross work, Christ has bequeathed the Holy Spirit, himself God, as the down-payment of the final inheritance that will come to Christ's people when he himself returns. The saving and transforming power of the Spirit displayed in the lives of Christ's people is the product of divine grace, grace alone - grace that is apprehended by faith alone. The knowledge of God that we enjoy becomes for us an impetus to missionary outreach characterized by urgency and compassion.[28]

Although the style is somewhat strident (*we insist*), over emphatic (*grace, grace alone - grace that is apprehended*) and prolix (passim) the evident intention is to be inclusive and irenic. This irenic approach was short-lived. Carson soon assails those who have transgressed his preferred borders for legitimate evangelical diversity, seeking to expose what he considers the disaster of theological accommodationism:

---

[26] Hughes, 1995: 10.
[27] See Hilborn (2000) for official legitimization of alternative interpretations by EAUK.
[28] Carson, 1996: 445.

> I worry less about the anti-intellectualism of the less educated sections of evangelicalism than I do about the biblical and theological illiteracy, or astonishing intellectual compromise, among its leading intellectuals... In the main, they think like secularists and bless their insights with the odd text or biblical cliché.[29]

Since Carey speaks of pan-Anglican co-operation in mission - "the Catholic, Liberal, Evangelical and Charismatic traditions merge to work together to bring Good News to this land." [30] - Carson concludes that none who have a clear grasp of the doctrinal heritage of evangelicalism can "thoughtfully embrace the Archbishop's enthusiasm. His utterance and declension are sad beyond belief." [31] Since Grenz rejects modern evangelicalism's use of "propositionalism" in interpreting the Bible,[32] Carson's can find no place for Grenz within the fold: "With the best will in the world, I cannot see how Grenz's approach to Scripture can be called 'evangelical' in any useful sense." [33] Since Stott and Pinnock espouse forms of annihilationism, Stott's exegesis of the disputed Scriptures "really will not do" [34] and Pinnock's exegesis "is close to wishful thinking".[35] Carson damns their approach to eternal judgment as "a reflection of this age of pluralism" and unfaithful to "the 'hard' lines of Scripture".[36] As to Pinnock's enquiry into the openness of God, Carson is dismissive, even derisory: "the most consistently inadequate treatment of both Scripture and historical theology dealing with the doctrine of God that I have ever seen..." [37]

In each area of debate, Carson cannot accept legitimate diversity or dialogue within, let alone beyond, evangelicalism. Carson's opponents are effectively set outside the camp by the strident and emotive tone of his rebuttal. Beyond his ostensibly irenic summary of evangelical convictions we find an instinctively separatist and exclusivist dogmatism that, as a logical consequence, requires minimal co-operation and respect for non-evangelicals, a commitment to propositionalist inerrancy,[38] an unyielding emphasis upon eternal torment in hell, and a readiness to un-church, or at least un-evangelical-ise, many senior churchmen and leading theologians from the wider evangelical tradition. Such stridency may be a product of temperament at least as much as theological tradition, but Carson acknowledges a further factor that shapes the tenor of his contribution.

---

[29] Carson, 1996: 483.

[30] English Churchman 7394 (January 20 and 27 1995).

[31] Carson, 1996: 460.

[32] Grenz, 1993: 70.

[33] Carson, 1996: 481.

[34] Carson, 1996: 527.

[35] Carson, 1996: 528.

[36] Carson, 1996: 536.

[37] Carson, 1996: 225. The book Carson condemns was published by IVP (USA) as was his own, reflecting the evangelical pluralism that he resists. IVP (UK) are much more conservative and published Carson's book, but not Pinnock on open theism.

[38] Carson, 1996: 450.

It is reflected in the widely recognized clamour for academic recognition among many of the younger evangelical intellectuals, in their drumming criticism of evangelical "fathers" (like immature adolescents who cannot allow any opinion other than their own to be respected), in their persistent drift from biblical authority, and, increasingly, from other doctrines as well. But most of them still want to call themselves evangelicals: that is their power base, that is their prime readership, and it is that group that funds many of the colleges and seminaries where they teach...the product is less and less "evangelical" in any useful historic or theological sense.[39]

Carson's extended (more than twenty pages) review[40] of Grenz's *Renewing the Centre*[41] is particularly trenchant, reflecting Grenz pre-eminence among postmodern evangelical theologians. Carson charged Grenz with drifting towards liberalism, domesticating the Gospel and needing to "re-think several matters of fundamental importance before he goes any farther down this path". For Carson, an engagement with postmodernity that entails a reappraisal of evangelical givens is necessarily a dilution and a mistake. He appears doubtful whether Grenz's theology still qualifies as an authentically evangelical.

Carson writes out of a sense of urgent apprehension that the conservative evangelicalism he seeks to defend is beginning to face the possibility of being overturned or dissolved by a new generation of progressive evangelical scholarship.[42] The evangelical tradition is in the process of re-inventing itself, as Bebbington demonstrated it has done repeatedly in previous eras,[43] loosing the grip of twentieth century conservative calvinistic hegemony, with its enlightenment epistemology[44] and exclusivist claims to represent the only authentic evangelical tradition.[45] Conservative perturbation mirrors substantive theological questioning among "post conservatives".[46] This term was coined by Roger Olson,[47] who freely

---

[39] Carson, 1996: 453.

[40] Carson's "Domesticating the Gospel" was reprinted, with amendments in Erickson, Helseth and Taylor (2004), a compilation of conservative critiques, mostly polemical, against post-conservatives.

[41] Grenz, 2000.

[42] Hunter (1983, 1987) had drawn a similar conclusion.

[43] Bebbington, 1989.

[44] Barr, 1977; Murphy, 1996; Knight, 1997; Dorrien, 1998.

[45] When discussing Loraine Boettner, Barth described them as neo-Calvinists (Church Dogmatics II/2, 46). Pinnock designates them paleo-Calvinist and speaks of the "scholastic Reformed roots of fundamentalist evangelicalism" that has not moved beyond the Westminster Confession (Pinnock, 2001: 14).

[46] The dominance of American voices in this process of self-criticism is striking. English evangelicals have a much less developed academic framework and vocabulary of self-criticism. Whereas in the States, for example, Mark Noll was appointed in 1998 to the Visiting Chair in Evangelical Theological Studies at Harvard Divinity School, there is no equivalent academic stature in the UK for Evangelical Studies. James Dunn and Tom Wright are prominent instances of a trend whereby scholars associated with the evangelical tradition tend to transition to the theological mainstream, thus reinforcing the suspicions of the evangelical right.

acknowledged many diverse emphases rather than a common agenda in this emergent reconstruction but claimed that such evangelicals are rejoining the academic mainstream as a distinctive tradition, tending to be more at home in the Evangelical Studies Group of the American Academy of Religion than in the American Evangelical Theological Society.

The American Evangelical Theological Society (founded 1949) has an inerrantist basis ("The Bible alone, and the Bible in its entirety, is the Word of God written and is therefore inerrant in the autographs. God is a Trinity, Father, Son, and Holy Spirit, each an uncreated person, one in essence, equal in power and glory." [48]), to which members must re-subscribe annually. This may explain Pinnock's retention of the term "inerrancy", albeit with a "nuanced, flexible definition", having previously demonstrated the lack of any direct biblical basis for such claims,[49] and may also have prompted Vanhoozer to affirm inerrancy and yet state that it is too narrow a concept to express the variety of biblical genres and the complex functions of language.[50] In November 2001, in a session entitled "Defining Evangelicalism's Boundaries" the ETS voted 253 in favour, 66 against, 41 abstentions (360 ballots cast from a potential 1,000) on the motion: "We believe the Bible clearly teaches that God has complete, accurate, and infallible knowledge of all events past, present, and future including all future decisions and actions of free moral agents." Wayne Grudem described it as an overwhelming rejection of open theism and a "gentle nudge" for open theists to change their minds or leave the organization. Clark Pinnock described it as more like a fatwa from the evangelical mullahs. In response, Roger Olson, Jonathan Wilson and Stanley Grenz together drafted "The Word Made Fresh: A Call for a Renewal of the Evangelical Spirit".[51] Signed by over 100 leaders, including William Abraham, Craig Blomberg, William Dyrness, Gordon Fee, Richard Middleton, Nancey Murphy, Robert Webber and Ben Witherington, this statement affirmed broad, historic evangelicalism with its tradition of "genuine diversity and fresh reflection" and "generous orthodoxy", founded upon submission to Christ and "the supreme authority of the canonical Scriptures". It deplored "militant, separatist habits of mind and heart" that cause some to return to "the more onerous attitudes of fundamentalism" and warned against "attempts to propagate rigid definitions of evangelicalism that result in unnecessary alienation and exclusion." Grudem's response was tart, objecting to slippery language and claiming that some signatories want "to ask evangelical institutions to include viewpoints that historically have not been included on their faculty... such as a denial of inerrancy, an advocacy of open theism, a denial of substitutionary atonement, a denial of hell [and] eternal punishment of unbelievers." [52] The battle lines have been drawn, and it

---

[47] Olson, 1995, 2000.

[48] http://www.etsjets.org. Accessed 5 August 2005.

[49] Pinnock, 1985: 78, 60.

[50] www.christianitytoday.com/ct/9t2/9t2038.html. Accessed 5 May 2003. *Christianity Today,* 8 February, 1999.

[51] Olson, Wilson and Grenz, 2000.

[52] Quoted in *Christianity Today,* June 10, 2002.www.christianitytoday.com/ct/2002/007/10.

is difficult to see how the post-conservatives can long stay in coalition with the uncompromising exclusivity Grudem represents. It remains to be seen whether the two factions will both lay claim to the term "evangelical": the Right may return to the term "fundamentalist" or clarify their identity as "Reformed and conservative evangelicals"; the Left may designate themselves as post-conservative evangelicals or ultimately conclude that it is not worth attempting to retain a descriptive term as imprecise and potentially pejorative as "evangelical". While the post-conservative theological agenda is much more fully developed in the States than in the UK, conventional American evangelicals are significantly to the right of the British mainstream, where inerrancy has never been avowed by the pan-evangelical bases of faith of EAUK and IVF/UCCF, and the legitimacy of non-literal interpretations of hell was given turn of the century official sanction by the Council of the Evangelical Alliance.[53] Following the so-called "culture war" between the religious right and the urban and secularized liberal elite, a further culture war *within* American evangelicalism seems almost inevitable.[54]

Building upon Ramm's pioneering departure from residual fundamentalism and Lindbeck's post-liberal critique of pre-modern cognitive-propositional and modern experiential-expressive theological methodologies, Grenz and Vanhoozer reject epistemological foundationalism, an evidentialist apologetic and propositionalism defined not as rejecting the possibility but rather the priority of propositional revelation with the attendant tendency to reduce narrative and other genres to an alleged propositional intent.[55] Webber goes further and rejects *sola Scriptura* and argues for the recovery of continuity with the patristic tradition, particularly *Christus Victor* and the *regula fidei*.[56]

Murphy modifies Lindbeck's approach, arguing that conservatives and liberals represent the bifurcated options of enlightenment foundationalism, with reductionist consequences in both camps.[57] She traces two enlightenment trajectories: Reid's common sense realism leads to Princeton and thence fundamentalism, while Kant leads to Schleiermacher and so to liberalism. Liberals adopted an experiential

---

18.html. Accessed 5 May 2003.

[53] Hilborn, 2000.

[54] Neuhaus, 1986; Wuthnow, 1988; Hunter, 1991.

[55] Ramm, 1983; Lindbeck, 1984; Grenz, 1993, 2000; Vanhoozer, 1998, 2002.

[56] Webber, 1999, 2002. See also Williams, 1999: 229-234. In calling for a catholic evangelicalism engaged in critical orthodoxy, Williams and Webber echo Florovsky: "The Church is apostolic indeed, but the Church is also patristic." (Florovsky, 1972:107). Signs of profound transition are found in the facts that Webber taught at Wheaton, long considered a centre of conventional conservatism and his father-in-law is Harold Lindsell, author of *The Battle for the Bible* (1976) and a leading influence in the attempt to return evangelicalism to a fundamentalist orientation. The late 1970s and early 1980s saw a "Canterbury Trail" from Wheaton into Episcopalianism as part of this quest for evangelical catholicity (Webber, 1985). In 1987, similar concerns resulted in 200 North American evangelicals being admitted into the Antiochian Orthodox (Gillquist, 1992).

[57] Murphy, 1996.

foundationalism, considered language to be subjective-expressivist, conceived theology and science as distinct categories of knowledge and saw divine action as immanentist. Conservatives held to scriptural foundationalism, considered language to be propositionalist, conceived theology and science as a single category of knowledge in which the Bible held authority over Darwinian theory, and saw divine action as interventionist. Murphy argues that post-enlightenment approaches to epistemology, language and metaphysics break the foundationalist bipolarity, facilitating a new theological spectrum, post-liberal and post-conservative.[58]

Middleton and Walsh, welcome the opportunities of postmodernity, (as do Grenz, Murphy, Vanhoozer and Webber) albeit not uncritically, and seek to reconstruct evangelical theology in the emergent cultural context.[59] In particular, Middleton and Walsh argue that the Bible delivers a non-totalising and counter-ideological meta-narrative that is sensitive to suffering, promises liberation for the oppressed and intends to align the reader with God's purposes of *shalom*, compassion and justice. This defence of the biblical meta-narrative as non-totalising does not, of course, exonerate the Church from the charge of promoting a plethora of totalising meta-narratives, from Constantinianism and Western imperialism to the marginalisation of women and non-whites. For Middleton and Walsh, truth and ethics are "stranger than they used to be", understood at least in part as social constructs shaped by "will to power". Implicitly, therefore, they recognise the need for aspects of the evangelical tradition, like any other religious tradition, to be expunged as totalising.

Vanhoozer critiques conventional evangelical theology as a stepchild of the enlightenment. He calls for a baptism of the imagination and proposes a "canonical-linguistic" approach to theology, grounded in the canon rather than the interpreting community, as an evangelical equivalent (inerrantist in Vanhoozer's case, but not necessarily so from the logic of his argument) to Lindbeck's post-liberal "cultural-linguistic" model.[60]

---

[58] Murphy rejects Olson's epithet, "post-conservative", arguing that "conservatism (favouring the past in a contest between traditional formulations and contemporary relevance) will continue to characterize one end of the spectrum" (1996: 90). She proposes instead "postmodern evangelicals" (1996: 90), but this carries its own ambiguities. For Murphy, the French postmodern tradition shares "too many assumptions with their modern predecessors to count as truly postmodern" (1996: 87, see also Murphy in Hauerwas et al, 1994). She argues that a more decisive break with the enlightenment is found in Anglo-American postmodernity - notably Quine and MacIntyre (epistemology), Wittgentstein and Austin, Rorty and Fish (language), R.W. Sellars (physical realism).

[59] Walsh and Middleton, 1984; Middleton and Walsh, 1995.

[60] While both Frei (1980) and Lindbeck (1984) argued that traditional conservatism as well as the dominant academic tradition of liberalism had eclipsed the biblical narrative, Frei called for a "generous orthodoxy" in his response to a Carl F. Henry lecture at Yale in 1985: "…split as we are, not so much into denominations as into schools of thought,…we need a kind of generous orthodoxy which would have in it an element of liberalism – a voice like the *Christian Century* – and an element of evangelicalism – the voice of *Christianity Today*." (Frei, 1993: 208). In similarly irenic fashion, Lindbeck suggested at the 1995 Wheaton Theology conference for evangelicals and postliberals that "if the sort of research program

Pinnock rejects classical theism as a pre-Reformation platonic cultural construct, assimilated uncritically by the Reformers and subsequently by evangelicals.[61] In attempting to systematise a theology of the openness of God and the hope of universal salvation, in express opposition to what he terms "paleo-Calvinism", he particularly seeks to refute the concepts of divine impassibility and divine existence outside time (which was conventionally deployed by Arminians as the basis for retaining divine foreknowledge while rejecting calvinistic predestination).

With a briskness liable to produce apoplexy among staunch conservatives, Volf sweeps aside the gender subordination within certain biblical texts as needing no further investigation because "culturally conditioned" and interprets them "within the framework of an egalitarian understanding of the Trinitarian relations and from the perspective of the egalitarian thrust of such central biblical assertions as the one found in Galatians 3:28".[62] He argues that the Scriptures "come to us in the form of plural traditions",[63] that this inherent plurality precludes a single systematic construct, and that Christian commitments are incomplete without being applied to social realities.[64] Further, the Christian calling is not merely to tell but to "do" truth,[65] and authentic Christian commitment to Christ who is the truth cannot be legitimately translated "into the claim that we possess the absolute truth".[66] Cognizant of but not constrained by Nietzsche's and Foucault's critiques of the often unconscious connections between truth claims and power assertions, Volf emphasises the intrinsic provisionality of truth claims and the importance of crucicentric and trinitarian political theology, over against the conventional, instinctive patriotism of Constantinianism. He is a natural heir of the European broad Evangelical tradition, a successor to Barth and Moltmann, remote from both North American fundamentalism and transatlantic conservative evangelicalism.

A leading British exemplar of these transatlantic debates concerning evangelical identity and progressive reconstructions is N.T. Wright. While describing himself as a "fellow evangelical",[67] Wright argues that evangelical theology often functions

---

represented by postliberalism has a real future as a communal enterprise of the church, it's more likely to be carried on by evangelicals than anyone else." (Phillips and Ockholm, 1996: 253). Hunsinger (Phillips and Ockholm 1996), building on Frei, argued that Henry's valuation of the Bible in terms of cognitive propositionalism, facticity and authorship is contingent upon rationalistic modernity's conception of objective, value-neutral and public truth. Hunsinger observed that not all evangelicals hold to a rigidly enlightenment-dependent construct of biblical authority and argued plausibly that such theologians, rather than those in the tradition of Henry are likely to develop evangelical expressions of narrative theology.

[61] Pinnock et al, 1994; Pinnock, 2001.

[62] Volf, 1996: 183.

[63] Volf, 1996: 183.

[64] Volf, 1996: 209.

[65] Volf, 1996: 261.

[66] Volf, 1996: 271.

[67] The phrase is used with telling force in Wright's *The Shape of Justification* (2001), a riposte to Australian Bishop Paul Barnett's *Tom Wright and the New Perspective* (2000) a toned down version of the earlier *Why Wright is Wrong*. (For a robust Reformed evangelical

within an "enlightenment straightjacket", instinctively loyal to traditional interpretation over against the meanings critical realism elicits from the Bible. Wright readily embraces critical historiography, rejecting the hyper-subjectivism of full-blooded postmodern interpretations that find meaning solely in the reader, without reference to authorial intent or historical context.[68] While opposing the reductionism of the *Jesus Seminar*, Wright advocates a variant of the new perspective on Paul, redefining righteousness primarily in relational rather than forensic categories and emphasising the corporate dimension of soteriology. For Wright, as for Dunn and Sanders,[69] Luther's individualistic crisis, however legitimate an extrapolation from Romans, has made individual salvation, rather than the inclusion by grace of outsiders, Jew and Gentile alike, a fundamentally distorting hermeneutic in Western Protestant readings of Romans. Justification by faith, in the Pauline context, is understood to be more directly concerned with inclusive ecclesiology than individualistic soteriology with a forensic orientation. Like Dunn, Wright does not preclude substitutionary and sacrificial dimensions from models of the atonement but, contrary to Calvin and his successors, they are no longer centre stage. Furthermore, Wright argues for an openness in understanding biblical authority, calling the church, as do Middleton and Walsh, not to a closed revelatory system but to faithful improvisation in the light of the biblical meta-narrative. While Crossan rejected Wright's interpretation as "elegant fundamentalism",[70] the conservative right, enlightenment and tradition-bound, view his analysis not as maverick orthodoxy but rather as neo-liberalism.[71]

Although these emergent theologies by no means cohere into a single postmodern evangelical construct, and indeed polyvalence may be considered intrinsic to any postmodern theology, it is not difficult to understand the perturbations of the Right. If traditional evangelical theology has unconsciously assimilated a neo-platonic theism, a Reformation forenso-centric soteriology, a Pietist individualism, an enlightenment epistemology and a pre-critical tendency to literalism, then

---

retort to Wright, see Hill, 2001, and for more measured debate Newman, 1999.) While accepting that the New Perspective has made a constructive contribution, Barnett critiques Wright's methodology. (For Wright, establishing a cultural context for Paul's thinking in second Temple Judaism and examining justification/righteousness in the word-group's cultural context are prerequisite to serious historical lexicography.) Further, Barnett argues that Wright drives a wedge between justification and the Gospel, which for Barnett is central to and almost synonymous with the Gospel. Barnett therefore concludes that the New Perspective denies assurance of salvation and is pastorally naïve, failing to grasp the universal allure of salvation by law and works. Wright's response is courteous but emphatic. In particular, he argues that when Paul speaks of "the gospel", he means not justification by faith, narrowly, but "the announcement that the crucified and risen Jesus is Lord." Therefore, "one is not justified by believing in justification by faith...but by believing in Jesus."

[68] Wright, 1992, 1996, 2003.

[69] Sanders 1977; Dunn, 1983, 1988a, 1998b, 1993, 1998; Wright 1991, 1996, 2002.

[70] Crossan's critique of Wright is sustained and vigorous (1998: *passim*).

[71] Barnett, 2000.

evangelicalism is a complex construct of historical theology, formulated through an often unperceived interaction with its cultural setting, rather than, in Packer's confident and unreflexive formulation, unadulterated, timeless and universally applicable distillation of the Gospel of Christ.

> You cannot add to evangelical theology without subtracting from it. By augmenting it, you cannot enrich it; you can only impoverish it…The principle applies at point after point. What is more than evangelical is less than evangelical. Evangelical theology, by its very nature, cannot be supplemented; it can only be denied.[72]

Should these post-Reformation, post-enlightenment and post-critical critiques prove persuasive, particularly in a period of rapid cultural metamorphosis, evangelicalism's most cherished assumptions become subject to rigorous deconstruction in the light of biblical exegesis (notably Dunn and Wright), hermeneutics (notably Thiselton) and postmodern reconfiguration (notably Grenz, Murphy, Volf) and recovery of the broad tradition of Trinitarian orthodoxy (notably Webber and Williams). None of these objections to evangelical theology are unfamiliar in the academy, but what is newly significant is a self-critique by those who endeavour to reconceptualise rather than repudiate the evangelical tradition. Wright exemplifies this new creativity and liberty in deconstructing the evangelical tradition:

> …my bottom line has always been, and remains, not a theory, not a tradition, not pressure from self-appointed guardians of orthodoxy, but the text of scripture…That's the kind of serious biblical scholarship the Protestant Reformation was built on, and I for one am proud to carry on that tradition – if need be, against those who have turned the Reformation itself into a tradition to be set up over scripture itself.[73]

The two horizons of canon and culture combine in an unprecedentedly far-reaching reappraisal of evangelical theology by self-designated evangelicals. For the

---

[72] Stott, 1970: 33, quoting from an address Packer gave to the Fellowship of Evangelical Churchmen, 20 March 1961, subsequently published as *The Theological Challenge to Evangelicalism Today*. Contrast Mannheim's sociology of knowledge: "Such a system of meanings is possible and valid only in a given type of historical existence, to which, for a time, it furnishes appropriate expression. When the social situation changes, the system of norms to which it had previously given birth ceases to be in harmony with it…an ontology handed down through tradition obstructs new developments, especially in the basic modes of thinking, and as long as the particularity of the conventional theoretical framework remains unquestioned we will remain in the toils of a static mode of thought which is inadequate to our present stage of historical and intellectual development. What is needed, therefore, is a continual readiness to recognize that every point of view is particular to a certain definite situation and to find out through analysis of what this particularity consists." (Mannheim, 1936, quoted in Gill, 1996:87, 90). Packer's conservatism precludes conceptual and linguistic contingency.

[73] Wright, 2001. This exemplifies the nineteenth evangelical principle of the *right and duty of private judgement in the interpretation of the Scriptures*, as explored in Chapter 7 below.

traditionalists, this represents catastrophic accommodationism, even the betrayal of authentic evangelicalism.[74] For the post-conservatives, it signifies liberation into a new authenticity, simultaneously more biblically honed and more culturally apposite, embracing the improvisations of a progressive and self-critical Trinitarian orthodoxy.

Methodology

This study appraises the reality of English evangelicals' perceived but partial success as a religious tradition in the late twentieth century, evaluates their apparent partial immunity to church decline and assesses their prospects of theological reconfiguration, or indeed bifurcation. The historical account is set within the context of an analysis of evangelicalism as a contested tradition, exhibiting progressive theological iteration, cultural accommodation - both intentional and the accidental consequence of pragmatic activism – and yet obdurately unyielding conservatism. The primary frame of reference is restricted to English evangelicals, rather than the wider British context, with specific reference to the trans-denominational formulations and initiatives that characterise the pan-evangelical tradition, rather than examining the specific contribution, political function and theological development of the evangelical party within any particular denominations. Two forms rose to notable prominence within English pan-evangelicalism in the mid to late twentieth century: the conservatives and the entrepreneurs. Both had significant success in reconstructing evangelical identity,

---

[74] *Modern Reformation* is a publication of the Alliance of Confessing Evangelicals which held its first meeting of "evangelical scholars" in April 1996. The *Cambridge Declaration,* presented at this meeting, called evangelical churches to reject the "worldly methods" recently embraced, recover the Biblical doctrines of the Reformation, and regain adherence to the five "solas" of the Reformation - *sola fide, sola gratia, solus Christus, sola Scriptura* and *soli Deo Gloria.* Stackhouse (2000: 49) cites this grouping as an instance of evangelical formalism, "...often dubbed the 'Truly Reformed' by those who have felt the sting of their criticism. These warriors not only claim to speak authoritatively and univocally for what is in fact a multistranded Reformed tradition, but presume then to go on to speak for all evangelicals..." See Erickson, Helseth and Taylor (2004).
Johnson and Fowler White (2001) deliver a still more emphatic and uncompromisingly Calvinistic polemic. Contributors assail not only Middleton and Walsh's (1984, 1995) postmodern re-articulation of biblical metanarrative and Pinnock's open theism, but also repudiate Arminians, revivalists, charismatics, church growth theory, religious marketing, therapeutic models of evangelical spirituality and pastoralia, seeker-services and also *Christianity Today.* Johnson warmly endorses Warfield's assertion "...Evangelicalism stands or falls with Calvinism...every proof of Evangelicalism is proof of Calvinism." (Warfield, 1970: 8-9). For their fellow hyper-calvinists, such obdurately defiant polemic is doubtless considered timely and essential. For others, this attempt to become the sole arbiters of authentic evangelicalism is sectarian. This is unapologetic Reformation-centricity; or, more precisely, calvino-centricity, absolutising the pre-critical insights and polemic of the Reformer as if unconditioned by his cultural setting.

generating new energy, focus and heightened morale. However, both were constructs of modernity. And both faced new scrutiny with the impact of accelerating church decline and postmodernity during the period 1980-2000, and particularly with the nascent emergence, not yet to an equivalent prominence, of post-conservative or progressive evangelicalism.

The research process commenced as an enquiry into the nature, degree and durability of the entrepreneurial boom in pan-evangelical religion in the late twentieth century. This historical narrative required a broader context that examined the fractures within the former conservative hegemony that caused it to be supplanted in pan-evangelicalism by the entrepreneurs. This in turn required a comparative analysis between mid- to late-twentieth century conservatism and the earlier pan-evangelical tradition, more moderate and inclusive, together with a consideration of the subsequent evolution of evangelicals during the entrepreneurial period into three distinct sectors: the neo-conservatives, the cautiously open and the progressives. We shall argue not only that conservative identity was supplanted by entrepreneurial identity, for which its own fragmentation unintentionally opened the door, but that the entrepreneurial concern with pragmatic cultural re-alignment, coupled with the inevitable demise of its own exaggerated claims of imminent success, unintentionally opened the door for the rise of the new progressivism.

In order to develop a conceptual framework for this analysis it was natural to turn to Bebbington, whose seminal history of evangelicals proposed a quadrilateral of enduring and characteristic convictions:

> *conversionism*, the belief that lives need to be changed; *activism*, the expression of the gospel in effort; *biblicism*, a particular regard for the Bible; and what may be called *crucicentrism*, a stress on the sacrifice of Christ on the cross. Together they form a quadrilateral of priorities that is the basis of Evangelicalism.[75]

There is much to commend the descriptive precision of Bebbington's analysis, which has been widely adopted. *Conversionism* is a classic evangelical emphasis and evangelicals have traditionally been emphatically orientated towards conversion as a crisis decision. Only in recent years have evangelicals become more sympathetic to notions of a conversion process and to the model of belonging before believing.[76] *Activism* is undoubtedly the prevailing evangelical mind-set, always busy and sometimes frenetic faced with a world to serve and to win. Hyperactivity may sometimes appear to have become a substitute for an authentic and holistic evangelical spirituality.[77] Not all evangelicals welcome the term *biblicism*, which

---

[75] Bebbington, 1989: 3.

[76] Finney's study (1992) has been widely influential.

[77] In personal conversation when I was his publisher in the early 1980s, Donald Coggan reflected upon Augustine's twin priorities - *semper agens, semper quietens*. Honesty required him to acknowledge that the evangelical tradition knew considerably more of *semper agens* than *semper quietens*.

resonates disconcertingly for some with Barth's critique of bibliolatry,[78] but Bebbington's assertion that evangelicals consider themselves grounded in the authority of Scripture is beyond dispute. *Crucicentrism*, traditionally expressed in terms of penal substitution, denotes evangelicals' emphasis upon the decisive impact and salvific objectivity of the cross.

In order to elucidate the dynamics of evangelical convictions, various enhancements have been proposed to Bebbington's model. Barclay argued, from the perspective of conservative evangelicalism, that the affirmation of three cardinal areas of doctrine - revelation, redemption and regeneration - would be better expressed by re-ordering Bebbington's sequence: biblicism, crucicentrism, conversionism, activism.[79] Although Bebbington's order does not appear to be shaped theologically, a post-Barthian evangelical would prefer to affirm the ultimacy of the personal revelation of the divine in Christ through the following sequence: crucicentrism, biblicism, conversionism, activism.[80] A post-Lausanne evangelical, committed to holistic mission, would prefer to place broad-based activism before the more specific and narrow emphasis upon conversion.

Barclay, McGrath and Warner have all argued that Bebbington's framework requires an additional and specific recognition of Christocentricity.[81] Evangelical preaching, piety and hymnody are characteristically, albeit not exclusively, Jesus-centred. Christocentricity is therefore an evangelical distinctive, even though more broadly characteristic of traditional Christianity - Catholic, Protestant and Orthodox - rather than a specifically evangelical formulation. This could be pushed still wider to encompass Trinitarianism, although the doctrine of the Trinity has frequently been neglected by evangelicals in favour of Christocentricity.[82]

Marsden identified five distinctive and foundational evangelical convictions, including the transformed life, which is absent from Bebbington's quadrilateral:
   - the Reformation doctrine of the final authority of Scripture;
   - the real, historical character of God's saving work;
   - eternal salvation only through personal trust in Christ;
   - the importance of evangelism;
   - the importance of a spiritually transformed life.[83]
This is an entirely persuasive addition.

Some have further argued for a distinctive evangelical emphasis upon revival.[84]

---

[78] Barclay, 1997.

[79] Barclay, 1997: 10.

[80] Calver and Warner, 1996: 94-98.

[81] Barclay, 1997: 11-12; McGrath, 1993: 51; Calver and Warner, 1996: 98.

[82] Zizioulas has charged Western theology more broadly with "an extreme Christocentrism – an *imitatio Christi* – lacking the essential influence of pneumatology" (1985: 20). Calvin's Trinitarianism is derivatively Augustinian, citing him far more than any other early church theologian. As Gunton argued (1991, 1993) Augustine's Trinitarianism is profoundly attenuated by his non-personal account of the Holy Spirit as the interface between Father and Son.

[83] Marsden, 1984: ix-x.

This reflects evangelicalism's roots in the Great Awakening. Irrespective of their theological distinctives, evangelicals tend to express an almost statutory enthusiasm for revival, even though there is reason to question how readily the historical models of revival can be transposed into a postmodern, post-Christian context.[85] However, revival also provokes vigorous internecine disputes: between Calvinists and Arminians;[86] between Finney's revivalist methodology[87] and those with a more calvinistic emphasis upon spontaneous divine eruptions;[88] between those in the Welsh revival who emphasised the centrality of preaching and those who found that intense experiential encounters tended to supplant preaching.[89] Inevitably, the more extremely polarised repudiate the rival faction's claims to revival as inadequate or even inauthentic. Therefore, while an emphasis upon revival can certainly be identified as an historic evangelical distinctive, this can be more precisely delineated as earnest aspirations and vigorous disputes about revival. Revival is certainly an evangelical distinctive, but one as likely to produce division as unity.[90]

McGrath proposed two further characteristic emphases, upon the Spirit and community.[91] While these are certainly current evangelical distinctives in some quarters, it is doubtful they can be credibly claimed as historically persistent evangelical priorities. From this review of various critiques of Bebbington we therefore find persuasive three additions to his quadrilateral: Christocentrism, the transformed life and revival aspirations.

Two further emphases function as organising principles for evangelical thought. First we can identify the centrality of the Protestant principle of *faith alone*. No matter how drawn to works righteousness evangelicals have often been - Bunyan's *Grace Abounding*[92] exemplifies the puritan conviction that a regenerate lifestyle, typically understood in highly legalistic terms, was the only persuasive evidence of election - *faith not works* is the pivot of the voluntarist and convertive piety by which evangelicals have routinely distinguished themselves from nominalism and ritualism. This emphasis is a constant within the evangelical mind-set, implicitly informing evangelicals' core convictions. The inherent individualism of the

---

[84] Calver and Warner, 1996: 99.

[85] Warner, in Walker and Aune, 2003; Heelas, Woodhead et al, 2005.

[86] Notably demonstrated in Charles Wesley's more polemical and anti-calvinist hymns and in the 1742 Scottish Presbyterian seceders' denunciation of Whitefield, a fellow Calvinist, for doctrines and evangelistic success they judged could only be diabolical (Noll, 2004:103-4).

[87] Finney, 1835.

[88] Murray, 1994.

[89] Evans (1969) argued that Evan Roberts' withdrawal from the Welsh Revival and subsequent breakdown may have been precipitated by Peter Price, a Congregational minister and rival revivalist, who repudiated Roberts' meetings as bogus exhibitionism.

[90] Edwards (1990) and Murray (1994) are prime examples of calvinistic-exclusivists whose accounts of revival minimize or even preclude any Wesleyan-Arminian, Finney-type revivalist or Pentecostal-Charismatic claims to be authentic inheritors of the revival tradition.

[91] McGrath, 1993: 51-80.

[92] Bunyan, 1955.

emphasis upon personal conversion was intensified by the theological independent-mindedness of the "right and duty of private judgment" and the related inclination to relativise denominational distinctives and loyalties. We will argue that in late-modernity this endemic tendency took on a distinctive form: autonomous consumers of commodified religion who were nonetheless conformist in their adherence to theological conservatism. We sum up this tendency, which continues to resonate with the slogan of "faith not works", by proposing the oxymoron of conformist (and indeed consumerist) individualism.

Stackhouse identified a distinct but complementary organising principle, namely "trans-denominationalism".[93] Extreme schismatics apart, evangelicals have certainly tended to relativise their own denominational identity at least to some degree in favour of pan-evangelical co-operation. This is apparent, for instance, in Whitefield's defiance of some fellow-Anglicans' complaints that he should not preach for dissenters,[94] and similarly the present day post-denominational trend among those evangelicals who migrate readily between churches with evident disregard for denominational specifics.[95] As Stackhouse convincingly argues, evangelicals bestow upon Bebbington's quadrilateral a distinctive centrality and are willing to make common cause with all Protestants who share these convictions, irrespective of denomination. Marsden made a similar point when he described evangelicalism as a "transdenominational movement in which many people, in various ways, feel at home…Institutionally, this transdenominational evangelicalism is built around networks of parachurch agencies." [96]

Table 1: Evangelical characteristics

Bebbington's quadrilateral	Three additions	Two organizing principles
Conversionism	Christocentrism	Faith not works
Activism	Transformed life	Transdenominationalism
Biblicism	Revival aspirations	
Crucicentrism		

More important than any of these additional core convictions is Marsden's concept of conflictual priorities within pan-evangelicalism.[97] Despite its cogency as a conceptual framework, Bebbington's approach represents less of a theological matrix than a static summation of the essence of the evangelical tradition, particularly in his more recent study of the nineteenth century as an era of evangelical dominance.[98] Tensions and diversity are marginalised, even though the

---

[93] Stackhouse, 2000: 42, 2002: 47-74, 164.
[94] Stout, 1991; Noll, 2004.
[95] Identified in interviews.
[96] Marsden, 1984: xiv.
[97] Marsden, 1984.
[98] Bebbington, 2005.

distinctives allow for a certain amount of interplay and rivalry. Marsden persuasively argued that the core convictions embraced by all evangelicals characteristically function as competing priorities. That is, they are elaborated, emphasised and combined with considerable variation by diverse evangelical groupings, producing significant internecine rivalry.

This study seeks to build upon Bebbington's magnum opus, *Evangelicalism in Modern Britain: A History from the 1730s to the 1980s*,[99] by developing an historical narrative of the late twentieth century as an era of entrepreneurial advance, set within the wider context of substantive transitions within evangelical theology and identity. We therefore propose a decisive modification of Bebbington's thesis, in which his somewhat static model is reconceptualised as twin and rival axes within pan-evangelicalism that energise the dynamic of evangelical rivalries, experiments and evolution. While all evangelicals would give assent to Bebbington's quadrilateral, the entrepreneurial pragmatists major upon the conversionist-activist axis, even as the more theologically oriented, whether traditional, cautiously open or progressive, major upon the biblicist-crucicentric axis.

When we identify the primary empirical data to be scrutinised in order to interpret these axes, two distinct methodologies are immediately apparent. Since the conversionist-activists are preoccupied with results, the numerical data - attendance, membership, subscriptions and professed conversions - tell their story and test their rhetoric of advance and success. Since the biblicist-crucicentrics are preoccupied with formulating and guarding the doctrinal core of evangelical convictions, their bases of faith can be subject to close textual analysis that elicits the hidden narrative of evangelical theological transitions. Calvinism and entrepreneurialism are not mutually exclusive (notably Whitefield[100]), and charismatic and entrepreneurial are by no means synonyms (since some charismatics are more oriented to liturgical, reflective and therapeutic spiritualities). Nonetheless, within the period under study the conversionist-activist axis was dominated by the charismatic-entrepreneurs and the biblicist-crucicentric axis was dominated by the calvinistic-exclusivists (although we shall also explore post-conservative experiments in reconfiguring this axis).

This book develops a sociologically informed historical analysis, that, while not in formal approach a classic participant-observer study,[101] draws upon the perspective of an observing-participant.[102] The primary source documents, supplemented by interviews with senior evangelical leaders of the late twentieth century and participant-observation of many pan-evangelical events and

---

[99] Bebbington, 1989.

[100] Stout, 1991. Contra Carson, 1996; Dallimore, 1970, 1980.

[101] Whyte, 1955; Coleman, 2000.

[102] Denzin defined participant observation as a "strategy that simultaneously combines document analysis, interviewing of respondents and informants, direct participation and observation, and introspection" (Denzin, 1989: 158). Compare Goffman, 1956; Gold, 1958; Bruyn, 1966; Denzin, 1970; Geertz, 1973; Spradley, 1977; Agar, 1980; Adler and Adler, 1994. On the ethics of observation, see Erikson, 1967.

organisations, comprise a unique and unprecedented access to the archives and personnel of contemporary pan-evangelicalism. Data is analysed from the following sources:

> Archival data was made available from the Evangelical Alliance, Spring Harvest, Scripture Union and the pan-evangelical monthly magazines. These primary sources were analysed to construct the historical narrative and evaluate and interpret the public claims of evangelicals against their own empirical data of growth, stasis and decline.

> A close textual analysis explores the evolving, and implicitly even rival, theologies of evangelical bases of faith.

> Semi-structured interviews were undertaken (see Appendix 1) with a wide range of senior evangelical leaders. Additional personal perspectives were gathered from many unstructured conversations, particularly among members of the Evangelical Alliance Council and speaker teams at the Evangelical Assemblies and the Bible Weeks referred to below. I also interviewed many evangelical leaders for a weekly programme on Premier Radio over a period of four years, which facilitated more informal access to their perspectives.

> I attended (and sometimes addressed) pan-evangelical national events 1990-2002, including Spring Harvest, Keswick, Easter People, Spring Harvest At Work Together, Baptist Union Assemblies, an Assemblies of God Bible Week, national Alpha conferences, the two Challenge 2000 events, New Frontiers Leadership events and two Evangelical Alliance National Assemblies.

> At various times within this period I was a trustee of Scripture Union, the Shaftesbury Society, and the Evangelical Alliance, a founding trustee of Rebuild - a national initiative sponsored by Shaftesbury and TEAR Fund, promoting social action from local churches within their local communities - and also of Renovaré UK - the national expression of an international charity promoting catholic spiritualities. In short, I participated in pan-evangelicalism at a strategic level, which gave me exceptional access to the data, archives and leading personnel, and thence a privileged standpoint from which to engage in critical reflection.

> A questionnaire exploring diversity of theological and ethical convictions was completed by the council and board of EA, the leadership teams of Spring Harvest, Scripture Union, UCCF, Tear Fund, YFC, the speaker team and delegates at a national Evangelical Assembly and other sectors within pan-evangelicalism, including students at London School of Theology, Moorlands College and Ridley Hall, Cambridge.[103] This data, indicating parameters of evangelical diversity, formed a secondary and background resource for the present study and commenced an ongoing research project exploring evangelical convictions and transitions, theological and ethical.[104]

---

[103] Warner, 2008.

[104] American questionnaire based studies reveal evidence of significant diversity of evangelical convictions and possibilities of cognitive negotiation with the prevailing culture

The privileged, and in some measure unprecedented, access to the archival data, senior personnel and oral histories of pan-evangelicalism, was combined in the research process with reflexive attendance at key pan-evangelical events, public conferences, councils and boards of trustees. Triangulation of research strategies[105] has been developed at two levels: archival-empirical and qualitative data within an interdisciplinary analytical framework, historical, sociological and theological. This reflects what Callum Brown has described as the new integration of history, sociology and religious studies in the examination of Christianity in the context of contemporary secularization.[106]

Secularization remains an indispensable framework of analysis for the development of religious traditions, even if highly contested.[107] The classical prescriptive theories[108] find their polar opposite in rational choice theory.[109] Martin provided a highly sophisticated descriptive formulation through studying the variables in church decline across Western Europe,[110] and more recently on a wider canvas.[111] Davie argued for residual religion notwithstanding a lack of active adherence,[112] while Gill argued that church decline was exaggerated by the excessive church buildings of the nineteenth century that have always known empty pews.[113] Brown argued for a catastrophic decline in church attendance in the sixties,[114] but failed to address longer-term patterns of decline,[115] and his claim that this is directly related to the emergent women's movement is less convincing, since such a rapid socio-cultural impact upon the general population, and churchgoers in particular, seems implausible. What is incontestable, in the context of Western Europe is that church attendance has declined dramatically through the twentieth century,[116] accelerating in the UK in the 1960s and quite probably accelerating again in the 1990s. Church influence has also declined, with a complete abandonment of the traditional *imperium* that considered religious discourse integral to and presiding over scientific, ethical and socio-political debate.[117] Nonetheless, churches and other

---

(Hunter, 1983, 1987; Smith, 1998, 2000; contra Penning and Smidt, 2000).

[105] Denzin, 1970.

[106] During a day conference at New College, Edinburgh, 15 April 2005.

[107] Swatos 2000; Davie, Heelas and Woodhead, 2003; MacLaren, 2004.

[108] Wilson, 1966; Berger, 1967; Bruce, 1996, 2002.

[109] Stark and Bainbridge, 1985, 1987; Stark and Finke 1992; Finke and Stark, 2000; contra Bruce, 1999.

[110] Martin, 1978.

[111] Martin, 2005.

[112] Davie, 1994, 2002.

[113] Gill 1993, 2003.

[114] Brown, 2001.

[115] Gill, 2003.

[116] Gilbert, 1980, Wolffe 1995.

[117] Chadwick, 1975.

religious groupings have negotiated a return to the public square,[118] albeit learning to acknowledge, at least to some extent, the new pluralistic context of many faith communities and many people with no faith allegiance.

Unmodified, prescriptive secularization theory has faced several significant critiques. First, secularization theory is charged with offering a prescriptive model, in which societal advance results in the sloughing off of religion as primitive and irrational superstition. Thus, secularization theory can itself be interpreted as a totalising, enlightenment meta-narrative, as coercive as Christendom. Second, secularization theory is Eurocentric, treating the European experience as normative and the summit of civilisation to which other societies will ultimately ascend. Third, secularization theory is, in Popper's terms, "unfalsifiable" [119] since for Wilson, Wallis and Bruce, any data that appear to contradict or modify secularization, including periods of church growth or even revival, are invariably utilised to reinforce their prescriptive orthodoxy. For Popper, scientific theory is intentionally falsifiable, thus permitting modified hypotheses through the examination of new data, whereas an unfalsifiable theory – Popper's prime targets were Marxism and Freudianism – is essentially pseudo-science. Fourth, secularization theory can have an implicit, or even explicit, ideological agenda: when Bruce writes a book entitled "God is Dead" [120] he demonstrates a similar category confusion to Richard Dawkins: neither sociological data nor evolutionary theory is capable of producing theological conclusions. Fifth, secularization offers a linear evolution that begins from a golden age of a Christianised monoculture, over-gilding Christendom and failing to offer an account of the original rise of Christianity.[121] Sixth, as we shall argue below, secularization theory has not always distinguished adequately between the various dimensions of secularization, which may have diverse trajectories.

The primary facets of the secularizing process have been variously defined, but the four most convincing are functional differentiation, in which life becomes compartmentalized into self-regulated specialisms, rationalisation that produces the disenchantment of the world and scientific explanations without reference to the supernatural, structural pluralism that separates the public and private spheres and individualisation in which religion is determined by personal choice rather than ethnic identity. Dobbelaere proposed an analysis of secularization in three distinct spheres, namely macro (societal), meso (cultural) and micro (individual).[122] The variations at the macro level are striking: for example, in the US separation of church and state combines with religious discourse as a legitimate dimension of the political process, whereas in the UK an established church is combined paradoxically with the systematic excision of religious discourse from the political sphere, keeping private religion strictly separate from public politics.

We now turn to the possibility of making distinctions between various

---

[118] Casanova, 1994.

[119] Popper, 1989.

[120] Bruce, 2002.

[121] Stark, 1997.

[122] Dobbelaere, 1981.

dimensions of secularization theory. Berger defined the "classical task of religion" as "constructing a common world within which all of social life receives ultimate meaning binding on everybody".[123] This is dissolved through the process of secularization: "by which sectors of society and culture are removed from the domination of religious institutions and symbols." [124] Wilson defined secularization as the process whereby religious thinking, practice and institutions lose social significance.[125] Developing Yves Lambert's refinement of Berger,[126] we can conflate Berger and Wilson's definitions to identify four aspects of secularization – religious institutions, religious thinking, religious practices and religious symbols. The West exhibits *pervasive freedom* from the old authority of religious institutions and interpretations. This is combined with *autonomous abandonment or assent* with regard to religious practices and symbols, neither being inevitable but the former predominant in Western Europe.

Table 2: Dimensions of secularization

Religious institutions	} freedom from old authorities
Religious interpretations	
upper pair an almost universal Western trend, *lower pair mostly abandoned in Western Europe*	
Religious practices	} autonomous abandonment or use
Religious symbols	

The broad concept of secularization may be interpreted as the universal phenomenon of functional differentiation and rationalisation applied to the religious sphere. This was previously interpreted eurocentrically as the death of religion because the diminished role of religion within multiple, voluntarist sub-systems is inimical to the unitary culture of Christendom[127] and to a Durkheimian view of the societal function of religion.[128] Differentiation and rationalisation may be conceived as inevitable processes at least within Western culture, but there is no necessary or universal correlation between these factors and the demise, resilience or even resurgence of religious symbols and practices, including church attendance.

This approach defends the partial retention of secularization as a prescriptive theory, with specific regard to autonomy from religious institutions and thinking, but rejects any assumption of prescriptive inevitability with regard to the future decline of religious practices and symbols, not least including spiritual experiences and

---

[123] Berger, 1967: 134.
[124] Berger, 1967: 107.
[125] Wilson, 1966: 14.
[126] Lambert, 2000.
[127] Wright N.G., 2000.
[128] Durkheim, 1912.

personal faith. We further conclude that the current vogue for such terms as resacralization and desecularization is misleading:[129] the death of religion has been greatly exaggerated, but there is no prospect of the resurrection of Christendom. Papal aspirations for the re-catholicisation of the New Europe, evangelical aspirations for European church growth on the American scale, and Milbank's aspirations[130] to abolish sociology of religion and insert other academic discourses under an Augustinian and neo-Constantinian theological primacy within the academy, all lack cultural plausibility. There are undoubtedly counter-secularizing tendencies, but religious institutions and mythological thinking have been definitively dethroned.

Although the secularizing processes are at least as old as Protestantism in the European context,[131] something new emerged in the mid to late twentieth century when social custom reversed polarities from religious to non-religious conformity. The highly secularized educated elite in the humanities, social sciences and media contributed to a culture with new norms, in which Christian faith becomes a legitimate or even habitual target for marginalisation, indifference or disparagement, to a degree perhaps unknown in Europe since the late Middle Ages, France in the Age of Reason excepted. Differentiation and rationalisation, individualism and relativism decisively undermine the Church's Constantinian or unitary aspirations. In a de-traditionalized, increasingly egalitarian, individualistic and neo-liberal context, the traditionalist and establishment credentials of Christianity combine with perceived ecclesiastical ineffectuality faced with decline to reinforce the new cultural framework and the perceived obsolescence of the Christian Church. Western Europe no longer functions under Berger's sacred canopy: the new cultural canopy is unambiguously secular.

This study constructs a revisionist account[132] of the historical narrative of pan-evangelicalism through a period of particular turbulence, growth, and, we shall argue, incipient decline. The historical analysis develops the following argument:

> Pan-evangelical origins in the mid-nineteenth century were expressly ecumenical, implicitly pre-critical, and emphatically Protestant and conversionist. This broad and minimalist orthodoxy was supplanted by the biblicist-crucicentric axis of the elaborated conservative hegemony of the mid-twentieth century that was predominantly anti-critical and calvinistic, with fundamentalising tendencies evident in a continuing rightwards drift. This hegemony finally collapsed in the mid-1960s under an excess of mutually exclusive certainties.

> After a period of loss of confidence in pan-evangelicalism, the conversionist-activist axis prevailed in an entrepreneurial *risorgimento*, combining the residual, moderate evangelicals, the previously marginalised Pentecostals and the emergent charismatics in a revitalised activism. This entrepreneurial axis tended to displace the previous

---

[129] Compare Fenn, 2001; Davie, Heelas and Woodhead, 2003.

[130] Milbank, 1990.

[131] Weber, 1958; or indeed Old Testamental, as Berger (1967) argued.

[132] Contra Tidball, 1994; Randall and Hilborn 2001.

centrality of the biblicist-crucicentric axis, preferring to emphasise unity in pragmatic activism while presenting a meta-narrative of present advance and imminent success. This resurgence, exemplified in the growth of EA membership and Spring Harvest attendance, reached a plateau around 1990, even though the subsequent decade saw a further heightening of the rhetoric of success. This brief eruption of evangelical resilience could reasonably be interpreted not so much as significant missiological advance, which remains the perception of many senior evangelical leaders, but as reactionary assertiveness against the libertarian secularity of the 1960s, combined with pragmatic, entrepreneurial drive, consonant with the Thatcherite 1980s. This short-lived success, primarily in reconfiguring the internal evangelical market, deferred but failed to prevent what increasingly looks like late-onset decline.

In the same period, post-conservatism began to coalesce around reformulations of the biblicist-crucicentric axis, theologically self-critical, remote from fundamentalising separatism, and sceptical of the entrepreneurials' late-modern rhetoric of success. It is too early to say whether post-conservatives will merge into mainstream (post-) liberalism or provide a coherently postmodern and reconstructed pan-evangelical identity, supplanting the conservative/enlightenment and entrepreneurial/late-modern identities that had become increasingly outmoded and self-attenuated. Simultaneously, and partly in reaction against post-conservative innovations, the neo-conservatives have continued to harden their fundamentalising tendencies. We conclude that bifurcation within pan-evangelicalism appears almost inevitable, even though its precise configuration is unresolved, depending on whether the cautiously open come to identify more with the neo-conservatives or the progressives.

Neo-conservatives have no adequate response to the last two hundred years of biblical criticism, taking refuge in a dogmatically *a priori,* inerrantist sceptical fideism,[133] an enlightenment preoccupation with epistemology supplanting the soterio-centricity of Trinitarian orthodoxy.[134] Similarly, the late twentieth century flowering of entrepreneurialism had no coherent response to the last two hundred years of secularization, defiantly adhering to a profoundly implausible rhetoric of imminent success, amnesiac to a prolonged history of failed initiatives and sustained decline. We conclude that while neo-conservatives and entrepreneurials will continue to construct ideological enclaves for their devotees, neither can plausibly construct future trajectories around which pan-evangelicalism is likely to re-cohere. The decay of the enlightenment and the demise of late-modern certainties leave the two expressions of pan-evangelical identity that were successively dominant in the late twentieth century increasingly culture-bound with diminishing plausibility beyond their coteries. We therefore identify a double tension within pan-evangelicalism in the late twentieth century, not only between the conversionist-activist and biblicist-crucicentric axes, but also within the latter axis, between three sub-types of evangelical: conservative, cautiously open and progressive.

In order to interpret the evolution of English pan-evangelicalism, we draw upon

---

[133] Presciently recognised in Hume's *Dialogues* (1779).
[134] Following Abraham, 1981; Dayton, 1991.

sociological analyses of the durability and transitions of conservative religion[135] within the evolution of American religion,[136] set in the wider context of European church decline.[137] This study refutes Kelley's thesis that traits of strictness deliver conservative Christianity's resilience[138] and Hunter's subsequent thesis that evidence of post-fundamentalist cognitive bargaining in the evangelical tradition produces inevitable consequences of decline in comparison with unreconstructed fundamentalism.[139] Tamney's emphasis on "modernized traditionalism" [140] and Heelas and Woodhead's "experiential religions of difference" [141] more plausibly describe the viability within contemporary evangelicalism, particularly its charismatic variants. However, Stark's free market thesis[142] seems to have applied in England primarily within the evangelical constituency, with shifts of allegiance between evangelical sectors rather than significant conversion growth, confirming Bibby's Canadian research on evangelical ghettoisation.[143] In particular, Roof's "spiritual quest culture" [144] and Hammond's analysis of the reconstruction of religion around personal autonomy[145] identify a *zeitgeist* that has been conducive to the commodification of evangelical religion, undermining pan-evangelical leaders aspirations to homogeneous mobilisation. We further identify the unfalsifiability of late-modern evangelical entrepreneurialism that, failing to take account of secularization, has embarked upon the futility of a rhetoric of denial, exemplifying the consequences of what Festinger termed "cognitive dissonance".[146] Building upon Bellah's proposal that the entrepreneurial and therapeutic dominate contemporary culture,[147] we conclude that the public rhetoric of pan-evangelical leaders and songwriters, insistently proclaiming entrepreneurial advance, given its acute implausibility, has almost certainly been transposed among at least some evangelical consumer-participants, under the guise of personal autonomy into a therapeutic religion of subcultural, escapist entertainment.[148] Integral to this exploration of

---

[135] Festinger, 1957, 1964; Kelley, 1972; Hunter, 1983, 1987; Smith, 1998, 2000; Woodhead and Heelas, 2000; Tamney, 2002.

[136] Marsden, 1984, 1991; Roof and McKinney, 1987; Wuthnow, 1988; Hammond, 1992; Bellah, 1996; Roof, 1999.

[137] Historical: Chadwick, 1975; Currie, Gilbert and Horsley, 1977; Gilbert, 1980; Wolffe, 1995; Brown, 2001. Sociological: Wilson, 1966; Berger, 1967, 1999; Martin, 1978; Stark and Bainbridge, 1985, 1987; Stark and Finke 1992; Finke and Stark, 2000; Davie, 1994; Bruce, 1996, 2002; Gill 1993, 2003; Casanova, 1994; Swatos, 2000.

[138] Kelley, 1972.

[139] Hunter, 1983, 1987; compare Smith, 1998.

[140] Tamney, 2002.

[141] Woodhead and Heelas, 2000.

[142] Stark and Bainbridge, 1985, 1987.

[143] Bibby and Brinkerhoff, 1973, 1974, 1983.

[144] Roof, 1999.

[145] Hammond, 1992.

[146] Festinger, 1957, 1964.

[147] Bellah, 1996.

[148] Compare Postman, 1985.

evangelical evolution is the much-debated relationship – historical, theological and sociological - between evangelicalism and fundamentalism.[149] Following Harris' significant modification of Barr's analysis, we argue that many evangelicals have fundamentalising tendencies without being unreservedly fundamentalists.[150] A new synthetic analysis is developed of evangelicals' threefold resilience: conservative, entrepreneurial and reconstructive. Historical and sociological typologies of evangelical identity and diversity[151] are evaluated in the light of the analysis of empirical data, and a modified typology - building upon Hunter's development of Weber's typology of ascetic Protestantism - is formulated,[152] accounting for historical and continuing evangelical diversity.

This study is distinct from many recent analyses of evangelicalism, being neither a partisan insider's selective and defensive apologia[153] nor a dismissive outsider's trenchant rebuttal.[154] Nor, however, should it be taken to represent post-evangelicalism, which remains an essentially inchoate reaction against a pluriform tradition.[155] While it is entirely possible to be post-conservative,[156] post-entrepreneurial, or indeed post-charismatic, the evangelical tradition, like the Roman Catholic, is too diverse, longstanding, and too capable of self-reinvention,[157] for the term post-evangelical (or indeed post-Catholic) to be enduringly coherent.

---

[149] Historical: Marsden, 1984, 1987, 1991; Rennie, 1994. Theological: Barr, 1977, 1984; Abraham, 1981; Ramm, 1983; Cohen, 1990; Kung, 1992; Murphy, 1996; Knight, 1997; Dorrien, 1998; Harris, 1998; Grenz, 2000. Sociological and anthropological: Bibby and Brinkerhoff, 1973, 1974, 1983; Bibby, 1987; Balmer, 1989; Ammerman, 1995; Bruce, 2001; Coleman, 2000; Bramadat, 2000; Hunt, 2001, 2004. Socio-theological: Walker, 1985; Marty, Appleby et al, 1991, 1993, 1993, 1994, 1995; Percy, 1996, 2002; Partridge, 2001, Watt, 1991. Evangelical defences against the charge of omni-fundamentalism: Packer, 1958; Stott and Edwards, 1988; Wells, 1993; Tidball, 1994; Calver and Warner, 1996; Randall, 2000.

[150] Harris (1998) builds convincingly on Barr, without the polemical edge. Barr (1977, 1984) is persistently polemical, tarring all evangelicals with a fundamentalist brush. See Quebedeux (1974: 19), Pinnock (1990: 40-1), Tidball (1994: 26), McGrath, (1994: 33). Nonetheless, Barr persuasively argues that fundamentalist theology is a rationalist, and therefore reductionist, enlightenment construct. Moreover, he identifies three distinct strands – the total fundamentalists, the maximal-conservatives, and the mildly conservative – correctly predicting future division but failing to see this was imminent. Percy (1996) argues persuasively for a broader, cultural-linguistic conception of fundamentalism over against Barr's narrowly noetic approach. Both dimensions are integral to the phenomenon.

[151] Marsden, 1984; Bebbington, 1989; Lints, 1993; McGrath, 1993; Dorrien, 1998; Stackhouse, 2000.

[152] Weber, 1958, Hunter 1983.

[153] Calver, 1993; Tidball, 1994; Brady and Rowdon, 1996; Calver and Warner 1996; Randall, 2000; Randall and Hilborn, 2001.

[154] Barr, 1977, 1984. Dorrien (1998) avoids polemic in an exceptionally perceptive account of evangelical theologies.

[155] Tomlinson, 1995; Hilborn, 1997.

[156] Grenz, 1993, 2000; Olson, 1995, 2000; Murphy, 1996; Webber, 1999, 2002.

[157] Edwards, 1987.

Developing Bebbington's thesis that evangelicalism originated as an enlightenment construct,[158] we argue that twentieth century entrepreneurialism was derivative, unawares, of late-modernity, with trajectories exemplifying the Weberian routinisation of charisma.[159]

Running as a subtext through our historical narrative will be the successive reinventions of identity within the evangelical subculture. American sociologists first developed the concept of "subculture" in the mid-twentieth century. Although much analysis has concentrated upon youth subcultures, the field of enquiry has much wider applicability. However, as Yinger observed,

> Few concepts appear so often in current sociological writing... The usages vary so widely, however, that the value of the term is severely limited.[160]

Despite the fact that the term is used in widely divergent contexts, an element of opposition to the majority culture is inherent, making the subcultural participants appear deviant in some way, whether in their own eyes or others'.[161] Gordon concluded that a subculture has an "integrated impact upon the participating individual".[162] Cohen argued that a subculture confers status upon participants who otherwise feel excluded from ways in which the prevailing culture confers status.[163] Jenkins similarly observed that in a subculture, those "from a position of cultural marginality and social weakness"[164] coalesce to "forge an alliance with a community of others in defence of tastes which, as a result, cannot be read as totally aberrant or idiosyncratic".[165] Thornton, building upon Bourdieu, developed the concept of "subcultural capital" as the "linchpin of an alternative hierarchy"[166] that "reinterprets the social world".[167] She cited hairstyles, idioms and CD collections as characteristic indicators of subcultural participation.[168] The predominant usages tend therefore to concentrate upon smaller groups within society that are in some measure marginalised or oppositional to the prevailing cultural consensus. Irwin describes subcultures as endowing participants with "an explicit lifestyle"[169] and a framework of "beliefs, values and cultural meaning".[170] Wolfgang and Ferracuti argued that a "subculture is only partly different from the parent culture".[171] Hebdige

---

[158] Bebbington, 1989.

[159] Weber, 1991.

[160] Yinger, 1960, in Arnold, 1970: 122.

[161] Gelder and Thornton, 1997.

[162] Gordon, 1947, in Gelder and Thornton, 1997: 41.

[163] Cohen, 1955, in Arnold, 1970: 32.

[164] Jenkins, 1992, in Gelder and Thornton, 1997:509.

[165] Jenkins, 1992, in Gelder and Thornton, 1997:509.

[166] Thornton, 1995: 105.

[167] Thornton in Gelder and Thornton, 1997: 208.

[168] Compare Hebdige, 1979.

[169] Irwin, 1970: 166.

[170] Irwin, 1970: 167.

[171] Wolfgang and Ferracuti, 1970: 136.

recognised that his partial discontinuity can result in "a process of recuperation" [172] in which the majority culture seeks to accommodate the subculture, removing the oppositional threat. (Hebdige provides a pertinent framework for a possible future study of evangelicals within Anglicanism and the historical dialectic they inhabit of denominational opposition yet participation.) Subcultures cannot be considered as hermetically sealed systems. Arnold observed that virtually every individual participates in several subcultures, albeit to a varying degree according to time, intensity or extensiveness.[173] Irwin similarly concluded that all but the most isolated subcultures therefore engage in a continuing process of "comparing, negotiating and sharing".[174] This, he argued, provokes a new self-awareness as the subculture and the participant's role within it become explicit.[175] Particularly in the context of high geographical and social mobility combined with sustained exposure to a plethora of subcultural alternatives through the media, the postmodern context inevitably introduces a context of pluralism and relativism that questions the normative force and conceptual plausibility of any subcultural lifestyle. Notwithstanding post-subcultural theory,[176] even in a fragmented culture subcultural analysis remains a useful, albeit problematized, tool of analysis.

What Percy observed with regard to fundamentalism, drawing on Lindbeck, is true of all the major evangelical sectors: they provide a cultural-linguistic framework and are not solely noetic.[177] Richard Lints argued that a doctrinal definition of evangelicalism is insufficient because it fails to "account adequately for the significant diversity of the movement",[178] and fails "to differentiate evangelicals sufficiently from non-evangelicals",[179] who may hold orthodox doctrinal convictions but have no desire to be associated with evangelicals. Lints claimed, "The doctrinal criterion is in fact tangential rather than central to the essence of the movement." [180] While evangelicals hold in common a number of theological beliefs that they agree are important, these fail to "inhere in any larger theological construct that could be accurately identified as 'evangelical theology' ".[181] For Lints, evangelicalism is best understood not in theological or ecclesiological but rather sociological terms:

> In reality, it is a diversity of theological frameworks that more nearly captures the essence of evangelicalism. The movement's unique identity is defined to a considerably greater extend by cultural, institutional and personal factors than by a narrow set of

---

[172] Hebdige, 1979.
[173] Arnold, 1970: 85.
[174] Irwin,1970: 167.
[175] Irwin, 1970: 169.
[176] Muggleton and Weinzierl, 2003; Cheney, 2004; Bennet and Kahn-Harris, 2004.
[177] Percy, 1996: 11-12.
[178] Lints, 1993: 30.
[179] Lints, 1993: 30.
[180] Lints, 1993: 30.
[181] Lints, 1993: 31.

common doctrinal beliefs.[182]

Similarly, Kenneth Myers argued that evangelicalism is a subculture, with behaviour patterns rather than doctrines as the basis of identity and cohesion.[183] Brian Haymes has described evangelicalism as an ideology rather than a theology.[184] Marsden has identified three kinds of evangelical, using sociological rather than theological distinctions:

> First, evangelicalism is a conceptual unity that designates a grouping of Christians who fit a certain definition. Second, evangelicalism can designate a more organic movement. Religious groups with some common traditions and experiences, despite wide diversities and only meagre institutional inter-connections, may constitute a movement in the sense of moving or tending in some common directions. Third, within evangelicalism in these broader senses is a more narrow, consciously 'evangelical' transdenominational community with complicated infrastructures of institutions and persons which identify with 'evangelicalism'.[185]

Something of what Lints, Myers, Haymes and Marsden propose as a general tendency, is echoed in Randall Balmer's description of his personal "immersion in the evangelical subculture"; an assimilation more to a conventional religious lifestyle than to a cohesive doctrinal framework:

> ...affiliating with a local church (not just any church, but a church that 'preached the Bible'), eschewing 'worldliness' in its many insidious forms, hewing to strict codes of personal morality, sending the kids off to Sunday School,...establishing a daily 'quiet time'...witnessing, 'sharing your faith' with non-Christians...feeling very guilty if you failed to do any of the above, or if you failed to do it with sufficient rigour and enthusiasm, for there were always spiritual athletes around to shame you - pastors, travelling evangelists, godly matriarchs in any congregation whose personal piety served both as examples worthy of emulation and implicit rebukes to your own spiritual lethargy.[186]

Kent Hughes has argued that in North America there is a clearly defined evangelical subculture, entailing conformity in vocabulary and behaviour, with a common heritage that gives a prevailing sense of identity. This subculture remains widely acceptable within the prevailing North American culture, away from the liberal and secularized elites of the urban centres. Identifying with the evangelical world can still be advantageous in American business and politics.[187] The price, according to Hughes, exacted by the acceptability of the evangelical subculture, is

---

[182] Lints, 1993: 31.

[183] Meyers, 1992: 48-49.

[184] In conversation. Haymes is a former Principal of Bristol Baptist College.

[185] Marsden, 1984: ix.

[186] Balmer, 1993: 4-5.

[187] Weber identified the same American correlation in *The Protestant Sects and the Spirit of Capitalism* (Gerth and Wright Mill, 1991: 302-22).

increasing cultural, theological and moral accommodation.[188] To be pro-American, pro-life and pro-gun appears to be the prevailing trinity of many American evangelicals and the quasi-established religion of middle America. We shall examine successive reconfigurations of the English evangelical subculture and identify evidence of diminishing subcultural capital.

The inevitable complaint against sociological analysis of a theological constituency is that it is reductionist, failing to take sufficient account of theological distinctives. Milbank and Carson are forcibly dismissive of sociological reductionism[189] - and rightly so if sociological analysis is intended to preclude or replace theological consideration. Conversely, we may argue that theological analysis becomes similarly reductionist should it claim to account for every tendency and divergence within evangelical identity.[190] A complex grouping, comprising both a mass-movement and a theological tradition, cannot adequately be interpreted without a multi-disciplinary approach.

During the research process I transitioned from the perspective of an observing-participant towards a participating observer. Sustained reflexivity and critical detachment cohered with growing alienation as multiform implausibilities and intrinsic intellectual deficiencies, theological and sociological, became acutely apparent in various schools of pan-evangelicalism. The study is therefore, in the terms of its own analysis, a post-conservative and post-entrepreneurial construct, hermeneutically closer to Gadamer than Hirsch and Vanhoozer,[191] while sociologically persuaded of the residual resilience of free market religion in the context of European exceptionalist and post-Constantinian secularization.[192] As McCutcheon argued, the insider / outsider problem has been persistent in academic debate since the emergence of religious studies as a discipline distinct from theology in the mid-nineteenth century.[193] We reject Weber's insistence that unqualified detachment from the religion under enquiry is the necessary prerequisite of

---

[188] Hughes, 1995.

[189] Milbank, 1990; Carson, 1996: 455-457.

[190] Theological reductionism is not a specifically evangelical deficit in appraising sociology of religion. Early critics of Milbank's (1990) critique of the allegedly reductionist tendencies of sociology, identified, alongside reservations concerning his idealized Augustinian aspiration for a new Christendom, an equivalent reductionism in his over-simplistic, anachronistic and polemical account of contemporary sociology as necessarily dependent upon an enlightenment-determined, positivist, implicit theology. See Williams 1992, Nichols 1992, Flanagan 1992. Aspirations to reinstate theology as the queen of the sciences are inescapably specious in a differentiated and secularized culture.

[191] Gadamer, 1975, 1976; Hirsch, 1967, 1976; Vanhoozer, 1998, 2002.

[192] Warner, 2006. Contra Bruce (2002) who projects the imminent extinction of religion; Davie (2002) who argues that Protestantism outside the state churches has little future in Europe; and Stark, Bainbridge and Finke (Stark and Bainbridge, 1985, 1987; Stark and Finke 1992; Finke and Stark, 2000) whose theory anticipates a religious market altogether more volatile and assertive than the secularized indifference of present day Western Europe. See Martin, 1978, 2002.

[193] McCutcheon, 1999; see also Arweck and Stringer, 2002.

objectivity, precluding personal belief,[194] and equally MacIntyre's argument that the insider and outsider's perspectives are essentially incommensurate.[195] We accept rather Berger's emphasis upon the importance of reflexivity for the insider within a faith community who nonetheless functions as an outsider, analysing from a vantage point within the academic community.[196] But we can take this iterative process further. As Collins argues, in the light of his own work as an anthropologist studying Quakers as a Quaker, "We each become simultaneously insiders and outsiders." [197] The reflexive process requires the insider to harness the benefits of privileged access and familiarity with subcultural language games, in tandem with critical reflection, the dialectic of observation and participation functioning in a mutually transformative iteration. This insider-outsider simultaneity may produce two kinds of suspicion. Participants in the religion under enquiry may suspect that any social scientific analysis of their faith and practices is essentially reductive: here we emphatically reject the reductive antipathy to social scientific method exemplified by Milbank.[198] Traditional non-religious social scientists may equally suspect that an observing participant, however reflexive, is compromised *a priori*. In identifying the transitioning locus of this study, from critical insider to reflexive observer, we adhere to the dicta of Bruce Lincoln with regard to the study of religions,[199] particularly that reverence is a religious but not a scholarly virtue; that rigorous critical inquiry is not intrinsically cynical or reductive; that social scientific analysis necessarily examines religion without ratifying its claim to be transcendent and sacrosanct; and that authentic scholarship cannot permit those studied to define the terms in which they are interpreted or suspend interest in the temporal and contingent. The participant-observer dialectic rejects the naïve positivism of presumed absolute neutrality, but also rejects the dogmatic postmodern relativism that collapses social scientific enquiry into subjectivism; this study seeks to do justice both to the hermeneutical and scientific dimensions of historical and social scientific investigation.[200] In Ricoeur's terms, a hermeneutic of suspicion will be employed together with a hermeneutic of willingness to listen.[201]

In Part One we examine the conversionist-activist axis in the period 1980-2000, when pan-evangelicalism recovered its nerve and reconfigured its prevailing identity after the public and resonant division within the biblicist-crucicentric axis in 1966-7. We reappraise the much-publicised rise of late-modern evangelical entrepreneurialism, demonstrating, notwithstanding the normative entrepreneurial rhetoric of imminent success, that the empirical data of trends in pan-evangelicalism are most plausibly accounted for by a theory of late-onset decline. We also find

---

[194] Quoted in Puttick, 1997: 6.

[195] MacIntyre, in McCutcheon, 1999: 37-49.

[196] Berger, 1979; compare Wilson, 1982.

[197] Collins, 2002: 92; compare Hufford (1995) on relflexivity.

[198] Milbank, 1990; compare Flanagan, 1992, McGrath, 2002.

[199] Lincoln, 1995.

[200] Feyerabend, 1988; Hufford, 1995; Robson, 2002.

[201] Ricoeur, 1970: 27.

significant evidence of "cognitive dissonance" in the period of plateau or decline in the 1990s. In this context, we review and develop sociological theories of evangelical resurgence and durability and examine the extent and causes of any degree of evangelical exceptionalism, in contrast with the prevailing European exceptionalism of religious decline in a world grown, in Berger's apposite phrase, "furiously religious".[202]

In Part Two we examine the biblicist-crucicentric axis. We demonstrate the rising dominance through the mid-twentieth century of conservative maximalism, supplanting the earlier tradition of relatively minimalist orthodoxy, and its subsequent self-inflicted fragmentation. We examine the late twentieth century emergence of post-conservatism, the neo-conservative reaction, and the resultant bifurcatory trajectories within pan-evangelicalism. We further demonstrate that biblical infallibility and penal substitution have been contested rather than universal convictions within pan-evangelicalism.

In the concluding chapter, we assess the conflictual identities within evangelicalism. This study of two failed experiments in pan-evangelical identity, driven by the successive dominance of the twin axes, biblicist-crucicentric and conversionist-activist, demonstrates that the period 1966-2001 represents an era of tumultuous upheavals within pan-evangelicalism. These twin axes should, however, like Bebbington's four primary emphases[203] from which they have been developed, be conceived as together integral to evangelicalism. The development of the tradition can only be adequately grasped by examining both in tandem. Our historical study also exemplifies the Weberian law of unintended consequences:[204] the conservatives opened the door unwittingly to the entrepreneurs who later did the same for the progressives and neo-conservatives. Building on Martin's assessment of the evangelical subculture,[205] we argue that these rival reconstructions of pan-evangelical identity have entailed a continuing depletion of subcultural capital. We then build upon Hunter's development of Weber's model of sub-groups within ascetic Protestantism[206] to identify seven micro-paradigms, grouped in three meso-paradigms.[207] We review the trajectories and potential coalitions between these sectors, concluding that the future of pan-evangelical identity may reside with the cautious conservatives, with the progressives and exclusivists exhibiting increasing bifurcatory pressure. We argue that late twentieth century English pan-evangelicalism was intrinsically pluriform and contested, frequently possessing fundamentalising tendencies without being universally fundamentalist, and yet in partial reflexive reconstruction. English pan-evangelicalism is therefore too conflicted and too rapidly diversifying to be capable of mass mobilisation. This religious sector thus achieves less than its leaders promise or some opponents may

---

[202] Davie, 1994, 2002; Berger, 1999:2.

[203] Bebbington, 1989, 2005.

[204] Weber, 1958.

[205] Martin, 2005.

[206] Weber, 1958; Hunter, 1983.

[207] This builds upon Kung's (1989) adaptation of Kuhn (1962).

fear. The twin axes of pan-evangelicalism that we have formulated and tested in this study, presently expressed in the progressive, cautiously conservative and exclusivist sectors, are found to foster pan-evangelicalism's evolutionary resilience yet dissipate evangelicals' convertive certainties in alternative, rival and even mutually exclusive convictions and priorities.

PART ONE

THE CONVERSIONIST-ACTIVIST AXIS

Late-modern charismatic entrepreneurialism in the context of church decline

Prelude

Hegemony Fractured

The mid-twentieth century hegemony of calvinistic conservatism came to an inevitable and self-inflicted demise through proliferating certainties, which, in 1966, risked the collapse of the Evangelical Alliance and the abandonment of pan-evangelical co-operation. We begin therefore with this crisis moment of internecine warfare, before turning to the entrepreneurial advance for which it had inadvertently opened the door by creating a leadership vacuum in pan-evangelicalism.

Inherent tensions within the calvinistic hegemony reached a seismic fracture point in 1966-7.[1] On 18 October 1966, D. Martyn Lloyd-Jones, the dominant calvinist-exclusivist nonconformist of the mid-twentieth century,[2] preached at Westminster Central Hall during the opening meeting of the Second National Assembly of Evangelicals. The First National Assembly, held in September 1965 had called for a commission to study evangelicals' various attitudes to "the ecumenical movement, denominationalism and a possible future United Church". Lloyd-Jones preached for an exclusively evangelical unity, arguing that schism could only take place between true believers, whereas separating from heretics and unbelievers was a Christian obligation. While the precise nature of Lloyd-Jones' call to an ecclesial unity is still contested, and may have been unclear to the Welshman, John Stott, the leading conservative evangelical Anglican of the mid-twentieth century,[3] felt obliged to refute the appeal as chairman of the meeting. (John Laird of Scripture Union commended Stott's timely intervention. Douglas Johnson of IVF, the conservative evangelical student organisation, complained that Stott appeared overheated and had abused the chair, further stating that several delegates had suggested to him that the meeting had been "rigged".)[4] Although Stott justified his interjection as a way of protecting earnest young Anglican curates unduly swayed by persuasive Welsh rhetoric, the Anglican course was already charted away from the Free Churches, since the National Evangelical Anglican Assembly was scheduled for 1967. The impact of Lloyd-Jones' appeal was negligible upon the historic denominations: no new fellowship of evangelical churches was established

---

[1] These events are documented from the perspectives of Lloyd-Jones (Murray, 1990-hagiography, Brencher, 2002 – critical study), Stott (Dudley-Smith, 2001 - hagiography) and Packer (McGrath, 1997 - hagiography).

[2] Murray, 1982, 1990; Brencher, 2002.

[3] Dudley-Smith, 1999, 2001.

[4] Dudley-Smith, 2001: 68-9.

and the calvinistic separatists withdrew into greater isolation, with diminishing influence upon wider evangelicalism.

What followed was a process of systemic isolation. On 16 October 1966, Lloyd-Jones persuaded Westminster Chapel's members to withdraw from the Congregational Church, and on 13 April 1967 to join the FIEC, the leading Calvinist-exclusivist network of churches. (In May 1968, Lloyd-Jones retired from leadership of the Chapel; not until 1990 did the Chapel join EA.) On 29 November 1966, Lloyd Jones unilaterally closed the Westminster Fellowship, a gathering of some 200 ministers, including Anglicans, founded in 1941 under his tutelage. In 1969 Lloyd-Jones resigned as chairman of the Puritan Conference, where Packer, the foremost Anglican neo-Puritan, had been his close colleague. In 1971 it was reconvened as the Westminster Conference, under Lloyd-Jones' leadership, sans Packer.

On 1 November 1967 Lloyd-Jones preached the closing address at a BEC conference. His topic was the 450th anniversary of Martin Luther's ninety five theses; his theme was double purity – theological and denominational. Lloyd-Jones declared that evangelicals outside the BEC were "mixed up with infidels and sceptics and denials of the truth".[5] Evangelicals in mixed denominations were deemed guilty by association, since separatism and opposition to the ecumenical movement were intrinsic to this version of evangelical orthodoxy. In 1977 Lloyd-Jones looked back to the Luther address as the defining moment concerning what he considered the "ridiculous position"[6] of Anglican evangelicals and the Evangelical Alliance with regard to mixed denominations and ecumenism. Notwithstanding Lloyd-Jones' championing of the BEC and the separatist cause, he became self-marginalised and never recovered influence among evangelicals in the historic denominations. In effect, Lloyd-Jones was replaying the pre-war north American fundamentalist disputes, accepting their logic of a double purity in theology and fellowship.[7] His initiative was impassioned, intransigent and ultimately as ineffectual within the wider church and the wider evangelical world as his fundamentalist forebears. However, these events should not be interpreted merely as the consequence of idiosyncratic, even quixotic, dogmatism when Lloyd-Jones assumed the fundamentalist mantle within British calvinistic conservatism. As we will demonstrate in comparing bases of faith, the conservative hegemony was intrinsically unstable and ultimately unsustainable: excessive and mutually exclusive certainties determined its inevitable demise. Mid-twentieth century calvinistic hegemony was fractured from within by inherent, unexpected and often fissiparous pluralism.

---

[5] Lloyd-Jones, 1991: 164.

[6] Brencher, 2002: 226.

[7] Marsden, 1980, 1987, 1991.

Chapter 1

Calverism and the Evangelical Alliance, 1982-2001

The conversionist-activist axis has been determinative for the initiatives, successes and ambitious claims that will be examined in this chapter. Given the high levels of churchgoing and belief in God in the United States and the rapid decline of both in Western Europe, the religious trajectory of the West and the exceptional case have been much debated. Is secularization the inevitable consequence of pluralisation, rationalisation and differentiation, in accordance with the older sociological consensus?[1] Or could the apparent inevitability of secularization prove a culturally specific European phenomenon?[2] Historical and sociological studies of church decline have often employed the data of church allegiance and church attendance,[3] and this study builds upon this methodology to scrutinise the empirical data of participation in British (and predominantly English) pan-evangelical activities. In order to examine the trajectories and ideology of the evangelical mass movement, we trace the spectacular rise of the Evangelical Alliance and Spring Harvest, chart the decline of traditional evangelical practices, and explore the effectiveness of late twentieth century evangelical initiatives in evangelism. This analysis enables us to examine to what extent evangelicals may indeed exhibit what has been claimed as a counter-trend to the prevailing Western European church decline.[4] We demonstrate that the conversionist-activist axis, predominantly charismatic in the period under consideration, was highly pragmatic and vigorously entrepreneurial, achieving remarkable successes within the internal, pan-evangelical market while articulating societal expectations that were adventurously assertive but risked proving inflated, quixotic or even delusional.

Personal Membership - Growth and Decline

For twelve years from the early 1980s, the Evangelical Alliance enjoyed sustained, indeed spectacular growth in personal membership.[5] Clive Calver was appointed as

---

[1] Wilson, 1966; Berger, 1967; Bruce, 1995, 1996, 2002; contra Stark and Bainbridge, 1985.

[2] Martin, 1978, 2005; Berger, 1999; Davie, 1994, 2000, 2002; Gill, 1993.

[3] Martin, 1978; Gilbert, 1980; Wolffe, 1994; Bruce, 2002; Gill, 2003.

[4] Bebbington, 1989; Tidball, 1994; Brady and Rowdon, 1996; compare Smith, 1998.

[5] Numerical data in this section is taken from the following sources. 1982-1991 data supplied by EA membership department. 1992-2001 data taken from membership statistics in the papers of the Executive Committee, Board and Council for the year ending 31 March. Where

General Director at the young age of thirty four in 1982, and only with his appointment did EA recover from the traumatic and public division of 1966. The previous year EA had 900 personal members. By 1996, when Calver began a new term of office for the period 1996-2000, personal membership stood at 51,925. To recruit 51,000 members from a base of less than 1,000 in fourteen years, was an exceptional achievement. These personal members had no constitutional status, no voting rights or power. However, they were a construct that engendered a sense of evangelical momentum, levered greater media and political influence, and created a new engine room of funding for EA's expansive aspirations.

Table 3: EA personal membership 1981-1996, plotted at five year intervals

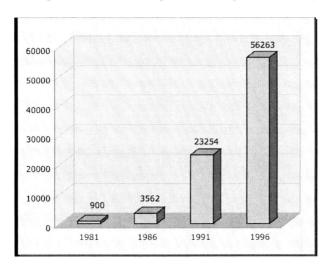

If we analyse personal membership in five-year periods, in numerical terms growth continued to accelerate: up 2,662 in the first period, 19,693 in the second and 33,009 in the third. However, in percentage terms the increase was 296% in the first period, rose to 553% in the second, but fell to a still strong yet relatively modest 142% in the third. The peak period for growth in EA membership was therefore the second half of the 1980s. While growth continued in the first half of the 1990s, it was slower than at any time since Calver had taken office.

In 1991, Calver's promotion of personal membership of the Alliance was typically robust, enthusiastic and demanding:

---

the two sets of statistics differ, presumably because the recent internal document used a different year end, I have used the year end statistics produced for the Board. The same statistics were used by Mark Birchall in a report entitled *Clearing the Decks*, dated 21 April 1997 in which he recorded the membership and financial data for 1992-1996. His title allegedly referred to an attempt to clear the cumulative financial deficit of the later Calver years.

There are tremendous challenges and opportunities ahead. But the Evangelical Alliance cannot respond without the support of at least 10,000 new members within the next year.[6]

Since the total increase from 1992-96, amounted to only 16,145, Calver's promotional rhetoric ran ahead of reality. If his analysis of the growth-rate required to seize the perceived opportunities was correct, we must assume that the Alliance was consistently incapable of delivering Calver's aspirations.

Table 4: EA personal membership 1992-1996, annual figures

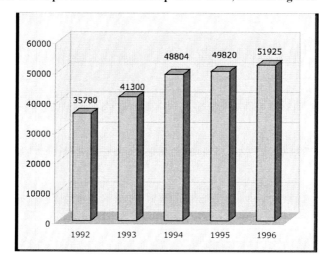

In 1995, the ambitious pursuit of growth intensified. The Council members were told at their September meeting:

> The vision of the EA Executive is to see 100,000 individual members by the end of 1996. The new campaign is 'Each One Get One' with EA writing to every member encouraging them to recruit new members.[7]

At this same meeting, EA Council were advised that 6,500 members had joined during that year, including 3,000 at Spring Harvest. This indicates the considerable synergy between Spring Harvest and the Evangelical Alliance that was pivotal to Calver's success, but demonstrates the Alliance was also securing substantial recruitment beyond Spring Harvest. The EA had plainly struck a chord with evangelicals, developing a remarkable momentum of sustained growth. Since the period from 1982 to 1995 had seen such explosive growth, a further doubling

---

[6] Spring Harvest Programme, 1991.
[7] EAUK Council papers, September 1995.

seemed only reasonable. Growth appeared guaranteed. The growth had been exponential, although growth would have needed further acceleration to achieve the target of 100,000 in the timescale proposed. The Executive clearly had no inkling that 1995 was the first year in which personal membership showed signs of reaching a plateau.

In the opening years of the 1990s, the growth of the 1980s was sustained. 1993 saw a 15.4% increase over 1992, 1994 saw an 18.2% increase over 1993. However, by the mid-1990s, when Calver was struggling with unstable blood pressure and a heart condition, the membership boom had stalled. In 1995, the increase was 2.1%. In the Assembly year of 1996, which involved high profile tours in celebration of 150 years of the EA combined with effusive promotional campaigns, membership increased by a modest 4.2%. The early to mid-1990s, even though membership was still growing, was a period in which EA recruitment dropped behind the exponential trend previously enjoyed. The last year in which EA membership grew rapidly was 1993-94. This new trend appears to have gone unremarked at the time within the organisation.

Table 5: EA personal membership 1981-1996

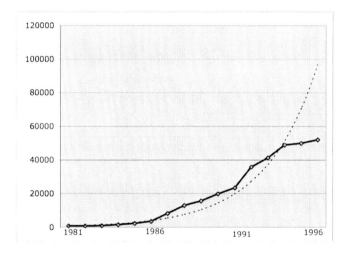

(The broken line indicates an exponential growth trend corresponding with the projected target of 100,000 agreed by EAUK Council in 1995.)

A further assertion well-publicised by EA in the mid-1990s was that they represented one million evangelicals. This number was reached by combining the attendees of the churches in membership, plus the members of the denominations in membership, plus those whose churches were not in membership who could nonetheless be identified as evangelical. Mark Birchall, who in the early 1990s chaired both the Evangelical group in the General Synod of the Church of England

and the Executive Committee of the Alliance, argued to the EA Executive[8] with characteristic enthusiasm that one million represented a considerable under-estimate of the real number of evangelicals in British churches and so the Alliance could pitch its claim still higher. The calculation of over one million evangelicals, the boom in personal membership and the indications in the 1989 church census[9] that church growth among evangelicals contrasted with numerical decline in the broader church, combined to make the early to mid-1990s a period of buoyant expectancy for EA. The 100,000 personal members was not considered a *terminus ad quem*, but rather an ambitious but achievable staging post on the way to bringing about a spiritual and ethical reconstruction in church and society.[10] Excitement ran deep. In 2001, by which time the campaign for 100,000 had been quietly dropped,[11] "one million voices" became a prominent theme in Joel Edwards' initiative, "movement for change". In short, once personal membership began to decline, the EA continued to base its campaigns on claims of numerical strength, emphasising a number sufficiently large to excite interest, but sufficiently vague as to be unfalsifiable. In Autumn 2002, EA publicity raised its claimed number of evangelicals to 1.5 million. This implied either severe under-counting in the recent past or a staggering rate of growth among evangelicals in the new millennium for which there was no corroborating statistical evidence. In January 2003 this higher claim was swiftly dropped. [12]

Securing political influence and media profile based on numerical support is one of five characteristic strategies employed by religious leaders. (i) Some derive influence from societal status, thus senior Anglicans enjoy a unique *ex officio* access to politicians and the media. (ii) Some derive influence from spiritual charisma, notably Basil Hume[13] or the Dalai Llama.[14] (iii) Some derive influence from intellect, notably Jonathan Sacks,[15] whose insights, redolent with the wisdom tradition, are found pertinent well beyond the world of Judaism. (iv) Some derive influence from their engaging, media-friendly personality, notably from the mid-1990s Steve Chalke, described by his organisation as the "TV Vicar".[16] (v) Some derive influence from their lobbying muscle, in terms of the number of people they represent. The increasing political and media access of the Evangelical Alliance ran parallel to and was dependent upon its growth in personal membership and its claim to represent a million evangelicals. The most significant unanswered question is not whether there were a million evangelicals - according to Brierley's statistics, there may well have been - but rather, on what basis and with what credibility the EA

---

[8] Indicated by him and others in interviews.

[9] Brierley, 1991a.

[10] Tidball, 1994; Brady and Rowdon, 1996; Calver and Warner, 1996.

[11] Indicated in interviews with senior EA staff.

[12] Indicated in interviews with senior EA staff.

[13] Hume, 1979; Howard, 2005.

[14] Dalai Lama XIV Bstan-'dzin-rgya-mtsho, 1999.

[15] Sacks, 2003, 2005.

[16] www.oasistrust.org. Accessed 5 August 2005.

could claim to represent a million evangelicals, when they had no access to most of them and no relliable way of canvassing their views or measuring their balance of opinion for particular policies or campaigns.[17]

Table 6: EA personal membership 1981-2001

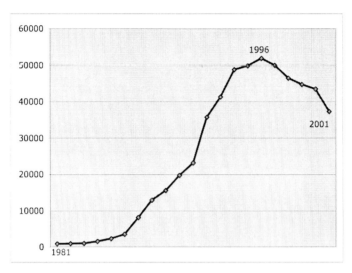

From 1991-96 personal membership grew by 28,671, whereas from 96-2001, personal membership decreased by 14,619. The figures for the year ending 31 March 2001 reinforced the mid to late 1990s turn down. Personal membership was 43,534, up a mere eighteen over the previous year, and church membership was 3,090, up ten. A further adjustment to remove non-contributory members reduced the total membership to 37,306. While not as dramatic as the preceding period of growth, the decline in the late 1990s was substantial. Half the growth of 1991-1996 was lost during 1996-2001.[18] After fifteen years of meteoric growth had apparently vindicated entrepreneurial evangelicalism's claims that success and advance were assured, this rhetoric's continued plausibility would have been severely dented had

---

[17] In the USA, Penning and Smidt (2002) demonstrate a strong and inter-generational consensus, Republican and ethically conservative on the evangelical right. However, Smith (2000) demonstrates wide divergence between evangelicals both in terms of social ethics and concerning the relative status of moral absolutes and individual freedoms in governmental legislation. He concludes that the self-appointed leaders of religious neo-conservatism are often more strident and absolutist than those they claim to represent.

[18] Churches in membership followed a different pattern in the late 1990s, continuing to grow, albeit slightly. Here too there was a dramatic shift. From 1991-96 church membership doubled (1,436 to 2,853), but from 1996-2001 the growth rate was just 8% (2,853 to 3,090), strikingly better than the personal membership decline of 28%, but still dramatically reduced from the earlier period. Institutional inertia means that churches are likely to cancel membership of any organization even more slowly than individuals.

these figures been widely known.

This turnaround indicates not merely a loss of momentum in garnering new members, but a loss of confidence on the part of existing members, who had committed to the Alliance as loose affiliates for the short term, rather than embedding themselves in the Alliance as a lifelong commitment. This short-termism is characteristic of the period. Previous generations of evangelicals, reflecting the general culture, made lifelong commitments to support their chosen charities, whereas the post-war generations proved more likely to donate to a particular project or endorse a particular personality, moving their support elsewhere once an initiative that caught their imagination had come to an end.[19]

Table 7: EA personal membership 1996-2001, annual figures

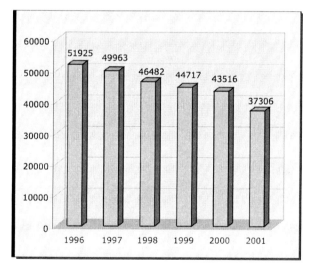

From the peak figure of 51,925 personal members in 1996, the actual membership in 2001 was 37,306, a return to the membership level of 1992. Calver had re-invented EA personal membership as the engine room of evangelical advancement. However, by 2001 EA could no longer plausibly aspire to become a mass membership organisation. In five years personal membership had haemorrhaged by 28% to little more than one third of the published target of 100,000. Although several senior evangelicals expressed to me during interviews the assumption that EA membership was assuredly around 100,000, the reality of a mere 37,000 is dramatically weaker. The conclusion is unavoidable: by the mid-1990s the spectacular growth was over. Rather than functioning as a launch pad for

---

[19] This trend was identified in conversations with senior staff at EMA, concerning changing donor patterns among their member agencies.

a subsequent acceleration of recruitment, the 1980s could now be reappraised as a short-term boom, a false dawn before postmodernity began to bite.

Denominational Profile

An analysis of the denominational profile of churches in membership of the Alliance in 2001 reveals three main contributors: Anglicans, Baptists and Independents.[20] Given the relative size of the Anglicans and the Baptists in the UK (1998 figures, Anglicans: 18,416 churches, 10,395 ministers; Baptists: 3,418 churches, 2,777 ministers[21]), one might reasonably suppose that the Anglicans would constitute a much larger grouping with the Alliance, even though the percentage of evangelicals is much higher among the Baptists. In fact, the denominational profile of church membership of EA indicates a substantial Baptist prominence,[22] comprising 25.84%, compared with 18.42% Anglican[23] and 18.49% Independent.

Table 8: Denominational profile of EA church membership, February 2001

Denomination	% of EA membership
Baptist	25.84%
Independent	18.49%
Anglican	18.42%
AoG	5.05%
Brethren	4.53%
NFI	3.73%
Elim	2.99%
FIEC	2.96%
Pioneer	2.03%

---

[20] Churches have been in EA membership since 1957.

[21] Brierley, 1999: 2.8, 2.10.

[22] The Baptist total figure is obtained by the addition of the Baptist Union of Great Britain 23.41%, and the Baptist Unions of Ireland, 0.19%, Scotland, 1.48% and Wales, 0.19%, the Grace Baptists, 0.16%, the Old Baptist Union, 0.03%, and Baptists who also have links to Ichthus 0.03%, and New Frontiers 0.35%. The total includes those who have new church links when their constitutional status remains Baptist. Local ecumenical projects including Baptists alongside other historic denominations comprise a further 0.44%, and the Independent Baptists provide 1.03%. If these other Baptist groupings are included, the total increases to 26.87%. The figure we have cited of 25.84% therefore probably represents a slight under-estimate of the Baptist contribution, which can broadly be expressed as just over one in four of the member churches of the Evangelical Alliance.

[23] By no means all evangelical Anglicans have proven willing to join EA, whether in its origins (Chadwick, 1966) or in the late twentieth century (Manwaring, 1985).

Methodist	1.9%
URC	1.61%
Other	12.45%

These proportions were little changed from 1995, when the figures were 27.94% Baptist[24] and 18.98% Anglican. Regrettably, data for the independents and new churches were combined in this analysis, which gave a largely meaningless figure of 30.03% for groupings quite different from one another.

The notable increases since 1995, although they are all relatively slight, are Assemblies of God, from 3.59% to 5.05%, Brethren, from 2.84% to 4.53%, and New Frontiers International, from 1.76 to 3.73%. This indicates the significant diversity of support for EA, since these three groupings are, respectively, Pentecostal, broadly non-charismatic, and new church.

Table 9: Denominational profile of EA church membership, February 1995

% of UK membership	Denomination	% of English membership
30.44%	Independent/none/new	30.03%
27.94%	Baptist	27.61%
18.98%	Anglican	20.61%
3.59%	AoG	3.48%
3.55%	Elim	3.52%
3.18%	FIEC	3.38%
2.84%	Brethren	2.79%
2.5%	Methodist	2.62%
1.76%	NFI	1.93%
1.42%	URC	1.52%
1.12%	Presbyterian & Congregational	0.7%
0.6%	Evangelical Free	0.53%
0.41%	Wesleyan	0.45%
0.34%	Pentecostal	0.37%

[24] The basis on which this composite figure was reached was not stated.

0.22%	Apostolic	0.2%
0.18%	Joint	0.2%
0.04%	Salvation Army	0.04%

Several conclusions can be drawn from these statistics. First, the Evangelical Alliance predominantly attracts a Free Church membership. Second, the Evangelical Alliance predominantly attracts believer-baptizing churches; few of the Independents are likely to be paedobaptist. Third, and paradoxically, the Evangelical Alliance is mainly comprised of evangelicals in historic denominations. Fourth, the two dominant denominations are the Anglicans and Baptists, together comprising nearly half the total membership, with nearly three Baptists for every two Anglicans. Fifth, three groupings, Baptist, Anglican and Independent, comprise 62.75% of EA church membership, and might reasonably be expected to wield the greatest influence and secure proportionate attention for their priorities and concerns. Sixth, these three groupings, representing two thirds of EA membership, comprise a wide range of ecclesiological contexts: majority evangelical denomination (Baptist), minority evangelical denomination (Anglican), and an exclusively evangelical independent sector.

The largest two new church representations in 2001 were New Frontiers (3.73%) and Pioneer (2.03%) with Ichthus delivering 1.19%, Salt and Light 0.51% and Covenant Ministries 0.19%. That means that for every one from Pioneer in membership of the Alliance, there were thirteen Baptists and nine Anglicans; for every one from New Frontiers, there were seven Baptists and five Anglicans. Thus, if EA drew accurately upon its membership in terms of its public representation and policies, we could reasonably expect the Alliance to emphasise, paradoxically, the historic denominations, the Free Churches and believers' baptism.

Faced with these conundrums of evangelical diversity, Calver proved an adroit politician. He made every effort to include senior Anglicans, shrewdly emphasising the established church dimension of the Alliance beyond their actual level of numerical involvement, considering Stott an informal ambassador for pan-evangelicalism among evangelical Anglicans[25] and securing George Carey to preach at the 150th anniversary celebration in London in January 1996. This reflected Calver's concern to counteract the drift of Anglicans away from pan-evangelicalism following the Lloyd-Jones and Stott controversy of the mid-1960s. Simultaneously, Calver gave deliberate and disproportionate prominence to the new churches, both within the Alliance and at Spring Harvest.

The Baptists have been a strong recruiting ground for EA because, of all the historic denominations, the Baptists have proven the most willing to participate and identify with pan-evangelicalism, probably in part because their distinctive denominational identity is much less strong than in other historic denominations.

---

[25] Indicated in interview.

The *Church Life Profile* concluded in 2002 that Baptists were "significantly different in many ways" from the other contributing denominations - Anglicans, Methodists, URC and Salvation Army. They placed particular emphasis upon the role played by God and their local church in their lives, but their denomination was less important than for those attending more institutional churches.[26] Nonetheless the Baptists seem to have been perceived as something of an Achilles' heel, since the Alliance chose to raise its profile by emphasizing the support of respectable bishops and radical new church leaders. The Baptists may have appeared too middle-of-the-road, carrying insufficient social status or entrepreneurial energy. According to some interviewees, EA preferred to invest its energies in the margins of its constituency.

Reasons for Growth

Calver's remarkable success in leading the EA to new prominence within and to some measure beyond the evangelical constituency demands explanation, particularly at a time of declining church attendance and socio-political influence. Reflecting upon the EA archives and the broader historical context alongside interviews and critical reflection as an observing-participant, and recognising that the initiatives of a charismatic leader both shape and are shaped by their micro and macro-cultural contexts, it is apparent that Calver's exceptional effectiveness is best interpreted as a confluence of personal charisma, the pan-evangelical context and wider cultural influences.

Interviewees observed that Calver possessed a rare force of charisma.[27] His presence could dominate a room or a platform, almost effortlessly. This was not an almost ethereal presence, in the sense of the Dalai Lama or Cardinal Hume, but more a force of personality sometimes found in leading politicians who dominate their party for a season. For Calver, this charisma of authority was reinforced by brinkmanship, a crisis-centred leadership style.[28] Those working closely with him became accustomed to a continuous turmoil of crises and deadlines, since Calver got the best work out of himself under acute pressure. Faced with this pattern of imminent crisis, EA's Executive and Council were usually willing to let Calver have his way. He developed a meta-narrative for the Alliance in which each urgent initiative he proposed was the only way for EA simultaneously to seize the moment and avoid disaster. At the time of his departure from EA, he painted evangelicalism's future prospects in almost apocalyptic terms:[29] either the million were about to be mobilised and the destiny of the nation transformed, or the various tribal groupings would, in a season of relative success, no longer need one another and fragment into disarray. There was no middle way with Calver: disaster and

---

[26] Escott and Gelder, 2002.

[27] Weber, 'The Sociology of Charismatic Authority', ET 1948.

[28] Indicated in interviews.

[29] In Calver's speech at his leaving party.

triumph were invariably imminent. Such a leadership style was intoxicating and exhilarating, but ultimately exhausting for his senior staff.[30] It also became increasingly unconvincing, at least for this participant-observer, who suspected from the early 1990s that a brief episode of meteoric growth had already passed.

Peter Meadows, co-founder of Spring Harvest who also worked with Calver at EA, recalls him tirelessly travelling the country, preaching at churches, and meeting strategic leaders.[31] Calver exhibited exceptional and sustained drivenness, determination and ambition as he wooed, cajoled and inspired the re-gathering of evangelicals under the banner of the EA. He was a highly effective builder of coalition, investing much time in the strategic leaders, or *tribal heads* in his terminology,[32] and persuading them to identify with the Alliance. In building bridges and developing coalition, Calver also understood the need for public recognition,

---

[30] Indicated in interviews.

[31] In interview.

[32] Calver enumerated "twelve tribes of evangelicalism" (Calver, Coffey, Meadows, 1993; Calver and Warner, 1996: 128-130).

    1 Anglican evangelicals
    2 Pentecostals
    3 Ethnic churches
    4 Renewal groupings
    5 Separatists
    6 Reformed evangelicals
    7 Evangelical majorities   e.g. Salvation Army, Presbyterian Church of Ireland and the Baptist Union
    8 Evangelical minorities   e.g. Methodist and URC
    9 Evangelical non-denominational groups e.g. Christian Brethren, FIEC, and Assemblies of God
    10 New Churches
    11 Independents
    12 Evangelical denominations   e.g. Free Church of England, Churches of Christ, and Independent Methodists

This categorisation is severely flawed. For example, the ethnic churches are overwhelmingly Pentecostal, and it is difficult to see why the Assemblies of God should be listed under non-denominational groupings when they are also the largest Pentecostal grouping in England. The Anglicans are listed as a separate category, reflecting their numerical strength, yet the Baptists are listed as one among many "evangelical majority" denominations, as if their majority status was more significant than their Baptist identity. If the broader categories pertain, the Anglicans should be listed among the "evangelical minority" denominations. However, Anglicans also encompass reformed evangelicals, renewal groupings, some ethnic churches and a small but vociferous number of calvinistic separatists. Similarly, to take a new church example, New Frontiers can be designated a renewal grouping, a reformed grouping, a new church, and also either a non-denominational grouping, by their own definition, or an evangelical denomination. This mythological twelve tribes categorisation is artificial: it seems likely that Calver began with a "twelve tribes" slogan and then arranged the evidence accordingly. It is also too static, failing to take account of the shape-shifting volatility of contemporary evangelicalism.

regularly commending senior evangelical leaders in his preaching and including them in his platform parties at Spring Harvest and EA events. Many leaders with diverse emphases were confident that Calver understood their concerns and was working for their best interests.[33]

Calver brought a fresh, contemporary edge, a missional pragmatism alongside ethical and theological conservatism. In his appointment the Alliance skipped a generation; in his disposition, he came as close as any evangelical of his generation to the prevailing radicalism of the 1960s; in his somewhat volatile temperament, Calver was considered energetic, even dangerous, such that London Bible College had received complaints about his suitability as a student from his more conventional peers.[34]

Calver was an exceptional intuitive, instinctively aware of the populist emphases and initiatives that would appeal among evangelicals, both clergy and laity. He understood the value of headline grabbing initiatives that demonstrated the EA taking a strong lead, not afraid to tackle controversial issues that the denominations failed to address. Opposition to the growing profile of Halloween and concerns about satanic sexual abuse ran the risk of looking juvenile and crowd-pleasing. Indeed one interviewee who required anonymity for this study but was closely linked with the EA at that time, feared that a campaign against satanic sexual abuse in the early 1990s came close to discrediting the EA with unsubstantiated scare-mongering. Nonetheless, such initiatives raised the profile of EA within the evangelical constituency.

Calver was strongly associated with evangelism,[35] having led British Youth for Christ and served as programme director for Billy Graham's Mission England (1982-3). His close links with the international evangelist Luis Palau and his enthusiasm for stadium evangelism meant that his track-record chimed well with the concern for evangelism among his two largest constituencies, the Baptists, who counted Billy Graham among their own, and the Anglicans, who had taken the lead in public commendation of the Billy Graham missions in the UK.

Calver was similarly emphatic concerning social action. With Peter Meadows he had attended the Lausanne Congress on World Evangelism in 1974 as part of a young team of UK delegates, and the emphasis upon holistic mission confirmed Calver's priorities. He habitually espoused the integral importance of social action through both EA and Spring Harvest, where the two annual offerings were for evangelism and social action. When he left EA for World Relief, an American evangelical development charity, this represented no change of emphasis but a further expression of long-standing convictions.[36] As a student of nineteenth century

---

[33] Indicated in interviews.

[34] Indicated in interview and recounted often in his preaching.

[35] Calver and Warner, 1996.

[36] Calver recalled in interview a Conservative cabinet minister expressing puzzlement that evangelicals combined a left of centre concern for social action with a right of centre ethical conservatism. What these two strands have in common is an emphatic emphasis on interventionism. Traditional evangelical activism has no time for *laisser-faire* economic

evangelical history, Calver argued that EA was grounded on the principle of united action and the practice of holistic mission. His historical awareness, albeit selective and polemical,[37] strengthened his case for the integration of evangelism and social action.

Above all, Calver instigated the remarkable EA-Spring Harvest interface. We will explore the story of Spring Harvest in Chapter 2, but here we note that this linkage proved extraordinarily effective: each year Spring Harvest functioned as a platform for the EA, not only to recruit new members, but also to present the vision of EA and to demonstrate the advantages of evangelicals working together enthusiastically. Spring Harvest expressed a trans-denominational (or even post denominational) ethos that expressed and strengthened Calver's vision for the EA. With Calver pivotal in both organisations, the relationship between EA and Spring Harvest was symmetrically symbiotic. More than any other single factor, this interface generated a unique and prolonged opportunity for Calver to grow and reposition the Alliance.

We turn now from Calver's leadership style and initiatives to contributory factors from the evangelical and wider cultural context. Calver came to the Alliance at a time, according to Ian Coffey (in interview), when evangelicals were coming out of their shells and growing in confidence and resolve to "make a difference in the nation". Calver's entrepreneurialism built upon a re-emergent assertiveness among evangelicals that achieved new public prominence in 1971 when over 35,000 Christians gathered in Trafalgar Square in what Malcolm Muggeridge described as a "Festival of Light". Prior to *March for Jesus* (1987-2000)[38], it was the largest pubic gathering of Christians in the UK in the twentieth century. The Nationwide Festival of Light grew out of this event and thence emerged CARE in 1983, which rapidly became one of the most prominent evangelical lobby groups, particularly against abortion and in favour of strong censorship controls. In describing the mood of the Festival, Lyndon Bowring, Pentecostal minister and longstanding executive

---

policy or libertarianism. EA has long been an instinctive exponent of big government.

[37] Wilberforce has been granted quasi-canonization among many evangelicals as their patron saint of social action, but his opposition to slavery was not integrated with an equivalent concern for social justice at home. He defended the Corn Laws, opposed the Reform Bill of 1831, and held a deeply patrician complacency about the allotted place of the lower classes (Noll, 2004: 240-242; Williams, 1944: 82). In religion, Wilberforce was strictly partisan in his view that the proper sphere of Christian influence was the National Church (*Practical View*, 1797, anthologised in Jeffrey, 1987: 515). Brown charged Wilberforce with being "steadily opposed to every serious political effort for the help of the oppressed lower orders" (Brown, 1961: 112). Indeed, Edmund Burke, the quintessential high Tory was reported to have read approvingly Wilberforce's *Practical View* on his death bed in 1797 (Pollock, 1977: 148). David Smith concluded that Wilberforce and the Clapham Sect identified the Christian Gospel with a social elite and patriarchal status quo, thus alienating the more radical social reformers and contributing to the long-term decline of Christian influence, notwithstanding the success of the abolitionist campaign (Smith, 1998: 19).

[38] www.jesusday.org ; www.grahamkendrick.co.uk. Accessed 5 August 2005.

chairman of CARE, identified a new mobilisation emphatically in reaction against the 1960s:

> At last many Christians were rising up to challenge the tide of morally liberal legislation introduced during the 60s and were committing themselves to standing for Christian values, marriage and family. The 'permissive society' had met with little opposition before this time, but God stirred hearts, challenging the Church to become more determined to raise a Christian voice in the nation.[39]

Terry Virgo, subsequently leader of New Frontiers International, the new church movement most closely associated with Lloyd-Jones' calvinist-exclusivism,[40] experienced this as an evangelical *risorgimento,* the birth-time of a new assertiveness:

> The wholehearted singing reflected new life emerging in the Body of Christ...The city of God was beginning to look good for the first time in my Christian experience...surely God was doing something new in the land.[41]

This renascent evangelical social agenda was essentially reactive, seeking a return to a pre-1960s era of legislated Christian conformity. Calver's entrepreneurial activism reinforced an existing expectation that evangelicals should and could rise up as a force of ethical conservatism to turn back the clock of social legislation.[42] This would inevitably result in a great deal of commonality and yet rivalry between CARE and EA, given the similarity in their agenda and rhetoric.[43] EA provoked rivalry in two ways: by stealing the thunder of CARE, which had since its inception been more prominent than EA in evangelical campaigning on such issues; and by offering a broader agenda of social policy, giving insufficient emphasis, from CARE's perspective, to anti-abortion and pro-censorship campaigns. The early 1980s saw in Britain a temporary return to tighter censorship, particularly in video distribution, which appeared to demonstrate the beginnings of new advances in evangelical influence. However, British society was already sufficiently secularized and libertarian to render the wholesale ethical reversion and enforcement cherished by many evangelicals an entirely naïve and unrealistic social policy.

Calver cultivated strategic friendships with influential evangelical leaders. He enjoyed strong support from his father-in-law, Gilbert Kirby, who had been General Secretary of the EA and then Principal of London Bible College during Calver's time as a student there. When Gordon Landreth, successor to Kirby's successor Morgan Derham, resigned as General Secretary of the EA, Kirby was the EA President and he identified what was wanted in Landreth's successor. Whether or

---

[39] Lyndon Bowring in a circular letter from CARE, September 2001.

[40] Virgo, 1985, 1996; Walker, 1989, 2002.

[41] Virgo, 2001: 87-8.

[42] For similar American emphases see Penning and Smidt (2002), although markedly different conclusions are drawn by Hunter 1983, 1987) and Smith (1998, 2000).

[43] Indicated in interviews.

not he had his son-in-law in mind, the similarities are unmistakable. The new General Secretary should:

> gain the ear of Christian people up and down the country...a reasonably young person, although not without some experience...hold the respect of the vast majority of Evangelicals...acceptable to charismatics and non-charismatics.[44]

Calver also gained the support of Sir Fred Catherwood, industrialist, Euro MP and, most significantly given the debacle of 1966-7, Martyn Lloyd-Jones' son-in-law. Catherwood became President of the EA and drove forward the development of local evangelical networks promoting social action. Given Lloyd-Jones' withdrawal from wider evangelicalism, Catherwood's continued involvement sustained an invaluable bridgehead to the reformed Right.

Calver drew upon friendships with fellow graduates of London Bible College, counting Ian Coffey and Joel Edwards among his closest EA colleagues. Another fellow student at LBC and close colleague was Lyndon Bowring, later a staff member at Kensington Temple, the leading Elim church in London, and Executive Chairman of CARE. Graham Kendrick, leading charismatic songwriter of the 1980s and 1990s,[45] was also a longstanding friend, with whom he had toured in an evangelistic team after leaving LBC. Kendrick became the leading modern hymn writer of his generation and a pivotal influence during the first decade of Spring Harvest. Calver had been converted under Roger Forster, founder of Ichthus, who was the first of the new church leaders to commit himself to wider evangelical co-operation, serving for many years on the Evangelical Alliance Council. At Calver's leaving party, Forster indiscreetly commended Calver for delivering "our" agenda.[46]

Strongly supported by his LBC comrades, Calver was also fortunate in his opponents. The year after he was appointed EA General Secretary, in 1984 David Jenkins was appointed Bishop of Durham. The media could rely upon the Bishop to deliver seasonal scepticism at Easter, Christmas or Epiphany, and Calver was always ready for gladiatorial combat, delivering a robust, traditionalist riposte. Each rallied his own troops; both were unlikely to convince their opponents. While moderate evangelical Anglican clergy had little time for Calver's robust conservatism, many Free Church evangelicals and many evangelical laity were pleased to have such a vigorous public advocate.[47]

Calver also benefited from the timing of evangelical initiatives and campaigns. Mission England (1984-5) and the Keep Sunday Special Campaign (1985-6) served to reinforce a sense of growing confidence and self-assertiveness for evangelicals, both in evangelism and in socio-political campaigning. Neither Jenkins' pronouncements, nor the Graham visit, nor the Sunday campaign were under Calver's control, but they all reinforced the entrepreneurial rhetoric that a new day

---

[44] *IDEA*, Winter 1982/3: 1.
[45] We return to Kendrick's contribution in chapter 2.
[46] Indicated in interviews.
[47] Both perspectives were voiced in interviews.

had dawned, with growing opportunities in the media and a renewed sense of mobilisation in evangelism and political lobbying. Calver conveyed the confident impression of evangelicals on the march once again, with EA blazing the trail.[48]

Calver's optimistic and visionary drive chimed well with a period in which evangelicals were emerging from a collective depression or loss of confidence in any broad and inclusive evangelical identity, following the Stott / Lloyd-Jones debacle which had resulted in the rekindling of separatism and the parallel withdrawal of evangelical Anglicans. He also bridged the gap between the historic denominations and the new churches and Pentecostals. In his convictions, Calver described himself as Reformed and charismatic. In his temperament he was a forceful extrovert, more similar to the leadership culture of the Pentecostals and new churches than the historic denominations. And yet, in his instinctive understanding of power and his evident appetite for church politics, Calver worked assiduously to integrate the historic denominations as well as the new churches. Although this resulted in some conservatives claiming that the Alliance had become the Charismatic Alliance[49], it meant that EA was able to welcome charismatics as equal partners in the evangelical movement at a time when other long-standing evangelical organisations, notably UCCF, were still trying to come to terms with the implications and legitimacy of charismatic expressions of the evangelical tradition. The collapse of the calvinistic hegemony resulted in the partial withdrawal from pan-evangelicalism of both the conservative evangelical Anglicans and the neo-fundamentalist calvinistic separatists, and this unintentionally opened the way, once EA recovered from this traumatic division, for the previously inconceivable full integration of Pentecostals, new churches and charismatics in Calver's reinvention of the Alliance.

The leadership style of this archetypal Weberian charismatic[50] correlated with the prominence in the 1980s of Margaret Thatcher and Richard Branson: strong, assertive, self-made and instinctively authoritarian. He was appointed as General Secretary, subsequently became General Director and eventually was designated Director General. Each re-entitlement indicated a further centralising of authority upon the charismatic leader. Evangelicals concurred with the wider cultural consensus in the Thatcherite years, seeing many advantages in "strong" leadership with authoritarian leanings. As one senior leader of the 1980s and 1990s put it in interview, "Clive was a benign dictator. We knew he was king, but he made space for others to make their contribution effectively."

Reasons for Decline

The assumption that the personal members would each recruit another evidently

---

[48] Calver and Warner, 1996.

[49] For example: "The Evangelical Alliance is in the hands of the charismatics." Thomas, 2000.

[50] Weber, 'The Sociology of Charismatic Authority', ET 1948.

sounded perfectly reasonable in the mid-1990s. But it didn't happen. EA assumed that it enjoyed an active membership, ready and willing to make an effort to recruit others. The failure of this campaign indicates a different kind of membership, essentially passive, willing to lend their names to the Alliance but insufficiently involved to become a cohort of voluntary recruiters.[51] At Spring Harvest, Calver regularly offered membership at a discounted rate from the normal level of suggested donation, which was already minimal. New recruits were offered a free video or book by evangelical luminaries. And they were told that their very presence in membership increased the influence of the Alliance. Evangelicals who had lent their name to a head count, with minimal financial cost and a free gift, could hardly be thought to constitute an active membership. They had done their bit already, and now it was up to the Alliance to deliver the goods. Calver claimed that 100,000 represented the critical mass that would deliver credibility in the eyes of the political parties and the mass media. The recruitment drive was impassioned and visionary. And yet it failed. If 100,000 members was indeed the minimum requirement to secure credible influence with the main political parties, even at its peak the Alliance fell short by nearly 50,000. We have identified one significant reason for the failure to sustain the period of meteoric growth: the personal members were passive, and unwilling to become active recruiters.

When Calver's re-appointment for the period 1996-2000 was being reviewed, Derek Copley, chair of EA Council, wrote a supportive letter to the Council in November 1993. Copley was defensive against the charge that this reappointment would demonstrate that the EA needed Calver. Nonetheless, Calver's adventurous vision, force of personality, enormous capacity for work under pressure, persuasive powers that drew diverse evangelical parties and "tribal heads" towards the Alliance, and his rhetorical gift for rallying the troops, together represented a rare and extraordinarily productive combination of gifts. In short, the most significant factor in the growth of EA was Calver. However, according to interviewees, he was growing restless. In the early 1990s, several of his senior team left EA, including Ian Coffey and Pete Meadows, and building a new team may have proved less rewarding than collaborating as pioneers.[52] Calver wanted to withdraw from the management of the Alliance, creating a role for himself as "Director General". Some said this would allow Calver to specialise in what he did best; others feared the prospect of semi-detachment between Calver and the EA.[53] At the same time, Calver's health broke down, as did Colin Saunders', EA's Chief Executive. Calver's hyper-active, crisis-driven, adrenaline-fed, another-mountain-to-climb model of management, while producing exceptional growth, and portentous expectations for the future, was proving unsustainable. Calver had generated the growth, but now the heightened expectations were producing an intolerable pressure upon Calver and his senior team. Calver could no longer function effectively as the inspirational dynamo,

---

[51] Compare Putnam, 2000.

[52] Indicated in interviews.

[53] Indicated in interviews.

attempting to recruit a further 50,000 members.

A related factor concerns the necessary transitions in management style as an organisation grows. Calver was an exemplary initiator, producing meteoric growth. But he was not a good consolidator, managing change and developing a stable and focused organisation.[54] In the period 1992-96, which enjoyed a 45% growth in personal membership, Alliance expenditure grew by 88.6%. Growth in staff and ancillary costs consistently ran ahead of recruitment. The cumulative deficit, 1992-1996, was £293K. If membership had reached a natural plateau, then so had willingness to give. The donors had dramatically increased their gifts, but could not keep up with the burgeoning expenditure. By the mid-1990s, the EA had lost its momentum of growth in membership but was sustaining its momentum of increasing expenditure and deficit budgets. Enthusiasm had parted company with reality.

As EA massively expanded both its donor base and the sums of money requested in its financial appeals, its member organisations began to see the EA as more of a threat.[55] It was no longer merely providing the umbrella under which the various "tribes" of evangelicals could meet together, but was starting to become a financial competitor, threatening its member organisations' fundraising with the increasingly high profile of its own appeals. Some member organisations were no longer confident that continued growth of the Alliance would necessarily benefit their own work.[56] At the same time, annual recruitment at Spring Harvest may have become counter-productive: all the adults among the 70,000 guests were hearing an impassioned promotion to which only 3,000 responded. For some, it presumably became a tiresome routine, even a discordant intrusion, to sit through an emphatic appeal to which they habitually declined to respond. Among some evangelical organisations, there was resentment that the Alliance had this most-favoured status at Spring Harvest, with attendant risks for other organisations' profile, support and income.[57]

EA also developed a church life team in the early 1990s, with a quasi-denominational programme of support for churches and their ministers. While for some, this was presumably invaluable or at least a useful supplement to their denominational resources, for others, it was irrelevant, since they were disinclined to look for such resources beyond their own denomination or new church network. As a result, there were suggestions that EA was empire building,[58] beginning to function as an alternative denomination, expanding into too many arenas and losing focus. When an organisation over-diversifies from its original focus, greatly expands its budget, and its new activities do not meet the needs of a significant proportion of its members, funding problems are inevitable.

Other factors in the inability to sustain growth were outside the direct influence

---

[54] Indicated in interviews.
[55] Indicated in interviews.
[56] Indicated in interviews.
[57] Indicated in interviews.
[58] Indicated in interviews.

or control of the EA. According to Brierley, there was a significant weakening in the growth prospects of evangelical churches during the mid-1990s.[59] Brierley presented these conclusions to EA Council in September 2000, and they proved unexpected, even unpalatable. Perhaps for the first time in a gathering of senior British evangelical leaders, the success-driven assumptions of the previous twenty years were brought into question. However, the meeting swiftly turned to more positive matters and failed to explore the disruptive implications of a potential paradigm shift.[60]

Spring Harvest was beginning to disengage from the special relationship with EA in the mid-1990s, although not from its version of "Calverism", severely curtailing EA's annual recruitment opportunities. Since Spring Harvest had delivered more new members and more high profile promotion for EA than any other event, the loss of this platform was a severe blow. No other event could compensate for the sustained high profile EA had previously enjoyed at Spring Harvest.

The new churches were beginning to make the inevitable transition towards second generation leadership. In the case of New Frontiers, this meant that while many of their churches came into membership of the EA, their separatist identity was consolidating.[61] In the case of Pioneer, explorations of heterodoxy that praised semi-Pelagianism, accompanied by a self-consciously postmodern identity, resulted in some prominent leaders within their network questioning whether "evangelicalism" had any real meaning or relevance to their younger adults, and even whether the network itself had a future.[62] This sharpening or consolidation of separate identities weakened any pan-evangelical identity, just as the evangelical Anglicans' sharpening of their denominational identity had precipitated their partial withdrawal from the wider evangelical world from 1966-67. EA was offering a growing range of pan-evangelical resources in an increasingly segmented evangelical market.

With the eruption of the so-called "Toronto Blessing" in 1994,[63] the Alliance faced *catch 22*. Anything less than denunciation would prove to some that EA had really become the Charismatic Alliance,[64] and uncritical supporters of every latest novelty. Anything less than enthusiastic approval would prove to others that the Alliance was quasi-denominational, capable only of institutional caution. The Alliance made every effort to make a constructive and irenic contribution,[65] but the impact of Toronto was problematic. While some evangelicals interpreted these

---

[59] Brierley, 2000.

[60] Eyewitness account.

[61] This was seen for example in the speaker teams during the last few years of Stoneleigh, their annual Bible week, apparently more comfortable with high profile overseas speakers than British speakers from outside NFI.

[62] Indicated in interviews.

[63] Hilborn, 2001; Warner, 2003.

[64] Thomas, 2000.

[65] Their contribution included an irenic statement on Toronto (Calver and Warner, 1996: 162-165), two days of consultation and a subsequent published symposium (Hilborn, 2001).

events as conclusive evidence that the charismatics had lost their heads, for some charismatics the expectations of imminent revival ran so high that the more ponderous approach of the Alliance made it seem less compelling, less important. Some parts of the evangelical coalition, charismatic and non-charismatic, perceived EA to be relinquishing their mutually exclusive perceptions of the centre stage.[66]

Before Calver left the Alliance his preaching was curtailed by failing health, and there were no other advocates on staff with a similarly prominent platform presence. His successor, Joel Edwards, was received warmly by non-evangelicals in the context of Churches Together,[67] who had always been wary of Calver, but was never going to be given the same preaching opportunities and profile as Calver at Spring Harvest and similar events. The Alliance saw itself not merely sitting at the top table of evangelical influence, but providing the table.[68] Others were more pragmatic: an Anglican vicar is obliged to invite the Bishop to take confirmation, but evangelical events accept no automatic obligation to give high profile to the senior staff of EA. Pan-evangelical profile is often conferred more by populist charisma than intellect or office.

Second generation charismatic renewal was showing signs of running out of steam. In parts it was re-vivified by Toronto, but that proved a blip. Since the growth of the Alliance had paralleled the growth of charismatic renewal, when renewal began to fade, there was an inevitable knock-on effect in perceptions of the Alliance.

The demise of John Major's government resulted in growing reservations about the nature and impact of evangelical influence upon national politics.[69] The MP with whom Calver had become most associated was Brian Mawhinney, previously a member of EA Council, who spoke at Calver's official celebration on his departure from EA. As Conservative party chairman, Mawhinney brought the abrasiveness of Northern Ireland to national politics and seemed incapable of addressing the endemic crisis of Tory sleaze. Mawhinney's failure to take a more robustly Christian stand may have diminished EA's credibility as well as his own: getting close to politicians is no guarantee of significant political influence. At the same time, Tony Blair's Christian faith was well known.[70] Some politically centrist evangelicals, disappointed by the failures of the Tory regime, may have diverted their hope for socio-political change from pan-evangelicalism to new Labour. Blairism, at least in its first term, looked more sophisticated, more contemporary, more likely to produce results than entrepreneurial evangelicalism, which, despite its concern for the developing world, remained rooted in reaction against the sexual revolution of the 1960s.

---

[66] Indicated in interviews.

[67] Indicated in interviews.

[68] Indicated in interviews.

[69] Indicated in interviews.

[70] Tony Blair was prepared for confirmation while an undergraduate at Oxford by his college chaplain, Graham Dow, presently Bishop of Carlisle and formerly of Willesden, who in the mid 1990s was a member of EA Council.

Calver was no longer the young radical. The EA had secured new access to church, media and politics, but it came with a price. The more influential Calver grew, the more respectable he became. Having rebelled against the traditions and institutions of traditional and establishment Christianity, by the mid-1990s the tables had turned. For the rising generation of idealistic, ambitious and impatient activists, Calver's generation was the new establishment.[71] Young evangelical leaders of one generation had aspired to speak at Spring Harvest; those in the next generation were more likely to complain about the event's old-fashioned deficiencies.[72]

In 1992 Calver produced his *Jerusalem Report* in which he identified the lack of theological undergirding as a critical weakness in contemporary evangelicalism. He argued that the current pragmatic indifference to theology was not characteristic of previous generations of evangelicals. As a result, ACUTE was established.[73] The most significant contributions of ACUTE have been a report on homosexuality that affirmed traditional Christian sexual ethics with a firm repudiation of homophobia,[74] and a report on hell that emphasised divine judgment but no longer required eternal suffering as the only legitimate evangelical interpretation of the biblical data.[75] Here we see the strengths of ACUTE: moderating a consensus and reaffirming evangelical unity faced with divergent interpretations. Hilborn, however, claimed too much when he suggests that ACUTE could resolve contemporary evangelicalism's theological deficit.[76] Calver recognised the inherent weakness in the activism he had espoused. However, the theological reconstruction of the evangelical tradition is unlikely to be generated by an institutional response. Calver's characteristically ambitious aspiration for the re-invigoration of evangelical theology is beyond the reach of a politically constrained, consensus-driven theological committee.

The winds of credibility were beginning to blow hard against the evangelical rhetoric of assured and imminent success. Charismatics and non-charismatics had, albeit unconsciously, endorsed methodologies dependent more upon late-modern presuppositions than distinctively biblical convictions. Few in Britain accepted Finney's theory of revival, in which the combination of key ingredients guaranteed mass conversions.[77] However, many had adopted formulaic methodologies that were implicitly built upon similar assumptions: church growth theory;[78] Wimber's

---

[71] Indicated in interviews.

[72] Indicated in interviews.

[73] The Alliance Commission on Unity and Truth among Evangelicals (ACUTE) was launched on 2 December 1993.

[74] ACUTE, 1998.

[75] Hilborn, 2000.

[76] Randall and Hilborn, 2001: 343.

[77] Finney, 1835.

[78] Originating with McGavran (1970), this approach sought to identify and replicate patterns of church life that allegedly assured numerical growth through conversions. See Gibbs, 1981; Pointer, 1984. The primary growth factors were modified significantly by Schwarz (1996), while retaining the underlying concept.

confluence of healing and evangelism;[79] church planting;[80] seeker services;[81] intercessory prayer and "spiritual warfare";[82] cell church;[83] restorationism;[84] prosperity teaching;[85] and even the traditionalist, unvarnished preaching of the calvinistic gospel.[86] These and many other strategies seemed, at least to their enthusiastic devotees, uncompromisingly biblical (notwithstanding the unprecedented novelty of many such programmes) and capable of assuring guaranteed success (notwithstanding the results of previous enthusiastically endorsed initiatives).

Many evangelicals had unconsciously made a transition from traditional evangelicalism that affirmed the truth of the gospel, to late-modern entrepreneurialism that assumed wholehearted adherence to the gospel guaranteed success for the church. The presumed problem was not to address secularization but to rediscover the formula for certain success.[87] The mechanical universe of late-modernity seemed, for a few years at least, to have been vindicated by the self-evident success of English evangelicals in the 1980s. The eager rhetoric of what we term *hyper-Calverism*, promising profound spiritual, moral and political influence just around the next corner of growth in EA membership, was unsustainable. In the years of dramatic growth, exemplified at both the EA and Spring Harvest, the experience of numerical advance seemed to vindicate the rhetoric. However, high-octane activism is more plausible over the short-term than the long haul. When local churches were not seeing dramatic growth, and when the impact of evangelicals on

---

[79] An emphasis on thaumaturgy as the key to effectual evangelism, of which the leading non-Pentecostal exponent in this period was John Wimber (1985, 1987). For a rigorous critique, see Percy, 1996.

[80] See below, Chapter 4.

[81] Exemplified by the growth of Willow Creek Church. See Hybels, 1995.

[82] This was often emphasised within March for Jesus (1987-2000), where "prayer for the nation" was accompanied by rhetoric of "claiming the ground" from the grip of evil powers. www.jesusday.org/history.php. Accessed 5 August 2005.

[83] A modification of church growth theory around structural principles grounded in small groups (Neighbour, 1990; Beckham, 1995).

[84] The assumption among some new church leaders that the New Testament provided a single blueprint of ecclesiology that could be directly implemented in late twentieth century Europe, thus guaranteeing the rapid advance of a vibrant church under apostolic leadership (Wallis, 1981; Virgo, 1985). For a critique, see Walker 1985, 2002.

[85] A predominantly Pentecostal variant, in which thaumaturgy is transposed into materialistic "blessings" characteristically considered consequent upon generous financial donations in support of its leading exponents, whose personal prosperity is beyond doubt. Notable exponents include Kenneth Hagin, Kenneth Copeland and Morris Cerullo. EAUK produced a theological critique (Perriman, 2003). For an anthropological critique, see Coleman, 2000.

[86] Murray, 1982, 1990, 1994, 2000.

[87] Peter Wagner exemplifies this late-modern methodological optimism, espousing a series of alleged growth guarantors with equal enthusiasm, for example: church growth theory (1984, 1987), church planting (1990), spiritual warfare (1990), spiritual gifts (1997), and new apostolic churches (1998, 2002).

the media and in politics looked increasingly minimal, with Christianity drifting to the margins of British cultural consciousness, the evangelical empire was considerably less poised for advance than the rhetoric had promised. In short, the EA failed to deliver, not because of lack of effort, but because its visionary goals were unrealistic, not merely in terms of prospects for future recruitment of personal members, but because of a wholesale failure to grasp the corrosive effects upon evangelical influence and identity of the ineluctable cultural transitions of secularization and postmodernity.[88] Evangelicals lacked a coherent socio-political critique[89] and had failed to come to terms with the implications of a secularized and pluralistic culture: enthusiastic rhetoric and ethical conservatism are no substitute for rigorous and reflexive analysis.

Calverism Meets Postmodernity

While EA was trying to change the post 1960s culture of late-modernity, a new culture was emerging, a seismic shift in the conceptual and ethical consensus that would erode still further the effectiveness of conventional evangelism and apologetics, and would respond with an indifference moving towards antipathy to the moral campaigns of Christians, whether anti-abortion, pro-traditional family, anti-euthanasia, anti-cloning, pro-censorship, or opposing full equality for homosexuals in age of consent, marriage, employment and church participation. The one notable exception to this catalogue of failure was the Jubilee 2000 campaign for debt cancellation in the developing world.[90] In this new cultural setting, evangelicals along with the wider Christian community were only likely to make a significant impact with their ethical campaigns when there was convergence between their moral idealism and a much broader post-Christian moral consensus. While some accounts of postmodernity emphasise amorality or a highly individualised morality,[91] a new collective morality appears to have been emerging[92] in which the primary virtues comprise individual liberty (doing what I want so long as no one gets hurt – J.S. Mill had supplanted Marx as the utopian ideal), human rights, tolerance, the exclusion of all prejudice (race, gender, class, sexual orientation), animal rights, and concern for the environment.

Calver's late-modern cultural captivity was such that he would be unable to provide coherent leadership in this new cultural context, for he set his face against post modernity with characteristic bravado:

---

[88] Bruce, 1996, 2002; Davie, 1994, 2002; Brown, 2001, 2006.

[89] Hilborn (2004) provides a prolegomena to this process. Compare Hauerwas, 2001; Avis, 2003; Storrar and Morton, 2004.

[90] www.jubilee2000uk.org. Accessed 5 August 2005. Jubilee 2000's successor organisation, *Make Poverty History* (www.makepovertyhistory.org. Accessed 5 August 2005.), recognised the need to build the widest possible coalition: the overtly Christian component was played down.

[91] Foucault, 1984.

[92] Baumann, 1991.

I believe that postmodern thinking is totally non-Christian, but I also believe in the power of the gospel.[93]

Those who marry their Christian faith to a specific cultural context are destined to self-marginalization when that culture fades. Late twentieth century evangelicals were not merely inhabiting an enlightenment construct,[94] shaped by conservatism in reaction against liberalism,[95] but were profoundly influenced and even captivated by a late-modern ideology of imminent success. By the turn of the century, the plausibility of this late-modern, entrepreneurial reconstruction of populist evangelicalism was severely attenuated.

Here is a classic example of over-reaching, more familiar in the City than the Church, where there are rarely instances of forceful entrepreneurial leadership. Future growth was projected in the light of past achievements on an exponential trend. The rhetoric of a million evangelicals meant that little or no consideration was given to the possibility that recruitment might already have peaked with nearly 60,000 personal members. Staffing and expenditure were expanding in line with what was taken to be assured future growth, on which was projected increasing societal impact, in politics and the media. Meanwhile, the Alliance was evolving in the eyes of other parachurch organisations from being an inspiration to an institution, and an increasing threat as a competing provider and fund-raiser within the evangelical market. Just as Thatcherism was built upon strong leadership but failed to resolve the economic cycle of boom and bust, Calverism was built upon strong leadership but suffered from recurrent vision inflation. The legacy of evangelical boom and bust is apparent: disappointed expectations, a sceptical distrust of subsequent expressions of ambitious vision, and a shift in attitude towards the Alliance so that allegiance to the organisation became more provisional, more episodic, more post-institutional.[96]

When many organisations and most churches were reporting declining memberships, Calver's inspirational leadership grew the Alliance with startling rapidity. The Alliance's subsequent decline meant a return to the normal contemporary pattern of postmodern membership of organisations: provisional, temporary, linked to vision not an institution, linked to a person more than principles, functioning as a secondary interest not one's primary identity. Similarly, once Tony Blair's luminosity diminished, New Labour's membership declined dramatically - from 420,000 at the time of the 1997 General Election to 254,000 in 2001.[97] Greenpeace also enjoyed spectacular growth that proved transient, tripling its North American membership from 1985-1990, followed by a collapse of 85% by 1998.[98] Putnam endorsed Bosso's conclusion that supporters of "mail order

---

[93] Calver, 1999.

[94] Bebbington, 1989.

[95] Barr, 1977.

[96] Compare Putnam, 2000; Bosso, 1999a, 1999b.

[97] *Tribune*, July 2001.

[98] Bosso, 1999a, cited in Putnam 2000: 156-8.

organizations" are less "members" than "consumers" of a cause, [99] providing only "cheque book affiliation".[100] Our analysis finds these conclusions apposite to Calver's EA as much as to Greenpeace. As Calverism began to suffer a loss of credibility, the Alliance ceased to go against the cultural norms of diminishing confidence in institutions and declining levels of personal membership in voluntary organisations. Evangelicals, in common with the majority culture, were increasingly "bowling alone".[101]

Copley was right to be defensive about the extent of EA's dependence upon Calver at the time of his final reappointment, for his contribution had been exceptional. However the decline of the Alliance began not with Calver's illness or departure, but with the policy, by then well established, of a relentless and ultimately unrealistic and unattainable pursuit of growth, in personal membership, staffing and activities, expenditure, and an equally inflated projection of impact upon the nation. Calver undoubtedly made the single greatest contribution to the Alliance's growth, revitalising an organisation subdued since 1966.[102] However, the inability of others to harness him effectively for a credible and sustainable new era in the early to mid-1990s meant the seeds of decline were already present in the fruit of success. Socio-political impact was proving difficult, media access was mainly oppositional and restricted (no regular EA contributors to *Thought for the Day*, *Any Questions* or *Question Time*, for example[103]), membership growth had stalled, and financial resources were over-stretched. Entrepreneurial evangelicalism had moved from an undeniable measure of success to inflated expectations. Calver had transformed the Alliance; however by the mid-1990s Calverism was unsustainable.[104]

---

[99] Putnam, 2000: 158; Bosso, 1999b: 467.

[100] Fowler and Shaiko, 1987: 490.

[101] The more apposite metaphor than Putnam's in the English context is perhaps "drinking alone", since, judging from supermarket sales of alcohol, there has been a dramatic shift from communitarian imbibing at a local pub to watching TV at home, beer in hand.

[102] Murray, 1990, 2000; Dudley-Smith, 1999; Randall and Hilborn, 2001.

[103] Neither Elaine Storkey nor Anne Atkins, though both evangelicals, were associated with the Evangelical Alliance in their contributions to *Thought for the Day*.

[104] Of course, Calver can be no more personally responsible for the excesses of Calverism than Calvin for the excesses of Calvinism.

Chapter 2

Spring Harvest: A Case Study in Evangelical Exceptionalism

Evidence of Exceptionalism

Within the context of European exceptionalism[1] we continue our assessment of the conversionist-activist axis and consider in our study of Spring Harvest the possibility of an evangelical exceptionalism, countering the majority European trend. We find evidence of exceptionalism in the patterns of late twentieth century growth, but this tends mostly to be restricted to shifting patterns of adherence within the internal market of pan-evangelicalism. At the same time, we identify an entirely non-exceptional conformity with Weber's transition from charisma to bureaucracy.[2]

Rapid Growth

Compared with the general condition of the churches of England 1980-2000, Spring Harvest[3] proved exceptional in several ways. The growth of SH in its first decade was dramatic. In 1979, 2,800 attended. By 1984 this had reached 21,000 and by 1989, 70,000. Throughout the 1990s, SH claimed an annual attendance of 60-70,000, some years reaching 80,000. The simultaneous explosion of personal membership of the EA meant that entrepreneurial evangelicals saw the 1980s as a vindication of their expectations of accelerating growth and rising societal impact.

By the late 1990s the team on site comprised 2,700-3,000 people, with 250-300 involved in year-round planning committees. From its inception, SH attendance has been mainly Anglican and Baptist. The Baptist percentage of guests has remained constant at 30%. The Anglican percentage increased between 1990-2001 from 36% to 40%. Although Calver gave high prominence to new church leaders at SH, one SH founder observed, "They never brought their churches."

Most guests attend SH for three consecutive years and then take a break. As a result, every year two thirds of the guests have attended the previous year. With an

---

[1] Berger, 1999; Davie, 2002.

[2] Weber in Gerth and Wright Mill, 1948.

[3] Spring Harvest will hereafter be generally referred to as SH. This analysis was made possible by generous access to the SH archives and a number of interviews, particularly with Alan Johnson (CEO), Clive Calver (co-founder), Pete Meadows (co-founder) and Ian Coffey (member of the new leadership team in the late 1990s and a long-term senior contributor).

average attendance of 60,000, over a three-year period the total number of people who attend could be as many as 100,000. Some guests come as individuals, or as an evangelical sub-group within a broader local church. Other parties comprise the core group of leaders and opinion formers in predominantly evangelical churches. These parties, in particular, influence whole churches in the light of their SH experience, taking home practical ideas, distinctive emphases, and, perhaps most frequently, new songs. The total number of Christians influenced by SH is therefore likely to be several times the 100,000+ who attend over a three-year period.

Table 10: Spring Harvest attendance, 1979 1989

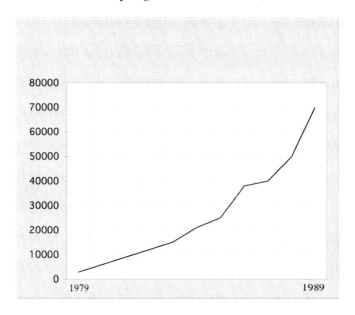

Entrepreneurial Leadership

The idea for SH germinated after Peter Meadows visited a Methodist event at Prestatyn to sell Buzz, his youth magazine.[4] Meadows raised the idea with Calver, who developed the concept of a week, networked a team of initiators and recruited Graham Kendrick, the guitarist with whom he had previously toured as an itinerant evangelist.

The pivotal influence of Calver and Meadows is universally acknowledged.[5] They were considered young radicals, bringing a newly assertive and optimistic mood to evangelical initiatives. They also brought new appetites and table manners: when Calver attended meetings where others brought sandwiches, he would devour

---

[4] Interviews with Calver and Meadows. See Ward, 2005.

[5] Indicated in interviews.

a take-away curry. Interviewees cited this incident as symptomatic of a man with the confidence to break unwritten rules. One senior evangelical leader described Calver as the "constitutional monarch" of EA and SH. Another described Calver in the 1980s as "pushy, seemingly unstoppable, yet insecure and always looking for conspiracies". That gave him the energy to be an exceptional entrepreneurial innovator, but made it difficult to address leadership succession.

Calver took time off from EA duties each year to write the SH seminar notes. Meadows combined work for both organisations. Colin Saunders was chair of Spring Harvest's executive from 1983 and was subsequently appointed Executive Director of the Evangelical Alliance. As we have noted, Calver used SH as the key annual means of recruitment of personal members for the Alliance, and extended main platform invitations to speakers he wanted to connect more closely with EA. It was Calver's EA role that enabled him to engage in "talent spotting" for new speakers. And it was Calver's status as General Director of EA, combined with his personal charisma, that enabled him to persuade senior evangelical leaders to speak at rain-swept and spartan holiday camps. SH depended upon EA for its vision and speaker team and provided the most fertile recruiting ground for EA. The two were intertwined and often treated synonymously. As one senior speaker observed in interview, "Everyone knew that Clive was really Spring Harvest."

Calver and Meadows established an environment of risk and adventure. Those involved in the first decade speak of a roller-coaster ride, an expectation that anything might happen.[6] Faced with an evangelical tradition firmly entrenched in a pre-1960s world of formality, conventionality and predictability, SH broke the bourgeois taboos. However, by the mid-1990s the young Turks had become the new establishment and SH was following a familiar pattern from year to year: it ran the risk of becoming the evangelical equivalent of Christmas TV repeats of familiar favourites. Nonetheless, in its first decade SH represented a new radicalism, a breath of fresh air erupting amid the confines of conventional, conservative religion.

Bellah argued that the two dominant categories of American life in the late twentieth century were the entrepreneur and the therapist,[7] and they have become the culturally apposite frameworks for recasting Christian faith. The originators of SH exemplified an entrepreneurial re-framing of the evangelical tradition. The multiple-choice approach of Spring Harvest's programme introduced many evangelicals to a commodified concept of worship and teaching: the autonomous individual makes an independent selection from the programme and may come to expect a similar autonomy in choosing local church activities.[8] At the same time, since therapies have moved from the rich and famous into the middle class mainstream, therapeutic categories have become increasingly familiar and compelling compared with conventional religious categories. Therapeutic religion tends to shift the focus from loving God, receiving instruction and serving others to finding and fulfilling my

---

[6] Indicated in interviews.

[7] Bellah, 1996.

[8] Hammond, 1992.

own potential; more about phobias, neuroses and the pursuit of personal happiness than sin and forgiveness, truth and obedience. Late-modern evangelicals appear to have been increasingly influenced by the recasting of religion in therapeutic terms, as a spiritual exploration of wholeness and self-actualisation. John Wimber, for example, explicitly presented Christ as the bringer of therapeutic salvation -

> Give him all your tears of sadness,
> Give him all your years of pain,
> And you'll enter into life in Jesus' name.[9]

As the go-getting entrepreneurial categories of Spring Harvest's main-stage speakers failed to deliver the promised advances, the guests may have increasingly recast the evangelical tradition as a smorgasbord of spiritual therapies.[10]

Contemporising Worship

Churches were exposed at SH to contemporary worship, thus increasing the pressure for traditional worship to give ground in the historic denominations. Many guests came from smaller churches, and for them in particular, worship with several thousand was an inspiring experience on a scale unparalleled during the rest of the year. In the first ten to fifteen years, the celebrations were a breakthrough, more contemporary than many local churches.[11] In later years some interviewees judged that the celebrations enshrined a new traditionalism, no longer pressing beyond local churches in creative experiment, but rather offering predictable presentations in the idiom of Radio 2 stadium rock. Uncertainty about how to develop these celebrations was implicit in the regular attempts to reinvent them.[12]

The contribution of Graham Kendrick in the first decade of SH was immense, often writing new songs to express the annual theme and sustaining SH as the market leader in contemporary evangelical worship. In the 1980s, no other Christian songwriter was as popular in the UK. Kendrick's songs facilitated the shift from the traditional hymn sandwich in many churches. The vocal range was limited, making them accessible for congregational singing when many traditional hymn tunes require too many high notes for an era with little adult singing outside churches and

---

[9] Wimber, "O let the Son of God enfold you," *Worship Today,* 320.

[10] Percy (1996) develops a critique of Wimberism in terms of power and control. While these elements are undoubtedly present in the public performance of cathartic ministry sessions, my own critique of Wimber focuses upon therapeutic subjectivism and the Californian quest for the permanently happy life. Beneath the rhetoric of divine power and physical healing, the underlying pre-occupation is at least as much upon "inner" healing and emotional well-being. With his laid-back style and Quaker acceptance of ambiguity, Wimber was closer, though this was not acknowledged by his advocates, to new age therapists than pentecostal thaumaturgists. He embraced uncertainty but appeared to offer an assured journey into personal wholeness and fulfilment.

[11] Indicated in interviews.

[12] Indicated in interviews.

football stadia. The diction was contemporary and fairly colloquial, but was also informed by biblical terminology: among contemporary Christian songwriters, Kendrick was unusually concerned, at least in some songs, to provide sung doctrine rather than mere enthusiasm. Moreover, some of Kendrick's material was not explicitly or exclusively charismatic, thus enabling non-charismatic churches to use his songs. Kendrick therefore gave expression to the worship of more contemporary Christians and yet for some traditional Christians proved the more acceptable face of new worship idioms. Eventually this proved the kiss of death for Kendrick's credibility with the rising generation of the 1990s: when *Shine Jesus Shine* became a regular choice on *Songs of Praise*, it was no longer fashionable to sing his songs in churches aspiring to a more contemporary approach. Contemporisation exacted the price of a severely reduced shelf-life for new songs.

The most influential SH publication has undoubtedly been the annual songbook, first published in the mid-1980s in both words and music editions. Subsequently, the growing use of overhead projectors in churches terminated the words edition. Each year SH requires 50% of the songs to be totally new in the UK. According to Johnson, sales have been fairly constant since the mid-1980s. In 2001, SH published *Worship Today*, a compilation of the currently most popular 500 songs and hymns. This represents a unique snapshot, not of the intentions of the editors as with a conventional hymnbook, but of the actual worship practices in 18,000 churches between October 1999 and March 2000. [13]

Worship Today includes 81 songs from the 1970s, 165 from the 1980s and 199 from the 1990s. Contemporary evangelical worship therefore has a very short shelf-life, longer than most pop songs but reflecting contemporary popular culture far more closely than traditional church culture. 60% of the songs used in this type of evangelical worship have been written in the last fifteen years, 20% in the last five years. Looking more closely at the last two decades, 65 songs have lasted from 1980 to 1985, 100 from 1985-1989, 102 songs from 1990 to 1994, and 97 from 1995-1999. This suggests the peak period for this upsurge of new Christian songs may have been between 1985 and 1994. Of the contemporary songwriters, Graham Kendrick contributed 68 to *Worship Today*, Noel Richards 23[14], Matt Redman 20 and Dave Bilbrough 18. From the 1970s, Kendrick contributed 4 out of 81; from the 1980s, 43 out of 165, a remarkable 25%; and from the 1990s, 21 out of 199. (These statistics do not, of course, indicate the number of songs Kendrick has produced, but rather the number still popular in 2000.) Kendrick's dominance, like most pop and

---

[13] Churches that register with the copyright license authority are asked to provide complete listings of all the songs in current use. *Worship Today* resulted from collating data from churches where all the songs are projected onto a screen with data from churches that also use one or more printed resources, presumably often including a traditional hymnbook. This analysis therefore reflects in particular the detraditionalized, post-hymnbook strand among British evangelicals. However, SH data indicates that the primary consumers of the brand are Anglicans and Baptists. *Worship Today* is therefore indicative of detraditonalized evangelical-charismatic worship within the denominational mainstream.

[14] In various collaborations.

rock stars of the 1980s, had waned considerably and rapidly.

Striking comparisons can be made with *Hymns of Faith*, a standard evangelical hymn book published in 1964 by Scripture Union and with *Hymns for Today's Church*, published in 1982 by Hodders on behalf of *Jubilate*, an evangelical group of predominantly non-charismatic, Anglican clergy. In *Hymns of Faith*, Charles Wesley had 47 hymns, Isaac Watts 27, Frances Ridley Havergal 17, John Newton 15 and William Cowper 10. In *Hymns for Today's Church*, Wesley had 26, Watts 20, Havergal 6, Newton 6 and Cowper 4.[15] The contrasts with *Worship Today* are stark. Wesley has 3 hymns, Watts 1, Havergal 0, Newton 1, Cowper 0. As to the Jubilate contributors, Dudley-Smith has 6 (46 in *HTC*) and Michael Saward 1 (27 in *HTC*). The earliest hymn in *Worship Today* was dated 1650, and the total number of hymns included from 1650 to 1930 is 27 out of 500.

Table 11: The demise of the classical hymnwriters

	Hymns of Faith, 1964	*Hymns for Today's Church*, 1982	*Worship Today*, 2001
Charles Wesley	47	26	3
Isaac Watts	27	20	1
Frances Ridley Havergal	17	6	0
John Newton	15	6	1
William Cowper	10	4	0
Timothy Dudley-Smith	N/A	46	6
Michael Saward	N/A	27	1

SH has promoted a profound detraditionalization of evangelical worship, which has, with the exception of a handful of rousing classics, severed itself from the long-standing tradition of hymnody. Moreover, while previously most hymn writers were clergy, the new lyricists are usually theologically untrained performers on the Christian music circuit: the musical laity have been empowered, but with the prospect that Christian music becomes a sub-genre of contemporary pop, uncritically dependent upon a narrowly contemporary frame of reference and shaped

---

[15] Jubilate heavily favoured their own brand of hymnody, including 46 by Timothy Dudley-Smith and 27 by Michael Saward. To give Saward more space than Charles Wesley indicates extraordinary disproportion in their selection criteria, given that they were ostensibly defenders of classical British hymnody. Although the editorial team chose each hymn on its merits, without the author being identified, their criteria were evidently heavily weighted in favour of their own contemporary variant upon the tradition they espoused.

neither by biblical literacy nor a coherent theological framework.[16] Traditional hymns are no longer a Christian *lingua franca*. There has been a dramatic rupture with the tradition, exemplifying evangelicals' customary capacity - the more conservative excepted - for pragmatic self-reinvention, assimilating more readily than most religious traditions to the detraditionalized cultural context.

Post-Denominationalism

SH established a new sense of vibrant hope and common identity among evangelicals. As Meadows observed in interview, before SH there was no one event where the majority of evangelicals might congregate. This claim is debatable, but it indicates the perceived innovations of late-modern pan-evangelicalism. SH therefore provided a new experience of evangelical solidarity; it was Calver's vision of pan-evangelicalism in conference form. As a result, SH accelerated the trend of post-denominationalism apparent among late twentieth century English evangelicals, where strong evangelical identity was allied to relative indifference to denominational contexts.[17] Nonetheless, there were discreet boundaries: both Meadows and Coffey acknowledged that Pentecostal speakers were rarely invited, presumably because their modes of discourse might alienate the Anglican and Baptist majority among the guests. Few church groups have attended from the Pentecostals, new churches and Methodists. (Also immune to Spring Harvest's appeal was the Anglican vicar[18] who explained he was unable to bring his church because Butlins failed to provide dessert forks...)

Pan-evangelicalism at SH was exemplified until the mid-1990s through the preaching of the "tribal heads" of Calver's mythological twelve tribes of evangelicalism.[19] Ian Coffey acknowledged that this emphasis has diminished in the post-Calver era. Perhaps some were less inclined to attend without Calver's persuasion, or perhaps the inclusion of "tribal heads" was less of a priority once SH was no longer a primary means of pursuing EA's avowedly pan-evangelical agenda.

Transitions

SH shifted key assumptions within the evangelical subculture. SH brought

---

[16] Compare Ward, 2005; Parry, 2005.

[17] One of the first evangelical exponents of denominational indifferentism was Whitefield, who recorded in his journal on 19 September 1740 his response to the Anglican clergy who examined him in Boston – "I saw regenerate souls among the Baptists, among the Presbyterians, among the Independents, and among the Church folks – all children of God, and yet all born again in a different way of worship: and who can tell which is the most evangelical?" (Whitefield, 1960: 458). The late twentieth century is widely considered to have seen unprecedented levels of denominational switching among English evangelical laity.

[18] Indicated in interview.

[19] Calver, Coffey, Meadows, 1993; Calver and Warner, 1996: 128-130.

charismatic renewal onto the agenda of many local churches.[20] In a survey of English evangelical leaders[21] I found a strong consensus accepting the availability of the full range of New Testament spiritual gifts today. SH probably contributed more to this shifted consensus than any other event. The new churches were brought into contact with the historic denominations, so that their insights and ethos could be received more widely and in a more palatable form. Social action was intrinsic to the event from the beginning, thus emphatically reinforcing the Lausanne agenda in the UK. For example the profits from the music album to commemorate the first ten years were given to international projects for Aids sufferers. It was similarly innovatory that women were from the early days considered integral to the speaker team, whereas at most traditional Bible Weeks preaching was strictly a male preserve. These shifts of emphasis meant that SH was inevitably subject to suspicion from more conservative and pre-charismatic evangelicals.

Marketing and Branding

The SH brand has high visibility. The logo appears consistently on the publicity, seminar resources, songbooks, and also on mugs, sweatshirts and other products. SH and *Alpha* have undoubtedly become the two most prominent brand names of British Christianity, with loyal adherents able to assert: "We're an *Alpha* / Spring Harvest church." Nonetheless, while the brand name is high profile and well marketed, Johnson stated in interview that Spring Harvest's avowed policy is to restrict merchandising. This distinctive emphasis upon branding rather than merchandising was exemplified for several years by handing out SH car stickers to departing guests. SH were maximising not the immediate commercial opportunity by selling the car stickers, but rather maximising the medium-term impact of their brand profile, building customer loyalty and repeat business. The entrepreneurial contemporaneity of SH broke new ground for British Christians.

Expansion

When Johnson joined SH there were six staff, compared with around forty by the turn of the century. Calver was the intuitive entrepreneur whose vision became unsustainable when EA and SH achieved market saturation. Johnson is the managerial entrepreneur, pressing to broaden the impact of SH after a decade of plateaued attendance. In the late 1990s SH embarked upon a policy of sustained expansion,[22] adding to its portfolio a specialist conference exploring work place issues, a book publishing imprint, a missionary conference in Dubai, worship projection software and other resources for local churches, a financial share in the leading evangelical magazine, *Christianity and Renewal*, and a relationship with

---

[20] Compare Scotland, 1995.

[21] Warner, 2008.

[22] Indicated in interviews and evidenced in the SH archive.

Premier Radio. SH is moving towards omnipresence in the evangelical media. With a finger in every communication pie, and an annual upgrade to the songbook, SH shows signs of becoming the Microsoft of entrepreneurial evangelicalism.

We have identified clear evidence of elements of evangelical exceptionalism at SH: dramatic growth for a decade; contemporising music in worship; giving expression to post-denominational evangelical ecumenism; effective marketing and branding; and above all, unusual entrepreneurial drive. A free market theory of religion recognises such factors as plausible prerequisites for any re-emergence of the post-Constantinian church in Western Europe.[23]

Evidence of Lack of Exceptionalism

In many ways, SH remains entirely unexceptional, within contemporary expressions of conservative religion, within the conversionist-activist axis, and in accordance with the Weberian transposition from charisma to bureaucracy.

Precedents

The evening "celebrations" at SH appeared radically new to many participants in the first decade, sweeping away the fustian formality and dog collars of traditional evangelicalism, preferring an absence of titles and a preponderance of woolly jumpers – although many contributors metamorphosed on the night they were preaching into a well-groomed appearance with jacket and tie. These evenings were typified by enthusiastic music, impassioned preachers using emotive anecdotes and raw eloquence, animated "altar calls" that became ever more inclusive until the front of the marquee was suitably packed with those making some kind of response, and protracted offering appeals. An earlier Christian tradition within the conversionist-activist axis combined these ingredients, namely North American revivalist camp meetings.[24] Spring Harvest's variants on the tradition are both telling: first, this English re-casting was definitely non-Pentecostal; second, the revivalists' ethos was now redeployed for a gated community of evangelicals on holiday.

Plateau

The fact that Calver regularly cited an attendance of 80,000 in the early to mid-1990s[25] suggests either that the event subsequently suffered a numerical decline that

---

[23] Stark and Bainbridge (1985, 1987) argued that unregulated religious markets permit religious entrepreneurs to extend market share and to reach new market sectors through diversification. Thus, the pivotal factor in European exceptionalism is the suppression of the free market through quasi-nationalised religious utilities (compare Martin, 1978, 2005). Nationalised monopolies are only overturned by privatisation (disestablishment), but can lose market share at the margins to vigorous entrepreneurs.

[24] Synan, 1971.

[25] In his preaching and presentations.

has never been acknowledged or that attendance reports have become more realistic. Johnson rejects any suggestion of decline, explaining that 80,000 could only attend when SH used 4 sites for three weeks which all happened to fall within the school holidays. In February 2001, Johnson indicated in interview that 80,000 was in principle the maximum attainable attendance, although the current capacity was 70,000. While the numbers may not have declined significantly, market saturation had been reached. In mid 2001, SH reduced its publicised annual attendance claim to 60,000.[26] The years of explosive growth ended in the early 1990s.

In the early days of SH, the event was considered upbeat, contemporary, open to charismatic renewal, and user-friendly to churches in the historic denominations.[27] The alternatives at that time were predominantly either strongly charismatic new church events, with an at least implicitly separatist agenda, or pre-charismatic Bible weeks. The 1990s saw the growth or emergence of Stoneleigh, New Wine and Easter People and also new growth at Keswick, the oldest English Bible week, and Greenbelt. SH had plateaued in a more competitive market: 60,000 at SH compared with 100,000 attending the other major events, not counting the denominational assemblies and conventions. The nearest competitor was NFI's Stoneleigh, which reached 27,000 in its final year, having plateaued from 1995-1999 at 20,000. SH therefore continues to be dominant, but its market share has declined.

Table 12: Bible week attendance, 2001[28]

Spring Harvest	60,000
Stoneleigh	27,000
Soul Survivor	16,000
New Wine	13,800
Keswick	12,000
Easter People	12,000
Greenbelt	10,000
Grapevine	4,000
Summer Madness	4,000
Flames of Fire	1,000

By the mid-1990s, most guests at SH would have been able to attend at least one other Bible week where they could feel at home. Since most participants take a

---

[26] Worship Today: 1-29.
[27] Indicated in interviews.
[28] Cited in Christianity and Renewal, May 2002.

break every three years, this means that SH remains dominant in the market but its popularity is considerably more precarious than during the 1980s. In a culture of declining brand loyalty and in a competitive and possibly fragmenting market, continued dominance cannot be assured.

Women Marginalised

Despite the early revolution of including women in the main seminar teams, women have made little contribution to the celebrations and Bible expositions. In some years, most women on the speaker team have been the wives of male speakers, suggesting either a dearth of other suitable women, or an inability on the part of SH to recruit beyond a narrow circle. Johnson defended the unrepresentative mix of main celebration speakers, emphasising they must be chosen by ability, not denomination. One senior speaker was less sanguine in interview than Johnson, concluding that, with no women Bible teachers in 2002, SH seemed to be slipping backwards rather than making progress.[29] Having opened the Pandora's box of promising equality in ministry, SH has discovered that a halfway house satisfies neither the traditionalists nor those expecting substantive change. Gender equality in public ministry is remote from the SH status quo, even though SH remains more sympathetic to women speakers than most evangelical Bible Weeks.

From Intuition to Planning

We can identify several pivotal changes in Spring Harvest's internal organisation. In 1990, Johnson became the first CEO; previously there had been a series of managers and administrators. In 1989-1990, Johnson's first major task was to analyse the executive and the contributions of the key players. This resulted in the executive being halved in number. In 1993, SH separated from its founding organisations, Elm House and Youth for Christ, having, in Johnson's phrase, "grown bigger than its parents". Here we note a twofold transition: a "shift to bureaucracy" in Saunders' unconsciously Weberian phrase,[30] with a paid centre for the organisation. In Calver's words, SH moved from being a "gathering" of evangelicals to "the event",[31] assuming a life of its own and taking itself more seriously as a separate centre of identity. One of the early leaders of SH concluded in interview that this transition marked a decisive shift in the organisation's direction and proposed an entirely different policy: "Instead of growing an administrative centre, we should have given it back to the Evangelical Alliance for them to develop."

In 1996-7 David Cormack, a Scottish management consultant, helped the executive develop a five-to-ten year strategic plan, against which the developments

---

[29] Elaine Storkey was the only woman Bible teacher announced for SH, 2003. Her longstanding participation had evidently thus far failed to open the way for an increasing contribution by women speakers.

[30] Indicated in interview.

[31] Indicated in interview.

of SH are measured in an annual report to their Council. This transition still provokes contrary responses. The turn of the century leadership team continued to refer to it as a yardstick for future development; several strategic papers written by Broadbent specifically built upon its emphases. However, such detailed planning was not congenial to Calver,[32] who preferred the earlier, year on year, more immediate ethos. Saunders described it as a shift towards long-term planning that meant less space for intuition. Meadows dismissed it as little more than rearranging the furniture.

We have traced a consistent pattern of transition: from entrepreneurs to managers, from intuition to planning, from charisma to bureaucracy. With Calver running out of steam with a heart condition in the mid-1990s, this was perhaps inevitable. SH was no longer a roller coaster ride - to use Ian Coffey's metaphor for the early years - and was more like a Volvo estate: a predictable and safe Easter holiday for the evangelical bourgeoisie.

Centralisation

The original owners of SH, Elm House and Youth for Christ, each supplied two executive members. Three supporting bodies released their national directors to help develop SH: Clive Calver - EA, Lowell Sheppard - YFC, and Dave Pope - Saltmine. SH gave platform presence to the organisations, annual promotional slots and provided training and ministry opportunities for their staff. From Spring Harvest's perspective, according to Johnson, the involvement was as individuals and not as "power blocks". From the perspective of the sponsoring organisations, however, the connection between SH and themselves was organic. Their contribution to SH was to assist the wider evangelical cause, but they saw their own organisations playing strategic roles in that wider arena. There was an unwritten quid pro quo: they contributed to SH which generated profile, volunteers, finance, personal supporters, and enlarged mailing lists for their organisations. When SH had no significant separate centre of identity, the model proved sustainable, albeit with other organisations privately complaining of exclusion from an inner circle of privilege and profile.[33]

Since 1999, SH has determined its own agenda and other organisations submit their possible contributions in support of that agenda. Such proposals are submitted for a single year, rather than within a continuing partnership. This indicates a shift from an alliance of organisations in sustained collaboration to an autonomous sponsoring organisation with competing client-providers. Their contributions are no longer granted automatic access but are only acceptable inasmuch as they conform to the sponsoring organisation's independently determined annual objectives. In particular, since Calver's departure, EA's profile at SH, its primary recruitment ground during fifteen years of substantial growth, has been severely curtailed. SH

---

[32] Indicated in interviews.
[33] Indicated in interviews.

also exercises considerable financial muscle: in the late 1990s it removed its long-term funding from many existing projects, preferring to invest mainly in initiatives that correlate directly with its own priorities, one year at a time. Power has been centralised, and the relationship with other organisations transformed. The top table no longer comprises an inner circle of partner organisations, but Spring Harvest's autonomous executive, and this organisational autonomy has inevitably attenuated the pan-evangelical coalition.

Institutional Leadership

Within a single meeting in 1998 the long-standing SH executive volunteered their resignations and a new team was appointed. Many outside the meeting expressed admiration that the old team relinquished powerful roles so graciously,[34] tempered with surprise that the momentous change of appointing a new team was accomplished the same day. There was no pause to recover from the shock of losing the old team, to review the proposed new team, or to consider candidates not around the table that day. Here was a curious yet characteristic impulsiveness, a hankering back perhaps to the former era of risk, unpredictability and intuitive leaps.

Saunders described the current team as stepping into a vacuum caused by the failure to establish a process of sustained transition in the early 1990s. One, Pete Broadbent, when subsequently appointed as a bishop, went against the Anglican convention of a new bishop relinquishing former responsibilities by affirming his desire to continue working with SH. One is a Baptist, Ian Coffey, who previously worked with Calver at the EA, and whose brother is General Secretary of the Baptist Union. The other three - Jeff Lucas, Gerard Kelly and Rachel Orrell - are all from Pioneer. The prominence of Pioneer is curious at a time when their own network has a lower profile than in the early 1990s, with some doubting that it will survive intact through the inevitable transition to second generation leadership.[35] The new team intended to hold office for around five years, with a phased handover. In June 2003, two long-standing Spring Harvest contributors, Steve Chalke (Baptist) and Ruth Dearnley (Anglican), were added, but by 2005 the new leadership team's "phased handover" had seen no voluntary retirements.

Calver brought together leaders from parachurch organisations for whom SH was a supplementary activity alongside their main ministry. He therefore ensured that SH was a constellation of leading evangelicals and evangelical organisations. What subsequently emerged was a more centralised organisation, more powerful in its own right, with a tendency to self-contained development, more distant from the parachurch organisations, denominations and local churches.

---

[34] Not that the subsequent handling of the transition was easy, according to interviewees. This could indicate inadequate pastoral support, ill-defined terms of service, or perhaps an ambiguous and unexamined attitudes to power and influence among senior evangelicals, perhaps reflecting Barr's plausible charge (1981: xvii-xix) that popular evangelicalism often functions as a religion driven by personality and power.

[35] Indicated in interviews.

The focus of SH, according to our analysis, has shifted from a gathering to an event, a coalition to an organisation, an exceptional intuitive to a highly competent manager, from charisma to bureaucracy, from a voluntary association of influential organisations to a separate centre of influence and control, from an unpredictable roller coaster to a centralised company with a five year plan. SH has become more powerful, but more self-contained. The primary transition is not from Calver and Meadows to Coffey and Lucas: it is from Calver to Johnson. This represents an entirely unexceptional, indeed predictable, organisational life cycle, and an archetypal Weberian transition from charisma to bureaucracy. [36]

Evidence of Problematic Exceptionalism

Expecting Assured Success

While the vast majority of SH speakers would not accept the mechanical revival theory of Finney,[37] the leading nineteenth century revivalist, there was a similarly pragmatic embrace in the 1980s of various mechanisms thought to guarantee church growth, from McGavran to Wimber, from restorationism to spiritual warfare.[38] At the first SH, Luis Palau, an Argentinean evangelist, fanned optimistic flames when he declared that SH presaged the re-evangelisation of Britain with all the success of Latin American evangelicals:

> What I see here reminds me of Latin America about 20 years ago. It started in many cases at conventions like Spring Harvest. I get the same feeling that I did in Latin America – that we are letting loose an army led by young leaders who could really take Britain for Christ in the next decade.[39]

The burgeoning and symbiotic growth of SH and the EA in the 1980s and early 1990s seemed to demonstrate that success was within the grasp of entrepreneurial evangelicalism. This reinforced a profound shift of emphasis among many

---

[36] Weber in Gerth and Wright Mill, 1948.

[37] Finney, 1835.

[38] See above, pp 62-3. This mechanical approach reached its apotheosis at SH in the mid-1990s when Ed Silvoso, a visiting Argentinean from California, explained, complete with diagrams ostensibly representing Pauline teaching, that human acts of reconciliation would bind Satan and thus allow God to move in revival power (Silvoso, 1994). The clinching argument for this speculative theory was that this methodology had secured revival in Argentina. Momentarily the Big Top seemed captivated by this astonishing reversal of authority in which God can be rescued from satanic domination by human initiative. Susceptible enthusiasts queued by the microphone to express their reconciliation. There is, however, no evidence that a mechanism assuredly producing imminent revival was thereby set in motion.

[39] Quoted in the Spring Harvest souvenir programme, celebrating the first decade, 1990: 36-39.

entrepreneurial evangelicals from the old conservative priority – defending the truth that endures – to a new expectancy – achieving the success that is assured. Delayed success rather than the delayed *parousia* became the primary provocation for mounting scepticism and disillusion in the late 1990s.

Activism Displacing Biblicism

While Bebbington identified four primary characteristics of evangelicals,[40] the twin axes we have identified function at times as rival polarities: some biblicist-crucicentrics exhibit a passivity that disregards the biblical emphasis upon orthopraxy; some conversionist-activists display a casual disinterest in biblical theology which suggests their evangelicalism is more a subcultural ideology than a coherent theological tradition. Within populist evangelicalism, theological convictions are shaped less by key theologians and senior leaders and more by personality preachers capable of compelling a crowd of several thousand.[41] Some of the popular celebration speakers make little non-eisegetical reference to the Bible.[42] The entrepreneurs of the conversionist-activist axis have substantially displaced the priorities of the biblicist-crucicentrics in some quarters of the evangelical subculture, resulting in impatience with critical reflection and an instinctive anti-intellectualism. While theological liberalism assimilates to high culture, entrepreneurial evangelicalism assimilates to mass culture, providing commodified religion repackaged for the TV age.[43] As a result of the entrepreneurials' pragmatic indifference to the inflexible prerequisites of the old conservatism, this activism made an oblique and unintentional, but highly significant contribution to the acceptability of the subsequent post-conservative reconstructions of evangelical theology.[44]

Subcultural Isolation

By using holiday camps, SH constructed an evangelical village for a week. Isolation was both its strength and its limitation. Its strength because it provided a powerful, positive reinforcement of the plausibility structures, or "sacred canopy" [45] of evangelicalism: for a week, at least, evangelicals inhabited an essentially mono-cultural community where their convictions and customs prevailed. This reinforced

---

[40] Bebbington, 1989: 3.

[41] For similarities in the United States, see Lints, 1993.

[42] On one occasion that I observed, a leading Spring Harvest personality explained at the adult speakers' prayer meeting, "We've done the Bible teaching this morning, tonight we get down to the real business of prophetic preaching."

[43] Oriented to the same conversionist-activist axis, the pragmatic entrepreneurialism of Latin American Pentecostals makes them early adopters of new communication technologies (Martin B., 1998; Martin D., 2002) .

[44] Hunter, 1983, 1987.

[45] Berger, 1967.

the enthusiastically promulgated but entirely implausible aspiration to move from a pluralistic society to an evangelical version of Christendom.[46] However, while evangelical parents could allow their children freedom within the relatively safe confines of a gated village, this meant the event was hermetically sealed from the host community. Whereas Easter People recruited volunteers from among its guests to serve alongside local churches in the host town, both in social action and evangelism,[47] SH talked about the need for engagement but provided a weeklong experience of isolation.

In 2002, SH secured a campsite in the Vendee for evangelical holidays beginning with the season May to October 2003.[48] This expansion served as a protection against any future loss of access to Butlins, or indeed the possible disappearance of the Easter break from the educational year.[49] It is likely to result in the further ghettoisation of some evangelicals, who will no longer need to endure contact with the unbelieving majority while on holiday. This looks less like a community gathering for advance than a remnant withdrawing into subcultural segregation.

Ecstasy and Illusion

Among leading post-Kendrick charismatic songwriters we can trace distinctive and novel emphases.[50] They recast Christian faith and motivation in terms of emotional intensity:

He has kindled a flame of passion[51]

I will run with all the passion you've put in me[52]

Nothing is hindering the passion in my soul[53]

Our passion is for holiness[54]

---

[46] Compare Smith, 2000.

[47] Indicated in interviews and observed directly.

[48] Although Johnson stated the French campsite "…will eventually be handled by a new group of people, and is structured within a totally separate legal entity," the publicity expressly presents the initiative as Spring Harvest Holidays, using Spring Harvest's branding and logo. Johnson was the most prominent individual in the first publicity for the initiative, which was explicitly linked with Spring Harvest's twenty fifth Anniversary year in 2003.

[49] Indicated in interviews.

[50] Despite the objection that it is unrealistic to apply close textual analysis to lightweight, popular songs, to do so is to treat them seriously as literary and theological constructs, the standard texts of contemporary worship. What follows does not attempt to provide an exhaustive thematic analysis, but focuses upon a novel, ecstatic triumphalism – cognitive dissonance in song. Compare Parry, 2005; Ward, 2005.

[51] Townend, "My first love," Worship Today: 298.

[52] Oakley, "Fire! There's a fire!" *Worship Today*: 93.

[53] Redman, "I will dance," Worship Today: 193.

This is grounded in a tendency to universalise the experiences of Pentecost:

> Let me feel your tongues of fire resting upon me,
>
> Let me hear the sound of your mighty rushing wind.[55]

Ecstatic intensity is presented as a universally attainable and repeatable spiritual experience. The ecstatic becomes normative. All believers can become a Saint Teresa d'Avila, with none facing a dark night of the soul:

> There's a fire, sweet fire burning in my heart[56]
>
> You have brought your holy fire to our lips[57]
>
> I'm opening up my heart
> Come make this joy complete...
> Let your rain flood this thirsty soul[58]

Ecstatic experience is celebrated as the source of dependable assurance:

> I can feel the power of your hand upon me[59]

Martin Smith, in particular, uses intense, evocative and compelling diction. The experience of God is sensuous:

> I have felt your touch, more intimate than lovers[60]
>
> You've burned the truth on our lips[61]
>
> You've set this heart on fire[62]

Responses to God are similarly centred upon emotional intensity:

> My heart is bursting Lord[63]
>
> It would break my heart[64]

---

[54] Smith, "The crucible for silver," *Worship Today*: 395.

[55] Oakley, "Fire! There's a fire!" *Worship Today*: 93.

[56] Oakley, "Fire! There's a fire!" *Worship Today*: 93.

[57] Smith, "The crucible for silver," *Worship Today*: 395.

[58] Townend, "Your love, shining like the sun," *Worship Today*: 500.

[59] Oakley, "Fire! There's a fire!" *Worship Today*: 93.

[60] Smith, "What a friend I've found," *Worship Today*: 457.

[61] Smith, "Men of faith," Worship Today: 292.

[62] Smith, "The crucible for silver," *Worship Today*: 395.

[63] Smith, "I could sing unending songs," *Worship Today*: 168.

I will open up my heart[65]

They will dance with joy like we are dancing now[66]

I could dance a thousand miles because of your great love[67]

When people pray, according to Smith, cloudless skies will break, echoing Elijah, kings and queens will shake and the church will see dead men rise.[68] When all saints join in one song to Christ, mountains, darkness and people will tremble, while the oceans and singers will roar.[69] The two most decisive Christian activities to bring in this new day of God appear to be prayer and singing. The church triumphant is but a song away.

Right praying and right singing secure a future destiny and a present-day experience. The destiny is for the individual Christian to become a history maker, a speaker of truth "to all mankind", which is certainly ambitious. As for the present, Smith invites churches to declare that the joy of God is in the town and everyone sees the truth.[70] Oakley similarly declares that all around the world a new day is dawning.[71] Not the new day of the in-breaking of the Kingdom of God, nor the new day of Pentecost, but the era of the successful church, which, he claims, has now demonstrably arrived. Future hope focuses more upon success than the *parousia*. Once again a key signifier of this hope is musical - "a new song rising up". Here is exuberance crammed with intemperate hyperbole. With intoxicating enthusiasm believers attempt to sing themselves into an alternate reality, where secularization is a myth and an evangelical-charismatic variant upon Christendom is imminent.

This kind of contemporary song promotes a universal ecstatic spirituality that promises a sustainedly passionate devotion to Christ, with the expectations that every believer will speak truth to all mankind and that whole towns are presently filled with joy and compelled by the Gospel. Neither the New Testament nor church history gives credence to such expectations. Given the current condition of the church in Western Europe such songs indulge a wilful disregard for reality. They represent a heady cocktail of the promise of an altered state of consciousness through exuberant singing - the charismatic equivalent of clubbing - combined with the exaggerated hopes of entrepreneurial evangelicals, persisting in denial faced with the failure of inflated promises.

The SH annual songbook has made a considerable contribution to the rapid reconfiguration of evangelical worship and has facilitated the emergence of new

---

[64] Smith, "What a friend I've found," *Worship Today*: 457.

[65] Smith, "Over the mountains," *Worship Today*: 343.

[66] Smith, "Over the mountains," *Worship Today*: 343.

[67] Smith, "I could sing unending songs," *Worship Today*: 168.

[68] Smith, "Is it true today," *Worship Today*: 215.

[69] Smith, "Did you feel the mountains tremble?" *Worship Today*: 70.

[70] Smith, "Well I hear they're singing," *Worship Today*: 456.

[71] Oakley, "All around the world," *Worship Today*: 4.

songwriters. It has also commodified music in worship, providing disposable worship songs with an imminent sell-by-date. Contemporaneity has been secured, while eccentricities of spirituality and exaggerated claims of present day success have been promoted. Here is a Mephistophelean pact with modernity: the hidden price tags are a ruptured tradition, a heightened potential for a *theologia gloriae* unfettered to a *theologia crucis*, a growing biblical illiteracy, a replacement of *parousia* hope with expectations of imminent success, and a quasi-gnostic, ecstatic and escapist spirituality.

Vision Inflation

According to Johnson,[72] the future vision of SH is twofold. First, to continue to equip the church. Second to "touch the nation". During the 1996 planning process, Johnson wrote himself a note "Spring Harvest, as it touches the nation for Christ", and kept it in his Bible. When a similar phrase emerged within the new executive, Johnson displayed his cherished note. His account of its significance is emphatic:

God's word to us has been that Spring Harvest is going to "touch the nation".[73]

Johnson describes as "scary, way beyond anything before" this new and portentous societal ambition. With talk of "touching the nation", SH is either graduating to a new level of cultural influence or succumbing to the characteristic extravagance of entrepreneurial evangelicalism in the 1990s, namely vision inflation. This recalls Adrian Hastings' charge that evangelicals often promise more than they deliver,[74] thus making evangelicalism prone to remain always a form of juvenile religion. SH is, after all, merely a Bible week, a holiday for evangelicals, which seems an implausible springboard for societal revolution.

Negative aspects of entrepreneurial evangelical exceptionalism therefore include the promotion of success that displaces the *via crucis*; the emphasis upon personality preachers that tends towards anti-intellectualism and the seductiveness of the superficial; ecstatic worship in denial; a widespread disregard for the church before 1980; and the distinctive vision inflation that tended from the early 1990s to intensify the entrepreneurial evangelical aspirations of imminent and immense advance, even as the cultural climate became more indifferent to the Christian church in all its forms.

---

[72] Indicated in interview.

[73] Quoted in an article on the new Spring Harvest executive in *Christianity* magazine, December 2000.

[74] "It seems characteristic of Evangelicalism both to appeal especially to youth and to make rather grand claims in regard to its advances... The consequence is that Evangelicalism looks like a tide always claimed to be just about to come in, yet never quite reaching the shore with the force proclaimed." (Hastings, 2001: xlv).

Entrepreneurial Rhetoric and Religious Recreation

Spring Harvest's transition from charisma to bureaucracy traverses familiar Weberian territory,[75] but entrepreneurial evangelicals produced an unusual variant: where second generation leaders typically emphasise steady progress, the entrepreneurial evangelicals combined centralisation and bureaucracy with an intensification of vision inflation, announcing ever greater expectations. To evangelicals who had enjoyed the dramatic growth of EA and SH, the 1980s seemed to promise imminent and extensive transformation of both church and society. However, the 1990s suggested that the condition of the church was less at Jericho's walls than by the waters of Babylon, less imminent conquest than prolonged exile.[76] The entrepreneurial evangelicals prominent in SH would not readily adjust to the realities of a church in cultural exile. By the late 1990s, as the credibility of the entrepreneurs' superheated promises burnt out, evangelicals may have begun to grow disillusioned with and sceptical of the entrepreneurial recasting of their tradition. The guests at SH who had filtered out the restorationist agenda from new church speakers in the 1980s, were now likely to filter the hyperinflation of the entrepreneurs, in preaching and in song. Notwithstanding the main-stage rhetoric of SH, transforming the nation had become a less plausible prospect than self-actualisation through therapeutic religion.

We can therefore identify two interwoven but contrary strands of evangelical exceptionalism at SH: a sustained exploration of possible cultural transpositions of the church;[77] and yet a self-attenuating predilection for the inconsequential enthusiasms of evangelical juvenilia.[78] The implausibility of the inflated entrepreneurial rhetoric may even have precipitated an unintended withdrawal into escapist religious recreation. While singing songs that herald an army mobilised to take the land, Spring Harvest's evangelicals functioned increasingly as a gated community, a ghetto on holiday.

The plateauing of Spring Harvest was an early indicator of the demise of the entrepreneurial dreams of accelerating evangelical advance. Evangelical decline in the 1990s was much less acute than among other traditions, but they exhibited no inherent immunity to secularization. Despite the pervasive rhetoric of success, evangelicals in the early twenty-first century, rather than enjoying an exceptional immunity, face at best attenuated decline, at worst late-onset decline into the free fall of other traditions, temporarily deferred by their subcultural cohesiveness and resilient certainties.[79]

---

[75] Weber in Gerth and Wright Mill, 1948.

[76] Brown, 2001, 2006; Gill, 2003.

[77] Warner, 1994; Gill, 2001, 2002, 2003.

[78] Hastings, 2001.

[79] Compare Kelley, 1972; Hunter, 1983, 1987; Davie, 1994, 2002, 2003; Smith, 1998, 2000; Bruce, 1996, 2002; Brown, 2001; Percy, 2003; Heelas, Woodhead et al, 2005.

Chapter 3

Evangelical Trends: Late-Onset Decline

We now turn to the trends in traditional pan-evangelicalism during the period of the boom and plateau for SH and the EA. Our examination of the sales of evangelical monthly magazines and Bible reading notes will demonstrate sustained decline in these substantive contributors to evangelical subcultural capital,[1] even though entrepreneurial evangelicalism, particularly on the conversionist-activist axis, consistently presented a public image of a rising tide of influence, numbers and success.

The Collapse of the Monthly Magazines

In the early 1980s, evangelical monthly magazines enjoyed a monthly combined UK distribution of over 72,000.[2] By 1990, sales of the equivalent range of magazines had reduced to 42,000, and by 1999 to 28,000. This represents a decrease of 61.4% in 20 years, which indicates a devastating collapse in the market.

In contrast, the leading North American monthly, *Christianity Today*, enjoyed average monthly circulation of 184,856 in 1980, 159,645 in 1990 and 163,128 in 2000. This represents a decline of 11.8% over twenty years, and an increase in the 1990s of 1%. These hardly represent exciting commercial trends, but indicate a markedly more stable cultural context for Christianity in general and evangelicalism in particular.

---

[1] Thornton, 1995; Gelder and Thornton, 1997; compare Irwin, 1970.

[2] Figures provided by Dave Roberts, previously editor of *Alpha Magazine* and subsequently an advisor to *Renewal*, and by John Buckeridge, editor of *Christianity and Renewal*, previously editor of *Christianity* and *Youthwork*. All figures represent official distribution. Rival editors are allegedly inclined to discount one another's figures for dumping, overseas distribution etc. The higher figures have been used throughout, to allow for proportionate "inflation".

Table 13: Estimated sales of evangelical monthly magazines

	Early 1980s	1990	1996	1999	2001
Buzz	28,000				
Christian Family	23,000				
Today	6,600				
21CC	19,000				
Alpha		17,000	10,000		
Christianity			10,000	5,000	
Youthwork				5,000	5,000
Christian Woman		16,000	12,000	9,000	9,000
Renewal	15,000	9,000	12,000	9,000	
Christianity & Renewal					14,000
Totals	72,600	42,000	34,000	28,000	28,000

In the period 1980-2000, *Renewal Magazine*, the only ecumenical monthly specifically serving charismatics, with a market primarily in the historic denominations and predominantly Anglican,[3] decreased by 40%. In 1996, *Renewal* enjoyed a strong, but temporary rise in sales. Although *Alpha* magazine, not to be confused with the evangelistic programme, gave prominent and positive coverage to Toronto, it was *Renewal* that enjoyed the growth in market share. This increase of 3,000 copies was not sustained, but *Renewal's* decline was halted so that its sales at the end of the 1990s matched those at the beginning of the decade. Leading book publishers of this period concluded by the late 1980s[4] that charismatic renewal was no longer generating new markets, and was struggling to develop a second generation identity. John Finney has argued that this may not signify failure since by their very nature, renewal groupings that successfully influence the wider church often consequently lose their *raison d'être*, unable to sustain the intense and focused enthusiasm of the founding generation.[5]

---

[3] As an editorial consultant to the magazine I was notified by the editors of such trends from 1982 onwards.

[4] In conversation and interview.

[5] Finney, 2000, drawing on Weber. While Foster (1998) argued that the charismatic tradition is one of the six great traditions of Christian spirituality, the New Testament emphasis upon the Holy Spirit's concern to focus attention towards the Son may suggest that charismatic renewal could be expected to have an inherent tendency to become re-oriented from Pneumatocentricity to Christocentricity. In short, authentic Holy Spirit movements may be intrinsically short-lived.

Table 14: Comparative sales, 1980-2000

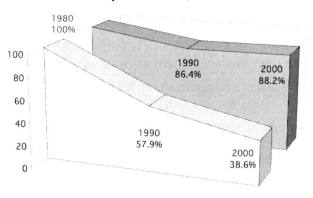

UK monthly magazines   *Christianity Today*

These twenty years saw an 83% decrease in the sales of broad evangelical magazines. The merger between *Christianity* and *Renewal* in 2001 signifies the demise of a separate market for the moderate, non- or pre-charismatic evangelicals, and probably also indicates the unsustainability of second generation charismatic culture. The last pre-merger editor of *Christianity*, John Buckeridge, who trained at Moorlands College and previously worked with Youth for Christ, became editor of the joint magazine and for a while also served as the part time leader of a Pioneer church. (The influence of Pioneer upon wider evangelicalism remained remarkably pervasive, given their modest numbers and the ambivalence about their network's viability voiced privately by several of their leaders.[6] They were the only new church stream represented on the Board of EA, as well as contributing three fifths of the turn of the century SH leadership team.)

Renewal Magazine's percentage of the market was 36.6% in 1980, 34.6% in 1990, but 66.7% in 2000. The slight decline in market share during the 1980s led to concerns on the editorial board, of which I was a member, that *Renewal's* contributors were ageing, overly Anglican for the broader market, and simplistically uncritical of charismatic renewal, with a frequent pursuit of the fashionable, the novel and the quick-fix. By 2000 *Renewal* had nearly doubled its market share in a decade, and became the bestselling evangelical monthly, not by addressing these issues but simply by maintaining sales. Over these two decades, the decline of *Renewal* was substantial, but the decline of the broad evangelical magazines was catastrophic and potentially terminal.

---

[6] Indicated in interviews.

Table 15: Comparative sales of *Renewal* and the broad evangelical monthlies

	Renewal	Today/21CC/ Alpha/Christianity
1980	15,000	26,000
1989	10,000	18,000
1990	9,000	17,000
1996	12,000	10,000
2000	9,000	5,000

Table 16: Changing market share, 1980-2000

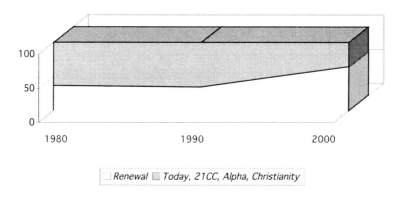

Renewal ▨ Today, 21CC, Alpha, Christianity

What factors produced this collapse in market? Were evangelicals simply not buying magazines, despite growth in magazine sales in the secular market? They were certainly difficult to purchase, since Christian bookshops were the only retail outlets. But the bookshops had always been few and far between, so this was not a new factor. The old distribution system through churches, where a willing volunteer handed out personal copies, seems to have collapsed. But this system only delivered distribution, without actively recruiting new subscribers. This period saw the new churches develop their own glossy magazines. While they eschewed denominational identity, they produced magazines that marketed their distinctive brand – Pioneer, New Frontiers - as God's prime regiment. Their products were more exciting to their brand loyalists than the broader magazines. However, the vast majority of subscribers to the existing magazines were not in the new churches. It may be there was simply a declining interest in the transdenominational evangelical subculture. This could indicate a journalistic failure to deliver commercial content. It could indicate a lack of evangelical leaders able to provide compelling and provocative articles. But what it suggests more broadly is diminishing pan-evangelical identity. Any such loss of identity would have been compounded by confusion about the ethos of the various magazines as a result of the regular mergers and re-branding, with sales continuing ineluctably to slide. Instead, of purchasing the same or similar broad-based evangelical magazines, those attending evangelical churches have become more likely to receive free literature that focuses upon the single issues or programmes in which they have a particular interest. For example, circulation of Tear Fund's magazine grew rapidly (from around 20,000 in 1979, to 170,000 in 2001), and so, subsequently, did HTB's *Alpha News*, achieving circulation of 250,000 by 2003.[7]

Table 17: Comparative decline of *Renewal* and broad evangelical monthlies, 1980-2000

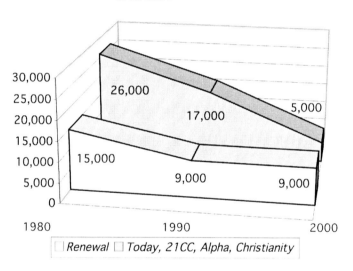

This represents a hidden crisis of communication and identity for evangelicalism as their internal market fragments. Without a broad-based and mass-market magazine, pan-evangelical consciousness is necessarily diminished. Evangelicals appear to have become more distant from any wider evangelical identity, beyond their local church (and for some, but by no means all, their denomination or network[8]). They will therefore become increasingly uninformed and distanced from any pan-evangelical agenda. The leaders of pan-evangelicalism have lost one of

---

[7] Booker and Ireland, 2003: 28.

[8] Certainly not the Baptists, among whom many individuals (and perhaps local churches) appear to be semi-detached from their denominational identity (Escott and Gelder, 2002).

their key platforms to communicate with and sustain their constituency. The vision of pan-evangelicalism is then more narrowly expressed through the inevitably limited number of preachers who are able, willing and invited to preach from the main platforms at the large venue evangelical and charismatic events.

Symptomatic of the demise of evangelical magazines is the collapse of the middle-brow. The American magazine, *Christianity Today* has always intended to include longer, more substantial articles,[9] while the main British monthlies have long subsisted on a diet of populism. Similarly, book publishers in the UK, both independent evangelical and broad-based commercial publishers of religious books,[10] while declining to make public specific figures, have spoken to me privately of the collapse of the middle-brow. The evangelical market has segmented into a growing specialist sector of academic publications and, on the other hand, lightweight testimonies and simplistic "how-to" guidebooks. Since there has been no equivalent collapse of the middle-brow in general publishing, this suggests that many evangelical readers have little appetite for serious reading that stretches them beyond the ephemeral and entertaining. Once popular notions of developing a Christian mind,[11] appear to have sunk without trace, not because of postmodern scepticism about the very notion of a world view but rather because evangelicals have lost their appetite for such intellection. Evangelical faith, at least in Britain, appears to have entered upon a consumerist trajectory, privately engaging but publicly irrelevant. The quest for an evangelical meta-narrative has been aborted in favour of inspirational entertainment. The secularizing process has produced evangelicals whose faith is compartmentalized and privatized according to the prevailing cultural pattern.[12] Perhaps it is the evangelicals, to adopt Postman's polemical description of TV, who are "amusing themselves to death".[13]

It would have been reasonable to assume that Meadows' marketing flair as a magazine publisher combined with Calver's entrepreneurial drive might produce a Spring Harvest inspired surge in magazine subscriptions. On the contrary, the

---

[9] Billy Graham's intentions were clear from the start of *Christianity Today*. "My idea that night was for a magazine, aimed primarily at ministers, that would restore intellectual respectability and spiritual impact to evangelical Christianity…" (Graham, 1997: 286.) The British evangelical monthlies have long held more tabloid aspirations.

[10] In conversation.

[11] Blamires, 1963, 2001; Guinness, 1995.

[12] Spring Harvest's *At Work Together* conferences represented at the turn of the century an attempt to reconnect faith and work. Significantly the most favoured explanation for the churches' disengagement was the impact of Platonic assumptions leading to a sacred-secular divide. The disengagement was thus the fault of the church and the problem could be solved by the church rediscovering the holistic approach of the ancient Jews. British evangelicals evidently find it more palatable to blame the church for failings that can consequently be self-corrected, than to engage with the sociological analysis of secularization. When cultural developments originate outside the church, the logical consequence is that the forces of fragmentation and differentiation are almost certainly beyond the power of the church to reverse.

[13] The title of Postman's (1985) trenchant polemic against television is apposite.

inverse relationship of their growth and decline is striking. While Spring Harvest grew from 2,800 in 1978 to 50,000 by 1988, an eighteen-fold increase, the magazines went into a tailspin almost halving their circulation from 72,000 in the early 1980s to 42,000 in 1990. If video killed the radio star, Spring Harvest may have killed the evangelical magazine.

Table 18: A family tree of evangelical monthlies

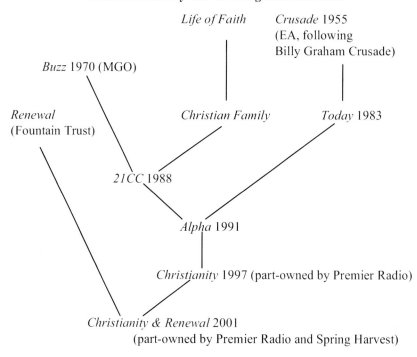

There was evidently more appetite for an annual inspirational holiday than monthly reading matter. If the evangelical subculture was losing its internal plausibility, the willing suspension of disbelief was more easily accomplished during a few days of hot-house religion at Spring Harvest than through a monthly magazine. It remains to be seen whether Spring Harvest's new investment in *Christianity and Renewal* in 2001 will bring about a resurgence in magazine sales, or whether it represents too little, too late. A complimentary copy was given to every adult guest at Spring Harvest in 2001, resulting in 1,000 new subscriptions[14] - a modest increase given the number of guests but substantial relative to the existing subscriptions. Evangelical magazines appear to have lost a generation who once subscribed (age 35-50) and to have never recruited the following generation (age 20-35). Even as the growth of EA membership and SH attendance seemed to vindicate aspirations for pan-evangelical mobilisation, evangelicals were turning their backs

---

[14] Indicated in interviews.

upon the transdenominational identity previously expressed through monthly magazines.

The Decline of the Quiet Time

Mid-twentieth century evangelical spirituality was centred upon the daily discipline of the "Quiet Time", which combined reading and reflecting upon a set portion of Scripture with time for personal prayer, emphasising adoration and thanksgiving, confession and intercession, but not usually meditation or contemplation. Origins of this discipline may be found in the Daily Prayer Meeting formed by evangelical students at Cambridge in 1862 and Torrey's emphasis upon the "Morning Watch", which during his 1911 mission to Cambridge resulted in 200 undergraduates committing themselves to a daily hour of personal prayer and Bible study.[15] Barclay records that in the mid-twentieth century undergraduates declined to attend "the chapel breakfast after Communion, because it could interfere with the Quiet Time".[16] At the 2001 EA Assembly, John Stott's contribution on video included a strong affirmation of this traditional evangelical discipline, but his enthusiasm had become passé. Stott's audience listened respectfully but the data we examine in this section demonstrates that evangelicals had become unconvinced of the necessity or sustainability of the traditional cornerstone of twentieth century evangelical spirituality.

As the long time market leader, positioned at the very heart of mainstream evangelicalism, the trends revealed by sales of Scripture Union notes are symptomatic of the vitality or even viability of mid-century evangelical spirituality.[17] SU identify their mission priorities as evangelism and teaching, with special reference to children, young people and their families, and Bible ministries. In the 1990s, the International Council of SU produced new working principles that continued to affirm a bibliocentric spirituality, but shifted the emphasis from "daily" to "regular" Bible reading:

> We are committed to Bible reading which is thoughtful, prayerful and regular and which enables the reader to respond to the message of the whole Bible rather than to isolated passages.[18]

This may indicate a new theological emphasis upon liberty rather than legalism. Or perhaps it reflects a realistic response to a new culture in which, for practising Christians as well as the wider society, time has become a scarce resource, with self-discipline no longer a familiar virtue.

In 1985, SU's adult Bible reading notes sold an average of 199,593 copies per

---

[15] Barclay and Horn, 2002: 19, 84.

[16] Barclay and Horn, 2002: 125.

[17] The raw data for this analysis, only available from 1985, was kindly provided by senior staff at Scripture Union.

[18] SU, 1995.

issue. Given that these sales are repeated quarterly, unlike the one-off purchase of a book, this represents substantial market penetration, far in excess of the evangelical monthly magazines. By 2000, total sales had declined to 98,380 per quarter. SU Bible reading notes still have a greater penetration of the evangelical market than the largest annual Bible Week, demonstrating the continued and regular, if not daily, practice of this spirituality within some sectors of evangelicalism. Nonetheless, while the market remains large, the scale of decline has been substantial: 50.71% between 1985 and 2000.

This pattern of decline is repeated across the range of SU materials. *Encounter with God*, the most demanding of these publications, saw a 41.3% decline. If we subdivide the period into three five-year sectors, the decline appeared to slow slightly in the early 1990s - down to 8.39% from 9.75%. However, the late 1990s saw an escalating decline of 16.9%. There was a slight increase in sales in 2000, up by 220 copies, but this change is too small to be interpreted as a reversal of long-term decline.

Closer to God, designed to be the most easy to use, most contemporary format, grew by 14.21% in 1985-89. However, in 1990-94 this was reversed with a decline of 27.26%. In October 1996, *Closer to God* incorporated a short-lived product, *Alive to God*, which had attempted to reach a more overtly charismatic market. Sales did not justify two separate products and SU concluded that a moderate renewal consensus was expressed through both publications.[19] This boosted sales of *Closer to God* from 28,951 in 1995 to 31,314 in 1997, the first full year after merger, but this temporary improvement failed to reverse the underlying trend, with the five-year period from 1995-99 showing a decline of 15.82%. Over the period 1985-2000, *Closer to God* declined by 40.4%. The most tabloid SU format almost exactly matched the decline of the most demanding (40.4%, compared with 41.3% for *Encounter with God*.)

SU's flagship Bible reading resource is *Daily Bread*. In 1985 it sold 115,236 copies, representing 57.7% of all notes sold by SU. In 2000 it sold 48,471, representing 49.3% of total sales. In 1985-89, sales of *Daily Bread*, declined by 9.35%, closely matching the 9.75% decline for *Encounter with God*. In 1990-94, the decline accelerated dramatically to 23.42%, compared with 8.39% for *Encounter with God*. In 1995-99 the decline accelerated again to 28.9%, compared with 16.9% for *Encounter with God* and 15.82% for *Closer to God*. The total decline is 57.9%. In short, the best-selling, middle-brow Bible reading notes declined the most rapidly.

When the total sales of SU notes have declined by 50.71% in the period 1985-2000, and the market leader, *Daily Bread*, has declined in this period by 57.9%, we draw the following conclusions. First, the sales of daily Bible reading notes have recorded long-term and remorseless decline, with the eventual prospect of their publication no longer being economically viable. Second, the influence of daily Bible reading notes upon the broad evangelical community has diminished apace.

---

[19] Advised in conversation.

Third, mid-twentieth century conservative evangelical spirituality, based around the discipline of the "Quiet Time" has become increasingly marginal.

Table 19: The decline of Bible reading notes, 1985-2000

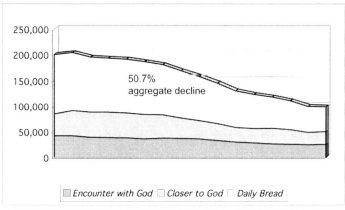

	1985-9	1990-4	1995-9
Encounter with God	-9.75%	-8.39%	-16.90%
Closer to God	+14.21%	-27.26%	-15.82%
Daily Bread	-9.35%	-23.42%	-28.96%
Total	-4.35%	-22.33%	-23.34%

Table 20: Comparative decline, 1985-89, 1990-94, 1995-99

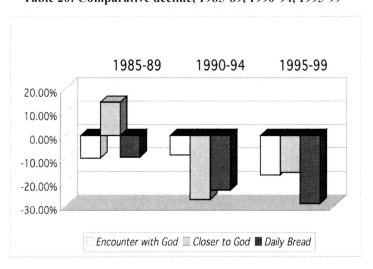

Evangelicals are either exploring other approaches to prayer and Bible reading[20] or the tradition is secularizing rapidly. Inasmuch as the "Quiet Time" promoted some measure of biblical literacy, albeit highly devotional and pietistic, the demise of this practice contributes to the perceived trend of growing biblical illiteracy among evangelicals.[21] The distinctive spirituality of the mid-twentieth century conservative evangelicals is being abandoned, presumably as no longer helpful, compelling or relevant. Bebbington's emphasis upon biblicism as an evangelical distinctive[22] appears to be in decline among contemporary English evangelicals: more observed in theory than in practice.

Behind EA's headlines of dramatic growth, evangelical organisations suffered a dramatic decline in Bible reading notes, magazine sales, and book sales, 1980-2000. This severe and sustained decline indicates a diminishing sense of pan-evangelical homogeneity as evangelicals transition into a loose coalition of diverse emphases, practices and spirituality. There is also evidence of an ageing donor base for many long-standing evangelical organisations[23] and a decline of 3% in evangelical church attendance during the decade to 1998.[24] The evangelical boom years may not so much have been "taking new ground", in the idiom of Kendrick's March for Jesus songs,[25] as walking on thin ice. Morale was raised with promises of imminent advance, but eyes were averted from the uncomfortable evidence that indicated the possibility of incipient decline.

While American evangelicals have constructed a well-delineated and self-sustaining subculture,[26] (such that Penning and Smidt's reworking of Hunter's survey of students at evangelical colleges confounds his predictions by identifying close theological and socio-political agreement between current evangelical college students and their parents[27]) the English evangelical subcultural identity is necessarily attenuated by the decline of the common currency of magazines and

---

[20] For example through Renovaré. See Foster, 1998.

[21] Such a trend, while not objectively quantifiable, was cited in interview by several senior evangelical leaders.

[22] Bebbington, 1989, 2005.

[23] Support base data was discussed in written and verbal form with a number of leading agencies, without being analysed at length in this chapter.

[24] The decline in Catholic churchmanship during the decade to 1998 was 48%, compared with 11% for liberal and 19% for broad church (Brierley, 2000). Evangelicals are therefore doing better than other traditions, even with 3% decline.

[25] www.jesusday.org ; www.grahamkendrick.co.uk. Accessed 5 August 2005.

[26] "…their own educational institutions, special interest groups, denominations, radio and TV programs, music, books and magazines. Children are socialized by attending evangelical schools, listening to evangelical rock music, reading evangelicals comic books and magazines, buying evangelicals toys and games, attending social events with other evangelicals, even attending evangelical colleges and graduate schools." Reimer, 1996, chapter 3, quoted in Penning and Smidt, 2002: 69. Compare Gordon, 1947; Cohen, 1955; Arnold, 1970; Irwin, 1970; Thornton, 1995; Gelder and Thornton, 1997; Muggleton and Weinzierl, 2003; Bennet and Kahn-Harris, 2004.

[27] Penning and Smidt, 2002; Hunter, 1987.

quiet times. Neither American subcultural isolationism nor English inflated entrepreneurialism is likely to transform the secularizing trends of the prevailing culture,[28] but American evangelicals are more likely to be able to sustain their discrete identity.[29] The English evangelical rhetoric of the 1980s and 1990s was upbeat, ambitious, entrepreneurial and filled with expectancy. The underlying statistical data indicate destabilisation, fragmentation and even decline. The first half of the 1990s, when SH plateaued, EA's growth slowed, and evangelical magazines and Bible reading notes declined faster than previously, therefore represents a seismic shift in evangelical prospects, and a further tipping point in the death of Christian Britain.[30] The social construction of evangelical subcultural reality, in terms of a pervasive identity and piety, was breaking down.[31]

---

[28] For the American paradox of self-sustaining subcultural strategies that are self-defeating of evangelicalism's mission aspirations, see Smith, 1998, 2000.

[29] Although Bramadat (2000) identifies bridging as well as fortress strategies among evangelical students at a secular Canadian university, he also notes that most of them were converted in childhood (p60), thus indicating a lack of effectiveness in student and adult evangelism in North America as well as on the students' mission to Lithuania (pp119-138).

[30] Brown, 2001.

[31] Berger and Luckmann, 1967; Thornton, 1995; Gelder and Thornton, 1997.

Chapter 4

Deconstructing the Decade of Evangelism

1994: The Year of Evangelistic Programmes[1]

Many British denominations and Christian organisations designated the 1990s the "decade of evangelism". Since church attendance had been in long-term decline[2] and for evangelicals there was no plausible successor to the high profile evangelism of Billy Graham, this was an ambitious declaration. In retrospect, the decade was less of a bang than a whimper.[3]

In 1994, the "decade of evangelism" seemed to be moving up through the gears. This year saw three major evangelistic programmes that won the support of many evangelical churches: *Jim* (Jesus in Me), *Minus to Plus* and *On Fire*. The Ecumenical Lent programme, *Have Another Look* was also run in 1994, but with little support from evangelical churches.

Jim was sponsored by the classical Pentecostal churches but welcomed involvement from other churches.[4] The aim of *Jim* was to see 250,000 new Christians during March 1994. This target derived from the vision of Wynne Lewis, then General Secretary of the Elim Pentecostal Church and previously the senior pastor of Kensington Temple, Elim's flagship metropolitan church. *Jim* attempted to use national resources and advertising to mobilise local church evangelism and raise interest in the wider community: a national training conference was attended by 3,000; a resource pack was produced for local churches; 40,000 copies of a manual on personal witness were distributed; 5,000 attended a nationwide tour for nurture group leaders; 15-20,000 prayer and evangelistic events were held; the organisers estimated that 500,000 people "received personal witness"; nine million copies of

---

[1] Statistical data taken from Earwicker and Spriggs, 1994. They surveyed 300 randomly selected EA member churches (10% sample), with a 44% response rate. The council membership of 60 proved a 37% response rate.

[2] Gilbert, 1980; Wolffe, 1994; Gill, 2003; Brown, 2001.

[3] T.S. Eliot's description in *The Hollow Men* of the world ending not with a bang but a whimper, was reversed by Ezra Pound's Canto LXXIV within the apocalyptic experience of the cage where he wrote *The Pisan Cantos* at the end of the Second World War. Whatever their validity in terms of a culture's decline, Eliot's version better characterizes the decay of the Western European churches in the late twentieth century. Like the closing cadences of a Tchaikovsky symphony, many traditional expressions of church may be facing a prolonged but terminal *diminuendo*.

[4] Data drawn from Earwicker and Spriggs, 1994.

Jim Times were distributed; 1,500 churches took part. Interviewees identified two major criticisms: *Jim* became too big for its own organisational resources - its popularity among non-Pentecostals resulted in administrative overload; and yet, paradoxically, it was not big enough - national advertising failed to reach critical mass and penetrate the unchurched consciousness.

Minus to Plus was the personal vision of Reinhardt Bonnke, a German Pentecostal evangelist who works mainly in mega-evangelism in Africa. Contrary to Hunt's suggestion, "Minus to Plus" was not a reference to declining church attendance,[5] but rather to the fullness of life available through Christian conversion. Bonnke's organisation, CfAN, Christ for All Nations, began with their existing networks that were mainly Pentecostal but their publicity achieved exceptionally high penetration of the pan-evangelical constituency. While *Jim* encouraged local evangelism with national training, resources and advertising, *Minus to Plus* had a quite different approach. A glossy booklet, written by Bonnke and anglicised in the light of advice from the Evangelical Alliance, was to be distributed by the Post Office to every home in the UK (and the Republic of Ireland) during Holy Week. Churches that registered as part of the project would receive the names of local people who returned a commitment card. CfAN projected a response rate of 20%, which therefore anticipated an astounding four million enquirers for churches. Late in the planning, CfAN changed distribution from the Post Office to an independent distributor; unfortunately, some churches claimed that no booklets at all appeared to have been delivered in their areas. 18,400 churches registered (15,400 of these in England) but a mere 30,000 responses were received.

On Fire was sponsored by self-styled "TV Vicar" [6] Steve Chalke's organisation, Oasis Trust, working through the official ecumenical channels. The aim was to encourage high profile events over Pentecost weekend in community buildings and parks, rather than in churches, followed by a fortnight of evangelistic activities, including guest services. The national organisers suggested a wide range of activities: but local churches apparently found this confusing rather than empowering and some claimed the initiative became too complex.[7] BBC's *Songs of Praise* provided an *On Fire* focus on Pentecost Sunday, but there was limited additional activity reported beyond the weekend. Perhaps because it rained on the Saturday, when many events were planned, there was less grass roots activism than had been anticipated. 1,648 churches took part, 1,627 in England, with many working together ecumenically for the first time.

In the immediate aftermath of these projects, the Evangelical Alliance surveyed member churches and Council members,[8] producing both objective data and subjective evaluations. Turning first to the objective data, publicity levels were high for all three initiatives and outstandingly high for *Minus to Plus* at 90% penetration

[5] Hunt, 2001: 4.
[6] The phrase has been used in Chalke's organisation's publicity. www.oasistrust.org. Accessed 5 August 2005.
[7] Earwicker and Spriggs, 1994.
[8] Earwicker and Spriggs, 1994.

of the evangelical constituency. Participation by 30% of EA churches was a success for *Jim*, extending their reach significantly beyond card-carrying Pentecostals. Participation in *Minus to Plus* was quite extraordinary at 98%. Clearly the high profile success of Bonnke in Africa, reputedly seeing mass conversions on a regular basis, produced very high credibility for his initiative, securing support way beyond the Pentecostals and charismatics. If this percentage of EA member churches is accurate, Bonnke's initiative secured more inclusive evangelical support than even the crusades of Luis Palau and Billy Graham. This may also reflect a sense of urgent need to try something new: implicit recognition that the long-standing evangelistic methods, from mass evangelism to door-to-door, were no longer culturally relevant, cost-effective or productive and that the cold winds of secularism were biting hard.

Table 21: Non-financial comparative data, 1994 missions

	Jim	*Minus to Plus*	*On Fire*
% of EA churches receiving publicity	81%	90%	77%
% of EA churches taking part	30%	98%	31%
Projected response per church enquirers/conversions	56/20	50/22	22/3
Actual response per church enquirers/conversions	17/3	3/0.4	8/0.14
Actual response as % of projected response enquirers/conversions	30% / 15%	6% / 2%	36% / 5%

Table 22: Financial comparisons, 1994 missions

	Jim	*Minus to Plus*	*On Fire*
Donation per enquirer	£27	£79	£23
Donation per church	£476	£235	£182
Total cost	£3 million	£3.75 million	£155,000

The two numbers in the projected response and actual response columns of Table 23-5 signify the ratio of enquirers to conversions. In each case the projected figures assumed more enquirers than conversions. *Jim* and *Minus to Plus* assumed ratios of 2.8:1 and 2.27:1, whereas *On Fire* assumed a much higher ratio of 7.33:1. In reality the ratios were *Jim* 5.67:1; *Minus to Plus* 7.5:1; *On Fire* 57.14:1. *On Fire's* ratio of enquirers to conversions was notably poor, indicating that it produced very few

102 *Reinventing English Evangelicalism*

conversions but relatively significant numbers of enquirers. In their projections of actual results, all three initiatives were lamentable. The most accurate projections were for enquirers, from *On Fire* (36% of projected numbers) and *Jim* (30%), but even these figures indicate a threefold over-estimate in the headline grabbing projections. As to conversions, *Jim* was the most accurate, but still achieved merely 15% of the projected results. The most inaccurate projections were from *Minus to Plus*, which achieved 6% of the projected enquirers and a mere 2% of the projected conversions. These unrealistic projections indicate that extreme optimism had parted company with reality. Some conversionist-activists had evidently become incapable of projections that took account of the cultural chasm between the English unchurched and any realistic prospect of Christian conversion.

Minus to Plus was the most expensive per actual enquirer (£79). Other evangelistic organisations estimated that they lost donations most to *Minus to Plus* (35%) and *On Fire* (36%). However, given the modest national costs of *On Fire*, these organisations' assessment seems to have been anecdotal rather than objective, reflecting the perceived threat of Chalke's escalating entrepreneurial profile. Taking account of the unrecorded costs of the local missions that were integral to both *Jim* and *On Fire*, the Evangelical Alliance estimated a total cost for the three events of around £8 million. Churches had donated generously, but it was hardly money well spent.

The following tables identify subjective evaluations of the three projects from EA churches and EA Council.[9] Since the Council figures represent only twenty two responses, they are not statistically significant but reveal some striking divergences from the churches.

Table 23: *Jim* evaluated

Jim	service quality churches / council	people mobilised churches / council	value for money Churches / council
very well	23% / 13%	39% / 13%	15% / 0%
well	25% / 6%	26% / 19%	28% / 31%
acceptably	35% / 38%	18% / 19%	28% / 31%
poorly	18% / 44%	18% / 41%	28% / 39%

[9] The actual questions were as follows: How well did the national organizers serve the network? Did the project help to mobilize your network in evangelism? Did the projects represent good value for money?

Table 24: *Minus to Plus* evaluated

Minus to Plus	service quality churches / council	people mobilised churches / council	value for money churches / council
very well	16% / 5%	7% / 5%	9% / 5%
well	24% / 14%	19% / 14%	13% / 9%
acceptably	25% / 9%	23% / 29%	26% / 5%
poorly	35% / 72%	51% / 52%	52% / 82%

Table 25: *On Fire* evaluated

On Fire	service quality churches / council	people mobilised churches / council	value for money churches / council
very well	14% / 23%	0% / 21%	22% / 25%
well	46% / 38%	23% / 21%	27% / 33%
acceptably	35% / 31%	40% / 7%	38% / 17%
poorly	5% / 8%	30% / 50%	14% / 25%

The Council responses were more negative than the churches. The peak figures from the churches indicate the highest service quality from *On Fire* (60% very well or well) and the worst from *Minus to Plus* (35% poorly). Council rated *On Fire* at 61% very well or well, but gave a much worse rating to *Minus to Plus* of 72% poorly. As to mobilisation, the churches rated Jim highest (65% very well or well) and *Minus to Plus* worst (51% poorly). Council agreed on *Minus to Plus*, giving a 52% poorly rating, but preferred *On Fire* (42% very well or well) to *Jim* (32%).

As to value for money, the churches saw little to choose between *Jim* (43% very well or well) and *On Fire* (49%). Council was more approving of *On Fire*, which was by far the cheapest project (58% very well or well). As to worst value for money, the churches saved their disapproval for *Minus to Plus* (52% poorly), to which Council gave its most robust condemnation (82% poorly).

Both the churches and Council gave generally favourable assessments of *Jim* and *On Fire*, rating *Jim* best for mobilisation and *On Fire* best for service quality and value for money. By far the least effective project, according to the churches, was *Minus to Plus*, receiving the worst ratings in all three areas. Council agreed in each case, but gave worse ratings each time; dramatically worse in the case of service quality, at a very high 72%, and even more so for value for money, at a condemnatory 82%. If the Sale of Goods Act applied to evangelistic initiatives, the churches would presumably have demanded their money back.

The survey also asked whether the projects had "affected the spiritual climate", without providing any definition or proposed means of measurement. Wittgenstein would no doubt have judged silence the only legitimate response.[10] Here we note, with surprise, that the Council members, tougher than the churches in objective assessment of results, were more optimistic than the churches in assessing putative spiritual impact This suggests that national evangelical leaders may find it harder than local church leaders to provide a blunt assessment of the secularized condition of late twentieth century Britain. The most striking divergence concerns *Minus to Plus* where 47% of EA Council concluded there was no benefit at all, compared with 67% of churches. The church assessment of *Minus to Plus* is stark: 98% of EA member churches took part, and 98% concluded that there was marginal or no impact upon the spiritual climate. These evaluations indicate that most considered themselves ill-advised to have been involved and that their investment of money and prayer had not paid off.

Table 26: Perceived impact upon the "spiritual climate"

	Jim	Minus to Plus	On Fire
Marginal (churches)	43%	31%	51%
Marginal (council)	60%	53%	67%
Not at all (churches)	50%	67%	29%
Not at all (council)	40%	47%	25%

Faced with such poor outcomes, the EA report concluded with a series of practical recommendations.[11] Major projects were asked to provide earlier consultation with church leaders and rapid notification of any changes in the project during its development, in order to avoid confusion and disenchantment. Member churches were advised to obtain independent advice about any proposed national project. The EA offered itself as a source of expertise for national initiatives, providing advice, consultancy, communication to members and direct involvement.

The report's most significant conclusions were as follows. First, EA Council were asked to consider adding an additional recommendation or even requirement that member organisations allow "independent verification of claims made both prior and subsequent to" their major projects. Second, EA insisted that the "long-term health of the church" requires that "claims ahead of the project are responsible and explainable" and "claims made during and after the project are demonstrable and open to independent verification", thus ensuring that "expectations are not heightened unrealistically" and "evangelicals are seen to be acting responsibly". Such recommendations were responsible, but untenably centralising. It was highly unlikely that member organisations would ever be willing to allow the EA to wield regulatory authority. Moreover, since EA had advised CfAN on the content of their *Minus to Plus* booklet, EA's involvement had evidently done little to address the

[10] Wittgenstein, 1922: 89.
[11] Earwicker and Spriggs, 1994.

problems its member churches and Council raised after the event. The third major conclusion rejected the rhetoric of instant success.

> It is important to recognise that in our present culture there are no easy routes to fast and numerous conversions.[12]

This was a salutary corrective to the quasi-revivalist expectations that had undergirded the anticipated response of four million to *Minus to Plus*. The report identified a particular missiological crisis:

> ...the confident ability of church members to build friendships and share their faith personally is an absolutely essential facet in the effectiveness of any evangelistic strategy.[13]

Here we should note a shift and an omission. The shift is towards relational evangelism, in preference to cold contact mass evangelism.[14] The omission is the failure to ask why church members lack that "confident ability". The report's solution is for local churches to emphasise "this aspect of evangelism training". This conclusion was characteristically superficial and sociologically uninformed. In a fragmented society, particularly in the urban and suburban setting, where people constellate in special interest groups but no longer have a sense of geographical community, the call to build friendships is easier said than done. Moreover, the perceived "lack of confidence" could be due not so much to believers' ignorance of their faith, as to the indifference of the unchurched resulting from the impact of secularizing cultural transitions that have rendered the Christian faith increasingly implausible as "public truth" for believers as well as non-believers.[15]

The disjunction between the projected and actual results of the 1994 projects was at least ridiculous, perhaps scandalous. Evangelicals had been inspired to make generous donations entirely disproportionate to the actual results. There had been a deeply misguided failure to take account of cultural realities. This risked a widespread collapse of credibility for any proposals for large-scale mission and requests for its financial support: churches who funded *Minus to Plus* discovered the projected results were a will o' the wisp. Disillusion leads easily to cynicism, especially in a climate where the secular media customarily report the imminent demise of the church. When it comes to extravagant promises about the imminent

---

[12] Earwicker and Spriggs, 1994: 14.

[13] Earwicker and Spriggs, 1994: 14.

[14] Finney (1992) had become widely influential.

[15] MacLaren, 2004; Bruce, 2002. For a post-Christian perspective on the religious contribution to public debate, see Rorty, 1999:168-174 - *Religion as Conversation-stopper*. Rorty argues that liberal democracy requires religious believers to trade privatisation of religion for a guarantee of religious liberty. He has no intention to exclude religious believers from the public square, but sees no place in public debate for specifically religious arguments that appeal to religious authorities. Casanova (1994) demonstrates and examines the return of religions to the public square.

conversion of England so long as enough money is given to support the latest ambitious project, grass roots evangelicals may have resolved, like a cynical electorate who have heard it all before, that they won't be fooled so easily or donate so readily again.

A still deeper crisis for evangelism than the absurdly unrealistic claims among some on the conversionist-activist axis of evangelicalism is the profound impact of the cultural transitions of secularization and post modernity.[16] In the brave new, post-Christian and post-Christendom world, people in a pluralist and relativist culture can no longer be called *back* to the faith in which they were nurtured as children, and no longer inhabit the unexamined givens that once shaped a Christianised culture. When Jonathan Edwards preached about sinners in the hand of an angry God at the beginning of the Great Awakening, his audience may have been religiously indifferent, but they broadly shared his assumptions about morality, conscience, judgment, God and Christ. The common currency of Christendom is no longer current coinage in Western Europe.[17] Culturally obsolete or inappropriate methods and grossly inflated expectations only make effective communication more difficult. Conversion has become a much longer journey than it used to be, and that requires a profound re-imagining of the tasks of evangelism and catechesis.[18] The shock of 1994, £8 million for very little return, indicated that many evangelicals were yet to come to terms with the acute cultural rupture within Western Europe.[19] Evangelicals were discovering they could not buy their way out of secularization.

The (Half) Decade of Church Planting

In 1992 "church planting" (that is the aim to establish new and culturally apposite local churches or congregations[20]), was placed centre stage in the decade of evangelism, not merely for the new church networks but to some degree across all the Protestant denominations. During the 1980s, some 3,100 churches were closed in the UK and 3,000 were planted.[21] The overall impact of church planting was therefore the replacement of expired churches, with at least some new initiatives presumably connecting more closely with their cultural context than some that had

---

[16] Bruce, 2002; MacLaren, 2004.

[17] Brown, 2001; MacLaren, 2004; Heelas et al, 2005. Of course, not all Christians see the death of Constantinianism as more of a problem than an opportunity (Wright, 2000; Murray, 2004)

[18] See Abraham, 1989; Finney, 1992.

[19] In June 2002, George Barna (2002) concluded that during the 1990s North American churches had spent more than $500 billion trying to influence American's spiritual convictions but his own surveys revealed no significant improvements. American profound cultural inertia begins, of course, from a very different starting point, when 43% of adults attend church on a weekly basis and 34% can be designated "unchurched" (notably increased from 24% in 1991).

[20] Wagner, 1990; Murray, 1998.

[21] Forster, 1995.

closed. Challenge 2000, the first national DAWN congress (an acrostic signifying a strategy designed to "Disciple a Whole Nation") was held in 1992. Delegates from across the Protestant churches met together to explore the principles of saturation church planting developed in the Philippines since 1975[22] and popularized by Jim Montgomery. Peter Wagner, North American church growth exponent and regular UK visitor at that time declared:

> Church planting is the most effective evangelistic methodology under heaven in all contexts and at all times.[23]

However, the UK hardly represents a cultural setting consonant with the Philippines. The concept of saturation church planting was almost certainly inapplicable to a post-Christian, multi-cultural society, in which church attendance is in dramatic decline.

In a conference of feverish excitement, expectations were intensified as the final goals from the different denominations were computed and collated. The event climaxed with the unveiling of a portentous slogan:

> 20,000 new churches by the year 2000, with 20% of the population attending church regularly.

Following this event, some denominations saw church planting re-emerge as a significant mission strategy, although others proved unwilling to nail their colours - or their budgets - to the church planting mast.[24] Even before these varied responses became apparent, the slogan contained three fatal flaws.

First, the year 2000 was a distraction, producing a short-term target when church

---

[22] In a document entitled, *It is a Dawn Strategy If*, the founder of DAWN, Jim Montgomery, wrote with great enthusiasm of Challenge 2000:

> In England the national Challenge 2000 (DAWN) committee spent many hours praying and poring over the data that had been gathered through their research project. They concluded that a goal of 20,000 new churches by AD 2000 seemed to be what the Spirit was saying. But they shared this goal with no one. Instead they had each denomination set their own goals at the Congress held in February, 1993. [actually it was 1992] When these individual goals were added together, the total came to almost exactly 20,000! It was great confirmation to all that this represented the mind of Christ. With this conviction, the multiplication of churches throughout England is overcoming many years of decline.

Montgomery describes himself as a pragmatic missiologist, but his idealised aspirations vastly exceed the reality of a failed UK initiative (www.dawnministries.org. Accessed 19/7/03).

[23] Forster, 1995: 4.

[24] For example, AOG, Methodists and Salvation Army adopted official church planting policies. The Baptists and Anglicans did not.

planting can only be credible as a long-term mission strategy. As one member of the Challenge 2000 organising team observed in interview:

> Church planting as a way of mission will only yield fruits over the medium to long term and as an approach it needs consistency, quiet faithfulness and an undergirding theological framework to keep it on track. For instance the work we did in "Newborough" has only yielded fruit over 20-25 years. The original 75 members of the church that became a source of church planting have now (25 years on) become 590 members.

As soon as the UK expression of DAWN reconfigured itself as Challenge 2000, the timescale was narrowed into a pre-millennium strategy that was short-term, intense, and therefore looking for immediate activism and almost instant results.

Second, the target of 20,000 church plants was extravagantly optimistic, compared with the 3,000 achieved in the 1980s. After a decade of decline, the churches of England were being asked to produce a sevenfold increase in church planting, with all the associated costs of time, personnel and money. In the heat of the conference the numbers evidently seemed compelling. In the cold light of day, a serious church planting strategy, designed to endure, would have required a substantive reconfiguration of the numerical goals and time scale. According to Challenge 2000's own calculation in 1995, the rate of church planting from 1990 to 1995 would require no less than sixty four years to establish the proposed 20,000 new churches.[25]

Third, the aim for 20% of the population to become regular churchgoers suffered from similar "vision inflation", running counter to all current trends. Challenge 2000 predicated external, conversion growth in the 1990s upon the internal, evangelical boom of the 1980s, seen most notably in the substantial growth of SH and EA. Far from discerning the signs of the times, entrepreneurial enthusiasm had lost touch with reality. Church decline would, in reality, accelerate in the 1990s and begin to impinge upon evangelical churches that had previously appeared immune to the general trend.[26]

A plausible case could have been made for a sustained, long-term, reflexive, strategic experiment in culturally engaged church planting. Instead, an inflated numerical target was linked to a short-term deadline and an entirely unrealistic projected level of resultant church attendance. The delegates' response, at the initial Dawn conference, was gasping enthusiasm. This subsequently turned to serious and uncomfortable questioning and, in short order, the inevitable demise of Challenge 2000.

For the second national conference in March 1995, Yonggi Cho, leader of the largest South Korean church, was brought in to boost the expectancy that the God of mega-churches in the developing world could re-energise the churches of Western Europe. Lynn Green a senior leader of YWAM (UK) and one of the Challenge 2000

---

[25] Forster, 1995: 44.
[26] Brierley, 2000, 2001.

leadership team, had been deputed to affirm the achievability of the goal of 20,000, explaining that the word "church" was inclusive of many different expressions of regular Christian gathering, such as home groups and prayer cells. The organisers would have been better advised to abandon their goal than attempt special pleading. In the event there was little or no more church planting in the 1990s than in the 1980s.[27] From Spring 1994, a novel focus emerged, particularly for the new church charismatics who had been pivotal in Challenge 2000. Toronto was in full flood[28] and by the time of the second Challenge 2000 national conference a new revivalism was erupting that would sweep church planting from centre stage as the fashionable methodology expected to deliver the almost instantaneous revitalisation of the church and the reconversion of England.

From extravagant projections to rapid disillusionment we trace a familiar pattern in the initiatives of the conversionist-activist axis. First, the quest for a quick fix, a short-term methodology that has, allegedly, produced exceptional results in another part of the world, which can be transplanted to the UK with more or less guaranteed results. Second, impatient expectations, in which leaders embrace a particular strategy with enthusiasm, only to abandon it when the fashion fades: while evangelicals marched for Jesus for a few years (1987-2000), Catholics make pilgrimage to a shrine for many centuries. Third, a naïve optimism that predicates substantial conversion growth as the rapid and direct consequence of the currently fashionable methodology; an expectation that had its roots in Finney's nineteenth century mechanical theory of revival.[29] Fourth, an inability or even refusal to recognise the severity of the cultural dislocation between the church and the prevailing culture. Fifth, a disinclination to engage in the necessary critical reflection prerequisite to more realistic, even chastened, long-term goals. Sixth, a tendency to claim to provide strategic thinking while actually functioning on intuitive impulse and high-octane rhetoric. Seventh, enthusiastic endorsement by high profile leaders of an ill-considered and unrealistic vision that quickly turns to dust.

These prominent and regular large-scale failures in the mid-1990s undermined the credibility of senior evangelical leaders and the plausibility of hopes for any significant advance in Christian mission. The reserves of confidence in evangelical entrepreneurialism built up during the 1980s – the new subcultural capital of pan-evangelicalism - had been rapidly depleted in extravagant claims and sparse results. Just as *Minus to Plus* failed to compute, *Challenge 2000* quickly proved to be a false dawn.

Social Action

We have demonstrated that in the early to mid-1990s evangelicals found evangelism

---

[27] Murray, 1998.

[28] Hilborn, 2001; Warner, 2003.

[29] Finney, 1835.

far more difficult than their public rhetoric allowed, but we should note briefly the relative burgeoning of evangelical social action. Earlier in the twentieth century many evangelicals accepted a false dichotomy - social gospel or evangelism.[30] However, Lausanne-1974 both affirmed and gave new impetus to an emphasis upon holistic mission[31] in which evangelism and social action function as integral partners in the mission of the church and in expressing the Kingdom of God.[32]

An indication of the strength of support for social action can be found in the budgets of Tear Fund and The Shaftesbury Society, the largest member organisations of the Evangelical Alliance. Shaftesbury's annual income and expenditure for the year ended 31 March 2000 was nearly £19 million.[33] Tear Fund had around 25 staff at their head office in 1979, 250 in 2001. Income was £3 million in 1979, £35 million in 2001. *Tear Times* circulation was 20,000 in 1979, 170,000 in 2001.[34] Although speakers at evangelical Bible Weeks still appeal for evangelicals to accept social responsibility within their local community and globally, the evidence suggests that many have long since embraced as integral to holistic mission what their conservative forebears derided as the "social gospel".

The social priority may prove increasingly problematic for local churches. The demise of volunteerism may be emerging, with the traditional church workforce of women at home diminishing rapidly. The turn of the century populist demands for state funding for church social projects[35] may indicate a dependency culture, quite unlike the self-financing philanthropy of much evangelical social action in previous generations. Moreover, the principle of structural differentiation which previously prompted local churches to hand over community initiatives to the civic authorities has been overlaid with increasing professionalisation in the provision of care. The local church may find it problematic to deliver social services with the required expertise.[36] Cox summed up the early twentieth century transition when church

---

[30] For example, in Basil Atkinson's 1933 revision of *Old Paths in Perilous Times*, which was given free to all CICCU freshers, he wrote:

> While believing that it is always a part of Christian duty to ameliorate distress, the CICCU cannot be enthusiastic about schemes for bringing world peace by means of political bodies such as the League of Nations, or social uplift by methods of reform. It holds that in the Gospel of Christ alone lies the only hope for the world by the regeneration of the individual. All else consists merely of 'dead works' without permanent value before God and may be written down as 'vanity'.

Quoted, without approval, in Barclay and Horn, 2002:131.
[31] Padilla, 1976.
[32] Bosch, 1991; Kirk, 1999; Hauerwas, 2001.
[33] Data from annual reports supplied by Shaftesbury.
[34] Data supplied by senior staff at Tear Fund.
[35] Spearheaded by Steve Chalke of Oasis Trust's Faithworks campaign.
[36] Morris (1992) demonstrated in his study of Croydon, 1840-1914, the trajectory of differentiation with the resultant handing over of social initiatives from the church to the newly emerging, state sector.

social provision faced an increasingly differentiated culture:

> In virtually every sphere of activity, the churches found that they were competing with
> a more specialised institution and they were generally... eager to hand over
> responsibility to a more effective body.[37]

What is certain is that the largest evangelical organisations, measured in terms of income and expenditure, are unambiguously committed to social action. In the case of Tear Fund, there has been a clear transition from providing crisis aid to working with local church partners in development projects. In recent years, particularly with its contribution to the Jubilee 2000 campaign to cancel international debt, and its successor *Make Poverty History*, Tear Fund has raised the profile of the third strand of its development work, namely the pursuit of international justice and fair trade.

Although some evangelicals inevitably disapprove such politicisation, the size and high profile of these social initiatives is beyond dispute. If it could have been claimed in the mid-twentieth century that evangelicals were indifferent to social action, the same charge could not reasonably be made at the century's end. There is a long-term approach, financial rigour and professional credibility found in these charities that has not always been evident in prominent evangelistic initiatives. In terms of budget and staffing, evangelicals are now investing more heavily, and in a more sustained way, in social action than evangelism. And it is evangelism that evangelicals are finding harder to accomplish effectively, notwithstanding the rhetoric of imminent advance.

Resilient Optimism

Recent UK church attendance surveys have indicated a sustained rise to prominence of evangelicals.[38] In 1989, evangelicals represented 30.1% of church attendance, compared with 39.4% for catholics, the largest sector.[39] In 1998, the catholic proportion had reduced to 26.4% while the evangelical had increased to 37.4%.

Table 27: The catholic and evangelical proportions of churchgoers

	1989	1998
catholic	39.4%	26.4%
evangelical	30.1%	37.4%

This evangelical ascendancy can be overstated. The decline in catholic

---

[37] Cox, 1982: 24.

[38] Brierley, 1991b, 1998, 2000. The detailed statistics interpreted in this section are taken from Brierley 2000.

[39] This represents not those who attend Roman Catholic churches but the larger number who identify their churchmanship as catholic.

churchmanship during the decade to 1998 was 48%, compared with 11% for liberal and 19% for broad church. The comparative decline for evangelicals was 3%. Therefore, while evangelicals have not declined at the catastrophic levels of other traditions, they still suffered shrinkage. They have become a larger proportion within the church, but have been unable to compensate for the decline in other sectors or even retain all their own adherents. Although their relative strength has increased, their perceived and oft-proclaimed capacity to deliver vibrant and sustained growth irrespective of cultural context is brought into serious question.

Table 28: Relative decline of traditions, 1989-1998

catholic	-48%
broad church	-19%
liberal	-11%
evangelical	-3%

Turning to future expectations, significant growth in the coming decade is expected even among the denominations who have experienced the greatest decline: by 11% of Roman Catholics, 14% of Methodists, and 29% of Anglicans. Among Baptists 50% expect significant growth, 87% among Pentecostals, and 89% among new churches. The sharp divide between the institutional and voluntarist[40] sectors is striking, although Anglicans were significantly more optimistic than other institutional churchgoers.

Table 29: Expectations of significant growth in the coming decade by denomination, 1998

Roman Catholic	11%
Methodist	14%
Anglican	29%
Baptist	50%
Pentecostal	87%
New churches	89%

When growth expectations are analysed according to churchmanship, 15% of catholics expect significant growth, compared with 51% of evangelicals. When the evangelical expectations are subdivided, 25% of broad evangelicals expect

[40] Troeltsch's (1911) categories of "church" and "sect" are more often used, but his alternative terminology has the considerable advantage of being more value neutral.

significant growth, compared with 43% of mainstream evangelicals and 79% of charismatics. Evangelicals are therefore considerably more optimistic than other Christians and charismatics are nearly twice as optimistic as other evangelicals. Many evangelicals would explain this optimism as confidence in the Gospel. Many charismatics would explain their heightened optimism as derived from their distinctive emphasis upon the continued outpouring of the Holy Spirit. However, these expectations are essentially unrelated to the actual growth and decline patterns of the previous decade.

This is particularly the case among charismatics. In 1989 charismatics were the dominant evangelical stream (631,200 compared with 384,600 mainstream and 414,600 broad). By 1998, the broad had declined by 47% to 217,900, the charismatics had declined by 16% to 527,900 and the mainstream had moved from third place to first with 645,500 and a growth rate of 68%. We therefore discover a striking contradiction between experience and expectations. Charismatics have experienced 16% decline in the 1990s but 79% expect significant growth in the coming decade, and Pentecostals 9% decline with 87% expecting significant growth, while mainstream evangelicals have enjoyed 68% increase but only 43% expect significant growth.

The prevailing disjunction between experience and expectations within contemporary evangelicalism is therefore greatly intensified among Pentecostals and charismatics, many of whom were prominent among late twentieth century exponents of the conversionist-activist axis. This indicates that optimistic expectations have become heightened beyond reality as a result of embracing late-modern assumptions of assured growth and success. Moreover, this ideology appears to have become unfalsifiable: if success is the automatic and intrinsic destiny of the true church, whenever churches suffer decline, it can only be, according to the law of inherent and assured growth, because they are not evangelical, Pentecostal or charismatic enough.

The characteristic response of evangelicals to the lean years of the 1990s and the growing resistance or indifference of Western European culture to the Christian Gospel, has been quite the reverse of their late nineteenth century predecessors' withdrawal into premillennialism.[41] Instead there has been a zealous stoking of vision inflation. Faced with the seismic shifts of postmodernity, when their growth expectations wantonly disregard the fact that the decade of evangelism proved to be a decade of decline, evangelicals in general and charismatics in particular appear to be in denial. A great deal of growth is projected where modest decline has been achieved.

Evangelicals, and particularly entrepreneurials and charismatics, who are closely related but not coterminous, therefore exemplify Festinger's account of the characteristic response to "cognitive dissonance" [42] - a defiant optimism that is essentially an escapist fantasy to sustain implausible convictions. We conclude that

---

[41] Bebbington, 1989; Noll et al, 1994.
[42] Festinger, 1957, 1964.

we have identified in their resiliently, indeed defiantly optimistic expectations the engine room for the conversionist-activists' pragmatic, non-reflexive entrepreneurialism. By the mid 1990s their reconstructions of evangelical identity had become increasingly project-driven and short-term. Ever amnesiac to past disappointments, they publicised and financed new programmes, confidently proclaiming that their latest initiative was sure to produce the assured advances in convertive piety they continued resolutely to expect. The conversionist-activist axis is remarkably resilient, but, in the context of secularization, shows evidence of delusional tendencies.

Chapter 5

Alpha: A Second Case Study in Evangelical Exceptionalism

Alpha's Growth

Alpha was the great success story of British evangelism in the 1990s.[1] Take away *Alpha* and there would be little left of the "decade of evangelism". The growth has been phenomenal. In the *Alpha* organisation's own words, "Since 1993, *Alpha* has grown beyond expectations. 5,000 courses were hoped for by the end of 2000. Over 17,000 courses were actually registered."[2] By March 2001, over 7,000 churches in the UK had registered to use *Alpha*, over 17,000 churches worldwide, in 121 countries and 34 languages.[3] At the 2001 *Alpha* UK National Strategy day, Nicky Gumbel cited *The Guardian's* estimate that 250,000 have come to faith in the UK on *Alpha* courses. In an anecdote reminiscent of claims for the impact of the Billy Graham Crusades in the 1950s, the strategy day was told that at one recent selection conference for Anglican ministry, "virtually all the candidates did *Alpha* as a starting point." It was further claimed that over 3.6 million people have "either done the course, or know someone who has".

To take two four year periods, from 1993 to 1996 registered courses increased by 4,800; from 1997 to 2000 by 10,500. The numerical advance year on year increased steadily: 1993 - 195 additional courses; 1994 - 550; 1995 - 1,750; 1996 - 2,500. Although 1997 saw the increase reduce to 1,500, the new promotional initiative in 1998 resulted in the annual increase escalating to 4,000. Growth stayed strong in 1999 (up 3,700) and 2000 (up 3,800). In percentage terms, however, the annual growth showed unmistakable signs of tailing off:

1996: 100%	1997: 30%	1998: 61%
1999: 35%	2000: 20%.	

---

[1] For critiques of *Alpha*, see Percy, 1998; Ward, 1998; Hunt, 2001, 2004; Booker and Ireland, 2003; MacLaren, 2004.

[2] Reported in the documents of the Alpha UK Strategy Day, 7 March 2001.

[3] Official statistics taken from Alpha News no. 24, March-June 2001.

Table 30: Registered *Alpha* courses, 1992-2000

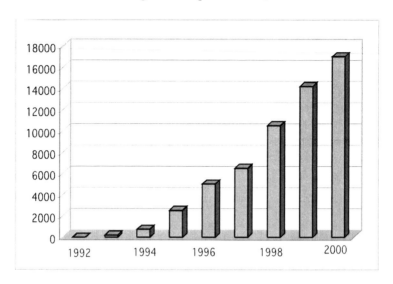

Table 31: Cumulative *Alpha* attendance, 1993-1999

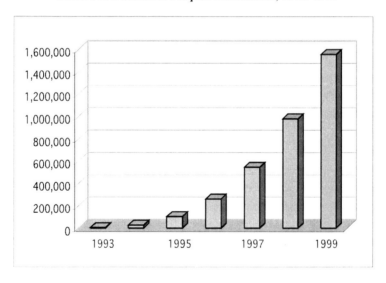

Large numbers of churches and new converts have voiced their enthusiasm for this remarkably popular and well-received evangelistic course. BUGB statistics for the year 2000 reported a 20% increase in baptisms.[4] While one year's figures may only be a blip, during the last fifty years significant increases in baptisms have been consistently linked to Billy Graham missions. By 2000 the Baptists had a higher proportionate adoption of *Alpha* than any other denomination. The Baptist Union Department for Research and Training in Mission suggested that, while it was too early to predict sustained conversion growth, and while the link with *Alpha* was not proven, the adoption of *Alpha* appeared to be the most likely source of this increase in baptisms.

The exceptional and pervasive impact of *Alpha* was exemplified in November 1998 by a *Newsweek* article featuring Nicky Gumbel. Significantly, the story was not featured under religion, but presented as the back page interview. This prestigious slot is generally reserved for high profile opinion formers who are considered to be changing or to have changed the face of their society. Gumbel was typically self-effacing, dismissing any suggestion that *Alpha*'s success had been enhanced by his own engaging style of communication. He chose to emphasise two key factors: first that the unchanging Gospel is deeply attractive to a generation searching for spiritual reality; second that the latest marketing and advertising methods are entirely appropriate as means of making the Christian message more widely accessible. *Newsweek* dubbed him "Adman for Christianity" and highlighted his emphasis upon promotion and marketing:

> All we're trying to do is take a message that's been around for 2,000 years and put it in [fresh] packaging.

The *Alpha* Initiative - "inviting the nation to supper" - was first run in September 1998. Over 4,000 churches supported a £1 million publicity campaign, using 1,700 large billboards, 5,500 poster sites and adverts in 850 local newspapers. ITV gave coverage on the *News at Ten*. BBC made *Alpha* the theme of a special *Songs of Praise*. The adverts were designed without charge by the advertising executives who had previously courted controversy with off-beat Christmas ads about the Virgin Mary's "bad hair day". Francis Goodwin, managing director of Maiden Outdoor, explained the intention to create advertising for *Alpha* that was contemporary, positive, non-threatening and non-abrasive, deliberately avoiding the traditional evangelical prominence of Bible verses or calls to repentance:

> We wanted people to feel that an *Alpha* course is a perfectly normal thing to do... We needed to establish the *Alpha* name in the world outside the church community and to link its logo with the name, thus helping create a brand image. We chose posters to give the campaign an impact at street level and to communicate with a large audience.[5]

These campaigns enjoyed some success in establishing product recognition. A

---

[4] Discussions with Derek Allen and Darrell Jackson of the Baptist Union Department for Research into Mission, May 2001, and with Nicky Gumbel.

[5] Quoted by Dominic Kennedy, *The Times*, 9 September 1998.

MORI poll in September 1999 found that 11% recognised the *Alpha* logo; 9% of those who had heard of *Alpha* knew it was a Christian programme; 66% of those recognising the product had either enrolled on a course or knew someone who had.[6]

Key Factors in *Alpha*'s Success

Many factors contribute to the unusual popularity of *Alpha*'s attempt to reconstruct plausible evangelism for the twenty first century.[7]

The fear of an unfamiliar, religious environment is defused by beginning each session with a meal. In an unchurched society, this is seeker friendly, putting people at their ease by providing a familiar social environment. The opportunity to relax over food and interact in an informal group gives time for the enquirer to evaluate the Christian participants as real people. Rather than sit passively in a pew, enquirers can actively assess the Christians' credibility. The whole experience is designed to be fun and friendly, down to earth and enjoyable, contrary to the religious stereotypes - dull, boring and irrelevant - acknowledged in Gumbel's introductory talk.

Deracinated postmoderns, particularly in the urban context, experience increasingly isolated lives. By meeting in groups that make friendships integral to the beginnings of a Christian lifestyle, *Alpha* provides an opportunity to develop a sense of belonging before believing in an age where some believe without belonging[8] and others, outside and within the church, perceive that believing is the prerequisite for any possibility of Christian belonging.

There is an interactive learning experience in the discussion groups. This corresponds with contemporary pedagogy both at school and in workplace training, and is more familiar to the unchurched than the traditional church passivity of preaching without feedback. The discussion groups also affirm the autonomy of the individual, a profoundly important value for postmodern generations.[9] Postmoderns want to know they can freely express their opinions and ask any questions they want. Open discussion respects people's integrity as free individuals, and recognises their need for space as they explore the often unfamiliar terrain of Christian faith. While there is opportunity for response, (considered by some modifiers of *Alpha* a premature opportunity[10]) the course is expressly designed to exclude anything forced or manipulative. There is no pressure to convert quickly, accepting that coming to faith is usually a process, rather than a crisis without due preparation. Moreover, in a culture where the Bible has become a thoroughly unfamiliar book, the weekly exposure to Bible passages is intended to unlock gradually the story of Jesus to the uninformed enquirer.

---

[6] Quoted in *Alpha News*, November 1998-February 1999, no 17: 1.
[7] Developed from my earlier analysis in Warner, 1999. See also Percy, 1998; Ward, 1998; Hunt, 2001, 2004; Booker and Ireland, 2003; MacLaren, 2004.
[8] Davie, 1994.
[9] Hammond, 1992.
[10] Indicated in interviews and conversations.

Within the conventional conservative evangelical apologetic there is a reasoned defence of the gospel, albeit pre-Kantian, but also an opportunity to encounter God in personal experience, strictly in terms of Wimber[11] rather than Schleiermacher[12] or Otto[13], particularly during the Holy Spirit weekend. The course seeks to provide enquirers with an opportunity to engage in a search for God that combines theoretical enquiry with experiential encounter. This holistic intention correlates more closely with new age spirituality than traditional, rationalistic evangelical apologetics, even though the dominant modes of discourse remain conventionally Protestant and evangelical: verbalist rather than visual, propositional rather than symbolic.

Alpha has secured widespread establishment support. The fact that Sandy Millar and Nicky Gumbel are former barristers, Eton and Oxbridge educated, doubtless makes the course more palatable in some quarters. Many senior church leaders have lent their endorsement: "Thrilling in prisons" was how the Acting Chaplain General, speaking at the March 2001 UK National Strategy Day, described the impact of *Alpha*. At the same event, Paul Boateng, Minister for Prisons, provided on video a politician's eulogy:

> I have been greatly impressed by all I have heard of *Alpha*'s contribution to the prisons. It is running in 121 prisons so far. I am also very grateful for the magnificent way in which some of the churches have responded to the enormous need to follow *Alpha* with practical help for newly released prisoners. My hope is that all of this work will continue and increase. I shall be watching its progress with great interest and support.

Clifford Longley was also quoted at the event, from an extended endorsement of *Alpha* in his *Daily Telegraph* column:

> ...an unqualified triumph. The reconversion of England...is suddenly almost believable... It makes the church seem professional, competent, self-confident and up to date... It is an idea whose time is long overdue.

Although an evangelical and charismatic course in origins, *Alpha* has assiduously sought to move beyond the evangelical boundaries. *Alpha* has almost certainly made greater inroads into non-evangelical parishes than among non-charismatic evangelicals, who have continued to express their reservations and prefer programmes of their own devising, most prominently *Christianity Explored*.[14] Leaders of *Catholic Alpha* stated at the March 2001 strategy day that their first wave of support was mostly among "charismatic Catholics". They were now "chipping away" at a second wave of the "middle ground". Their conviction was that *Alpha* would contribute to the Catholic bishops' development of a strategy for the re-

---

[11] Wimber, 1985, 1987; see Percy, 1996.

[12] Schleiermacher, 1799.

[13] Otto, 1923.

[14] Tice and Cooper, 2002.

evangelisation of the UK. Just how comfortable the Catholic hierarchy will prove to be if a course that originated among Protestants continues to gain popularity among Catholics remains to be seen.

In many churches, *Alpha* is laity led. This is sometimes to the relief of over-pressed clergy, sometimes with clerical bemusement at its popularity.[15] *Alpha* gives a clear role to many lay leaders, and this will intensify if HTB succeed in establishing a national team of regional co-ordinators. Running three times a year, as HTB recommend, an organising group are unlikely to have much time for other avenues of service.

The growth of HTB alongside the growth of *Alpha* helps participating churches garner confidence, feeling that their local evangelism is part of a national initiative that has proven success and wide credibility. HTB are practitioners of *Alpha* on a huge scale, expecting 700-800 to attend *Alpha* weekends (from whom they anticipate only one or two negative reactions) and the average age of their guests at *Alpha* is twenty seven. Few churches will run *Alpha* with such numbers or such a young clientele, given that the twenties are the least churched generation in England.[16] Nonetheless, the renowned success of HTB endows *Alpha* with a persuasive plausibility. *Alpha* and HTB provide substantial confidence building measures to beleaguered and defensive churches in an era when intensifying secularization means that many Christians have become reluctant witnesses to their increasingly marginalised faith. Far more than any one-off evangelistic course or event, *Alpha* offers a pervasive and sustained subcultural identity to keen advocate-participants.[17]

Alpha has become the most well-known and widely visible Christian brand. The *Alpha* catalogue offers books, videos, publicity (invitations, posters, car stickers, banners, balloons, booklets), training resources (for *Alpha* course teams, worship, prayer ministry and prayer for *Alpha*), HTB worship recordings, marriage and divorce resources, a post-*Alpha* programme based on Philippians (video, audio, a manual and a book), and specialist materials for youth, students and prisons. *Alpha News* has become the most widely distributed Christian tabloid[18] providing in a post-denominational age, a sense of identity and encouragement for those within the highly focused *Alpha* movement. The tenor of *Alpha* communication is enthusiastic, vital and optimistic. In person and in print, *Alpha* representatives breathe confidence and hope into local churches. The assurance of gathering momentum and the prospect of increasing future success are communicated with confident conviction. The resources and promotional materials are produced to consistently high standards. In an image conscious era, when the church is hardly renowned for professional PR, *Alpha's* packaging functions as a culturally apposite form of pre-evangelism. In the age of the logo, *Alpha* is the exemplar of effective marketing in

---

[15] Indicated in interviews.

[16] Brierley, 2000.

[17] Thornton, 1995; Gelder and Thornton, 1997.

[18] Booker and Ireland, 2003.

the Christian world.[19] Nothing else comes close.

Gumbel is a highly engaging, populist communicator, in person, on video and in print. His books were reputedly removed from the UK Christian bestseller list on the grounds that they were curriculum resources, since otherwise there would have been months when almost no other books were featured.[20] Gumbel's encyclopaedic supply of quotations, anecdotes and witticisms means that *Alpha* has been able to build in quality control for the speakers at local *Alpha* courses. Where local churches choose not to use the Gumbel videos, the weekly talk is still designed to be accessible, practical, jargon-free and shot through with Gumbel's humour and illustrations. As Gumbel observed to *Newsweek* in November 1998, "They are giving pretty well the same talk."

Just as Spring Harvest arose when there was a gap in the market for a contemporary Bible week that took account of charismatic renewal, *Alpha* arose as a more contemporary form of evangelistic programme - taking account of charismatic renewal and conceiving conversion as a relational process - and enjoyed a similar pattern of rapid growth. Spring Harvest subsequently had to come to terms with competition from new conferences, both charismatic and non-charismatic, that had learned from its approach. It seems reasonable to infer that the growth curve of *Alpha* and its emulators will follow a similar pattern.

Theological Critiques

From calvinistic neo-fundamentalism, unreservedly anti-Catholic and anti-charismatic, *Alpha* is denounced in predictably vituperative terms:

> ...over-manipulative, man-centred, minimalising the sin question and over-emphasising the charismatic element, especially with the notorious Holy Spirit weekend. The fact that Roman Catholic churches can use it without any qualms demonstrates its dismal lack of doctrinal content.[21]

> The God of *Alpha* is not the God of the Bible, the plight of man in *Alpha* is not as serious as in the Bible, and the Jesus Christ of *Alpha* is not the Jesus Christ of the Bible.[22]

The uncompromising sectarianism of these denunciations is nothing new: Whitefield faced similar acidity.

> Mr Whitefield is no minister of Jesus Christ; that his call and coming to Scotland are scandalous; that his practice is disorderly, and fertile of disorder; that his whole doctrine is, and his success must be, diabolical; so that people ought to avoid him, from

---

[19] Ward, 1998; Hunt, 2001, 2004.

[20] Advised in conversation by leading publishers.

[21] Hunt, 2001: 48, from an anonynmised interview.

[22] Hunt, 2001: 50, quoting C. Hand, *Is Alpha leading people astray?*

duty to God…[23]

Percy produced an early mainstream theological critique of *Alpha*, arguing that it fails to give sufficient space to the Trinity, baptism, communion, community or social justice. His critique is trenchant:

> The Spirit on offer obviously arises from a personable, therapeutic, home-counties context that is concerned with the individual. [24]

Percy's characterization of *Alpha* as "join the dots Christianity" recalls H. Richard Niebuhr's critique of Billy Graham:

> Graham offers Christian evangelism even less complicated answers than it has ever before provided.[25]

Building on Percy, we offer the following theological critique of *Alpha*. Reflecting its origins in early charismatic renewal, *Alpha* places a disproportionate emphasis on glossolalia and healing is emphasised without a balancing exploration of suffering in the way of the cross. The experiential component of encountering the Holy Spirit - quite alien in most non-Pentecostal churches in previous generations - draws heavily upon Wimber's idiosyncratic model of thaumaturgy. As Percy argued, the understanding of the Spirit is individualistic and therapeutic and *Alpha* omits exploration, for example, of the Spirit and social justice, ecology, creativity or aesthetics. At the same time, core doctrines of orthodoxy are under-represented (hardly surprising in a fifteen-session course), most notably the Trinity, ecclesiology, sin and repentance. Moreover, *Alpha*'s apologetic and emphases, excepting the charismatic overlay, are thoroughly conventional within the arena of modernistic conservative evangelicalism, drawn from the Bash camp syllabus of talks, quotations and anecdotes.[26] *Alpha* can therefore be summed up as Bash camp rationalistic conservatism combined with Wimberist charismatic expressivism operating within the milieu of late twentieth century marketing. This is a highly unusual, even paradoxical hybrid. Pragmatic evangelism colonises its host cultures, enlightenment and existential, with an urgent and opportunistic zeal.

---

[23] From the title of Adam Gib's denunciation, published on Whitefield's return to Scotland in 1742 (cited in Noll, 2004:103-4).
[24] Percy, 1998:16, see also Percy, 1996.
[25] Quoted in Graham, 1997: 301.
[26] The "Bash" camps were run by Eric Nash as mid-twentieth century recruitment holidays among public schoolboys for conservative evangelicalism. Prominent participants included John Stott, Michael Green and David Watson.

Surveying *Alpha*

The EA/EMA Strategic Commission Report, 1998

The Inaugural Annual Report of the EA/EMA Commission on Strategic Evangelism in the UK published in March 1998 demonstrated the growing prominence, indeed market domination, of *Alpha*.[27] In a survey of 192 EA churches, 90% were very aware of *Alpha*, way ahead of the other evangelism programmes in the survey, namely Evangelism Explosion (15%), Good News Down Your Street (13%), Just Looking (19%) and Person to Person (23%). Just 1% said they were unaware of *Alpha*, compared with 35% for EE, 52% for GNDYS, 47% for JL and 44% for PP. This heightened awareness of *Alpha* was not simply a matter of HTB publicity. The impact of its direct mail placed *Alpha* in third place, cited by 22%, compared with 29% for JL and 32% for PP.

The three areas in which *Alpha* scored most highly were bookshops, cited by 12%, reflecting the huge success and profile of Gumbel's books, where the only other programme in double figures was GNDYS (10%); denominational recommendation, where *Alpha* scored 19% and the next highest were JL and PP, both on 8%, thus indicating a unique measure of endorsement through official channels; and word of mouth recommendation, where *Alpha* scored a massive 85%. All the other programmes received their highest score for word of mouth, indicating that personal recommendation is the most pervasive means by which awareness of evangelistic programmes moves from church to church. However, all the other programmes received substantially lower word of mouth ratings, demonstrating that *Alpha* had become the talk of the church (EE - 62%; GNDYS - 55%; JL - 54%; PP - 54%). Since this survey was completed in the summer of 1997, before the national initiatives that dramatically raised the profile of *Alpha* and resulted in far more churches taking part, the awareness of *Alpha* has presumably increased still further.

Turning from awareness to use, 69% of EA churches in the survey had used *Alpha* during the last five years. The next highest ranking methods of relational evangelism were "guest services" at 59%, marriage preparation at 41%, birth / infant baptism at 28%, PP at 24% and bereavement at 21%. Only *Alpha* and guest services ranked higher than the rites of passage of marriage and birth. When asked what approaches they planned to use in the next few years, *Alpha* went up by 6% to 75%, while everything else declined except for Emmaus, which went up from 2% usage to a still modest 6%. Guest services were down 19% to 40%; marriage preparation down 12% to 29%; birth / infant baptism down 14% to 14%; bereavement down 8% to 13%; PP down 13% to 11%.

If these responses are stratified according to the size of church, subsidiary trends can be identified. *Alpha*'s greatest penetration was in churches of 100-199. The greatest anticipated growth was in churches of 70-99. The only expected reduction in the use of *Alpha* was in churches of 200+. A shift in the size of church using

---

[27] Evangelical Alliance, 1998. They surveyed 300 member churches as a 10% random sample, plus 98 churches identified in the 1997 General Survey as "especially 21 to 40 friendly", plus 24 churches nominated by commission members (1998:11).

Alpha appears to have commenced by 1998. In previous use, the second highest was churches of 200+. In projected use, the second highest was churches of 70-99. Compared with churches of 200+, projected use was higher among churches of less than 40 and equal among churches 40-69. These statistics suggest that larger churches had adopted *Alpha* earlier and by 1997 were beginning to consider moving on from *Alpha*, whereas smaller churches had adopted more slowly but were now accelerating their adoption. *Alpha* has clearly persuaded churches of all sizes of its suitability, with later adoption among smaller churches.

Table 32: Previous and planned use of evangelistic programmes

Church size	Alpha	Guest services	Person to Person	Marriage	Birth / infant baptism	Death
0-39	58%	52%	24%	19%	16%	14%
	72%	34%	18%	19%	10%	6%
40-69	67%	48%	19%	32%	27%	16%
	71%	33%	4%	28%	14%	11%
70-99	67%	59%	29%	35%	28%	18%
	78%	39%	17%	27%	16%	9%
100-199	78%	64%	23%	56%	30%	22%
	79%	39%	7%	33%	16%	18%
200+	77%	79%	26%	68%	38%	40%
	71%	63%	14%	43%	15%	21%
Totals	69%	59%	24%	41%	28%	21%
	75%	40%	11%	29%	14%	13%

As to guest services, a substantial fall in projected use was recorded across all sizes of church. This suggests that the Willow Creek model of seeker services had not taken root widely, despite the high profile of Willow Creek related conferences in the UK.[28] Perhaps the more sophisticated and hi-tech model of seeker services, using computer graphics and the performing arts, has produced a loss of confidence in more traditional guest services. Or perhaps the rapid decline of guest services reflects a lack of demand, with churches struggling to persuade their congregations to bring any guests. Churches over 200 report a reduced use of guest services (down 16%) but this represents a much smaller fall than churches of 100-199 (25%) and 70-99 (20%). In churches under 200, between 33% and 39% anticipated using guest services, compared with 63% for churches over 200. Guest services therefore have become a predominantly larger church strategy. However, since churches over 200 reported the only reduction in use of *Alpha* (down 6%) as well as a reduction in the

---

[28] Hybels (1995) recounts the evolution of the model and the subsequent mega-church.

use of guest services (down 16%), many churches appeared to anticipate reduced evangelistic activity beyond 1998.

Turning to the rites of passage, these are still seen to be aspects of relational evangelism by a minority of churches, but the perception of their usefulness has declined rapidly. Marriage preparation was down from 41% to 29%, rites of infancy down from 28% to 14% and bereavement down from 21% to 13%. Bereavement shows the smallest rate of decline (down 8%), but from the lowest previous levels. The fall in expected use is much higher among churches over 200 (down 19%), bringing their figures into line with churches of 100-199. Previously 40% of larger churches saw bereavement ministries as a useful dimension of relational evangelism, compared with 22% among churches of 100-199. Only churches of 100-199 anticipated a greater future ministry through bereavement than through rites of infancy.

Infant baptism recorded the highest overall rate of decline among the rites of passage.[29] Where previous generations had their children "done" as a normative religious activity even among non-churchgoers, this residual cultural aspect of Christendom has largely expired. The rapid growth in the number of children born outside marriage has presumably reinforced this trend. The expected evangelistic significance for rites of infancy has become fairly constant across the different sizes of church at 14-16%, excepting churches under 39 who projected the smallest decline but still project a lower rating at 10%. Since the smallest churches also project the lowest ratings for marriage and infancy, this suggests that very small churches have often become the most severely disconnected from the wider community in terms of rites of passage.

Marriage preparation was much higher in churches over 100 than in smaller churches. However, while marriage preparation recorded an over-all projected decline slightly lower than rites of infancy (12% compared with 14%), the projected decline was much higher in churches of 100-199 (23% compared with 14%) and slightly higher in churches over 200. Although marriage preparation receives a much higher average rating (29%) than infancy (14%) and bereavement (13%), whereas infancy rites occur more or less equally across the churches, marriage preparation is cited in 19% of churches under 39, rising to 33% for churches of 100-199, and 43% in churches over 200. Larger churches may have become significantly more attractive to couples seeking marriage preparation.

In sum, larger churches were doing far more in terms of bereavement and marriage preparation than smaller churches. However, the rites of passage faced the greatest projected decline in churches over 200 and the second greatest decline in churches over 100. This indicates not only that many smaller churches are already disconnected from the wider community but larger churches are likely to follow in an accelerating trend.[30]

---

[29] Brierley (1998, 1999, 2001) demonstrates the sustained decline in infant baptism through the twentieth century. See also Gill (1993, 2002, 2003).

[30] Compare Brown, 2001; Bruce, 2002; MacLaren, 2004; Heelas and Woodhead et al, 2005.

This survey demonstrated that almost every evangelistic initiative was expected to decline except *Alpha*. We may draw several conclusions from these trends. First, churches were realistic in expecting a continuing decline in demand for "hatch, match and despatch" ministries. Second, users of PP and guest services were either withdrawing from evangelistic programmes or transferring their efforts into *Alpha*. This could suggest that churches were putting all their eggs in the most successful basket, or that the demands upon *Alpha* volunteers leave little opportunity for other activities. The widespread adoption of *Alpha* is striking, achieving 69% penetration of the churches surveyed, with a projected penetration of 75%. The apparent success of *Alpha* contrasts with the withdrawal from other forms of evangelism, together with a diminishing market for Christian rites of passage, previously the bread and butter of parish evangelism.[31]

In terms of church mobilisation, numbers of unchurched contacted, and those led to faith, *Alpha* rated highest. More than twice as many church people were involved compared with any other programme, and nearly twice as many converts resulted compared with the next most fruitful programme.

Table 33: Average numbers involved in evangelistic programmes

	Trained	Involved	Contacted	Converted
Alpha	15.8	43	129.4	14.4
EE	11.3	9.8	43.3	3.6
GNDYS	10.2	11.5	59.2	7.5
JL	5.9	15.1	23.7	4.9
PP	23.1	18.1	85.4	3.5

Users of the programmes during the previous five years were asked to state whether the various programmes had made a constructive contribution in six areas: mobilising members, fostering prayer, conversions, ease of use, excellent resources, and being contemporary and relevant. In each area *Alpha* was the top-rated programme, except for ease of use, where GNDYS scored 81% against *Alpha*'s 76%. *Alpha*'s lowest strength rating was for conversions, at 61%. However, this factor produced the lowest ratings for almost every programme, and the other scores were substantially weaker than *Alpha*: EE - 43%, GNDYS - 25%, JL - 19%, PP - 12%.

Users were asked three further questions about level of satisfaction, the service provided by the sponsoring organisation and value for money. Perhaps not surprisingly, *Alpha* scored consistently high ratings. 93% were very satisfied or satisfied. 92% rated the quality of service as well or very well. 84% considered *Alpha* very good or good value for money. In the most negative ratings, *Alpha* scored 1% for very dissatisfied, 1% for poor service and 0% for poor value for money. *Alpha*'s performance ratings are consistently and exceptionally high.

---

[31] Compare Booker and Ireland, 2003.

Comparisons with the 1994 projects are salutary. For quality of service, *Alpha*'s 92% (very well or well) contrasts with, using the more generous church figures, *On Fire* - 60%, *Jim* - 48%, and *Minus to Plus* - 40%. 1% for poor service compares with *On Fire* - 5%, *Jim* - 18%, and *Minus to Plus* - 35%. As to value for money, *Alpha*'s 84% (very good or good) contrasts with *On Fire* - 49%, *Jim* - 43% and *Minus to Plus* - 22%. In part these figures may demonstrate the difference between the delivery of an ongoing product and a special event. The other evangelistic programmes do not rate as highly as *Alpha*, but they also rate more strongly than *Jim* and *Minus to Plus*. Only *On Fire*, which adopted a strategy of high profile, low national budget compared favourably with the rolling evangelistic programmes as a service provider and in terms of perceived value for money.

In short, *Alpha* achieved the highest ratings of awareness and approval. Users also reported the best quality of support and the greatest numbers mobilised, contacted and converted. The popularity of *Alpha* is therefore based upon all-round strengths that vindicate its position as the market leader among evangelistic programmes.

The EA Strategic Commission Report (1998) identified several shifts of emphasis in evangelism: from crisis to process; from specialist evangelists to whole church witness; from mass to relational strategies; and towards more contextualised approaches. They also commended organisations that developed high quality programmes and fostered a continuing relationship with local church users. Their report therefore represented a resounding, albeit implicit, endorsement of the methodology of *Alpha* and an invitation to other organisations to emulate the approaches *Alpha* had developed so effectively.

In addition to its appraisal of current evangelistic programmes, the Commission expressed concern about what it called "the growing culture gap". The report concluded that this was likely to result in Christians losing confidence:

> While few might say so publicly, believers are struggling with sharing the gospel in a culture which is frequently represented as pluralistic and multi-faith. [32]

It also warned that church events and services "are increasingly distant from the understanding of unbelievers", noting that this was particularly the case for those under 40, whom "the church is failing to attract and hold". The report's prognosis was grave. Since the "values and norms in today's culture" are increasingly shaped by those under 40, "the church of tomorrow may be even less accessible to those outside it." [33]

The EA/EMA Commission identified two trends in tension. On the one hand, it charted the extraordinary rise to prominence of *Alpha*, with performance ratings way ahead of any other evangelistic enterprise. On the other, it identified an underlying and growing dislocation between church and society. Inasmuch as cultural

---

[32] EA, 1998.

[33] EA, 1998. Compare Brown, 2001; Bruce, 2002; MacLaren, 2004.

engagement is prerequisite to effective evangelism,[34] unless the church proved willing to engage in a quantum leap of reflexive re-imagining, things could only get worse.

American Presbyterians and English Springboard, 2001

Alpha News in March-June 2001 carried the headline: "Independent surveys show '*Alpha* is good for churches'." In the United States, a survey for the Evangelism office of the Presbyterian Church received responses from 62 out of the 119 churches that were using *Alpha*. 98% said users either liked the course or liked it very much. 97% said they were planning to use the course again. 90% said they would recommend *Alpha* to other churches. 58% said their congregations had grown as a result of *Alpha*. 94% said *Alpha* participants "now think more seriously about spiritual issues" and 27% said their church as a whole had "experienced a spiritual awakening". Allowing for the naturally buoyant optimism of American religious culture, reflected in the emphatically positive responses to the more subjective questions, *Alpha* has evidently been very well received.

The UK *Alpha* survey, overseen by Peter Brierley of Christian Research, in association with Springboard, the Archbishops' evangelism initiative, was part of a larger survey on church growth in the 1990s. 8,861 churches answered the 1998 survey and its predecessor in 1989. 21.5% had used *Alpha* at least once. Those who used *Alpha* for one or two years performed no differently than other churches in terms of Sunday attendance. Those who had run *Alpha* courses for three to six years enjoyed better dividends.

Table 34: Relative performance of *Alpha* and non-*Alpha* churches

	Non-Alpha	Alpha 1-2 yrs	Alpha 3-6 yrs
% grew	21	21	26
% static (=/- 10%)	12	14	20
% shrank	67	65	54
sample size	6,815	602	1,264

Alpha News conflated the figures for growing and static churches to conclude:

With many UK churches still declining in numbers, 35% bucked the trend if they had held *Alpha* for one year; while 51% bucked the trend if they had held *Alpha* for six years...with 46% either remaining static or growing if they had run the course for five years. [35]

---

[34] Kraft, 1979; Stott and Coote, 1981; Donovan, 1982; Bosch, 1991; Warner, 1994.
[35] *Alpha News*, March-June 2001.

In the same edition of the promotional tabloid, Robert Jackson and Canon Robert Warren, both of Springboard, provided an article evaluating these results, and declared:

> For the first time, we have demonstrated statistically on a national basis that *Alpha* is good for church growth.[36]

Jackson and Warren acknowledged that half the *Alpha* churches are in decline, but they contrasted this with the two thirds of non-*Alpha* churches in decline. One in five non-*Alpha* churches is growing, compared with one in four *Alpha* churches. While acknowledging that *Alpha* by itself does not reverse overall decline and is not the only answer to decline, they felt able to commend the cumulative impact of *Alpha* and urged churches to "keep on plugging away year after year":

> ...a church that has done *Alpha* at least three times is more likely to grow and less likely to shrink.[37]

Proponents almost inevitably reach for conclusions that exceed the objective evidence of statistical data. Several key variables must be taken into account. First, churches that have been growing over three to six years may have other growth enhancing factors in common. *Alpha* may be the factor determinative of their growth, but alternatively other factors that are their primary growth determinants may have prompted their early adoption of *Alpha* as an evangelistic strategy and their subsequent growth. *Alpha* may therefore have been the key cause of their growth, or its adoption may have been consequent upon other key and determinative growth factors not identified within this survey. Second, concerning these early adopters, we do not know the pattern of growth or decline they were experiencing when they had only done *Alpha* once or twice. This information would allow objective comparison with those who have currently used *Alpha* once or twice, to see whether the short-term impact of *Alpha* is constant between the two types of church and periods of time. Third, for those churches that have only done *Alpha* for one or two years, other factors may have determined their lack of growth or decline. Prolonged used of *Alpha* may have little benefit, if unrelated growth inhibitors are the determinant factors in their current plateau or decline.

The published data provides no analysis of ways in which recent adopters of *Alpha* may differ substantively from the early adopters. The 1998 EA Commission certainly indicated a shifting centre of gravity since a growing proportion of smaller churches were planning to adopt the programme. As *Alpha* has raised its profile, it has persistently sought to recruit churches beyond the evangelical-charismatic stable of HTB and *Alpha News* asserts that more traditionalist Anglican and Roman Catholic churches have adopted *Alpha* more readily in recent years. Without an objective comparison of the churchmanship, ethos and size of churches that have

---

[36] *Alpha News*, March-June 2001.
[37] *Alpha News*, March-June 2001.

adopted *Alpha* in different periods, the growth of the early adopters cannot logically be predicated as the automatic benefit for recent adopters simply as a result of persisting with the programme, notwithstanding the organisation's assurances. Other factors that recent adopters may have in common could invalidate expectations derived from those who have been running *Alpha* for several years. More research is needed to develop and examine comparative data on the impact of *Alpha* in different kinds of church, by denomination, size, locality and tradition.

The Futures of *Alpha*

Expansive Vision

Alpha's new millennium vision, re-affirmed in March 2001, is the "re-conversion of England and the British Isles". Nicky Gumbel declared at the *Alpha* UK Strategy Day his enthusiasm for "a national day of prayer" that would focus specifically upon *Alpha* - "for the nation and for the Initiative". Gumbel described himself as frustrated with the pace of growth and stressed the need to accelerate.

Referring to Hunt's recently published *Anyone for Alpha*,[38] Gumbel cited the author's self-description as an "agnostic sociologist". While stressing that "there are always things we can learn," he summed up this book as a parallel to Sanballat and Tobiah's hostility to Nehemiah. Like Nehemiah, *Alpha* should not be put off by "sneers, ridicule and opposition". However, Gumbel was pleased to quote Hunt's observation that, if the leaders of *Alpha* have got it right, "a religious revival may be just around the corner." [39]

Concerning the ITV *Alpha* series planned for summer 2001, Gumbel emphasised that it was one factor among many, and not to be relied upon exclusively. Having employed the barrister's familiar rhetorical device of stealing his opponents' thunder pre-emptively, he then described it as a "great opportunity" and declared, "This year an extraordinary door has opened." Gumbel acknowledged his anxieties that a negative approach on TV "could sink the ship". This remark suggests an unexpected, underlying sense of fragility in the *Alpha* enterprise. Gumbel's aspirations for the impact of *Alpha* included "prisons emptying", "the divorce rate coming down", and "many young people in full churches".[40]

The intention was to pursue "growth and quality", with an *Alpha* adviser in every town, developing a regional strategy over the next five years. HTB wanted to encourage twenty to thirty churches in an area to pray and work together around *Alpha*. They aimed for 500 town co-ordinators or regional advisors, facilitating local *Alpha* initiatives. The advisers would be approved by HTB with the tasks of being

---

[38] Hunt, 2001; see also, Percy, 1998; Ward, 1998; Hunt, 2004.
[39] For sceptical assessments of the missiological and sociological prospects for Christian revival in Western Europe see Warner 2003; Heelas and Woodhead et al, 2005; Martin, 2005.
[40] In the event, the TV series proved neither momentous nor disastrous. Late night and erratic scheduling probably disrupted any positive and negative responses in equal measure.

the point of contact for *Alpha* courses in the area, supporting and advising new courses, conveying the vision of *Alpha* to churches, and linking with *Alpha* HQ at HTB. Gumbel suggested they might in turn recruit *Alpha* Partners at a local level - business people willing to finance evangelism in their community or region. Gumbel was aiming for 10 regional conferences each year to 2005, hosted by dioceses or denominations. New materials were promised on "developing an existing *Alpha* Course" and "maximising the potential of *Alpha*". Evangelistic events would also be provided by *Alpha*. Gumbel described *Alpha* as a lay movement, a grass roots movement. He stated, "We could see things happen faster than we think, with everyone involved." There could be "no limit to what could happen... No political party has one million activists working for them." The figure of one million seems to have particular allure for evangelicals, given its prominence in EA promotions 1995-2001. Even if one million activists is an implausible aspiration, *Alpha* has more chance of generating a movement than most Christian organisations, with its sharp focus and well-branded, high profile product.

The *Alpha* Supper Initiative in 2000 was described by HTB, unsurprisingly, as the "best initiative yet". Participating churches saw an average growth of 21% in numbers of the unchurched attending courses. In 2000, the promotional costs were split 60% HTB and 40% churches, with HTB providing nearly £1 million, representing 30% of the budget for high profile publicity. In 2001, churches made no contribution to central costs: HTB planned to give £1 million to the initiative once again, while seeking to raise £2-4 million from a new group of "*Alpha* Partners". At the first fund-raising dinner, over £1 million was given.

September 2001 also saw a nationwide training initiative and a nationwide prayer initiative. The number of prayer meetings devoted to *Alpha* rose to over 250 in 2000, which HTB took to be a key indicator of support and growth. Gumbel stressed the need to "stick at it" in the long-term process of developing *Alpha* in the local church by persistently running the course for several years. He also promoted the HTB training events as an essential component of the programme: "Running *Alpha* without going to a Conference is like driving a car without taking lessons." The phrase had begun to appear frequently on *Alpha*'s publicity literature. This decision to raise of the importance of the training events indicates a modified strategy faced with many participant churches not enjoying conversion growth: the subcultural capital of Alpha was being strengthened by direct encounter with Gumbel's preaching and HTB.[41]

Trajectories

In examining *Alpha*'s methodology, we trace familiar tensions. The remarkable popularity of *Alpha*, widespread and sustained, provokes an inevitable tension between inclusive and exclusive trajectories. In pursuit of inclusivity, *Alpha* has been careful not to identify itself too explicitly as evangelical, even though the Bash

---

[41] Thornton, 1995; Gelder and Thornton, 1997.

camp origins of its conservative apologetic pre-date the charismatic movement and the entry of moderate evangelicals into ecumenical co-operation. However, exclusivity is also at work, for the control of *Alpha* is firmly in the hands of HTB. The copyright statement that seeks to regulate and minimise adaptations of the course is designed to provide quality control, ensuring that all *Alpha* courses are consistent and reliable. As Sandy Millar observed,

> We have always been keen to allow individuals who are running an *Alpha* Course the flexibility to adapt where it was felt necessary to allow for locally felt needs and where there was the desire to retain the essential elements, nature and identity of the course. Experience has shown though that this has been misunderstood and the resulting loss of integrity in some courses has given rise to considerable confusion. Now that *Alpha* is running all around the world we have reluctantly had to draw up a copyright statement more tightly in order to preserve confidence and quality control. [42]

The copyright statement itself, in the version revised 28 October 2000, includes the following restrictive clauses:

> 4) Holy Trinity Brompton asks that the name '*Alpha*', or names similar to it should not be used in connection with any other Christian course. This request is made in order to: avoid confusion caused by different courses having similar titles; ensure the uniformity and integrity of the *Alpha* course; and to maintain confidence in courses listed in the *Alpha* register.

> 5) Holy Trinity Brompton accepts that minor adaptations to the *Alpha* course may occasionally be desirable. These should only concern the length of the talks or the number of sessions. In each case the essential character of the course must be retained. *Alpha* is a series of about 15 talks, given over a period of time, including a weekend or day away, with teaching based on all the material in Questions of Life. If the *Alpha* course is adapted the person responsible must: only use such a course in their own church or parish; not allow such a course to be used elsewhere; and not publish or promote such a course. [43]

However well intended, such detailed requirements are inevitably controlling and may appear unduly heavy-handed. The inclusivity of *Alpha*, its deliberate avoidance of denominational specifics, has resulted in widespread popularity and thus diversification. Nonetheless, the shaping of the vision and any official adaptation of the content remains firmly in the hands of HTB. Here is franchise evangelism: visit any McDonalds and get an identical Big Mac, visit any "*Alpha* church" and get the same *Alpha* course. [44] As Ritzer observed:

> McDonaldization has shown every sign of being an inexorable process by sweeping

---

[42] *Alpha News*, March-June 2001.

[43] *Alpha News*, March-June 2001.

[44] Ward, 1998.

through seemingly impervious institutions and parts of the world.[45]

Nonetheless, despite *Alpha's* avowed policy and contrary to the McDonaldization thesis,[46] many churches disregard these attempts to control their localised variations of *Alpha* and some that benefit most from the course have amended it substantially. According to the EA's 1997 survey, the churches that enjoyed the highest conversion rate from *Alpha* have either amended *Alpha* "not at all" (average 14.8 conversions per church) or "very much" (average 18.6 per church). Furthermore, according to this survey, more than 94% of churches adapt *Alpha* at least a little, and 32% adapt *Alpha* much or very much.[47]

Alpha has enjoyed remarkable and rapid growth as the innovative market leader, but now faces a growing range of approaches to evangelism and catechesis that have learned from its didactic methods and branding. Two early emulators were *Emmaus*, sponsored by broad Anglicans and published by Church House Publishing, and the *Y Course* from Peter Meadows, using Spring Harvest speakers on video. 2001 saw the launch of *Christianity Explored*,[48] jointly sponsored by All Soul's Langham Place and St. Helen's Bishopgate with a significant shift of titular nuance but not dogmatic substance, from an earlier programme, *Christianity Explained*. This conservative evangelical course uses the same techniques of glossy promotion, branding and course books. However, the fact that Rico Tice, its author, is concerned to emphasise judgment and repentance at the very beginning of the course is unlikely to make it palatable to postmoderns, nor to churchgoers outside the traditional conservative evangelical stable. His summary of Mark's gospel as "repent and believe to be saved from hell"[49] is exegetically implausible, derived more from his theological system than the Marcan text.[50] 2002 saw the publication of *Essence*,[51] Rob Frost's experimental journey into Christian faith with a new age resonance. CPAS, the broad evangelical Anglican charity published the Methodist evangelist. Just as the second decade of Spring Harvest saw the emergence of many alternative Bible weeks, *Alpha* will face an increasingly competitive and diversified market in contemporary, group-based evangelistic programmes.

Like the Evangelical Alliance in the mid-1990s, *Alpha* is now predicating future impact upon the growth pattern of the boom years. This could prove another

---

[45] Ritzer, 1996: 1, see also Ritzer, 1998.
[46] Conventional evangelical individualism has doubtless been reinforced by the cultural imperative to recast religion under the *imperium* of personal autonomy (Hammond, 1992; Smith, 2000).
[47] Included in the EA Evangelism Report, 1998: 53.
[48] Tice and Cooper, 2002.
[49] In personal interview.
[50] γεεννα only appears 3 times in Mark, all within a single pericope (9:43, 45, 47). More convincing summaries of Marcan intentions would focus upon the Messiah who suffers; discipleship in the way of the cross; or divine power and divine servanthood (Guelich, 1989; Evans, 2000; France, 2002).
[51] Frost, 2002.

example of entrepreneurial over-reaching. As the programme has developed, it has required more support staff and the annual promotions have become more elaborate and expensive. *Alpha* will need to wrestle with an inevitable tension: attitudes that from a partisan perspective represent an admirable focus, from a detached perspective are more likely to signify isolationism, empire-building, tunnel vision or narrowness. We have previously identified several more characteristic consequences of meteoric growth: over-bureaucratization; over-inflated expectations, leading to disillusionment; and the need for leaders to develop, or employ those possessing the skills necessary to provide the management, co-ordination and envisioning of what has inevitably become a far more complex organisation.

Hazards as well as opportunities arise from becoming a powerful institution. We have seen that Spring Harvest rapidly transitioned from a creative new experiment to the largest annual conference of evangelicals, and thereby became the new evangelical establishment. We also noted that the Evangelical Alliance became less appreciated by some of its member organisations when it grew large enough for them to fear it might compromise their own fund-raising capacity. Similarly, while the popularity of *Alpha* makes the very practice of evangelism more plausible for some Christians and the prospect of attendance at *Alpha* more attractive for some non-believers, now that *Alpha* is aiming to raise several million pounds annually, other charities are likely to grow increasingly threatened and defensive. Alternative evangelistic initiatives will surely be squeezed, while social action initiatives are certain to make increasingly vocal suggestions of better ways to spend several million pounds each year. Because of their size and wealth, HTB and its network of churches have been described as a diocese within a diocese.[52] If *Alpha* is successful in establishing town and regional *Alpha* advisers, who in turn secure substantial donations for local *Alpha* initiatives, *Alpha*'s national network may begin to seem quasi-denominational, an *ecclesiola in ecclesia*. If other leaders' power and influence, financial support, or mission initiatives feel threatened by the continued growth of *Alpha*, this could provoke a backlash against *Alpha*'s dominance. The very success of *Alpha* sows seeds of discontent.

While Gumbel has expressed an impatient desire for the growth of *Alpha* to accelerate, the precedents of Spring Harvest and the Evangelical Alliance - and, indeed, the mid to late twentieth century Billy Graham missions - suggest the inevitability of market saturation and an end to meteoric growth. We have identified a common tendency for entrepreneurial evangelicals to over-estimate the professed conversions resulting from evangelistic initiatives and a similar tendency to over-estimate the future growth and impact of their organisations. When expectations become unattainable and over-inflated, short-term enthusiasm risks being supplanted by disillusionment and a collapse of credibility.

Alpha has now been running long enough for a group to have emerged who thoroughly enjoy *Alpha* but have not yet been converted to the weekly pleasures of

---

[52] In interviews and conversations.

traditional church.[53] Their return trips to *Alpha* may be constructive in terms of evangelism if they bring unchurched friends with them. But *Alpha* has not convinced them that conventional church is other than dull, boring and irrelevant, despite Gumbel's protestations. We can trace four possible trajectories for these *Alpha* devotees. First, the path of assimilation: they may learn to love the church through habituation. Second, the path of reconstruction: they may contribute to the re-imagining of church, transplanting applicable aspects of *Alpha*'s methodology. Third, the path of dissolution: when *Alpha* eventually fades away - for every evangelistic project necessarily expires - those *Alpha* adherents who have failed to connect with a local church may be reabsorbed into secularity. Fourth, the path of separate development: when Wesley developed class meetings more relevant to the felt needs of eager converts than the parish church, these meetings gradually became the primary focus of their Christian loyalty in a trajectory that led ineluctably towards the birth of a new denomination. Notwithstanding the innate and emphatic Anglican loyalties of *Alpha*'s founders, and HTB's policy of dissuading what they call "*Alphaholics*" from repeated course attendance, if traditional churches remain unable to change sufficiently to address the needs of *Alpha* adherents, *Alpha* could yet spawn, however unintentionally, a new Methodism for the twenty-first century.

Normal social processes will make it increasingly difficult for *Alpha* still to be considered a work in progress, responding to constructive criticism and the changing cultural context as happened during its first decade. It certainly evolved considerably during the 1980s. John Irvine, yet another former barrister, who joined the staff of HTB as a curate in 1981 and was appointed Dean of Coventry Cathedral in 2001, expanded *Alpha* during his time in charge of the programme from a four to a ten week course and added the Holy Spirit weekend. It may prove increasingly difficult for the guardians and promoters of such a successful product to retain that sense of a work in progress. The success of *Alpha* is probably the greatest pressure towards the institutionalisation that would hasten its - eventually inevitable - obsolescence and demise.

The conviction of the *Alpha* organisation is that their dramatic success thus far represents but a foretaste of the re-evangelization of the UK - empty prisons, full churches and the nuclear family renewed. *Alpha* has undoubtedly provided one of the most effective plausibility structures for Christian faith and witness in the postmodern world and therefore, at least in the UK, the most widely popular and attractive evangelistic programme among the churches. Without *Alpha*, the "decade of evangelism" would have been almost invisible. Nonetheless, the seeds of the future decline of *Alpha* may have been sown in its years of success - centralised control, ambitious and expensive expansion, a dated apologetic, a pneumatology that overstates *glossolalia* and thaumaturgy, an accelerating bureaucratization, and a self-referential subculture that may make future modifications increasingly elusive. Above all, neither *Alpha* nor any other church initiative appears capable of reversing

---

[53] In interviews and conversations.

the tide of secularized alienation from traditional religion.[54]

At the turn of the millennium, *Alpha* was evidently for many churches the most effective buttress against a widespread Christian withdrawal into privatized and hidden faith. The continued credibility of *Alpha* is dependent upon attracting the unchurched and drawing them into living faith. In some churches, at least, the initial impact has been "inward evangelism", reaching out to nominal churchgoers and to those on the fringe of the local church. The unanswered question is whether *Alpha* is capable of attracting growing numbers of the unchurched.[55] This will require existing churchgoers to find the courage to invite them, but despite the continuing willingness of Christians to attend evangelistic events, they commonly exhibit a diminishing capacity to invite friends, neighbours and work colleagues.[56]

Faced with a cultural climate increasingly resistant to Christian conversion and church growth, *Alpha* has made a contribution to evangelism and catechesis that its users appreciate highly and consider far more effective than any other programme. There is, however, no objective evidence that *Alpha* can reasonably be expected to reverse the trends of Christian decline in Western Europe that have been sustained for over a century,[57] accelerated in the 1960s,[58] and appear to have accelerated still further in the 1990s.[59] Indeed, if *Alpha* has already peaked, as did EA and SH a decade previously, diminishing returns are in prospect for English churches' evangelism in the early twenty-first century.

According to the UK Alpha Survey published in 2001, 54% of churches using *Alpha* for three to six years have continued to decline.[60] Therefore, more than half of the churches using *Alpha* have either not seen conversions and recommitments through *Alpha*, or their inflow of new attendees has been exceeded by the outflow of those leaving the church. *Alpha* is no panacea. It cannot guarantee to halt decline or deliver growth in every church that uses it. When we strip away the rhetoric of success, the data reveals that 74% of churches using *Alpha* for three or more years are not growing. Among non-*Alpha* churches the number static or in decline is 79%, which is also the figure for churches that have used *Alpha* for one or two years. The explosive growth in the adoption of *Alpha* and its relatively high conversion-yield among early adopters, could easily beguile enthusiasts into premature and exaggerated expectations, similar to the pattern we have identified in other forms of evangelical entrepreneurialism.

For all its efforts to secure adoption in non-evangelical churches, our analysis demonstrates that *Alpha* typifies the conversionist-activist axis of evangelicalism, pragmatic and experimental, entrepreneurial and aspirational. Like EA and SH, *Alpha* has enjoyed a period of escalating adoption within the existing market for its

---

[54] Brown, 2001, 2006; Bruce, 2002; MacLaren, 2004.

[55] Booker and Ireland, 2003; MacLaren, 2004.

[56] EA 1998; Pete Meadows in personal interview.

[57] Gilbert, 1980; Wolffe, 1994; Gill, 1993, 2003.

[58] Brown, 2001.

[59] Brierley, 2000.

[60] *Alpha News*, March-June 2001.

type of religious practice, and has unusually extended its reach beyond the pan-evangelical sector, while promising a far more grandiose future impact. In contrast to Stark's theory of a self-regulating religious economy,[61] the English data raises severe doubts whether – notwithstanding their rhetoric - the conversionist-activist axis is any longer able to access the unchurched persuasively and in significant numbers. The socio-cultural trajectories of secularization have been untroubled by the growth within the Church and pan-evangelical subcultures of *Alpha*, SH and EA.

Moreover, we note a diminution in the breadth of the identity constructed, from pan-evangelicalism to a single-issue project. We have identified similar patterns of aspiration and ambition, a similar inclination to vision inflation, a similar blurring of growing market share within the church enclave with claims to wider societal impact. However the focus has been sharply narrowed. This new construction of subcultural identity is no longer pan-evangelical but centres upon *Alpha* exclusively. With the eventual and inevitable demise of this single-issue project, the subcultural identity thus constructed is more likely to evaporate than evolve into new formulations of the conversionist-activist axis.

---

[61] Stark and Bainbridge, 1985, 1987.

Chapter 6

Sociological Perspectives on Entrepreneurial Evangelicals

The conversionist-activist axis of English pan-evangelical entrepreneurialism is a productive test bed for sociological theories of evangelical durability. Kelley proposed that conservative churches grow because of traits of strictness; they convey meaning to adherents by combining absolutist convictions and rigorous lifestyle demands.[1] Hunter built on Kelley's work, arguing that the moderating trends among evangelicals that his surveys identified necessarily diminished their prospects for future growth.[2] Smith observed that while relatively conservative churches are growing, the strictness theory proposed a direct correlation between strictness and growth potential. However, evangelical churches are less strict than fundamentalist churches and yet this "religious tradition enjoys a significant margin of vitality above and beyond that of fundamentalism".[3] Even so, in the UK we have traced the dramatic growth of EA which far exceeded the more fundamentalist BEC. Similarly, Spring Harvest deliberately established a more contemporary, culturally connected ethos than the older Bible weeks that were more conservative in theology, worship and lifestyle requirements. To be sure, Calver was an authoritative leader, but he also instigated Spring Harvest's provision of optional seminars and alternative celebrations: the ethos of the event was more consumerist than conformist, more voluntarist than coercive. While Kelley may at least partly account for the continuing appeal and growth of authoritarian calvinistic-exclusivism –

---

[1] Kelley, 1972.

[2] Hunter, 1987. Penning and Smidt (2002) reject Hunter's conclusions. They repeated his survey to produce longitudinal comparative data that suggests high continuity of convictions among students at evangelical colleges, with the exception of a rightwards migration in politics and in their formulation of biblical authority. However, Penning and Smidt may not be comparing like with like. The validity of their comparisons with Hunter and their conclusion that the evangelical tradition is in theological and socio-political stasis (of which they approve wholeheartedly) would require further analysis to establish the social equivalence of the two cohorts of students. What they may be recording is not a tradition that is immune to change, contra Hunter, but a shift among users of evangelical colleges towards that sub-sector of the evangelical tradition where views have remained highly conservative or fully fundamentalist. Since Penning and Smidt teach in this sector, they have a personal interest in establishing that such colleges sustain rather than unintentionally subvert the evangelical tradition, which was Hunter's thesis.

[3] Smith, 1998: 85.

Lloyd-Jones, FIEC, Reform among Anglicans and NFI – his theory fails to account for the data of the evangelical majority, where cultural connectedness has prevailed over isolationist strictness. It is reasonable to conclude that Hunter's identification of a transition is more persuasive than Kelley's original thesis. However, contrary to Hunter's interpretation of this data, this shifting emphasis may contribute towards the cultural realignment of moderate evangelicalism. As Smith and Tamney argue,[4] this transition may increase evangelicals' potential effectiveness or at least their durability when functioning within a resistant culture, precisely by creating distance from Kelley's fundamentalistic "traits of strictness".

Tamney concluded, contrary to Kelley, in the light of his study of conservative Protestant churches in "Middletown" that modernized traditionalism, accommodating the "self-realisation ethos and the affluence ethic" was more likely to prosper than unreconstructed conservatism. [5] In particular, he suggested that charismatic evangelicalism was the religious variant most apposite to the prevailing culture – "in touch with their feelings…value individuals…preserve the environment."[6] Woodhead and Heelas similarly argue that "experiential religions of difference", are the kind of religion most likely to do well in the West, because they cater for an "expressive turn *and* for structure and transcendence, and they help followers cope with the modernizing process by socializing them into democratic and capitalist virtues; empower and guide, offer support and community in a world of rapid change".[7] Stripped of its tendencies to hyper-entrepreneurialism and anti-intellectualism, Spring Harvest has almost certainly contributed to the emergence of such trends among evangelicals. Despite its historic grounding in experience – the "felt Christ" of the Great Awakening – the evangelical tradition encountered a second subjective turn, over against the rationalism of the fundamentalists,[8] the Princeton School, American neo-evangelicals and British conservative evangelicals,[9] not through Schleiermacher but a century and a half later through charismatic renewal. We have further identified an associated responsiveness in this sector to the wider cultural turn towards the therapeutic and existential.[10] Non-triumphalist, non-coercive, non-separatist, non-illuminist, therapeutic charismatic renewal may be evangelicalism's closest correlative with the wider holistic trends in Western culture and spirituality.

While Martin identified a correlation between post-Protestantism and secularization in northern Europe,[11] Porterfield argued that America is post-

---

[4] Smith, 1998, Tamney, 2002.

[5] Tamney, 2002.

[6] Tamney, 2002: 251.

[7] Woodhead and Heelas, 2000: 494. See also Heelas, Woodhead et al, 2005, although the data could be interpreted not as a "spiritual revolution", as they argue, but rather, in the wake of secularization, as a spiritual residue.

[8] Barr, 1977.

[9] Knight, 1997; Harris, 1998; Grenz, 2000.

[10] Bellah, 1996.

[11] Martin, 1978

Protestant, having seen the demise of the *de facto* establishment, but has experienced a late twentieth century awakening, a multi-religion rediscovery of spirituality, transcendence, beauty and wholeness.[12] For Porterfield, New England Transcendentalism connects this pluralistic revitalisation of religion with the Evangelical Awakening and American Puritanism, even as contemporary fundamentalists represent a cognitive and moralistic conception of evangelical religion that also claims to be derived from the evangelical and puritan legacy but is profoundly alienated from the new spiritual awakening. While not providing empirical data to establish the scale of these trends, Porterfield provided a fresh perspective on the resacralization thesis, at least where there is a free market in religion and an intriguing parallel between the rise of new age spiritualities and charismatic renewal.

Tamney also argued against the linear assumptions of conventional secularization theory, proposing that North American atheism may have peaked when Christianity "was perceived as thoroughly reactionary – about one hundred years ago." [13] If that is correct, and if Europe and America are on the same trajectory, which may not necessarily be the case, then we may build on Tamney to suggest that America is in advance of Europe, where hostility to Christian faith may have been deferred, with the notable exception of France, and thence ultimately prolonged, by the Constantinian settlement and the resultant socio-cultural preferment granted to Christianity as the established religion.[14]

English entrepreneurial evangelicals during last two decades of the twentieth century exemplify the Weberian routinisation of charisma[15] and the interaction of conceptual thinking and cultural context.[16] Their vision inflation represents a distinctive variant of Festinger's cognitive dissonance, seen here not in terms of defiant adherence to increasingly implausible beliefs, but as a heightening within the subculture of claims of success, present or imminent.[17] Above all, the resurgent entrepreneurialism reflected the neo-liberal social context, in parallel with the Reaganite-Thatcherite revolution. However, while Stark concluded that a free market in religion produces experimentation to connect with innate religiosity in the untapped market among the unchurched,[18] late-modern English evangelical entrepreneurs showed more success at reconfiguring their own constituency than evangelising beyond it. Where the internal evangelical market was amenable to newly acculturated initiatives, there was significant growth in relative market share. However, the wider arena of the unchurched remained inhospitable cultural territory, perhaps less antagonistic than indifferent to Christianity in general, but with growing suspicions that evangelicalism is a Christian variant of the excesses of

[12] Porterfield, 2001.
[13] Tamney, 2002: 260.
[14] Compare Martin, 1978, 2005; Casanova, 1994.
[15] Weber in Gerth and Wright Mill, 1948.
[16] Mannheim, 1936.
[17] Festinger, 1957, 1964.
[18] Stark and Bainbridge 1985, 1987; Stark and Finke 2000.

resurgent fundamentalism evident across the world religions.[19] The modernized conservatism of the entrepreneurs produced a rhetoric of certainty and conquest, compelling at least in the short-term to many of the subculture's participants, but implausible and even distasteful or alienating to non-evangelical Christians and inhabitants of secularized postmodernity.

As Smith argued, the paradox of high tension yet high integration with mainstream society produces high resilience for the evangelical subculture.[20] However, the aspirations to social change do not result in effective action, partly as a result of instinctive dependence upon personal influence strategies, and the paradoxical combination of an absolutist morality with a voluntarist – and individualist - conception of church and personal morality.[21] Where fundamentalisms aspire to enforced absolutism, evangelicalism is characterised by the paradox, or perhaps oxymoron, of voluntaristic absolutism. The public rhetoric of the campaigning leaders may be absolutist, but the instincts of voluntaristic autonomy subvert the apparent non-negotiables and produce ethical and cognitive bargaining.[22] For example, while Catholics remain officially opposed to abortion and birth control, few British evangelical leaders any longer argue for absolutist restrictions on abortion or voice qualms about birth control.

Bibby described "religion *à la carte*",[23] in which preferred products are selected by the religious consumer. Roof denoted American baby boomer religion as a "spiritual quest culture" [24] prizing personal choice and sceptical of institutions. The English conversionist-activists' construction of an equivalent ethos was exemplified at Spring Harvest: a conservative theology was qualified by a praxis grounded in the growing affirmation of personal autonomy. Hammond argued[25] that the rise of personal autonomy produces less local ties, adherence to situational morality and a concomitant diminishment of church involvement, since church is a "symbol of conventionality" in doctrine, ethics and practice. This new voluntarism produces what he calls the "third disestablishment in America" in which church becomes increasingly individual-expressive rather than community-expressive. Building on Hammond's persuasive account we observe that the voluntarist-individualism of evangelicalism is particularly correlative with a culture of personal autonomy: the less rigidly conservative aspects of the tradition readily adapt to the individual-expressive culture and are melded by it. Of course, heightened emphasis upon personal autonomy is likely to result in an increasingly severe attenuation of

---

[19] Ammerman, 1990; Marty and Appleby, 1991, 1993, 1993, 1994, 1995; Percy, 1996; Armstrong, 2000; Bruce, 2001; Partridge, 2001; Percy and Jones, 2002.
[20] Smith, 1998.
[21] Smith, 1998, 2000. On voluntarism and individualism see Hammond, 1992; Penning and Smidt, 2002.
[22] Hunter, 1983, 1987; Smith, 1998, 2000.
[23] Bibby, 1987: chapter 4.
[24] Roof, 1999.
[25] Hammond, 1992.

subcultural capital.[26] This suggests at least the possibility of the subversion and continued dissipation of the pan-evangelical subcultural identity from within: commodified spirituality is the *à la carte* menu for religious postmoderns whose autonomy is sacrosanct.

Entrepreneurial evangelicals, just as much as new agers, are quintessentially free market religious activists. Their inability to attend a single Bible week (or even a single meeting at a Bible week given the proliferation of multiple seminars and celebrations since the inception of Spring Harvest) or employ a single programme of spirituality or evangelism, denotes pan-evangelicalisms' chaotic vibrancy. This generates their persistent capacity for self-reinvention and yet, through lack of reflexivity and unconscious accommodationism, produces an inevitable tendency to self-attenuation. Evangelicals are invariably less homogeneous, more capable of diverse, competing and even contradictory initiatives, than their advocates may wish or their opponents may fear. Berger's analysis of pluralism can be applied to contemporary evangelicalism, identifying the trenchant irony of the entrepreneurials' capacity to subvert the conservative hegemony that preceded their late twentieth century dominance:

> ...in this situation it becomes increasingly difficult to maintain the religious traditions as unchanging verity. Instead, the dynamics of consumer preference is [sic] introduced into the religious sphere.[27]

The sanctity of personal autonomy produces entrepreneurialism's accidental anarchy and their deconstruction of conservative conformity. These trends self-negate the rhetoric of evangelicals' aspirations to function as a coherent and homogeneous mass movement. Pan-evangelicalism's innate destiny, whether in evangelism or socio-political campaigns, may be privately thriving yet collectively ineffectual: entrepreneurial and consumerist autonomy generates heterogeneity. The conversionist-activist axis is self-attenuated by the pragmatic commodification of *à la carte* evangelicalism.

Although the old sociological orthodoxy of a universal and inevitable prescriptive secularization has been supplanted by the case for a nuanced and descriptive European exceptionalism,[28] the secularizing trends within Europe appear set to continue ineluctably. Notwithstanding their buoyant rhetoric, English evangelicals appear more likely to be facing late-onset decline as secularization gathers pace, rather than functioning with immunity to secularizing tendencies. Jamieson's New Zealand study observed that while evangelical churches "...are growing rapidly it appears, at least in the West, that these same churches also have a wide-open back door through which the disgruntled, disillusioned and disaffiliated leave." [29] Jamieson concluded that for many postmoderns, rigorously conformist and

---

[26] Thornton, 1995; Gelder and Thornton, 1997.
[27] Berger 1969: 144.
[28] Martin, 1978, 2005; Davie, 2000, 2002.
[29] Jamieson, 2002: 11.

conservative churches may increasingly be seen as "faith limiting environments".[30] Hastings similarly critiqued the evangelical predilection for religious juvenilia, consistently promising more than they prove able to deliver.[31] By the end of the twentieth century, English evangelicals were beginning to show signs of Davie's "believing without belonging".[32] Some, including evangelists working with national organisations, were said to be withdrawing from local churches that were perceived to be increasingly culturally alien,[33] and many were evidently declining to join the EA.

Bibby's analysis of Canadian evangelicals indicates a crisis of ghettoisation: more than 90% of evangelical growth was through transfer and offspring; 72% of recruits joined from other evangelical churches; of the 28% who were new converts, 20% were from evangelical families.[34] Despite their grandiose rhetoric, late twentieth century English entrepreneurials experimented with an enclave of free market religion operating within an internally segmented religious ghetto, but they failed to impact significantly the increasingly secularized majority culture.

Voas[35] has demonstrated that late twentieth century church attendance patterns across Western Europe indicate decline among women as much as ten years later than among men. This appears to lend new support to Brown's thesis that since the 1960s women's rejection of patriarchal religion and wider participation in the structurally differentiated context of the secular workplace have combined to alienate them from the conventionally feminised church subculture and have thus accelerated the death of Christian Britain.[36] Just as Voas found evidence of deferred decline among women, the data we have examined indicates the possibility of a late-onset decline among evangelicals that may finally have taken hold in the 1990s.

Of course, this analysis of contemporary trends does not account for the late nineteenth century period of decline, following the period Bebbington has termed the "dominance of evangelicalism".[37] The Free Churches suffered particularly rapid decline,[38] perhaps in part because they had become too wedded to the ethos of the mid-Victorian lower middle class and failed to find an adequate intellectual response to the widespread cultural collapse of confidence in biblical authority after Darwin and in the face of imperialistic modernity.[39] At the same time, following the era of "Palmerston's Bishops" - a cadre of evangelicals appointed under the influence of Shaftesbury - almost no evangelicals were appointed as bishops in the following generation. This indicates not only that the rise of Anglo-Catholicism decisively

---

[30] Jamieson, 2002: 122.

[31] Hastings, 2001: xlv.

[32] Davie, 1994.

[33] Indicated in interviews.

[34] Bibby and Brinkerhoff, 1974; see also Bibby and Brinkerhoff, 1973, 1983.

[35] Voas, 1995.

[36] Brown, 2001.

[37] Bebbington, 2005.

[38] Gill, 2003.

[39] Chadwick, 1975.

shifted the centre of gravity within Anglicanism, but also that, once in power, the evangelicals seemed to have little idea what to do with it.[40] (It remains to be seen whether history is repeated among Carey's Bishops.) We conclude that claims of evangelical immunity to church decline are illusory: evangelicals were full and even early participants in late nineteenth and early twentieth century decline and may now have entered late-onset decline in the face of late twentieth century accelerating secularization.

By the turn of the millennium, while *Alpha's* growth was sufficiently new for its burgeoning vision to remain convincing at least for a while among its devotees, there was no evidence that EA's ostensibly mobilised million or Spring Harvest's aspiration to "touch the nation" were plausible or compelling to the vast majority of evangelicals. Over-heated entrepreneurial evangelicalism was moving from boom to bust. In the context of chronic church decline, a more credible orientation was needed for the conversionist-activist axis beyond the temporarily mesmeric and beguiling but ultimately quixotic and untenable promises of the amnesiac entrepreneurs.

The pressing issue for any aspiration to an authentic and responsible entrepreneurialism (often but not necessarily an oxymoron) is how to avoid the over-centralising and inflationary tendencies we have enumerated. Centralisation compromises the intuitive creativity that characterised the early growth of Spring Harvest, *Alpha* and Calver's reinvention of EA. Vision inflation ultimately backfires by creating disillusion and even cynicism among the very people the leaders intended to inspire. Enthusiastic rhetoric that promises imminent results produces ready recruits with a short credibility span. Just as postmodernity demands a chastened theology, freed from the extravagant certainties of the enlightenment, the combination of secular culture and church decline demands a chastened entrepreneurialism, with no place for the beguiling illusions of vision inflation and the superficial religious recreation of hype without reality.

Hunter considered much of evangelicalism to have repositioned itself as a therapeutic religion, tailored to the perceived needs of an age of selfism and subjectivism.

> The fascination with the self and with human subjectivity has then become a well-established cultural feature of Evangelicalism generally in the latter part of[41] the twentieth century, not simply an ephemeral fashion among the younger generation.

Within the conversionist-activist axis, pragmatism and voluntarism were decisive and instinctive priorities that generated this major transposition. In Bellah's terms, the therapeutic reconfiguration of religion may have proven more enduringly plausible than the entrepreneurial.[42]

The entrepreneurial reconfigurations of evangelical identity colonised the pan-

---

[40] Chadwick, 1966, 1970; Bebbington, 1989.

[41] Hunter, 1987: 69.

[42] Bellah, 1996.

evangelical terrain made available following the fragmentation of conservatism. Nonetheless, their advance has proved volatile, transient and self-limiting, promising levels of success that proved untenable. By relativising traditional evangelical convictions, theological and ethical, through pragmatic experimentation and a persistent emphasis upon contemporaneity and cultural engagement, the entrepreneurs opened the door, however unintentionally, for the subsequent emergence of progressive reconfigurations of evangelical identity, when the biblicist-crucicentric axis began to return to prominence. Just as Stott and Lloyd-Jones unintentionally opened the door to the charismatic entrepreneurs, they in turn unintentionally opened the door to the progressives. However, before we consider the nascent reconstructions of the progressives, we turn first to the dominant identity of the mid-twentieth century, the conservative hegemony.

PART TWO

THE BIBLICIST-CRUCICENTRIC AXIS

From pre-critical inclusivity to the self-attenuated calvinistic hegemony, and the subsequent emergence of post- and neo-conservatism, with bifurcatory prospects

Chapter 7

Foundations of Evangelical Ecumenism, 1846-1912

Pan-evangelicalism, particularly in terms of its biblicist-crucicentric axis, has characteristically and repeatedly sought to describe itself and denote its boundaries through requiring formal assent to a basis of faith. In this chapter we explore the developments and tensions between these various bases and the extent to which the alternative formulations of evangelical identity interact both with wider theological debates and the internal politics of the evangelical domain. An analysis of evangelical bases from their origins in 1845 provides the necessary broader context for the study of key documents within the focal period for this study, 1966-2001. Close textual analysis will demonstrate that the origins of evangelical co-operation were broad and ecumenical but that the fundamentalising tendencies of twentieth century calvinistic conservatism moved the evangelical consensus increasingly rightwards. Thereafter we trace the trajectories of evangelical re-engagement with church, theology and culture and the neo-conservative reaction. Through analysing the diverse formulations of the biblicist-crucicentric axis we demonstrate that penal substitution and infallibility/inerrancy are contested rather than universal convictions within pan-evangelicalism. We further demonstrate that bifurcation between the neo-conservatives and progressives appears inevitable, with the composition of any future evangelical coalition dependent upon the primary allegiance of the intermediate sector whom we designate the cautiously open.

In order to establish the context for the division of 1966-7, we begin by considering the drafting of a theological framework for the putative World's Evangelical Alliance in 1845 and the formal adoption of an agreed basis in 1846. John Angell James, a Congregational minister, contributed the first recorded proposal, during a meeting of the Congregational Union in May 1842, that a united evangelical body should be constituted, specifically among dissenters, with a view to combating infidelity and also Popery, Puseyism and Plymouth Brethrenism.[1] Hostility towards the Brethren, subsequently a dominant force within evangelicalism for the next century, often in tandem with Anglicans,[2] arose from their anti-denominationalism and rejection of ordained ministry. Opposition to Popery and Puseyism was mentioned in the preparations for the inaugural conference of 1846, but others declined to adopt the contentious "third P", which rapidly disappeared from view.[3] However, both the draft and the adopted basis contained a strong

---

[1] Rouse and Neill, 1954: 318.
[2] Price and Randall, 2000.
[3] Kessler, 1968. Edward Bickersteth, chairing the 1846 meeting that adopted the basis, emphasised the positive nature of the basis, preferring this to any political crusade against

affirmation of the two Protestant sacraments and the ordained ministry, and so a measure of resistance to Brethrenism remained implicit in the founding documents.

A preparatory conference was held in Liverpool, 1-3 October 1845, at which 216 leaders represented twenty denominations, including the Church of England and the Church of Scotland. The letter of invitation, sent in the name of the Scottish evangelical churches, stated the intention to "associate and concentrate the strength of an enlightened Protestantism against the encroachments of Popery and Puseyism." The conference chose to avoid an oppositional basis, accepting the plea of John Angell James that evangelical unity should be centred upon love, rather than controversy with other groups. This preparatory conference also accepted the name "Evangelical Alliance" for the body it intended to form and approved a provisional basis of faith. R.S. Candlish, prominent within the Disruption of 1843 from the Church of Scotland, was appointed reporter for the drafting sub-committee, and in presenting their draft, he explained two of their key intentions: first, rather than conflate the historic confessions, to frame a new wording "to suit the exigencies of modern times"; second, to make a "general statement" rather than an exhaustive and formal creed, "which could not be mistaken by parties who acted in good faith and which should indicate with sufficient clearness what sort of persons ought to be entitled to compose this union." [4]

This draft basis therefore had three distinctives of lasting significance for the character of inclusive evangelicalism. First, its status was deliberately self-relativised by stating that it was a document appropriate to immediate historic circumstances. twentieth century evangelicals became more inclined to absolutise the status of their bases of faith.[5] Second, it was presented as a document that made no attempt to provide an exhaustive listing of doctrinal convictions in a complete and distinctively evangelical creed, preferring to provide a broad basis on which to secure maximum co-operation among evangelical Protestants. In the steady proliferation of additional clauses, compilers of subsequent evangelical bases of faith proved unable to resist the temptation to become more comprehensive in their doctrinal coverage. Third, it agreed to eschew any attempt to develop a distinctively evangelical ecclesiology. In the second half of the twentieth century, evangelicals would attempt to add a modicum of non-controversial ecclesiology to their bases.

In April 1846, the provisional committee added an explanation that doctrines omitted from this basis were not considered unimportant,[6] and also that the basis was not attempting to define the limits of Christian brotherhood, but rather intending to indicate "the class of persons whom it is considered, on the whole, desirable and

---

Popery, even though he thought the EA would help "Christians" withstand "Infidelity and Romanism" (Evangelical Alliance, 1847). George Eliot (1855) recorded a similar hostility to "Romanists, Puseyites and infidels" in the preaching of John Cumming at the National Scottish Church in London, which indicates the continuing resonance of these enmities.
[4] EA, 1845: 57.
[5] One notable example was the IVF policy of only using speakers willing to sign their basis.
[6] Wide concern about the absence of any clause affirming Sabbath observance was addressed within a companion set of practical resolutions.

right to embrace within the Alliance." In August 1846, two further amendments were made: the Scottish secured the addition of "his mediatorial intercession and reign" in order to express a more complete Christology; the Americans secured an additional clause concerning eternal blessedness and punishment.

At the inaugural conference, 19 August to 2 September 1846, over fifty denominations were represented. Around 84% of the delegates were British, 10% American. The fact that the International Congress of the Communist League was held in London in June 1847, resulting in Marx and Engels' *Communist Manifesto*, indicates the common currency of a new internationalism and an appetite for definitive documents of international unity in the period before the European revolutions of 1848. There was, of course, no intimation of revolutionary consciousness in the formulations of the assembled evangelicals.

Despite concerns about the increased length of the basis, the clause concerning ministry that might exclude the Quakers and the Brethren, and the absence of any statement about moral character, which was deemed beyond the jurisdiction of such an Alliance, the Basis was accepted without dissent. The only changes at this conference were to move the "private judgment" clause up to second place and to elevate the new American clause before the original ministry and sacraments clause. J. Howard Hinton, General Secretary of the Baptist Union, then proposed that slave owners should be excluded from membership of the Alliance. The Conference agreed to condemn "slavery and every form of oppression", and to exclude slave owners. This debate was already raging within America. In 1844 the American Methodist Church divided over slavery into southern and northern divisions reflecting the political consensus of each region.[7] Similarly in 1844 the American Baptist Foreign Mission Board ruled that no slave owner could be appointed as a missionary, and in Spring 1845 the Home Mission Society agreed to subdivide into northern and southern divisions.[8] However, in the international context, Americans refused to countenance what they considered an imposition that failed to take account of their particular context. As a result, the attempt to establish a World's Evangelical Alliance collapsed, replaced by the intention to create a loose affiliation of national bodies. For some, Howard Hinton's contribution aborted the opportunity for the first experiment in worldwide ecumenism. For others, it was a triumph of principle over pragmatism, an insistence that orthodoxy is incomplete without orthopraxy.

Unresolved tensions are apparent not only between the Americans and the British, as yet the dominant party, but more profoundly between the contrary trajectories of inclusivity and exclusivity. The provisional committee had raised the import of the basis, from a broad indicator of those for whom membership was appropriate to an overtly exclusive approach - "such persons only as hold and maintain evangelical views, in regard to the matters of doctrine understated". While the intent of this sharpening of the introductory rubric is unambiguously more

---

[7] Synan, 1997: 19.
[8] Ammerman, 1990: 31-2.

exclusive, it was counterbalanced by the first supplementary note, which rejected any notion of treating the basis as a "creed or confession". Moreover, the "private judgment" clause was retained within the basis itself, and its importance was emphasised by making it the second clause. Even though, as Bebbington observed,[9] its original intention was anti-Catholic, the agreed phrasing provided a much wider remit for independent interpretation and conviction. While Kessler argued that this second drafting was more exclusive and narrow,[10] we might rather see an implicit tension between the inclusive and exclusive emphases. If anything, at this stage in the development of English evangelicalism, a stronger emphasis upon inclusivity rather than exclusivity is evidenced by the prominence within the basis itself of the unambiguous assertion of the right and duty of private judgement, which inevitably relativises somewhat the subsequent doctrinal clauses.

Bickersteth's introductory remarks from the chair in 1846 confirm an anti-Roman nuance to the "right of private judgment", since he contrasted it with the recent Roman encyclical that "denied the Scriptures to the laity". Bickersteth resisted the charge of Protestant fragmentation consequent to private judgment by citing the genuine unity found within the nascent Evangelical Alliance.[11] Despite Bickersteth's more narrow definition, John Angell James had long argued for a much broader freedom of biblical interpretation and religious conscience based upon this principle, describing it as one of the two principles, the other being the authority of Scripture, upon which Nonconformity rested.[12] The eviction of the Congregationalist Samuel Davidson, from the chair of biblical literature at the Lancashire Independent College, near Manchester, and his subsequent defence by Thomas Nicholas (1860), including the principle of private judgment, may have influenced the later tendency to de-emphasise and then abandon this early evangelical principle, seen increasingly as a Trojan horse for liberalism. (Wesley exhibited a Lockean epistemic confidence in the empirical certitude and universal applicability of the conversion experience. Even so, the right and duty of private judgment logically extends the emphasis upon freedom of religious conviction found among the early Baptists to encompass Locke's emphases, notably in his *Letters Concerning Toleration* (1689-1693): freedom of religious conscience; churches as voluntarist associations that should be free from any coercion by individuals or the state; and the exclusion of the state from any religious interventions.) F. D. Maurice concluded that what Aristotle was to the German in the sixteenth century, Locke was to an Englishman in the nineteenth noting that orthodox dissenters, Unitarians and practical men opposed to Hegelian mysticism all depended upon his thought.[13] Among these, in terms of private judgment, we may certainly include the broad evangelicals.

John Henry Newman unhesitatingly deemed the right of private judgment to be antithetical to Catholicism, in an appendix to the second edition of his Apologia in

---

[9] In personal conversation, July 2002.
[10] Kessler, 1968.
[11] Evangelical Alliance, 1847.
[12] James, 1834b.
[13] Maurice, 1853.

1864.[14] Newman considered it characteristic not of evangelicalism but rather of religious liberalism. Twentieth century reformed evangelicals and fundamentalists were inclined to agree with the Cardinal. It is highly ironic that the EA produced a phrase that unconsciously echoed Spinoza's biblical hermeneutic in his *Tractatus Theologico-Politicus,*[15] and anticipated John Stuart Mill's radical defence of individual liberty.[16] However, late twentieth century evangelical campaigns for state-regulated conservative traditionalism, not only in ethics but also in religious regulation, notably the retention of a blasphemy law that appears logically untenable in a pluralistic culture, indicate that the principles of Locke had been forgotten, in favour of the restrictive authoritarianism of Calvin.

Despite Calver's blithe description of "an alliance to unite Anglicans and Dissenters",[17] Chadwick notes that most Anglican evangelicals thought the Evangelical Alliance was tainted with disestablishment and so "conquered their sympathy for its aims and refused to touch it".[18] Even so, the *Christian Observer* attacked those Anglicans willing to co-operate with the Alliance for "fraternizing with Anabaptists".[19] In short, the mutual antipathy which erupted in 1966-7 burned bright in the 1840s, even as it did in the 1790s when, as Hylson-Smith argued,[20] Simeon and his fellow-Anglicans rejected the pan-evangelical approach to overseas mission in pursuit of the establishment of the Church Missionary Society (which grew out of the Society for Missions to Africa and the East, founded 1799), over against the pan-evangelical London Missionary Society (founded 1795). Of course, Anglicans were not alone in denominational consciousness, since the Baptist Missionary Society had been established in 1792. The 1790s and 1840s thus demonstrate that the mutual incompatibilities of 1966-7 were not a fleeting aberration, but are intrinsic to the contested tradition of pan-evangelicalism.

Ten critical factors can be identified concerning the inclusions and variations between the phrasing of 1845 and 1846.

1) Both begin by making an affirmation about the Bible rather than God, an order reversed by IVF in 1959 and EA in 1970. However, despite its pre-eminence, the clause concerning Scripture restricts itself to affirming inspiration, authority and sufficiency. There is an absence of the terminology that characterizes bases of faith constructed in the wake of fundamentalism, notably "infallibility" and "inerrancy". Later preoccupations were not yet considered essential, fundamental or non-negotiable in the mid-nineteenth century.

2) The reference to human sinfulness is emphatically calvinistic. If anything, the phrase "utter depravity" out-Calvins the Calvinists' emphasis upon "total

---

[14] Newman, 1956: 275-7.
[15] Spinoza, 1670, 1951:119; see Spinoza's chapter 20 for an admirable, early promulgation of radical freedom of thought and speech.
[16] Mill, 1859.
[17] Calver in Brady and Rowdon, 1996: 148.
[18] Chadwick, 1966: 441.
[19] Balleine, 1908: 254; quoted in Smith 1998: 41.
[20] Hylson-Smith in Brady and Rowdon, 1996: 143.

depravity". This is the one clause in the agreed draft of 1845 that is narrowly determined by a particular school of evangelical theology. We should also note, and this will characterize all subsequent evangelical bases of faith until the late twentieth century, that a negative anthropology is not counter-balanced by any positive affirmation of the *imago Dei*.

3) The reference to the atonement is restrained, affirming objectivity without specifying the characteristic twentieth century evangelical preoccupation with penal substitution.

4) The work of the Spirit is rather narrowly defined in terms of conversion and sanctification. The initial drafting in 1845 used the more technical term "regeneration", but the delegates preferred "conversion". It may be, in their commendable concern for brevity, the drafters considered other dimensions of the work of the Spirit - to empower for work and witness, to provide assurance, and so on - were either implicit or secondary. Or perhaps in binitarian days they went unnoticed.

5) In the light of the twentieth century tendency to consider evangelicals narrowly conformist and exclusivist, we should note the surprising inclusion of the right of private judgment, made all the more emphatic by the addition of the phrase "and duty". This serves to relativise the basis of faith itself and affirm the importance of the mind and continued theological reflection. It is a Reformation principle made new. The elevation of the clause to second place in EA-1846 made this affirmation of individual freedom of conscience all the more emphatic. The contrast with the subsequent, conformist climate of fundamentalism could not be more acute. However, this is the last major evangelical basis of faith to include any affirmation of freedom of thought and conscience.

6) Given the deliberate avoidance of ecclesiological controversy in this new minted evangelical ecumenism, it is perhaps surprising to see an emphasis upon baptism, eucharist and ministry: an implicit corrective to non-sacramental Free Churches that would logically have excluded Salvationists and Quakers from the EA until the new basis in 1970. This was, however, set within the context of the delegates' *a priori* acceptance of denominational diversity.

7) The *parousia* is entirely omitted from EA-1845. It is tacitly re-inserted in 1846, by the reference to the "judgment of the world by our Lord Jesus Christ". Either this was an accidental omission, or the second coming was considered secondary in their doctrinal framework, or perhaps the rising tide of nineteenth century pre-millennialism made the evangelical coalition unwilling to be more specific, for fear that some delegates would attempt to insert their particular millennial schemas into the clause. In contrast with the premillennial preoccupations among some nineteenth and early twentieth century evangelicals, these pan-evangelicals showed a measure of eschatological indifference.[21]

8) The 1846 version demonstrates a problem that would plague later revisions of

---

[21] This observation remains true whether their omission of any direct reference to the *parousia* was intentional or an oversight.

bases of faith. The brevity of the original wording was intended to be advantageous, but those working on later drafts found further details and clarifications irresistible and apparently essential. Moreover, lobby groups would be inclined to offer their own, well-intended additions, further elaborating or even distorting the existing draft. Such emendations risk distorting the original intention of providing a broad outline of evangelical orthodoxy. The Scottish addition - "and His mediatorial intercession and reign" - while filling out the Christology of the basis, is guilty of superfluity according to the intentions of the original draft.

9) The American clause was more detailed than the rest of the basis and was phrased in such a way as to be less able to function as an inclusive and enduring expression of diverse evangelical convictions. It replaces a succinct phrase with a more exhaustive catalogue of statements -

> The immortality of the soul, the resurrection of the body, the judgment of the world by our Lord Jesus Christ, with the eternal blessedness of the righteous, and the eternal punishment of the wicked.

More significantly, this clause contains two contentious phrases. First, "immortality of the soul" is careless, having more to do with Platonic notions of the soul than Hebraic unitary conceptions of human existence. Second, "eternal punishment of the wicked", while intended to provide completeness and clarity, served to provoke subsequent conflict. [22]

John Angell James indicated the difficulties raised by this clause: the Aggregate Provisional Committee debated its inclusion for "four anxious hours". [23] The British contributors to the 1846 debate resisted its inclusion: Byrth argued that "those Truths only which were absolutely essential to salvation ought to be included"; Hinton argued nothing should be adopted that would exclude a single believer, although he added that, even though some Roman Catholics may be "real Christians" there had never been any intention to include them; Binney argued that the basis should be "the simplest possible, consistent with essential Truth", therefore rejecting the ninth clause or any other addition on the grounds that a minimum number of essential articles of faith would ensure maximal inclusivity of believers.

---

[22] Later in the nineteenth century, this became a theological storm centre among evangelicals, leading to the resignation of T.R. Birks as Honorary Secretary of WEA (Randall and Hilborn, 2001: 119-132).

[23] References throughout this paragraph from Evangelical Alliance (1847). John Angell James' bestselling evangelistic pamphlet, *The Anxious Enquirer* (1834) emphasized the legitimate anxiety of the unbeliever faced with "everlasting torments", which is an indication that this traditional belief was commonly held among British evangelicals. However, wide assent to this conviction was not considered necessarily to require its specific inclusion within the new basis as a fundamental and non-negotiable article of evangelical faith. The logic of Birt's argument against introducing a clause that required adherence to a belief not specified by any denomination would apply with equal force to the twentieth century evangelical preoccupation with inerrancy/infallibility and penal substitution, neither of which is included in the historic ecumenical creeds.

Birt warned that many denominations required adherence to other doctrines not mentioned in the basis, which were therefore considered secondary to evangelical unity, but he knew of no denomination in which eternal punishment was a required article of faith: the ninth clause therefore constructed a new and divisive criterion of fellowship and he feared the consequences. The Americans, however, were forthright and adamant. Cox accepted the ninth clause had been "impugned by some honoured and learned Brethren", but considered it "a synopsis, a miniature of Revelation's glory"; he claimed he could almost worship the clause, and was willing to be a martyr for it. Beecher argued that since the clause had been raised for public consideration, "it could not be rejected, without implying, as the public mind would feel, ... sanctioning the doctrine of the non-eternity of punishment." He further argued, with a contradictory emphasis that the Evangelical system could not stand "if this doctrine were omitted". However reluctantly, the British acceded to American demands.

In 1853, when F.D. Maurice articulated his rejection of a literal understanding of eternal punishment, he charged the Evangelical Alliance with introducing a novel harshness into orthodoxy that was "outrageous...contemptuous to human sympathies and conscience":

> This tenet must be accepted with *greater* precision now than in the days gone by. The Evangelical Alliance, longing to embrace all Protestant schools and parties, makes it one of its nine articles of faith, one of those first principles which are involved in the very nature of a comprehensive Christianity. It is clear that they are not solitary in their wish to give the doctrine of everlasting punishment this character. Your orthodox English Churchman, though they may dissent from some of their opinions as too wide, will join heart and soul with them whenever they are narrow and exclusive.[24]

While they did not adhere to Maurice's emphasis on the sole priority of divine love, it is striking that British contributors to the pan-evangelical debate in 1846 anticipated much of his critique.

Had Howard Hinton interpolated his proposed exclusion of slave owners earlier in the series of meetings in 1845-6, the Americans would have abandoned the EA before the final basis was agreed. Without the American clause, British evangelicals would not have been locked into an approach to eternal judgment that was explicitly asserted as the only legitimate evangelical interpretation within the EA basis of faith until 1970. Not until the end of the twentieth century would EAUK explicitly endorse approaches to final judgment that do not insist upon a literal hell or eternal suffering as integral to evangelical orthodoxy.[25] Just as the British in 1845-6 were content not to include any reference to the *parousia*, they had evidently not felt obliged to include any details concerning the consequences of final judgment.

10) There is no reference to the two practices that would characterize mid-twentieth century evangelicals, namely systematic biblical exposition as the

---

[24] Maurice, 1853: 378.
[25] ACUTE, 2000.

preferred mode of preaching and the priority of evangelism, whether at large scale events or in personal witness. This is a further indication of the extent to which the evolution of the evangelical movement marks it as a child of its times.

The 1846 basis of faith was retained until 1970. However, a much more concise and inclusive form of membership was introduced in 1912. Its precise constitutional status seems unclear, since it was, at least officially, meant to be used alongside the existing basis.

> All are welcomed as members of the Evangelical Alliance (British Organisation) who, acknowledging the divine inspiration, authority and sufficiency of the Holy Scriptures, believe in One God; - the Father, the Son, the Lord Jesus Christ our God and Saviour who died for our sins and rose again; and the Holy Spirit by whom they desire to have fellowship with all who form the One Body of Christ.

Hilborn argued, "The Alliance could consequently be said to have lost some of its theological distinctiveness during this era."[26] On the contrary, this represents the fullest expression of the inclusivist principle within evangelicalism, as articulated by some British contributors in 1846. Even as the tide was running towards fundamentalism in the United States, British evangelicalism strengthened its ecumenical inclusivity. Here are none of the controverted preoccupations of evangelical exclusivity, neither calvinistic, nor nineteenth century, nor twentieth century: total depravity, eternal suffering of the damned, biblical inerrancy, penal substitution. For those who conceive evangelicalism, whether as critics or exponents, through the narrowness of fundamentalism and calvinistic-exclusivism, such an irenic approach - requiring allegiance to a minimalist statement of Trinitarian orthodoxy, the objective atonement and biblical inspiration - may come as a considerable surprise.

The more elaborate the later evangelical bases of faith became, the more likely they were to exclude those who were fully within the compass of this "generous orthodoxy".[27] This statement could be read as the revenge of the British: American slave owners had pressed them towards a more rigorous and exclusive basis of faith, before walking out on the nascent World's Evangelical Alliance. Now the British found a way to moderate that agreed basis. The right of private judgement was no longer needed as an explicit clause in the new form of membership, since the details this clause implicitly qualified were now, if not expunged, then certainly marginalised among the secondary convictions of the inclusivist evangelicals.

---

[26] In an unpublished manuscript.

[27] Frei's call for a generous orthodoxy, (1993: 208), included the assertion that some evangelicals could be expected to make a valuable contribution on this putative wider ecumenical stage.

Chapter 8

EA-1970 and the Conservative Undertow, 1928-1981

EA-1970 – The Stott Revision

Following the public dispute between Stott and Lloyd-Jones in 1966, the Evangelical Alliance was in considerable disarray, with many separatists suspicious of affiliation with such a "broad" organisation. Out of this climate of division and distrust there emerged a wholesale reconstruction of the grounds of evangelical orthodoxy, producing the single most radical re-drafting in the history of any British evangelical organisation's basis of faith. In identifying the contrasts with EA-1846, we also need to take account of the two major bases of faith of the intervening years, IVF-1928 and WEF-1951. These documents, and the European fallout from WEF-1951, clearly contributed to EA-1970.

We first identify the major contrasts between EA-1846 and EA-1970, working through in EA-1846 order:

1) The new basis begins not with the Bible but with God, following the precedent set by the 1959 revision of the IVF basis.

2) Whereas EA-1846 contains no reference to divine sovereignty, this is inserted in EA-1970, following the precedent of WEF-1951 and IVF-1959, which added sovereignty to IVF-1928. However, the emphasis is shifted by the additional phrase "and grace" which makes EA-1970 more complete, and more generous in tone.

3) Although the Bible clause eschews "infallibility", affirmed in IVF-1928 and WEF-1951, it considerably strengthens the existing clause with the phrase "and its consequent entire trustworthiness"; it underlines authority with the adjective "supreme"; and it adds the further clarification "in all matters of faith and conduct". Since WEF-1951 includes the phrase "entirely trustworthy" and both IVF-1928 and WEF-1951 include the phrase "supreme authority in all matters of faith and conduct", the convergence is obvious. The EA-1970 clause gets as close to its counterparts as possible, without using the word "infallible".

In order to understand this reluctance, we need to refer back to persistent controversies that were brought to a head around the formulation of the WEF-1951 basis. In 1951, the World Evangelical Fellowship was being established[1] and agreeing a formulation concerning the Scriptures proved contentious. A preliminary statement drafted the previous year had affirmed "the divine inspiration and entire trustworthiness of the Holy Scriptures as originally given and its supreme authority

---

[1] In 1953 the original WEA of 1846, subsequently known as the Evangelical Alliance (British Organisation) became EAUK, obviating confusion with the new international organization.

in all matters of faith and conduct". This moved beyond EA-1846 with an emphasis upon the original autographs, echoing IVF-1928, which combined the claim of infallibility with the phrase "as originally given". However, in 1951 the American delegation secured the insertion of "infallible", just as Americans had added the eternal damnation clause in EA-1846. Several European delegations complained that this modified clause was mechanical or fundamentalist in its understanding of biblical inspiration. The following year they abandoned the fledgling World Evangelical Fellowship, forming the European Evangelical Alliance, with a basis of faith that avoided any assertion of infallibility. In 1968 the World Evangelical Fellowship eventually admitted the European Alliances on the grounds of their allegiance to the historic ecumenical creeds and their agreement to a statement affirming the entire trustworthiness of the Bible that avoided the touchstone of infallibility. This rapprochement and the statement that secured mutual acceptance had been brokered by the British Evangelical Alliance. It was therefore inconceivable that the British would employ the word "infallible" in their own revised basis of faith, just two years later. The new EA clause is best understood as an attempt to bridge the gap between the infallibilist and non-infallibilist schools of evangelicalism, taking as much as possible of the wording of the infallibilist bases of faith, without using the actual word "infallible".

In reaction against the perceived rising tide of liberalism, IVF-1928 was intended to clarify existing evangelical convictions rather than introduce theological novelty. However, IVF-1928 produced a narrower and more prescriptive definition of biblical inspiration than EA-1846. The demarcation between conservative and liberal evangelicals became a second front of theological controversy in the early days of IVF.[2] Defensive orthodoxy defined its boundaries more narrowly, excluding liberal evangelicals as well as mainline liberals.

If evangelicals ground their theological distinctives in EA-1846, "infallibility" is not an intrinsic, primary or universal evangelical conviction. But when self-definition begins with IVF-1928, "infallibility" is deemed non-negotiable. "Infallibility" can be interpreted as an attempted clarification in the context of controversy, not only with mainstream liberal theology but also with more liberally inclined evangelicals, resulting in a more conservative and circumscribed definition of biblical revelation and authority. Controversy provokes the need for a sharper self-definition and risks producing a legacy of polemic, inviting successive generations to continue to fight and be defined by the theological battles of a previous era. In affirming "infallibility", IVF-1928 intended to do no more than defend biblical orthodoxy. However, by redefining biblical inspiration in the light of current conflict, debate and division, the tradition was inevitably modified and narrowed. In this clause, at least, IVF-1928 was certainly closer to the fundamentalists than EA-1846, even though most British evangelicals declined overt identification with American fundamentalism.

Where EA resisted the novelty represented by the term "infallible", preferring to

---

[2] Barclay, 1997: 13.

retain the older terminology of "divine inspiration", IVF would resist the later American preference for "inerrancy" in their 1981 revision. Four inevitable dangers arise from focus upon a single descriptive term of this kind. First, the measure of orthodoxy is reduced to assent to a single word or concept. Second, when the key descriptive term is a negative and absolute assertion, it only requires a single contradictory instance for its claims to be overthrown or discredited. Third, in order to counterbalance this risk, an additional phrase is added - "as originally given" - which commences the theological journey of a thousand qualifications, in which theologically literate evangelicals who choose still to employ the requisite formulation tend to do so in an ever more metaphorical manner. Fourth, as I.H. Marshall observed, some of the more conservative can risk becoming more committed to their formulaic model of revelation than the actual biblical text.[3] The "inconvenient" complexities of the actual Bible become subsumed under conservatism's idealised rhetoric.

4) Returning to our comparisons after that divagation on infallibility, the right of private judgment, promoted from clause 7 in EA-1845 to clause 2 in EA-1846 is dropped in EA-1970, in accordance with IVF-1928 and WEF-1951. The conservative hegemony evidently preferred conformity rather than the heterogeneity consequent upon private judgment.

5) The harshly negative, calvinistic phrase from EA-1846, "utter depravity", is dropped[4] and replaced by "universal sinfulness and guilt of fallen man". (Inclusive language was not yet an issue for evangelicals in 1970.)

6) The EA-1846 phrase, "work of atonement" is replaced by "substitutionary sacrifice", with the additional clarification, "sole and all-sufficient ground of redemption". This explicit and exclusive endorsement of the substitutionary model of the atonement was proposed by the Pentecostals.[5] IVF-1928 had referred to "the sacrificial death (as our Representative and Substitute)" and WEF-1951 to "His vicarious and atoning death". As with the Scripture clause, EA-1970 was more rigorous, more conservative. Since Lloyd Jones and his followers were increasingly remote from EA, working instead within the separatist BEC, EA presumably felt vulnerable faced with lobbying from the Pentecostals. Their membership was retained but a more specific and narrower approach to the atonement was endorsed.

7) The EA-1846 phrase "by faith alone" is replaced by the more precise "solely by the grace of God through faith in Christ". The Pentecostals also requested this explicit Christocentricity. Following the phrase "sole and all-sufficient" in the previous clause, this repetitious and over-insistent use of "solely" serves to make the tone of these two clauses more emphatically Protestant than EA-1846.

8) The work of the Spirit is developed more fully, recovering the word "regenerating" that had been dropped from the early draft in EA-1845, and adding the words "illuminating" and "indwelling". The language is more precise, the clause

---

[3] Marshall, 1982.

[4] The phrase is also absent from IVF-1928 and WEF-1951.

[5] Elim and Assemblies of God.

more comprehensive, although the absence of any reference to spiritual gifts would cause continuing disquiet among Pentecostals and charismatics.

9) The "American clause" is dropped, thus excluding any reference to the "immortality of the soul". Judgement is referred to in terms of "God's wrath and condemnation", rather than "the judgment of the world by our Lord Jesus Christ". The explicit reference to the eternal punishment of the wicked is omitted, being replaced by reference to the "eternal consequences" of sin. Although this new clause was consonant with Stott's later rejection of a literal approach to hell and eternal torment,[6] it should not be interpreted as a novel formulation expressly designed to accommodate Stott's convictions. IVF-1928, which seems to have been the main template for EA-1970, was equally accommodating, whether or not intentionally, of the more moderate perspective, at least in this regard.

10) The "church clause" was effectively reversed, affirming the priesthood of all believers rather than "the divine institution of the Christian ministry". Although IVF-1928 omitted any clause about the church, subsequent IVF bases made reference to the "universal church, the body of Christ" and WEF-1951 referred to "the church, the body of Christ". EA-1970 therefore closely echoes these statements, but chooses to refer to "believers", whereas IVF-1928 and WEF-1951 both speak of "true" believers, reflecting their more exclusive approach. The church clause also emphasises worldwide Gospel proclamation, a priority omitted from EA-1846, and perhaps more surprisingly from IVF-1928 and WEF-1951. There is no reference to ministry and sacraments in EA-1970, in accordance with both IVF-1928 and WEF-1951, but unlike EA-1846. This may indicate a diminishing interest among evangelicals in ecclesiology or a greater concern to include non-sacramental groupings, such as the Salvation Army, although they have always remained marginal as a proportion of EA membership.

11) A second coming clause is added, whereas EA-1846 omitted, neglected or chose to subsume this doctrine under the reference to "the judgment of the world by our Lord Jesus Christ". IVF-1928 ends with the phrase, "The expectation of the personal return of the Lord Jesus Christ." WEF-1951 includes a Christological third clause, which ends with the phrase "His personal return in power and glory". EA-1970 conflates these two, beginning with IVF-1928 and ending with the WEF-1951 phrase "power and glory". Between these phrases EA-1970 inserts "visible", presumably with the intent of making the clause yet more emphatic.

EA-1970 demonstrates some of the characteristic tendencies of such a process of revision. In EA-1846, the revised version was the target of complaints that it was longer than EA-1845. Revisers are always inclined to pursue clarity through additional phrases and clauses. The development of a more comprehensive statement tends to distract from the original intention to produce a minimal basis to maximise evangelical ecumenicity. Each subsequent revision, as we shall see with IVF, tends to become yet more exhaustive and expansive and is likely to exclude some who could accept the previous formulation.

---

[6] Stott and Edwards, 1988; compare Hilborn, 2000.

Comparison with EA-1846 is complex, since some clauses are strengthened, two softened, and one inverted to bring about an entirely different emphasis. These changes, tightening yet loosening the previous wording at different points, can be tabulated as follows:

Table 35: Comparisons, EA-1846 and EA-1970

Loosened	Tightened	Added	Dropped
Utter depravity	Divine sovereignty	Fuller account of work of Spirit	Right and duty of private judgment
Eternal punishment	Biblical inspiration	Priesthood of all believers	"Scottish" Christological detail
	Substitutionary atonement	Gospel proclamation	"American" immortality of the soul
	Solely by grace through faith in Christ	Second coming	Ministry and sacraments

The two loosenings from EA-1846 represent a broadening in line with the inclusive intentions of the founders of the Evangelical Alliance, removing an overly calvinistic phrase and the contentious American interpolation. The four additions enrich the balance of the document, although the founders of the EA clearly preferred brevity to comprehensiveness, outlining the broad parameters of inclusiveness rather than providing a more exhaustive, and therefore more exclusive, quasi-creedal document. The rejection of immortality of the soul represents an overdue elimination of residual Platonism. However, the exclusion of ministry and sacraments reflected twentieth century evangelical indifference to ecclesiology, and the exclusion of the right and duty of private judgment was a severely retrograde step, pushing evangelicalism towards the narrowing conformity of neo-fundamentalism. Where the document is most significant is in its tightening of EA-1846. In particular, the theological models employed to describe biblical inspiration and the atonement had become more specific and narrow.

The underlying tension between purity and engagement is apparent and acute. While the EA basis was tightened in 1970, thus emphasising purity, there was a simultaneous initiative, spearheaded by Stott, particularly through his Anglican initiatives, to encourage evangelical engagement with wider denominational life and mainstream theology. In consequence of this engagement, the traditional conservative evangelical models of biblical inspiration and the atonement would come under increasing scrutiny. Ironically, Stott's revision of the basis of faith emphasised a more conservative understanding of evangelical convictions, even as his call for engagement encouraged the growth of self-questioning evangelicals who became increasingly sceptical of mechanical models of inspiration and atonement. Stott's evangelical "offspring" would therefore experience increasing distance from one another, even mutual incomprehension - conservatives in their unyielding and unchanging purity and moderates in their engagement with other theologies and the broader contexts of church and culture.

Major Variants – IVF-1928 and WEF-1951

We now consider IVF-1928 and WEF-1951 in the light of EA-1846 and EA-1970, first making a series of comparisons in the order of IVF-1928, and then drawing conclusions about the sources and intentions of EA-1970. Both IVF-1928 and WEF-1951 are more conservative than EA-1846. They both combine "infallible" with the qualifier, "as originally given", and WEF-1951 adds "entirely trustworthy". WEF-1951 also adds a Christological clause (3), which adds "in power and glory" to the affirmation of the personal return of Christ. In this same clause, WEF-1951 includes "virgin birth", a traditional but imprecise way of asserting the virginal conception and incarnation.

IVF-1928 is more emphatic with "universal sinfulness and guilt" than WEF-1951's "lost and sinful". While IVF-1928 describes the consequence of fallenness to be "God's wrath and condemnation", WEF-1951 defers any description of consequences until its last clause, where it refers uncompromisingly to the "resurrection of damnation". IVF-1928 concentrates on God's response to sinfulness rather than specifying the consequences of divine judgment.

IVF-1928 speaks of Christ as "Representative and Substitute", whereas WEF-1951 uses "vicarious", thus providing a narrower emphasis upon substitution. Both are insistent concerning the means of salvation, IVF-1928 italicised the word "only" in clause d), whereas WEF-1951 affirmed salvation "by faith apart from works".

The Spirit is given two clauses in IVF-1928, but only one in WEF-1951. However, the previous clause (4) in WEF-1951 refers to regeneration. WEF-1951 omits "granting repentance...and faith" from IVF-1928, perhaps indicating that North American evangelicalism was less influenced by Calvinism. However, WEF-1951 gives a fuller account of the ongoing work of the Spirit, for while IVF-1928 simply refers to "indwelling", WEF-1951 specifies the Spirit enabling believers to live a holy life, to witness and to work.

IVF-1928 omits any reference to the church, which is reinstated by WEF-1951, which then makes this clause more separatist by stating that the universal church comprises all "true" believers.

Finally, while WEF-1951 concludes with a clause affirming two resurrections, IVF-1928 concludes with the second coming, correcting the most obvious omission of EA-1846. There is, however, a slightly indirect approach to this last clause in IVF-1928, which was purged in UCCF-1981 when the revisers removed the phrase "the expectation of", previously included before the direct reference to the parousia.

These comparisons indicate that IVF-1928 and WEF-1951 had different opponents in their sights. IVF-1928 had a clear primary target in liberalism, with an implicit secondary target of liberal evangelicalism. Its underlying assumptions combined conservative evangelicalism with a moderate Calvinism. WEF-1951 is less calvinistic, avoiding phrases in EA-1846 and IVF-1928 that have an obviously calvinistic provenance. By strengthening the IVF-1928 clause on infallibility and by reasserting eternal suffering, WEF-1951 is more exclusive, less willing to legitimise diversity. Although WEF-1951 shared the target of liberalism, it is also more self-consciously Protestant in its insistence that works make no contribution to salvation and that the universal Church comprises "true" believers. WEF is more obviously anti-Catholic, more directly influenced by fundamentalism and allows no leeway for neo-orthodoxy. Unsurprisingly, neither has any place for the right of private judgment.

Although the distinctions are nuanced, and the specific categorisation of any particular element can be debated, the general pattern is clear. The most moderate of the major bases considered thus far is EA-1846; but for the interpolated "American clause", it would be consistently more moderate than any of the mid-twentieth century bases. The most conservative is consistently WEF-1951. The post-war hegemony of the United States was evident not only in politics and economics but also, with fundamentalising trajectories, in world evangelicalism.

Table 36: Relative conservatism compared, EA-1846, IVF-1928, WEF-1951 and EA-1970

	Moderate	Intermediate	Conservative	Strongly Conservative
Bible	EA-1846	EA-1970	IVF-1928	WEF-1951
Atonement	EA-1846		IVF-1928 EA-1970 WEF-1951	
Judgment		IVF-1928 EA-1970		EA-1846 WEF-1951
Second Coming	EA-1846	IVF-1928	EA-1970	WEF-1951

While EA-1970 incorporates individual supplementary phrases direct from WEF-1951, the two bases that are closest to each other are IVF-1928 and EA-1970, reflecting Stott's active contribution to both organisations. Three clauses are taken almost word for word from IVF-1928 (clauses 2, 3, 8), and the general order is very similar. In reality, EA-1970 is not a revision of EA-1846, but rather an update of IVF-1928, more emphatic with regard to the second coming, very similar in terms of atonement and judgment, more moderate with regard to biblical inspiration.

EA-1970 sought to establish the closest proximity to IVF-1928. Where EA-1970 is more conservative or more detailed than IVF-1928, it tends to draw upon WEF-1951, which suggests a secondary intention of strengthening global evangelical commonality. In part this reflects the fact that IVF-1928 was a more comprehensive basis of faith than EA-1846 and more attuned to the mid-twentieth century endemic opposition to liberalism. "Popery" was evidently much less prominent than liberalism as the prime target of mid-twentieth century British evangelicalism.

The new proximity between the bases of faith had a political dimension: Stott and Lloyd-Jones both had a profound influence within IVF, which had never joined the Evangelical Alliance, tending to suspect that the older organisation ran the twin dangers of being too broad and preferring the activism of "muscular evangelism" to doctrinal precision. In the newly divided evangelical world after 1966, for EA to produce a new basis of faith as close as possible to IVF's was to affirm the close theological proximity of the two leading pan-evangelical organisations, with neither being conceded as the sole preserve of the separatist neo-fundamentalists.

Although EA-1970 was marginally to the left of IVF-1928, considerably to the left of WEF-1951, and substantially to the left of the bases of FIEC, BEC and EMW (see below), it was nonetheless, although the most moderate among its contemporary bases of faith, a shift to the right from EA-1846, which, under American influence, had itself shifted to the right of EA-1845. Even though British evangelicalism was concerned to distinguish itself from fundamentalism, there was a discernible hardening of the theological arteries, a trend towards exclusivity. Whether under pressure following the 1966 debacle, fearing that any leftwards revision would result in further haemorrhaging of EA membership in the direction of Lloyd-Jones and his followers, or whether in reaction against the assertive theological liberalism of the 1960s[7], EA's basis of faith had been moved, subtly but significantly, to the right.

Separatist Bases

The separatist bases of faith need not be scrutinised so closely, since our focus is formulations intended to foster pan-evangelical identity. Three separatist groupings produced noteworthy bases: the British Evangelical Council Doctrinal Basis (1953), the Statement of Doctrinal Belief of the Evangelical Movement Of Wales (1955) and the Fellowship Of Independent Evangelical Churches: Doctrinal Basis (1922, revised 1991)[8]. By definition, statements that seek to reinforce exclusivity are more exhaustive, since detail serves to sharpen the distinction between the "elect" and the excluded. We will examine key phrases with regard to biblical inspiration, the

---

[7] The greatest public prominence attached to Robinson's (1963) popularization of Bultmann and Bonhoeffer.

[8] FIEC references are to the 1991 version. Not surprisingly this basis does not reflect the new moderation of non-separatist bases in the 1990s that we examine later.

atonement and divine judgment, previously identified as key delineators in the more inclusive bases, and then enumerate the most telling distinctives of these separatist alternatives.

The Bible is described as "without error" and the "final authority" by FIEC, "inerrant", the "supreme authority" and "the only rule of faith and practice" by BEC, and "infallible" and the "sole authority" by EMW. Two years after the European Evangelicals balked at "infallible" in WEF-1951, BEC tightened the emphasis with "inerrant" and "only rule". EMW's use of "sole authority" appears to exclude conferring any authority to reason, tradition or the decrees of the Church. Ironically, the status given to the EMW statement of faith appears to contradict this narrow biblicism, since it functions as a subsidiary centre of authority, requiring the signed assent of all who wish to participate in EMW.

The atonement is described as Christ "bearing God's punishment for their sin" (FIEC), Christ's "substitutionary and atoning death as a sacrifice for sin" (BEC) and Christ's "substitutionary, atoning death on the cross, where He triumphed over Satan, sin and death" (EMW). All three are equally emphatic in terms of substitution. FIEC spells out penal substitution explicitly. However, EMW is the most comprehensive, including affirmation of *Christus Victor* over Satan, sin and death.

As to final judgment, FIEC states "the wicked will be sent to eternal punishment", BEC asserts "the everlasting punishment of the lost" and EMW states, more fulsomely but with more or less identical emphasis, "The unbelieving will be condemned by Him to hell, where eternally they will be punished for their sins under the righteous judgment of God." There is no room for ambiguity, no inclusion of the possibility of a non-literal, non-eternal approach, such as that provided, perhaps unintentionally by IVF-1928 and EA-1970.

These separatist bases are well to the right of EA-1970, let alone EA-1846. They are also to the right of IVF/UCCF. Since BEC is effectively a rival to EA,[9] this points towards an additional pressure upon IVF/UCCF. Where EA-1970 moved slightly to the right, in part to minimise further departures in the wake of Lloyd-Jones' separatist call, UCCF would face more direct pressure from evangelicals within BEC, FIEC and EMW, at least some of whose members saw themselves as lobbying EA from without, UCCF from within. By the 1980s, UCCF had accommodated the Right but had not yet come to terms with the charismatics and newly emerging open evangelicals; warnings from the Right had greater resonance within UCCF than innovation on the Left.

We can identify three distinctive contributions in these bases. First, they still fight Reformation battles, with emphatic repudiation of anything "Papist". For example, FIEC's account of the sacraments is as much concerned to deny as to affirm:

---

[9] Its aims include: "To advocate Christian principles and to resist the progress of atheism, ungodliness and loose morality which have become so great a threat to the Christian mode of life in our times." and "To represent the Evangelical viewpoint to governments and public bodies regarding matters of common concern at home and abroad."

Baptism is a symbol of union with Christ and entry into his church but does not impart spiritual life. The Lord's Supper is a commemoration of Christ's sacrifice offered once for all and involves no change in the bread and wine. All its blessings are received by faith.

EMW is similarly insistent in its description of the basis of salvation and the separation at the final judgment:

...that through faith (and only faith) in the Lord Jesus Christ... Salvation is therefore by grace and not by human merit.

... He will divide all men into two, and only two, categories - the saved and the lost.

Second, these bases are emphatically anti-ecumenical. FIEC affirms, "True fellowship between churches exists only where they are faithful to the gospel." BEC expressly states that its objectives include "To awaken Christian people to the insidious dangers of all departures from the Evangelical faith and of that form of ecumenicity that is achieved at the expense of vital Christian truth" and to avoid "entanglement with churches or religious groups that are unfaithful to Evangelical principles". Such anti-ecumenism is blunt, uncompromising and indifferent to any offence caused by the language used. The Reformation's anti-Catholic rhetoric is extended to assail all official ecumenical bodies and theologically mixed denominations.

Third, and perhaps surprisingly, FIEC affirms human dignity in creation:

All men and women, being created in the image of God, have inherent and equal dignity and worth. Their greatest purpose is to obey, worship and love God.

Although the emphasis shifts immediately to the dominant evangelical categories of fall and redemption, and there is no exploration of the implications for racism, sexism or economic exploitation, this instance of positive anthropology is all the more striking since it remained absent from EA-1970 and UCCF-1981.[10] We should further note that the general omission of the doctrine of creation, save for the single word "creation" without an indication of any substantive theological implications, demonstrates that young earth creationism, beloved of fundamentalism, was by no means *de rigeur*, nor even worthy of mention among English evangelicals.

Given the extent to which the Right still functions with reference to the controversies of the Reformation, it will be clear that David Watson's reservations about the "mistake" of the Reformation expressed at NEAC, Nottingham-1977 were considered an outrage,[11] demonstrating irrefutably to calvinistic and cessationist separatists the dire theological consequences of mixed denominations and charismatic renewal. Watson was judged to have slighted and abandoned the

---

[10] Not until the 1990s would moderate evangelical bases articulate a positive anthropology and explore the Gospel's socio-political implications.

[11] Capon, 1977; Murray, 2000.

indispensable Reformation heritage. Underlying this insistent and unyielding anti-ecumenism is not only separatism but an unreconstructed anti-catholicism. It is within these right wing groupings, hyper-calvinistic and exclusive, that evangelicals and fundamentalists become more or less synonymous categories, albeit not coterminous.

IVF-1974 and UCCF-1981

EA-1970 was the last twentieth century revision of the EAUK basis of faith. However, IVF changed its name to UCCF in 1975 and produced two further revisions of its basis.[12] While EA-1970 effectively abandoned EA's original basis, preferring maximal proximity to IVF-1928 and secondary proximity to WEF-1951, IVF/UCCF adopted an entirely different approach. IVF-1974 and UCCF-1981 both retain most of the existing basis, word for word, adding further phrases and clauses to provide clarification and tackle controversies previously unaddressed.

IVF-1974 is an extremely modest revision of IVF-1928. The wording is identical, save for two clauses and the introductory rubric. The rubric refers to "the fundamental truths of Christianity", rather than "the truths of Christianity". In a non-theological context, the word "fundamental" would merely indicate that what follows is not exhaustive but focuses upon pivotal convictions. However, in the light of the ambivalent inter-connectedness between evangelicalism and fundamentalism, this represents a curious insistence upon a controverted term, presumably on the pedantic ground that fundamental truths of Christianity are not synonymous with the excesses of fundamentalism. This is surely confusing, even provocatively and pedantically impolitic, given the polemical insistence of some opponents of evangelicalism that evangelical and fundamentalist are invariably theological synonyms, equally anti-intellectual, intolerant and discredited.[13]

We turn now to the additions. Clause b) adds to the conventional evangelical emphasis upon revelation, redemption and final judgment a new, albeit succinct, reference to creation. EA-1970 cited creation and providence, but IVF-1974 cites only creation. Similarly, EA-1970 paired sovereignty and grace, but IVF-1974 emphasises sovereignty alone. The IVF/UCCF church clause (i), asserts, like WEF-1951, that the universal church comprises "true" believers. There is no reference to ministry and sacraments, as in EA-1846, nor to the "priesthood of all believers" and the evangelistic task of the church, both included in EA-1970. The IVF-1974 formulation shows minimal interest in the Church, reflecting IVF/UCCF's non-ecclesial function as an evangelistic and catechetical organisation. In sum, the minor revisions of IVF-1974 did little to diminish the rapprochement established by EA-1970 with IVF-1928, although the new elements of divergence, while modest,

---

[12] A further modification in 1995 made no theological changes to UCCF-1981 but employed inclusive language and a simpler, more direct form of expression, intended to require less theological literacy. Not until 2005, reflecting its cultural conservatism despite being theologically more moderate, did EAUK adopt inclusive language.

[13] Most notably, Barr, 1977, 1984.

confirmed IVF/UCCF's position to the right of EAUK but to the left of WEF.

The ten clauses of IVF-1974 were replaced by 11 clauses in UCCF-1981. Five of the clauses remain unchanged from IVF-1974, being the first four plus the church clause. Of the remaining six clauses, one is modified very slightly, changing the phrase "death of Christ" to the broader "work of Christ", three are given more elaborate additional phrases, one is entirely and one almost entirely new. The characteristic problem with evangelical bases of faith is that every revision becomes more comprehensive and thence more verbose. EA-1845 comprised 111 words, EA-1846 153 words, and EA-1970 182 words. IVF-1928 comprised 149 words (165 words including the introductory rubric), IVF-1974 180 words (199 including the rubric), and UCCF-1981 292 words (311 including the rubric).

Turning to the additions, clause f) adds "once for all time" to "sacrificial death", and also a supplementary final phrase, "the only mediator between God and man". Clause i) adds "in all those thus regenerated" to "the indwelling of the Holy Spirit" and provides an explanation of the indwelling in terms of sanctification and empowerment for witness. Surprisingly, given the meticulous precision of this revision, "increasing likeness to Christ" appears to be presented as an automatic consequence rather than a possible outcome. Clause k) deletes the phrase "the expectation of" before "the personal return", and adds a detailed explanation of the last judgment and its consequences. Unlike WEF-1951, UCCF-1981 avoids specifying a literal hell or eternal suffering as the consequence of "just condemnation on the impenitent". It ends on a positive note, affirming the prospect of "eternal glory".

The first additional clause (e), replacing the previous clause f) that simply affirmed the resurrection of Christ, is Christological, essentially parallel to WEF-1951, similarly affirming "virgin birth" rather than "virginal conception" but also adding the "present reign" of Christ, an emphasis last seen in the Scottish amendment in EA-1846. The second (g) is a Pauline soteriological clause, succinctly employing the righteousness / justification terminology of Romans and Galatians, as interpreted in traditional evangelical exegesis. This recalls and resists, whether consciously or unconsciously, two trends evident at Nottingham-1977 among emergent post-conservatives, namely a diminished emphasis upon penal substitution and a questioning of what was previously considered the self-evident centrality of Romans and Galatians to Pauline thought, to New Testament interpretation and to authentic evangelical theology.[14]

UCCF-1981 is more exhaustive than IVF-1928 and IVF-1974, and more polemical. In the two clauses that address soteriology in terms of objective, substitutionary atonement and imputed righteousness, there is one occurrence of "once for all time", one of "alone" and two of "only", compared with one solitary "only" in IVF-1928 and IVF-1974.[15] This heightened insistence suggests a new and urgent need to delineate the boundaries of conservative evangelicalism. Similarly,

---

[14] See Wright, 1991, 1996, 2002; Dunn, 1983, 1988a, 1998b, 1993, 1998.

[15] It was italicised in 1928, but not in 1974.

the additional and rather antiquated phrase, "in all those thus regenerated" that qualifies the "indwelling of the Holy Spirit", suggests an insistent corrective whether against universalism, ecumenism or, most likely, charismatic inclusiveness. UCCF-1981 is still marginally to the left of WEF-1951, but is more insistent, more rigorous, and more exclusive than its forebears.

The elaborations of UCCF-1981 indicate that calvinistic conservativism had grown more assertive. This could suggest a more confident era, or a more defensive climate. By the early 1980s, UCCF was facing three new pressures:[16] a rising tide of biblical illiteracy among students, resulting in an inclination to be less doctrinally discriminating than previous generations of ardent young evangelicals; the emergence of post-conservative evangelicalism, evidenced at Nottingham-1977; and the increasing influence of charismatic renewal, which was generally, at least in the historic denominations, less theologically conservative and more ecumenically inclined than traditional evangelicalism. UCCF was still uncomfortable with charismatics and unsure how to encompass them within its distinctive form of pre-charismatic pan-evangelicalism. The full impact of charismatic renewal, and of Spring Harvest and Calverism was yet to be felt, but at a time of nascent evangelical resurgence, in morale if not in numbers, the wider influence of UCCF was diminishing, even as it tightened its own basis of faith.

While the modifications of IVF-1974 had been moderate and did little to diminish the convergence initiated by EA-1970, UCCF-1981 elaborates the exclusivities of calvinistic conservatism. Far from establishing a minimal framework for maximum evangelical inclusiveness, this basis is more strident, more concerned with the rigorous establishment of clear boundaries that minimise legitimate evangelical diversity.

UCCF-1981 represents the high watermark of Lloyd-Jones' influence on UCCF, a deliberate withdrawal from the centre stage of pan-evangelicalism, a tendency to put purity before engagement, exclusivity before inclusivity.[17] Three outcomes were inevitable: those within the rising trend of moderate evangelicalism were likely to conclude that UCCF was becoming too hard-line; uncompromising charismatics would eventually establish an alternative student organisation;[18] and UCCF would ultimately face an identity crisis – pan-evangelical or calvinist-exclusivist - in which separatists and conservative traditionalists would want to continue to tighten the boundaries of evangelical identity, while broad evangelicals would want to extend inclusivity beyond IVF-1928 and IVF-1974, let alone UCCF-1981. In the following twenty years, IVP-USA adopted a much broader strategy, publishing authors - charismatic, post-conservative and open theist – judged inadmissible within the narrowing domain of IVP-UK.

---

[16] Identified in interviews.

[17] Robin Wells, UCCF General Secretary at that time, saw himself, according to a staff worker from that period whom I interviewed, as Lloyd-Jones' "man for the job".

[18] *Fusion*, primarily sponsored by Arminian new churches, was launched in 1996-7.

Inherent Tensions and Fragmentation

Our investigation is now sufficiently advanced to make several critical observations concerning the characteristics, omissions and trajectories of evangelical bases of faith. The bases demonstrate the inclusive/exclusive dialectic within evangelicalism. There is an acute tension between a framework that facilitates cooperation and a quasi-creedal statement that in its elaboration serves to define more prescriptively the boundaries of "true evangelicalism". On the Right this is resolved by minimising the concern for inclusivity: rigorous doctrinal conformity takes precedence over irenic inclusivity. On the Left, the most radical solution was in the early twentieth century, when the Evangelical Alliance espoused a minimalist Trinitarian orthodoxy in order to maximize inclusivity.

Just as EA-1970 represents a move to the right from EA-1846, UCCF-1981 represents a move to the right from IVF-1928 and IVF-1974. In the closing decades of the twentieth century, influential American formulations would continue this conservative trend even as post-conservatives began to emerge on both sides of the Atlantic.

While EA-1970 and IVF-1974 represent the high point of convergence between the two main pan-evangelical bases of faith in the UK, UCCF-1981 denotes the reassertion of conservative exclusivism, disinclined to converge any further with, let alone join, the older and broader evangelical organisation. The specific echoes of BEC-1953 - the Christological clause of UCCF-1981 recalls the BEC-1953 Christological clause, and BEC-1953 similarly included a reference to "imputed righteousness" - may have been intended to delineate an intermediate role for UCCF, more inclusive than BEC, but to the right of EA. UCCF-1981 indicates an inclination to re-run the polarisation from early IVF days between conservative and liberal evangelicals. Oliver Barclay, IVF General Secretary 1964-1980, specifically interpreted late twentieth century diversification among evangelicals in these anachronistic categories.[19] Far from setting the agenda for the coming decades, UCCF-1981 represents the high watermark of a retrenched calvinistic conservatism that was already beginning to lose influence in English pan-evangelicalism as the entrepreneurs of the conversionist-activist axis rose to new dominance.

Although late twentieth century English apologists for the evangelical tradition often emphasised its Trinitarianism,[20] the predominant orientation of evangelical bases of faith is not the Trinitarian schema underlying the ancient Christian creeds but rather the Reformation triad: *sola scriptura, solus Christus, sola gratia.*[21] That is

---

[19] Barclay, 1997.

[20] Notably, among English evangelicals, Packer, 1978; McGrath, 1994; Wright 1996; Stott, 1999.

[21] Milne (1982) and Grudem (1994) follow the conventional conservative foundationalist pattern, seen in the earlier bases by beginning their systematic theologies with the doctrine of an infallible and inerrant Scripture. Grenz (1994) writing as a post-foundationalist, begins with God in Trinity. He considers the doctrine of Scripture in Part Four as a sub-section within his Pneumatology, to the chagrin of traditional conservatives.

not to suggest that the evangelical tradition has not been Trinitarian, but rather that a thoroughgoing Trinitarian grounding to their theology is a distinctive emphasis of some contemporary evangelicals, in accordance with broader theological trends, rather than a consistent and distinctive emphasis of historical evangelical theology. Until the 1990s, the Trinitarian aspect within evangelical bases of faith was accorded a decidedly secondary emphasis.

The consistent absence of the "right and duty of private judgment" from the twentieth century bases of faith may indicate the pervasive influence of fundamentalism. The fear of mid-twentieth century evangelicals was presumably that "private judgment" ran the risk of becoming nothing less than doubters' acid, corroding assent to a basis of faith into little more than metaphorical orthodoxy. In the postmodern context, which strongly affirms the autonomy of the individual and the validity of diverse convictions,[22] evangelicalism may find the seeds for any postmodern reconstruction of their tradition, not in twentieth century conservative formulations, but in the remarkably prescient, pre-fundamentalist basis drafted in 1845. The enduring, pervasive legacy of fundamentalism, an aberrant offshoot that generated a new and reactionary interface between enlightenment rationalism and traditional, reformed evangelicalism,[23] can be traced in the rightwards drift of mid to late twentieth century evangelical bases of faith.

The diversity of these bases represents an implicit problem for evangelicals given their characteristic claim to stand for biblical Christianity, unadorned by church traditions and cultural influences. By the late twentieth century evangelicals could choose between EA-1970 (quite different from and to the right of EA-1846), UCCF-1981 (close but to the right of IVF-1928), WEF, FIEC, BEC and EMW. This wide range of expressions of evangelical identity - some demanding rigorous conformity, others accommodating theological diversity - undermines any claim to evangelical uniformity. Since evangelicals were unable to codify a single confession of faith that secured universal pan-evangelical assent, this exposes a greater degree of diversity within the evangelical tradition (and by implication within the biblical data[24]) than some evangelicals would admit or tolerate. While the bases of faith proclaim an absolute confidence in revealed truth, divergence between the bases serves to relativise their formulations, demonstrating substantial diversity and dispute between different groupings who claim with equal confidence to be authentic exponents of evangelical convictions. When diverse evangelical sectors were equally certain about differing conclusions and emphases, dogmatic exclusivism grew less plausible with every new basis of faith.[25] In contrast with the earlier evangelical pursuit of a minimalist and thereby inclusivist orthodoxy, elaborated conservative certainties produced mutual exclusivities and rival groupings and thus served unintentionally to emphasise the evangelical heterogeneity their proliferating

---

[22] Hammond, 1992.
[23] Murphy, 1996; Dorrien, 1998.
[24] Dunn, 1977; Marshall, 1982; Goldingay, 1987.
[25] The equivalent relativising consequence of proliferating denominations is an integral part of orthodox secularization theory. Bruce, 2002; contra Stark and Bainbridge, 1985.

certainties intended to repudiate. Even within the mid-twentieth century period of calvinistic hegemony, the evangelical tradition, almost despite itself, was intrinsically heterogeneous, multi-vocal and contested.

Chapter 9

Emergent Openness, 1967-1977

Keele-1967

The Anglican event at Keele in 1967 was described by Hastings as "one of the more important ecclesiastical documents, not only of the sixties but of this century", which "made it possible for non-Evangelicals to be on the same wavelength as Evangelicals".[1] Keele prepared the way for Lausanne in Stott's own development, but we should note a significant dislocation between Stott's role in international evangelicalism and Stott's role in English evangelicalism. In Lausanne-1974, Stott worked ecumenically. In Keele-1967 Stott's energies were focussed upon rehabilitating the evangelical contribution to Anglicanism. Stott retained a pan-evangelical perspective from his global involvement. However, some of his co-denominationalists operated increasingly within horizons more exclusively Anglican.

The Keele statement was in five sections: the Church and its Message (clauses 1-17); the Church and its Mission (clauses 18-36); The Church and the World (clauses 37-52); the Church and its Structures (53-63); the Church and its Worship (64-80); and the Church and its Unity (81-102).

Section one functioned as a contemporary exposition of evangelical faith, albeit prefaced by a sentence of appreciation for the creeds and 39 articles. The Bible is affirmed as "authoritative divine teaching" so that "to differ from the Bible is to deviate from the truth." However, while the Bible is "the supreme authority in all matters of faith and practice" and "the wholly trustworthy oracles of God" there is no reference to infallibility, original autographs or inerrancy. While scholarship that promotes "a more precise understanding of holy Scripture" is affirmed, there is no explicit acknowledgement of the hermeneutical disciplines of interpretation and application that would take centre-stage at Nottingham-1977. This section of Keele-1967 is close to EA-1970: they share Stottian DNA.

Concerning the cross, Keele-1967 provides an uncompromising defence of penal substitution, as the central model of the atonement:

> The atonement can be fully understood only when Christ is seen as bearing the penalty of our sins in our place. This is the deepest, though not the only, significance of the

---

[1] Hastings, 2001: 554.

divine love demonstrated in the cross.[2]

As to spiritual gifts, in a terse phrase Keele-1967 indicates discomfort among evangelical Anglicans in the late 1960s with the emergent charismatic movement.

…we have no united opinion as to whether current 'charismatic' manifestations are of the same sort as the corresponding New Testament 'gifts of the Spirit' or not.[3]

At Nottingham-1977, although Stott expressed concerns about contemporary prophecy, he insisted, "We are over the hump." [4] George Carey expressed his conviction that "there are a terrific number of evangelicals at this congress who have been influenced and helped by the charismatic movement." [5] In subsequent articles in the *Church of England Newspaper*, Colin Buchanan declared, "The charismatic divide is all over bar the shouting", and Michael Harper announced, "The charismatic divide was given the last rites." [6] While debates would continue, the tone had shifted considerably. A joint statement, *Gospel and Spirit*, signed by seventeen evangelical Anglicans and one Church of Scotland minister, resulting from four short conferences sponsored by the Church of England Evangelical Council and the Fountain Trust, and published shortly before Nottingham-1977 had established a new tone of mutual acceptance. We note the absence of signatories from the other historic denominations, the Pentecostals and the new churches. Rather than working pan-evangelically, most obviously under the aegis of the EA, evangelical Anglicans in the 1970s, non-charismatic and charismatic alike, were more inclined to function unilaterally. The greatest divide at this time concerned not charismatic renewal but churchmanship. Anglicans and separatists alike were pursuing separate development, and both remained aloof from the theologically mixed historic Free Churches.

Sections two and three explored mission and ethics. Mission is presented as transformational - "to bring all aspects of human life under the Lordship of Christ." This entails a responsibility upon Christians to "promote justice and meet human need in all its forms. Evangelism and compassionate service belong together in the mission of God." Here we see a dramatic step forward from the mid-century bases of faith and a repudiation of the crude polarisation between evangelism and the "social gospel". This section anticipates Lausanne's synthesis, but the approach to social action is essentially high Tory, philanthropic and ameliorative. Marx cast no shadows at Keele.

Up until clause 25, Keele-1967 could have been an ecumenical statement of moderate evangelicalism. In clause 25, world mission through missionary societies is affirmed for the Church of England, and in clause 27 dioceses are called to

---

[2] From Clause 9, Keele-1967.
[3] From Clause 14, Keele-1967.
[4] Capon, 1977: 58.
[5] Capon, 1977: 60.
[6] Quoted in Capon, 1977: 63.

designate "special mission areas" among the poor. Thereafter the content is more broadly applicable again until clause 34 which declares "...we seek renewal for ourselves as Evangelicals within the Church of England". Here we should note a typical use of the word "evangelical" within Keele-1967 as a noun, signifying the Evangelical Party. Later Anglican formulations generally preferred to use "evangelical" as an adjective, describing a particular sector within Anglicanism: "evangelical tradition" is said to have become a characteristic self-designation for the *cognoscenti* at Nottingham-1977.[7]

Section three addressed a number of social issues in calling Christians to face up to the ethical implications of evangelical doctrines. Lausanne-1974 and EA-1996 are prefigured in the willingness to "confess to our shame that we have not thought sufficiently deeply or radically about the problems of our society". [8] Turning to specific policies, on abortion Keele-1967 stands considerably to the right of later evangelical thinking:

> We therefore urge that questions such as alleged rape, the possibility that the embryo might be malformed, and social considerations, should not be regarded as grounds for abortion unless the mother's health is in danger.[9]

Given that 1967 was also the year of David Steel's sponsorship of new abortion legislation, Keele-1967 was whistling in the wind.

On other social policies, the document was curiously naïve , perhaps reflecting the long absence of evangelicals from socio-political debate. Government is asked to "take the necessary steps" to address "inadequacies and gaps in welfare services" and is also asked to address the problem of "hardship caused by the high price of land and property". The preservation of Sunday is commended as "the national day of rest", racial discrimination is condemned "in all countries", nuclear disarmament is called for, pre-marital and extra-marital "intercourse" are condemned as "responsible for much unhappiness", and so is drug addiction. In espousing full engagement rather than withdrawal from society, Keele's social policies assume that Christendom still exists and the Church has the right, even duty, to impose Christian values on a secular society. Reactionary neo-Constantinianism was sure to make little headway during the ethical revolution of the 1960s.

Section four turned to the internal issues of Anglicanism, proposing structural reforms including the modification of parish boundaries and freeing bishops from administrative responsibilities, while commending the continuance of the establishment and patronage. Keele-1967 thus offers a package of conservative reforms, affirming the priority of mission but otherwise supporting the status quo of the established church.

Section five continued with internal Anglican concerns, affirming the need for liturgical revision but condemning the latest revisions of the communion service for

---

[7] Manwaring, 1985.
[8] Clause 37, Keele-1967.
[9] Clause 43, Keele-1967.

including prayers for the dead and an "offering of the bread and the cup to God", which was considered quasi-Roman, while failing to emphasise the "once-for-all sacrifice of Christ upon the Cross" and omitting any "adequate reference to the Second Coming". Infant baptism is affirmed, but with a narrowly covenantal implementation - "only the children of parents who profess to be Christians are fit subjects for this rite." As to communion, while the traditional "westward position" is commended, Keele-1967 embraces the Anglo-Catholic principle of a weekly Eucharist as the primary act of worship of the local church:

> We determine to work towards the practice of a weekly celebration of the sacrament as the central corporate service of the church.[10]

Paradoxically, Keele-1967 was proposing a reform of the sacraments in opposite directions: concerning baptism, towards the restrictedness of Reformed covenantal theology; concerning communion, towards alignment with Anglo-Catholic practice, which subsequently provoked a new tension between "Keele evangelical worship" centred on the Eucharist, and "Reformed evangelical worship" centred on expository preaching. [11]

Section five also contained a terse counterblast to the standard baptismal practice of the majority of evangelicals, possibly in England by 1967 and indisputably in the world.

> We reject rebaptism as unscriptural. It is destructive of the sacrament, makes it a sign of our faith rather than God's grace, and removes its once-for-all character. It is also hurtful to the unity of God's people.[12]

Keele-1967 was irenic towards non-evangelical Anglicans and keen to promote new dialogue with Roman Catholics, but there was evidently no readiness for mutual dialogue or even respectful disagreement with those who rejected the validity of paedobaptism. Although Stott would later designate baptism as a secondary issue on which evangelicals could disagree without diminishing their unity in primary convictions,[13] the tone of Keele-1967 effectively precluded dialogue. For Keele, rebaptism is "destructive of the sacrament" and "hurtful" to unity. For practitioners of believers' baptism, as was apparent in Baptist responses to *Baptism, Eucharist and Ministry*, the WCC Lima Statement,[14] paedobaptism is considered to be less than full baptism, and so they reject the very term "rebaptism". While Keele repudiated what it termed "rebaptism", it failed to recognise that fellow evangelicals in believer baptising churches were capable of rejecting paedobaptism with equal

---

[10] Clause 76, Keele-1967.
[11] Manwaring, 1985.
[12] Clause 75, Keele-1967.
[13] Stott, 1999: 142-3.
[14] WCC, 1982; BUGB in WCC, volume 1, 1986: 70-77; various Baptist groupings in WCC, volume 2, 1987: 227-263.

force as "destructive of the sacrament" and "hurtful" to unity.

Section six turns to unity. Keele-1967 insists that Christian unity cannot be pursued without "holding fast to truth", "seeking holiness" and "practising evangelism" (in describing mission, Keele-1967 tends to revert to the old evangelical formula: mission equals evangelism). Nonetheless, Keele-1967 expressed a desire to enter fully into ecumenical dialogue and to practise an open communion table.

While concern was expressed about Anglican "chaos in doctrinal matters",[15] their faithful adherence to Anglicanism was an emphatic and explicit repudiation of Lloyd-Jones' preaching the previous year: "We do not believe secession to be a live issue in our present situation." [16]

Reunion was explored in terms of the Free Churches, Rome and, with greater detail given the then current negotiations, the Methodist Church, where an aspiration to eventual union was balanced by a disingenuous intention to "oppose any scheme that will have the effect of needlessly dividing Methodism for the sake of union with us". The clause concerning "fellow evangelicals" was much more terse and offered no specific ways forward:

> We value our present fellowship and co-operation with our fellow evangelicals in other churches, to whom we are specially bound by a common understanding of the faith, and we desire a strengthening of these relations.[17]

Nottingham-1977's "Twelve Declarations of Intent" recognised diminishing commonality with non-Anglican evangelicals:

> In grief that we find ourselves at a distance from our evangelical brothers in other denominations, we undertake to seek closer fellowship and co-operation with them in informal consultation, in shared worship and in united outreach.[18]

Stott publicly acknowledged in the opening session of the Nottingham Congress "the degree of estrangement that has occurred since Keele".[19] Two years previously, Raymond Brown, principal of Spurgeon's College, had launched his Presidency of the Evangelical Alliance with an appeal to Anglican evangelicals, "not to grow away from their brothers in the Free Churches".[20] The resurgence of Anglican identity had inevitably diminished pan-evangelicalism.

Keele-1967 is a prelude to Lausanne-1974 and the 1990s bases that represent a thoroughgoing reconstruction of English pan-evangelicalism. It anticipates the later formulations in its call to holistic mission and its aspiration to constructive

---

[15] Clause 86, Keele-1967.
[16] Clause 87, Keele-1967.
[17] Clause 93, Keele-1967.
[18] Quoted in Capon, 1977: 65.
[19] Capon, 1977: 65.
[20] Capon, 1977: 67.

engagement with the wider church, culture and theologies. However, in re-affirming their denominational allegiance, Keele-1967 inaugurated a period of separate development for evangelical Anglicans. This was understandable ever since Lloyd-Jones had presented one half of a polarisation in which the Stottian alternative was re-engagement with one's denominational setting.[21] Rejecting evangelical separatism, the Anglicans tended to give no more than marginal acknowledgment to more moderate expressions of non-Anglican evangelicalism. Rejecting obscurantist neo-fundamentalism, the Anglicans committed themselves to a moderate and engaged evangelicalism of which they were the majority exponents within the UK: it felt natural for them to go it alone. Rekindling their Anglican identity, their approach to ecumenism was more likely to accept the horizons of Anglicanism in which the Roman Catholics and Methodists were the most immediate ecclesiological neighbours. Whereas Anglicans had worked closely with Brethren leaders in the development of Keswick and IVF, and with Baptists in the Billy Graham "Crusades", these groupings with the highest proportion of evangelicals outside the Anglican Church would for a generation register only marginally on the evangelical Anglican ecumenical radar. Steadily improving opportunities of preferment would lead some Evangelical Anglicans to be more concerned to cultivate their Anglican credentials than devote time and energy to working with non-Anglican evangelicals. Once evangelical Anglicans sought reintegration within broad Anglicanism, the socio-cultural commonality of Anglican clergy, in terms of class and education, reasserted itself over against the relatively undistinguished social and educational status still predominant among Free Church pastors. Evangelical Anglicans thus entered on a process of re-engagement within Anglicanism that resulted in their self-marginalisation from their fellow evangelicals.[22] Calver subsequently inherited a vacuum of pan-evangelicalism from which the two most dominant figures of the 1960s had withdrawn their cohorts,

---

[21] It remains a matter of debate whether Lloyd-Jones precipitated this division in 1966 by speaking intemperately, or whether Lloyd-Jones was simply speaking to a theme others had proposed for him and was unintentionally strengthening the evangelical Anglican case for their congress already planned for the following year (Murray, 1990; McGrath, 1997; Dudley-Smith, 2001; Brencher, 2002). Lack of foresight by the EA, intemperate rhetoric by the preacher and over-intrusive chairing by Stott who later apologised to Lloyd-Jones for his interjection, combined in this debacle.

[22] Dudley-Smith presents this controversy as Anglicans against the Free Churches (2001:70-71). Murray as independents against the mixed historic denominations, led by a coalition of evangelical Anglicans and the Baptist evangelist Billy Graham (2000:4-50). The Baptists, Methodists and URC fell between the cracks as the Anglicans and Independents turned in upon themselves as more or less exclusive cadres. The Baptists, the largest evangelical sector, were effectively marginalized by both Stott and Lloyd-Jones. The Anglicans were suspicious of Baptists who stood over against the establishment and paedobaptism, while the independents were suspicious of Baptists as insufficiently Reformed and theologically compromised in a mixed, albeit broadly evangelical, denomination. The calvinistic conservatives' bifurcation paved the way for Calver's subsequent coalition of moderates and charismatics.

intentionally in the case of Lloyd-Jones, perhaps an unintended consequence for Stott. Separatists and Anglicans alike left an empty stage for the conversionist-activist entrepreneurials of the parachurch agencies, the charismatics and Pentecostals, and the new churches and to develop new constructs of evangelical identity.

Within Anglicanism, the impact of Keele-1967 is still debated.[23] Philip Crowe surveyed delegates three years after Keele to ask what difference it had made to their parish, and most answered "None" or "None that I know of." [24] However, those who chart the rising proportion of evangelical ordinands and bishops conclude that Keele-1967 marked the decisive dawn of the evangelical Anglican resurgence. Thus Saward:

> Year by year the percentage of male ordinands in the evangelical theological colleges moved up one or one-and-a-half points until by the late 1980s the figure was well over 50 per cent. By 1993 this figure had reached 56 per cent, as compared with 27 per cent in 'Central' colleges and 17 per cent in Anglo-Catholic colleges... Growth can also be identified with regard to the hierarchy. The total in 1967 was a tiny handful. By 1987 there were seven diocesan bishops, seven suffragans, three deans, and thirteen archdeacons. At the beginning of 1995 these figures had risen to thirteen, thirteen, eight, and twenty respectively.[25]

Even Saward tempered his enthusiasm by acknowledging, "The interpretation of 'evangelical' in these figures is, however, perhaps over-generous." [26] Unconvinced by these advances in preferment, the more conservative Anglican evangelicals came increasingly to express concern that the price of unreserved immersion in mainstream Anglicanism was the dissolution of full-blooded evangelical convictions and identity. Their suspicions were no doubt increased three months after Keele, when the Anglican liberal evangelicals closed their separate organisation as no longer necessary.[27] Just as Gorbachev's *glasnost* could be interpreted as the rebirth of Russia or the death knell of the Soviet system, there was an ambiguity in the Keele-1967 trajectory that could be interpreted as contributing to the reconstruction or even the dissolution of evangelical identity. Subsequently, while one evangelical Anglican theological college (Oak Hill) moved to the right, identifying with the strongly Reformed emphasis of the Sydney diocese, one (St John's, Nottingham) became linked with a new questioning of penal substitution[28] and several, notably Ridley, became increasingly identified with "open evangelicalism". Both sectors of

---

[23] See Yeats, 1995 (dialogical); Manwaring, 1985 (devout); Barclay, 1997 and Tinker, 2001 (both sceptical from the perspective of neo-conservatism).

[24] Capon, 1977: 176.

[25] Saward, in Yeats, 1995: 33-4.

[26] Saward, in Yeats, 1995: 34.

[27] D. Smith (1998: 90) concluded, "To a significant degree the agenda of Liberal Evangelicalism had been adopted at the Keele Congress."

[28] Goldingay, 1995. Goldingay was Principal of St. John's College, Nottingham 1988-1997, and subsequently a Professor of Old Testament at Fuller.

an increasingly divided evangelicalism among Anglicans (pro-NEAC evangelical Anglicans and wary-of-NEAC Anglican evangelicals) seemed equally inclined to write off one other.[29]

For all its innovations, Keele-1967 represents a lost opportunity in the reconstruction of pan-evangelicalism. If the congress had been divided into two sections: the first reformulating evangelical convictions; the second addressing denominational specifics in several, simultaneous streams, Keele-1967 might have brought forward the impact of Lausanne-1974 by several years and facilitated an earlier formulation of the "new face" of evangelicalism that emerged in the 1980s and 1990s. By conflating general evangelical issues and Anglican specifics, Keele-1967 distanced its insights from the broader evangelical constituency. Keele-1967

---

[29] In *Has Keele Failed?* (Yeats, 1995) - David Holloway made the case against on behalf of Reform, which had been established in 1993. He charged senior evangelical bishops with failure to take a stand against David Jenkins' outspoken heterodoxy in their report *The Nature of Christian Belief*, and failure to defend the biblical prohibitions on homosexual practices, in their report *Issues in Human Sexuality*. Holloway claimed that when the former Bishop of Durham had publicly questioned the bodily resurrection and then, in an address to the General Synod had scathingly dismissed "the divine laser beam type of miracle" as "a cultic idol" or "the very devil", it was an evangelical bishop who had been a Keele man who was "seeming to lead the applause". He further concluded that "the bishops are seeming to validate homosexual sex." For Holloway, the "biblical and apostolic" values of evangelicalism had been exchanged for modern Anglican values that are "neo-gnostic, neo-Arian, and neo-Deist". If not since Keele, then certainly since Nottingham-1977, Holloway detected a theological transposition among evangelical Anglicans in high office.

Peter Baron, a curate who had campaigned vigorously against Reform during 1994 in the pages of the *Church Times*, responded to Holloway. Baron emphasised the importance of opposition to the ordination of women in the foundation of Reform. He then argued that Reform's approach to biblical interpretation was "stuck in a reaction to modernity" and that their understanding of the church was too centred upon the local congregation. Baron set up a contrast between the purists who inhabited an evangelical ghetto before Keele-1967 and the open evangelicals who embrace the wider world of church and theology after Keele. For Baron, Reform holds to "an outdated and redundant hermeneutic", untenable and inappropriate in the postmodern world that turns interpretation into "an over-confident dogmatism". The fact that Reform failed to understand "how different interpretations can come from the same text, and how different texts require different rules of interpretation", demonstrated that the Nottingham-1977 call to develop a new hermeneutic had not been heeded.

For Anglican evangelicals like Holloway, re-engagement with the Anglican Church had been intended to produce a more recognisably evangelical denomination. For evangelical Anglicans like Baron, re-engagement with the wider church, the wider academic community and the wider cultural context produced a reconstructed evangelicalism with no desire to re-assert, let alone attempt to impose upon the wider church, the excessive, outmoded and implausible dogmatism of "closed evangelicalism". For Baron, Reform is fundamentalism in Anglican vestments. For Holloway, "open evangelicalism", at least in Baron's formulation, represents little more than emperor's clothes for a neo-liberal, postmodern and post-evangelical Anglicanism.

precipitated an evangelical Anglican form of separatism, not from co-denominationalists but from co-evangelicals, ironically an equal and opposite isolationism to Lloyd-Jones on the reformed right. At Nottingham-1977, Michael Green declared that he was "appalled at the insularity of this congress", since Festo Kivengere was the only overseas Christian to have been asked to contribute. Writing in *Idea*[30], Malcolm Hanson, who had beenthe URC observer at Nottingham, identified a different kind of isolationism:

> Presbyterians have lived for more than three hundred years without bishops or patronage, but with a strong emphasis on the eldership and on conciliar government. Yet apart from frequent references to Calvin, NEAC showed little awareness of traditions like these.[31]

This second insularity, isolated from non-Anglican evangelicals, would inevitably diminish the coherence, development and impact of English pan-evangelicalism, in the years from Keele-1967 through the rise of Calverism. If the mid-century growth and influence of IVF had been built upon a Brethren-Anglican axis, the dominant contributors to Calverism represented a new prominence for the para-church agencies and the new churches, particularly Ichthus and Pioneer.

Hastings argued that evangelicalism in England faced only two options by the time of Keele-1967: either "an intellectually archaic and fundamentalist sectarianism" or "absorption as a Conservative and biblically conscious wing within an ecumenical Catholicism upon the other".[32] Hastings' bipolarity is an over-simplification, tacitly acknowledged in his rider, "...for America it would be hard to say the same with any confidence." [33] What emerged subsequently was not merely a retreat into the sectarian ghetto of neo-fundamentalism, nor a thoroughgoing absorption resulting in the dissolution of any evangelical distinctives. Rather, we identify two quite distinct, additional trajectories: an assertive eruption of entrepreneurial pragmatism, and a progressive reconstruction, albeit preliminary and tentative, of evangelical theology.

Lausanne-1974

The Congress on World Evangelism, held in Lausanne, 16-25 July 1974, brought together 2,473 participants from 150 countries and 135 denominations. While the Billy Graham Evangelistic Organisation was the chief financial sponsor of the event,[34] John Stott chaired the drafting committee. In theological terms, Stott was the greatest influence in formulating the Lausanne statement.

Lausanne was described at the time by *Time* magazine as "a formidable forum,

---

[30] This was EAUK's official magazine at the time.
[31] Capon, 1977: 70.
[32] Hastings, 2001: 618.
[33] Hastings, 2001: 618.
[34] $2,272,000 towards a total budget of $3,000,000.

possible the widest-ranging meeting of Christians ever held" [35] and later by Derek Tidball as "the most significant gathering of evangelicals this century".[36] In the UK, it was spurned by some senior evangelical leaders, who disapproved of such an expensive global gathering, perhaps reflecting their sense of displacement in world evangelicalism with the rising stock of the United States and the developing world. As a result, the British delegation included two younger leaders, Clive Calver and Peter Meadows, for whom Lausanne was a breath of fresh air that confirmed and shaped their subsequent socially-engaged agenda for British evangelicals.[37]

The distinctive emphasis of the Lausanne Covenant, comprising 2,700 words, becomes apparent when placed beside EA-1970. Lausanne's main focus is upon mission, overwhelmingly in terms of evangelism, taking new account of global co-operation, cultural sensitivity, and appropriate methodologies. It concludes with a call to "work together for the evangelisation of the whole world". Rene Padilla described it as "little more than a detailed outline for an evangelical theology of mission".[38] For him, Lausanne-1974 eliminated several dichotomies: between evangelism and social involvement; between evangelism and the process of discipleship; and between evangelism and church renewal, particularly in terms of Christian unity.[39] A further seminal contribution was the novel recognition of the impact of cultural conditioning upon any expression of Christian faith and the consequent need to explore appropriate contextualisation in all cross-cultural mission. As Stott later observed, "Only, I suspect, as a result of the Lausanne Congress on World Evangelization in 1974 has the evangelical constituency as a whole come to acknowledge the central importance of culture for the effective communication of the Gospel." [40]

Table 37: The clause sequence of Lausanne-1974 and EA-1970

Lausanne-1974	EA-1970
The purpose of God	The nature of God
The authority and power of the Bible	The authority of the Bible
	The universality of sinfulness
The uniqueness and universality of Christ	The uniqueness of Christ / atonement
	Justification by faith
The nature of evangelism	
Christian social responsibility	
The Church and evangelism	The Church and evangelism (EA
Co-operation in evangelism	clause 7)
Churches in evangelistic partnership	

[35] Padilla, 1976: 10.
[36] Tidball, 1994: 190.
[37] Stated in interviews.
[38] Padilla, 1976: 15.
[39] Padilla, 1976: 11-13.
[40] Stott and Coote, 1980: vii.

The urgency of the evangelistic task	
Evangelism and culture	
Education and leadership	
Spiritual conflict	
Freedom and persecution	
The power of the Holy Spirit	The work of the Holy Spirit
The return of Christ	The return of Christ

Lausanne decisively re-integrated evangelism and social action. This was not strictly a new initiative; among British evangelicals, for example, Tear Fund had been launched in 1968.[41] Nonetheless, Lausanne represented a root and branch repudiation of the early to mid-twentieth century evangelical suspicion or rejection of "the social gospel". The drafting process of Lausanne reveals evangelicals in transition. The phrase "social action" was replaced by "socio-political involvement". Direct references were added to "alienation, oppression and discrimination", the concept of opposing sin was extended from the individual to the societal, and the clause was elevated from seventh to fifth. As a result, there was new prominence to the assertion that "evangelism and socio-political involvement are both parts of our Christian duty." [42]

The statement gives clear indication of several positions that it sought to counter. From the Right, there was a continued repudiation of the socio-political, but the statement calls for penitence for the attitude that had considered evangelism and social action to be mutually exclusive. From the Left, there was a growing suggestion that evangelism and social action were synonymous, but the statement insists that the two are distinct but complementary. There was a further debate about the boundaries of the Kingdom. From the Left, all acts of social justice were considered expressions of the advancement of the Kingdom of God on earth. From the Right, this inclusive approach was repudiated on the grounds that the Kingdom of God is entered by faith in Christ and the Kingdom is therefore a salvation category rather than a justice category. Once social action had been fully rehabilitated as integral to Christian mission, Lausanne seemed to side, as did Stott[43] with the more conservative approach, in its affirmation that "when people receive Christ they are born again into his kingdom."

There has continued to be much debate among evangelicals whether evangelism is the primary task of the church, or whether evangelism and social action are twin and equally prominent aspects of an integrated mission.[44] Lausanne was ambivalent in this regard, elevating social action to a new prominence, but nonetheless devoting most of its clauses to specific consideration of evangelism. The implicit logic of the Lausanne statement would therefore appear to be that both social action and

---

[41] The name was an acrostic denoting its origins: The Evangelical Alliance Relief Fund.
[42] Lausanne Covenant, Clause 5.
[43] Stott, 1975.
[44] Stott, 1975; Sider, 1987; Samuel and Sugden, 1999; Kirk, 1999; Tinker 2001.

evangelism are integral to Christian mission, as was affirmed by the Lausanne continuation committee in 1982,[45] but that eternal reconciliation with God is the ultimate centre of Christian service and proclamation. In short, in re-combining evangelism and social action, Lausanne sought simultaneously to conserve as much as possible of the emphases of conservative evangelicalism: notably the priority of evangelism and the Kingdom of God as the domain of believers. The risk was that far from uniting evangelicals, Lausanne offered a middle way that might alienate the Right - still suspicious of anything other than direct evangelism - and also the Left – providing what they would consider an inadequate shift of emphasis, thus prompting them to forge ahead independently with a more politicised, social justice oriented conception of Christian mission.

Several further aspects of Lausanne impinge upon our analysis of subsequent bases of faith. First, there was a repeated note of shame and contrition for evangelical deficiencies in theology and practice. Here was an expression of evangelicalism neither triumphalistic nor absolutising its own convictions and activities, but re-engaged with the self-critical process of *semper reformanda.* This is far from the oppositional dogmatism and absence of humility typical of fundamentalism. The self-critique is trenchant and remorseless; the intention was to produce a chastened, more humble, less strident and overly self-assured, culturally sensitive evangelical theology, scrupulously non-manipulative and with rigorous integrity.

Second, an emphasis upon religious liberty was included in clause 13, specifically in terms of governmental responsibility to provide freedom of religion in accordance with the Universal Declaration of Human Rights. However, there is no reference to the religious liberties of followers of other world religions, nor any appraisal of the legitimacy of an established church. With Stott so closely involved, the Free Church majority of world evangelicalism was hardly going to be allowed to critique the state churches bequeathed to Europe by the magisterial reformers. Further, in contrast with EA-1846, there is no reference to religious liberty within pan-evangelicalism, no re-affirmation of the right and duty of private judgment.

Third, the phrase "eternal separation from God" (Clause 3) expressed the emphasis characteristic of subsequent moderate evangelical bases, emphasising the finality of judgment rather than the duration of a literal hell.

Fourth, the characteristic evangelical emphasis upon the objective atonement was retained - "died for our sins" (Clause 4) - without elaborating, defining or preferring any particular theory of the atonement.

Fifth, Lausanne emphasised the importance of rejecting every cultural captivity of the church. Clause 6 insisted that the church "must not be identified with any particular culture, social or political system, or human ideology". Clause 10 complained that Christian missionaries "have all too frequently exported with the gospel an alien culture, and churches have sometimes been in bondage to culture rather than to the Scripture". For a post-imperial recognition of legitimate and

---

[45] Lausanne, 1982: 21-4.

necessary diversity within world evangelicalism, these insights were foundational. For the subsequent disentanglement of evangelicalism from modernity, they would be critical. Evangelicals who had previously accepted the givenness of their own cultural expressions of Christian faith as normative and untainted by cultural influences, were invited to relativise every cultural expression of the church and the gospel, including their own. For a conference with North American sponsorship to reach such conclusions, in a period of expansive American religious imperialism, was quite remarkable. (In the same era, Hal Lindsey's *Late Great Planet Earth* sold several million copies, presenting the cold war in terms of an apocalyptic last battle.

> The military capability of the United States, though it is at present the most powerful in the world, has already been neutralised because no one has the courage to use it decisively. When the economy collapses so will the military. The only chance of slowing up this decline in America is a widespread spiritual awakening.[46]

For Lindsey, therefore, a "spiritual awakening" might well lead to the decisive use of American military capability. Come to Christ and nuke the commies, apparently. Populist north American fundamentalism had little in common with Lausanne-1974 and its stringent critique of evangelicalism's endemic tendency to unconscious cultural captivity.)

One direct consequence of Lausanne-1974 was the 1978 *Willowbank Report on Gospel and Culture*, which included a rigorous critique of the Western missionary movement as a "mono-cultural export system".[47] Lausanne provoked a new awareness of cultural captivity - an essential factor in the development of a new hermeneutic. The very suggestion that there is no culture-free expression of the Christian Gospel marked a remarkably innovatory starting point for post-enlightenment and post-colonial evangelical missiology.

Sixth, sexism and racism are repudiated since all people are made in the image of God (Clause 5). However, these themes are not developed and there is no acknowledgment of sexism and racism within the church. There was also an absence of inclusive language, understandably since this was only just emerging in the secular culture, and no recognition of ecological responsibility. These issues remained essentially uncharted waters for evangelical bases of faith until the last decade of the twentieth century.

Seventh, while the main thrust of Lausanne-1974 is to move evangelicalism to the left, opening a much broader agenda of co-operative mission, much to the disquiet of the right of centre reformed evangelicals,[48] the Scripture clause is to the

---

[46] Lindsey, 1971: 184.

[47] Stott and Coote, 1981. Note the delay in publication. This was not yet a theme of perceived relevance among western evangelicals and, according to the publisher, probably would not have been published commercially without Stott's persuasive requests.

[48] Iain Murray, biographer of Lloyd-Jones, in his account of evangelicalism 1950-2000, in which he functions as an apologist for Lloyd-Jones' separatist tradition, concurs with the charge that Lausanne "made concessions to those who did not want to affirm the verbal

right of EA-1970. We have demonstrated that the Stott revision of the EA basis continued the earlier pattern of excluding the word "infallible", but employed phrasing characteristic of more conservative bases, thus moving to the right of previous EA bases while remaining to the left of IVF-UCCF, and the more conservative bases. Lausanne-1974 includes the word "infallible", but in a modified context. While UCCF-1981 speaks directly of the "divine inspiration and infallibility of Holy Scripture as originally given", Lausanne-1974 uses the term more narrowly, in terms of "the infallible rule of faith and practice". The phrase "without error in all that it affirms" may appear at first sight almost synonymous with previous conservative assertions of infallibility and inerrancy. However, some lassitude is garnered with the phrase "in all it affirms". For the pre-critical and anti-critical conservatives, infallibility was taken to exclude not only factual error but also any redactional modification or pseudonymity. The phrase "in all it affirms" thus has a threefold significance: at first sight, it is an emphatic reinforcement of the phrase, "without error"; however, it implicitly insists upon rightful interpretation of the biblical text, rather than legitimising a naïve absolutism that claims inerrancy for every literalistic interpretation; it therefore provides significant room for manoeuvre for those who conclude that a more precise reading of the text, according to its genre, authorial intentions and cultural setting, will not necessarily require, for example, Mosaic authorship of the Pentateuch, a literal, historicist understanding of Job or Jonah, a single Isaiah or Paul's authorship of the Pastorals. As the Willowbank Report observed:

> The Lausanne Covenant declares that Scripture is "without error in all that it affirms" (para. 2). This lays upon us the serious exegetical task of discerning exactly what Scripture is affirming.[49]

This clause therefore pushes simultaneously, and rather awkwardly, in opposite directions. By introducing the words "infallible" and "without error", it moves to the right of EA-1970, seeking to establish such terminology as the universal currency of world evangelicalism. This would be to the inevitable disquiet of those who had previously eschewed "infallibility" as the proposed prerequisite of evangelical orthodoxy. At the same time, Lausanne-1974 remains to the left of the IVF/UCCF, WEF and separatist bases, by shifting the locus of infallibility from the text itself to its unique contribution as a rule of faith and practice, and by adding the considerable elasticity of "in all that it affirms". The clause thus indicates a high degree of unresolved debate among evangelicals. Its formulation is probably best understood not as an attempt to resolve the inflammatory theological issues of biblical inspiration and authority, but rather as a diplomatically crafted exercise in evangelical politics.

According to Arthur Johnston, a north American participant in the Congress,

---

inspiration of the Scripture, and to ecumenical theology in the statements on social action and on the need for 'church unity' " (Murray, 2000: 50).

[49] *Willowbank Report* in Stott and Coote, 1981: 315.

Lausanne reaffirmed a strongly conservative, neo-fundamentalist position:

> The planning of Lausanne isolated the heretical views of the ecumenical movement, exposed their non-biblical foundations, and strongly reaffirmed the primacy of proclamation evangelism.[50]

On the evidence of the Lausanne Covenant itself, Johnston's views appear to demonstrate the triumph of subjective preconceptions over objective reality. He may have wanted Lausanne to do such things, but in reality, under the influence of Stott, Lausanne was moving the centre of evangelical gravity to the left, integrating evangelism and social action and calling for a new self-critical separation of essential gospel convictions from secondary cultural expressions and accretions. For Iain Murray, apologist for Lloyd-Jones and calvinistic separatism, Stott was returning to the "slippery slope" of liberal evangelicalism in the early twentieth century.[51]

David Edwards made the generous, alluring but overstated claim that Lausanne-1974 was the Vatican II of world evangelicalism.[52] There was, however, no equivalent in the loose coalition of evangelicals to Roman Catholicism's binding, ecclesiastical assent. The fluidity of evangelicalism makes co-ordinated and sustained reform difficult, even though evangelicalism is constantly evolving and being reinvented. The slightly ponderous and prolix diction of Lausanne inevitably limited its capacity to capture the imagination as western culture entered the era of the slogan and sound-bite. Nonetheless, Lausanne-1974 did propose a "new face of Evangelicalism",[53] more self-critical, more holistic, and extricated from the ghetto of neo-fundamentalism. Lausanne may not have delivered the death of the old conservatism; but it certainly heralded a new kind of evangelical identity. Just as fundamentalism was the source of the mid-twentieth century evangelical rightwards drift, Lausanne-1974 is the seminal preparatory formulation for the emergent, progressive evangelical consensus of the 1990s.

Nottingham-1977

Reservations about the conventional mid-twentieth century articulations of the biblicist-crucicentric axis became more apparent in the various drafts concerning biblical authority at the next NEAC, Nottingham-1977. The first draft stated, "the Bible is authoritative." The second referred to "unique authority". Later was added "divine inspiration, entire trustworthiness, and the sufficiency of its teaching for salvation". Still further phrases were then added: "unique and reliable witness to

---

[50] Johnston, 1978: 299-300.

[51] Murray, 2000: 50. For Murray, Adrian Hastings' conclusion that Stott was steering evangelicalism away from fundamentalism serves to prove his exclusivist point.

[52] Edwards, 1987: 417.

[53] This was the title of a subsequent book of essays reflecting upon the Covenant (Padilla, 1976).

God's self-revelation in Christ", "reliable in all that it genuinely affirms", and "authoritative for guidance in doctrine and behaviour". Similarly, the introductory statement was reinforced. Stott's phrase "To discover Christ's will we read the Bible" was replaced by "In order to discover his will we turn mainly to the Bible as God's Word written for our instruction," and this in turn became "In all matters of faith and conduct, the Bible is our supreme authority and guide, for Scripture was written for our instruction." [54]

This rephrasing is indicative of several factors. First, a tendency when working on draft documents through sub-plenary sessions, to revert to conventional descriptions of biblical authority. Second, a sustained avoidance of the language of infallibility or inerrancy, which had the effect of positioning Nottingham-1977 to the left of Lausanne-1974. Third, an emergent, post-conservative group that wanted a minimalist formulation concerning biblical authority.

At Nottingham-1977, Michael Sadgrove and Tom Wright, a generation younger than Packer, were leading influences in drawing post-conservative conclusions about the authentic trajectories of evangelical theology. In their presentation to the Assembly they explained their reasons for rejecting evangelicals' "traditional dive for Romans",[55] proposing instead that each New Testament document "must be allowed to speak for itself".[56] Although the Reformers had "made Romans the key to understanding the rest of the Bible", in their view, "it is better to allow the gospels and other epistles equal standing." [57] This indicates a hermeneutic of diversity, rather than a homogenising hermeneutic around a single theme or book. Moreover, while stating there are "no promises of salvation for those outside the Church", they suggested that the New Testament is "universalistic".[58] While avoiding a categorical universalism, they emphasised, in contrast to GC-1999 (see below), an inclusivist understanding of the atonement.

The debates at Nottingham-1977 revealed widespread, and strongly held, differences of opinion.[59] The modified draft statement declared: "In particular we continue to regard the death and resurrection of Jesus as the heart of the Gospel of salvation." Contrary to Capon, this was by no means "mealy mouthed",[60] but rather affirmed the centrality of the atonement to the Gospel without emphasising any particular model of interpretation. Here we see a double contrast with GC-1999, which emphasises the salvific nature of Christ's life as well as his death and makes penal substitution central. The drafting process at Nottingham-1977 indicates the divergent nuances of opinion. The final draft stated:

Nevertheless, we give different emphasis to the various biblical expressions of

[54] Capon, 1977: 56.
[55] Capon, 1977: 44.
[56] Capon, 1977: 45.
[57] Capon, 1977: 45.
[58] Capon, 1977: 46.
[59] Draft and final wordings quoted in Capon, 1977: 49.
[60] Capon, 1977: 49.

atonement. Some wish to see the truth that Christ died in our place as the central explanation of the cross, while others, who also give this truth a position of great importance, lay greater stress on the relative significance of other biblical pictures.

The second draft had included the phrase "penal substitution" at the request of some delegates, but this had been modified subsequently to "Christ died in our place." Similarly, the Declaration of Intent was changed from "through substitutionary redemptive death and risen life" to "through his death in our place and his risen life". These formulations indicate an engagement with contemporary New Testament scholarship, a willingness to critique, reappraise and establish a new distance from the assumptions of the Reformers and previous generations of evangelical theologians, and an inclination to describe the New Testament models of the atonement not as propositional formulations of systematic doctrine, but as "biblical pictures". While all were ready to assent to "dying in our place", whether as the central or as one aspect of the atonement, some were not prepared to assent specifically to the elaboration of that principle in terms of penal substitution.

Thiselton was a seminal contributor to Nottingham-1977 [61] where the term "hermeneutics" first entered common evangelical currency,[62] and he became the pre-eminent guide for British Evangelicals in the terrain of philosophical hermeneutics.[63] Within his somewhat opaque diction, Thiselton appears to agree with Gadamer, for whom meaning always exceeds authorial intent, that there is no presuppositionless interpretation and meaning is always open, incomplete and can only be determined in an open, iterative process, within which textual understanding is always creative and not merely reproductive.[64] Stott endorsed Thiselton and popularized the hermeneutical turn among evangelicals. However, while Stott is too sophisticated to suggest that the original meaning can be read off the written page without careful scholarship, and does not suggest that any such meaning can be implemented without carefully considered cross-cultural interpretation and application, he nonetheless follows the highly traditionalist hermeneutic of Hirsch: "...a text means what its author meant." [65] Neither Stott[66] nor Vanhoozer[67] has any sympathy with the death of the author espoused by Derrida[68] and Fish.[69] Harris' charge is therefore persuasive: cautiously open evangelicals typically employ a "trivial" and "often disingenuous" use of phenomenological hermeneutics that is only allowed to inform the application, not reconstruct the meaning.[70] Many evangelicals like Stott who

---

[61] Thiselton, 1977.

[62] Capon, 1977.

[63] Thiselton, 1980, 1995.

[64] Thiselton, 1980: 300-326; Gadamer, 1975, 1976.

[65] Hirsch, 1967: 1.

[66] Stott, 1992: 214-5.

[67] Vanhoozer, 1998, 2002.

[68] Derrida, 1974.

[69] Fish, 1980.

[70] Harris, 1998: 279-312.

reject a narrow literalism tend to be highly selective in their use of a more subtle hermeneutic, eventually legitimising women's ordination, but inflexibly traditionalist in most aspects of ethics and doctrine. Notwithstanding Thiselton, Nottingham-1977 marked a preliminary and truncated acceptance of the new hermeneutic that would later take progressives far beyond Stott's instinctive conservatism.

There were, by Nottingham-1977 at least four distinct groups among evangelical Anglicans: the right of centre grouping, who would want to affirm infallibility or even, with Packer, inerrancy; the new middle ground, in line with EA-1970 and Lausanne-1974; the new left wing, looking for a minimalist declaration of biblical authority; and an emergent fourth group who would become increasingly identified with a broadly orthodox and Anglican theology rather than a specifically evangelical orientation. If Keele-1967 represented Anglican evangelicals in the image of Stott, Nottingham-1977 represents evangelical Anglicans beginning to migrate beyond the mid-century conservative consensus Stott had espoused. Engagement with church, theology and culture was producing new expressions of evangelicalism that were growing more disparate from one another and distanced from Stott's moderate conservatism. He had taken evangelicalism to the left and into engagement, but the trajectories thus instigated would take some evangelicals much further, theologically and ecclesiologically, than Stott himself had been prepared to journey.

Chapter 10

The Conservative Counter-Trend, 1978-1999

The two most prominent documents of the conservative counter-trend are American, each focussing upon one dimension of the biblicist-crucicentric axis. We turn first to the Chicago-1978 reassertion of inerrancy.

Chicago 1978 - Inerrancy

In 1976, Harold Lindsell, former editor of *Christianity Today* published *The Battle for the Bible*, in which he attempted to make "inerrancy" a prerequisite for authentic evangelicalism. He launched a battle not so much for the Bible as for the dogma of inerrancy:

> It is my conviction that a host of evangelicals who no longer hold to inerrancy are still relatively evangelical. I do not for one moment concede, however, that in a technical sense anyone can claim the evangelical badge once he has abandoned inerrancy.[1]

Lindsell targeted Fuller Theological Seminary, often considered the American seminary most similar to British mainstream, broad evangelicalism, as a centre for the sub-evangelical thinking he opposed. From Nottingham-1977 some evangelical Anglicans were beginning to question whether the term "evangelical" should be retained since it carried negative, sectarian, anti-intellectual and obfuscatory connotations. However, in the United States, the term "evangelical" was being questioned by some who considered it too broad, vague and inclusive. In 1979, Lindsell's *The Bible in Balance* went so far as to propose the reinstatement of the term "fundamentalist", rather than "evangelical", as part of a renewed defence of inerrancy.[2] Carl Henry, leading theologian of the new evangelicals who had extricated themselves from fundamentalism, supported inerrancy but objected to the abrasive methods and divisive consequences of Lindsell's polemic.[3] Lindsell was by no means alone. Francis Schaeffer, widely influential in the 1960s and 1970s for his new apologetic, also became a champion of inerrancy as a non-negotiable prerequisite:

---

[1] Lindsell, 1976: 210.
[2] Lindsell, 1979: 319-322.
[3] Henry, 1976: 30. Lindsell (1979: 20) considered Henry's position a dereliction of duty, arguing that if inerrancy is essential, as Henry agreed, it demands a vigorous defence even at the risk of dividing evangelicalism, which Henry denied.

...the Bible is without error not only when it speaks of values, the meaning system, and religious things, but it is also without error when it speaks of history and the cosmos... Here then is the watershed of the evangelical world. We must say most lovingly but clearly: evangelicalism is not consistently evangelical unless there is a line drawn between those who take a full view of Scripture and those who do not...[4]

The origins of this controversy were longstanding. In 1966 a conference at Wenham, Massachusetts was convened as a debate between inerrantists and representatives of Fuller, which was seen to be softening its approach to Scripture. Fuller academics were accused of duplicity by some present, no agreement on inerrancy could be reached, and the final statement merely affirmed the "entire truthfulness" of Scripture. The inerrancy debate may have been partly symptomatic of an internecine rivalry between American seminaries, with Trinity Evangelical Divinity School seeking to replace Fuller as the leading post-fundamentalist centre of evangelical theology. According to McGrath, a northern evangelical establishment was seeking to impose its technical terminology upon all evangelicals.[5]

In 1977 the International Council on Biblical Inerrancy was established.[6] It held three summit meetings in Chicago (1978, 1982, 1987) and two Congresses (San Diego 1982 and Washington 1988). The Chicago Statement on Biblical Inerrancy (1978) was described by *Christianity Today* as second only in significance to Lausanne-1974, indeed "running a close second".[7] This was hardly the European or British evangelical consensus.

Packer was a key contributor, drafting the Chicago-1978 "exposition". His understanding of biblical inspiration had been elaborated much earlier in *Fundamentalism and the Word of God* (1958), when he sought to draw a clear distinction between fundamentalism and conservative evangelicalism, in defence of IVF's position. In 1965 he contributed *God has Spoken* to the Christian Foundations series, in which his robust defence of biblical authority was allied to a "demonstration of the Bible-based, Bible oriented character of the Church of England formularies (the Thirty-nine Articles of 1563, the 1662 Book of Common Prayer, and the Homilies attested in Article 35)".[8] The echo of the Tractarians is unmistakable: Packer's aspiration at that time was to bring Anglicanism back to its evangelical roots and heritage which he considered intrinsic to the 39 Articles. Just as Stott's work at Lausanne was prefigured in Keele-1967, Packer's work at Chicago was prefigured not only in these publications but also in a 1962 debate concerning the IVF doctrinal basis with Hugh Montefiore, when Packer defended both infallibility and inerrancy:

---

[4] Schaeffer, 1984: 57, 64.

[5] McGrath, 1994.

[6] Packer provided European representation.

[7] Christianity Today, 1999: 1.

[8] Packer, 1979: 7.

'Infallible' means 'not liable to be mistaken or to mislead'; 'inerrant' means 'free from all falsehood'. Both words express negatively the positive ideas that the Bible is entirely reliable and trustworthy in all that it asserts.[9]

This willingness to use both infallible and inerrant and to ascribe meanings that are distinct but complementary was reiterated in almost identical terms in Packer's Chicago exposition, sixteen years later. Packer's convictions had evidently not shifted since their original formulation in the mid-twentieth century:

> *Infallible* signifies the quality of neither misleading nor being misled and so safeguards in categorical terms the truth that Holy Scripture is a sure, safe, and reliable rule and guide in all matters.

> Similarly, *inerrant* signifies the quality of being free from all falsehood or mistake and so safeguards the truth that Holy Scripture is entirely true and trustworthy in all its assertions.

> We affirm that canonical Scripture should always be interpreted on the basis that it is infallible and inerrant.[10]

The wording of Chicago-1978 is a good deal less felicitous and more ponderous than Lausanne-1974. It comprises "the statement", "a short statement", "articles of affirmation and denial", and an "exposition". The articles of affirmation and denial follow the convention of the Barmen declaration in pairing positive and negative statements. However, while Barmen sought to extricate the Confessing Church from Nazism through five paired statements, Chicago-1978 explicates a single conviction through no less than nineteen paired statements. Self-consistency is sustained; repetition is rife.

Four aspects of Chicago-1978 typify its approach. First, a literalistic handling of Scripture is commended (in the fifth short statement) as the direct consequence of affirming inerrancy:

> Scripture is without error or fault in its teaching, no less in what it states about God's actions in creation, about the events of world history, and about its own literary origins under God, than in its witness to God's saving grace.

The twelfth article reinforces this statement

> We further deny that scientific hypotheses about earth history may properly be used to overturn the teaching of Scripture on creation and the flood.

Taken together, these assertions appear to commend anti-evolutionary creationism, preclude pseudonymity and leave little place for source and redaction criticism. The

---

[9] Packer, 1962: 15.
[10] Packer, 1979: 152.

model of inspiration apparently requires an individual author for every biblical text, neither working from existing sources nor being subject to later editing within the community of faith.

Second, the statement recognises that inerrancy applies strictly to the original autographs, and emphasises that the Bible contains writings in many genres. Attempting to take account of the actual Bible, the following defence is made in Article XIII:

> We deny that it is proper to evaluate Scripture according to standards of truth and error that are alien to its usage or purpose. We further deny that inerrancy is negated by Biblical phenomena such as a lack of modern technical precision, irregularities of grammar or spelling, observational descriptions of nature, the reporting of falsehoods (e.g. the lies of Satan), the use of hyperbole and round numbers, the topical arrangement of material, variant selections of material in parallel accounts, or the use of free citations.

Packer's exposition takes up this theme:

> When total precision of a particular kind was not expected nor aimed at, it is no error not to have achieved it. Scripture is inerrant, not in the sense of being absolutely precise by modern standards, but in the sense of making good its claims and achieving that measure of focused truth at which its authors aimed.

The exposition further warned:

> ...persons denying the full truth of Scripture may claim an evangelical identity while methodologically they have moved away from the evangelical principle of knowledge to an unstable subjectivism, and will find it hard not to move further.

In the North American context, it would not be difficult to read this as an avowedly epistemological tilt against Fuller and similar seminaries. Given that Packer wrote the exposition, it can also be interpreted as an oblique critique of Thiselton's presentation of the new hermeneutic that was influential, albeit in a preliminary manner, at Nottingham-1977.[11] McGrath records that, while Packer had never discounted the importance of hermeneutics, he held grave concerns about the consequences of Thiselton's approach:

> ...risked generating a relativistic mind-set, which could pervade every aspect of theology. Having 'battled for the Bible' for twenty years, Packer felt that this new turn threatened to undo his work...[12]

The statement specifically insists upon the importance of adherence to inerrancy:

> We gladly acknowledge that many who deny the inerrancy of Scripture do not display

---

[11] Thiselton, 1977.
[12] McGrath, 1997: 218-9.

the consequences of this denial in the rest of their belief and behaviour...

With a similar attempt to be irenic, the nineteenth article denies that confession of inerrancy is "necessary for salvation", but then adds an emphatic rider:

> However, we further deny that inerrancy can be rejected without grave consequences, both to the individual and to the Church.

From the perspective of Chicago-1978, inerrancy is intrinsic and foundational to biblical orthodoxy: the compilers presented their convictions as evangelical essentials. From the perspective of mainstream English pan-evangelicalism, "inerrancy" was considered extrinsic, novel, and a divisive distraction from biblical orthodoxy: most deemed Chicago-1978 best ignored.

The paradox of inerrancy is made manifest. Full-blooded fundamentalism wanted a Bible for which divine inspiration could be proven by its demonstrable inerrancy. However, while insisting upon inerrancy, Chicago-1978 allows two caveats. First, "standards of truth and error that are alien to its usage" do not refute inerrancy. Thus, logically, there is no obligation for inerrantists to adhere to a literal flat earth and firmament. Second, the Scripture is inerrant in "achieving that measure of focused truth at which its authors aimed". However, if inerrancy is measured in terms of authorial intent, centre stage must logically be taken in conservative theology (which could hardly be expected to be sympathetic with the "death of the author") not by the concept of "inerrancy" or "infallibility", but by biblical criticism, in order to determine as precisely as possible that original intent. [13]

Authorial intent could be mythological rather than cosmological, for example in Genesis 1, but Chicago-1978 emphasises inerrancy "in what it states about God's acts in creation"; "what it states" appears to mean the literal meaning of the text, without consideration of genre and intentions. Authorial intent could include pseudonymity, within say the Isaianic prophetic tradition, but Chicago-1978 excludes pseudonymity *a priori*. Authorial intent could be typological, notably in the book of Daniel, rather than being misinterpreted through naïve apocalyptic time-tabling; it could incorporate perspectives in tension, as in the theocracy-monarchy traditions underlying 1 Samuel; it could even expose in the book of Job the naïve inadequacies of the earlier wisdom tradition. Although at first sight Chicago-1978 presents itself as a definitive articulation of biblical inspiration, because it repudiates simplistic fundamentalism it represents a tradition in tension. Biblical criticism that elucidates authorial intent, whether of a single author, a prophetic school, sources in tension, or later redaction, will almost inevitably subvert traditionalist presuppositions, inasmuch as neo-fundamentalist exegesis has often been naïve ,

---

[13] Critical theory debates whether such a thing as authorial intent is objectively determinable or a plausible regulator of textual meaning (Derrida, 1974; Gadamer, 1975; Fish, 1980; Vanhoozer, 1988). However, even with the most traditionalist understanding of authorial intent that would be unproblematic to highly conservative evangelicals, a scholarly examination of such intent subverts fundamentalistic literalism.

superficial, and yoked to a predetermined theological schema. In short, inerrancy doesn't work. It either precludes biblical criticism, thus collapsing back into the modernist captivity of fundamentalism, or it shifts its focus from propositionalism to authorial intent in such a way as to promote the very biblical criticism its more reactionary exponents had intended to preclude, indirectly promoting at least a measure of return to the scholarly mainstream.

Chicago-1978 was a blind alley, up which almost all English evangelicals declined to follow Packer. At first sight, Chicago-1978 has the appearance of securing rigorous homogeneity among its adherents. In reality there are two schools of inerrantists: the literalists, who are anti-critical and the intentionalists who are, at least moderately, pro-critical and thus, if they choose to use the term "inerrancy" do so in a broader sense. Chicago is therefore more symbolic than substantive, redoubling the emphasis upon infallibility and disregarding the older evangelical tradition that had avoided such terms. Chicago-1978 builds a new alliance between conservatives and fundamentalists. It represents the reassertion of the Right against the trajectory of Lausanne-1974. Here is a new oppositionalism, not only against the "old enemy" of liberalism, but also against Lausanne's new face of evangelicalism.

Stott expressly rejected inerrancy with five arguments.[14] First, God's self-revelation is too rich to be reduced to a string of true propositions: inerrancy is too narrow a category. Second, the word is a double negative, of which Stott disapproves linguistically, citing in preference Packer's positive formulation, "total trustworthiness as a consequence of entire truthfulness".[15] Third, it promotes a defensive attitude that concentrates on explaining "apparent discrepancies" rather than reading the Bible to grow in grace and knowledge of God. Fourth, it is neither wise nor fair to turn acceptance of the word "inerrant" into the litmus test of evangelical orthodoxy: Stott emphasised submission to the Scripture over subscription to "an impeccable formula about the Bible". Fifth, Stott observed bluntly, "It is impossible to prove that the Bible contains no errors."

Stott is both a diplomat and a conservative. While by no means a comprehensive assault, his critique leaves inerrancy with broken wings. However, he prefaces his demolition with the statement that inerrancy "makes me uncomfortable": this softens the assault, by introducing an element of subjective and personal disquiet. Moreover, immediately following his five charges Stott quotes from the North American document, *Evangelical Affirmations*, co-sponsored in 1989 by the National Association of Evangelicals and Trinity Evangelical Divinity School. Stott applauds their statement as "fine, comprehensive". He then quotes their positive declaration, which echoes his earlier quotation of Packer,

Evangelicals hold the Bible to be God's Word and therefore completely true and trustworthy...

---

[14] Stott, 1999: 73-74.
[15] McGrath, 1997: 201. Quoted from Packer's Regent College lecture course, Systematic Theology I: Knowledge of God, Fall term, 1987.

Having assailed inerrancy and then affirmed this American statement, Stott
completes his quotation with their explanatory phrase: "(and this is what we mean
by the words *infallible* and *inerrant*)."

Two discrepancies in Stott's argument are inescapable. First, Stott assails
inerrancy and then affirms a statement that includes the term, which cannot but be
self-contradictory. The diplomat is building a bridge so that inerrantists may still
make a positive affirmation of biblical inspiration, while being invited to abandon
their negative term. Second, the logic of Stott's critique of "inerrancy" is equally
applicable to "infallibility". For some of the more conservative English evangelicals,
the word inerrancy was not imported after Chicago-1978 because it was not seen to
add anything to their existing affirmation of infallibility. Stott accepts the view that
the terms are essentially synonymous when, in his introduction to his critique of
inerrancy he states, "whose equivalent in the British debate has been 'infallibility'."

It would be highly unlikely that Stott was unaware of the logic of his own
argument, or that his express inclusion of the word "infallible" was accidental.
Indeed he makes the parallel all the more explicit by describing "infallible" as
"equivalent" to "inerrant". Stott's demolition of inerrancy, albeit couched in terms
of making him "uncomfortable", simultaneously functions as an oblique assault, but
with equal force, against the term "infallible". This is all the more striking when we
note that this book was published by IVP, UCCF's publishing arm and Stott's
favoured conservative publishing house. IVP have customarily required their
authors' assent to the IVF/UCCF basis of faith, which includes the word "infallible".
The implicit logic of Stott's argument was that the time had come for UCCF to drop
the word "infallible" which had been integral to its bases of faith since IVF-1928.

In his diplomatic promotion of maximum evangelical unity, Stott seeks to affirm
the inerrantists and infallibilists as much as he can. In his conservatism, he seeks to
defend a high view of Scripture, but in positive terms and with an emphasis upon
practical, personal submission. But in his theological integrity, Stott clips the wings
of right-leaning evangelicals, exposing the deficiencies of their negative
formulations. Stott and Packer are both conservatives, but what marks out Stott is an
approach that can be described as instinctively conservative yet cautiously open. He
therefore affirmed inherent provisionality in the construct of evangelical faith –

> They have always expressed their readiness to modify, even abandon, any or all of their
> cherished beliefs if they can be shown to be unbiblical. [16]

Packer, by contrast, has never moved from his early convictions of uncompromising
conservatism.

> You cannot add to evangelical theology without subtracting from it. By augmenting it,
> you cannot enrich it; you can only impoverish it…The principle applies at point after
> point. What is more than evangelical is less than evangelical. Evangelical theology, by

---

[16] Stott, 1970: 32.

its very nature, cannot be supplemented; it can only be denied.[17]

Packer's doctrine of revelation endowed evangelical systematics with an absolutist epistemological exactitude and certitude. His calvinistic metanarrative is unambiguously totalising.[18] Packer leaves no room for Stott's acknowledgment of provisionality, and therefore for the continued evolution of the evangelical tradition. While Bebbington and Edwards concluded that the capacity to evolve was endemic to evangelicalism as a living theological tradition,[19] for Packer change implied retraction, evolution necessarily indicated departure from the evangelical givens and thus impoverishment. Packer was therefore inclined to endorse the exclusivities of north American neo-conservatism. Stott's call to engagement was seminal for the emergence of an open evangelicalism that subverted Packer's dogmatism with the charge that it was a good deal more culturally conditioned and thus less unassailably biblical than the Right had supposed.

Counter-trends are inevitably complex. Packer may appear to be a neo-fundamentalist, given his championing of biblical inerrancy, his partnership with Lloyd-Jones in the promotion of Puritanism (until excluded by the Welshman), and his reservations about the agenda of Nottingham-1977 (particularly in its innovatory tendency within evangelicalism to establish a new critical distance from the Reformation and in what he feared would prove a relativisation of biblical authority through the new hermeneutic). However, Packer has also faced accusations of being no longer fully conservative: in the 1960s from Lloyd-Jones' school given his willingness to work collaboratively with Anglo-Catholics, and in the 1990s from anti-Catholics given his willingness to engage in dialogue with Roman Catholics.[20]

---

[17] Stott, 1970: 33, quoting from an address Packer gave to the Fellowship of Evangelical Churchmen, 20 March 1961, subsequently published as *The Theological Challenge to Evangelicalism Today*. Contrast Mannheim's sociology of knowledge: "Such a system of meanings is possible and valid only in a given type of historical existence, to which, for a time, it furnishes appropriate expression. When the social situation changes, the system of norms to which it had previously given birth ceases to be in harmony with it...an ontology handed down through tradition obstructs new developments, especially in the basic modes of thinking, and as long as the particularity of the conventional theoretical framework remains unquestioned we will remain in the toils of a static mode of thought which is inadequate to our present stage of historical and intellectual development. What is needed, therefore, is a continual readiness to recognize that every point of view is particular to a certain definite situation and to find out through analysis of what this particularity consists." (Mannheim, 1936, quoted in Gill, 1996:87, 90). Packer's conservatism precludes conceptual and linguistic contingency.

[18] Packer not only acknowledged his particular dependence upon Calvin's *Institutes*, (Milne, 1982:6), but in the introduction to his bestseller, *Knowing God*, dismissed Arminianism and Deism as equivalent errors (1973:7). The notion that Arminians, unlike Deists, can claim legitimacy as a major sector within the evangelical tradition, let alone within Trinitarian orthodoxy, is rejected cavalierly by this calvinist-exclusivist.

[19] Bebbington, 1989; Edwards, 1987: 416, 431.

[20] McGrath, 1997.

Packer's contribution is simultaneously combative within evangelicalism, yet ecumenical beyond: paradoxically he has therefore faced severe criticism from both the evangelical left and the evangelical right. Notwithstanding the complexities of Packer's contrarian contribution, it is clear that Lausanne-1974 and Chicago-1978 offered mutually exclusive trajectories for evangelicals in the late twentieth century.[21]

Gospel Celebration 1999 - Penal Substitution

The Gospel of Jesus Christ: an Evangelical Celebration was published as a special supplement by *Christianity Today* on June 14, 1999.[22] Within North America many evangelicals and fundamentalists united around this document. *Christianity Today* promoted GC-1999 as a unifying document equivalent in stature to Lausanne-1974 and Chicago-1978. To reinforce these claims of historic significance, David Neff, Executive Editor of *Christianity Today*, in asserting that this publication was momentous, cited an anonymous church historian: "When, since *The Fundamentals*, has something like this happened?" The very comparison with the source documents of fundamentalism is indicative of the huge cultural chasm between English and American evangelicals. For many moderate English evangelicals to draw a parallel with *The Fundamentals* is sufficient to raise acute disquiet rather than expectancy.

The pivotal emphasis in GC-1999 is justification. It could more precisely be described not as "Gospel Celebration" but rather "Justification Celebration". Within the statement this is quite explicit, acknowledging "our extended analysis of justification by faith alone". Not only is justification by faith described as "essential to the Gospel" [23], but the doctrine of the atonement is said to require an acceptance

---

[21] The influence of the Chicago Statement, or at least its accurate representation of prevailing conservative convictions in the United States is demonstrated by the move to the right of students at evangelical colleges (Hunter, 1987, Penning and Smidt, 2002). The percentage agreeing with the following two statements shifted significantly in the inerrantist direction.
1) The Bible is the inspired Word of God, not mistaken in its statements and teachings, and is to be taken literally, word for word.
          1982   38%   1996   47%
2) The Bible is the inspired word of God, not mistaken in its teachings, but is not always to be taken literally in its statements concerning matters of science, historical reporting, etc.
          1982   50%   1996   41%
[22] Timothy George, Dean of Beeson Divinity School, announced In *Christianity Today*, 7 February, 2000, it had by then been endorsed by more than 200 evangelical leaders. This assemblage represented a strong North American coalition of conservatives and neo-fundamentalists. The drafting team, 'The Committee on Evangelical Unity in the Gospel', included Don Carson, Thomas Oden and James I. Packer. Signatories among evangelical theologians include Donald Bloesch, Gerald Bray, Wayne Grudem, Ron Sider and David Wells; among conservative preachers and leaders Bill Bright, Chuck Colson, Jerry Falwell, Jack Hayford, Bill Hybels, Tim LaHaye, Billy Graham, Luis Palau and Charles Swindoll.
[23] GC-1999. Since the statement is available in various formats, there is no standardised

of, using an Anselmic-Calvinist composite phrase, "substitutionary satisfaction of divine justice accomplished vicariously".[24] Any rejection of this model of the atonement is expressly stated to be incompatible with the Gospel.[25]

In his commentary on the statement, Timothy George identified a key influence in the development of this emphasis:

> But, as Jim Packer has reminded us, there are moments in the history of the church when the primacy of God's grace must be emphasised against elements that would dilute or qualify it. In our present culture of post modernity, we must not neglect a leading word about justification.[26]

Thus, GC-1999 endorses the agenda of the reformation and blithely assumes that this agenda has equivalent relevance faced with post modernity. Indeed it is reasonable to suppose that it is reactive against any contemporary distancing from, or relativising of, Reformation perspectives and emphases. It therefore makes assumptions that have been subject to considerable dispute in recent years in New Testament theology: that the theme of Galatians-Romans is central to Paul's teaching, rather than a distinctive emphasis of this particular correspondence in response to local needs; that this Pauline theme is the sole legitimate defining centre for New Testament soteriology and a canon within the canon; and that the Lutheran concept of justification is fully authentic and reliable as an interpretation of the New Testament, over against the new perspective on Paul.

When GC-1999 defined the Gospel so rigorously and exclusively in terms of justification, it implicitly acknowledged that justification has become its guiding interpretative principle, employing a calvinistic hermeneutic:

> This Gospel is the central message of the Holy Scriptures, and is the true key to understanding them.[27]

Just as justification by faith was understood by the reformers to be a central tenet and hermeneutical pivot of the New Testament, and the Gospel was articulated in such terms for their cultural setting, justification is now considered to be the necessary and only legitimate focal point for any postmodern interpretation or communication of the Gospel. The concept of diverse modes of discourse within the New Testament, consonant with different cultural contexts and equivalent to one another as parallel and alternative means of articulating the mystery of the Gospel is alien to GC-1999. Any divergence from calvinistic emphases is considered to entail a departure from the Gospel itself.

---

pagination to permit referencing by line number. See, for example, (accessed 15 May, 2007): http://ctlibrary.com/2231; http://members.aol.com/augusteen/EvanUnity.html; http:www. thiswebelieve.com/statement.htm.
[24] GC-1999.
[25] GC-1999.
[26] George, 2000.
[27] GC-1999.

Justification by faith is understood by GC-1999 specifically in terms of imputed righteousness.[28] Gundry argued that the reason the document repeatedly emphasises the salvific consequences of the life of Christ is this recurrent emphasis upon imputed righteousness, thereby endorsing a specific theological system that goes beyond the New Testament, which consistently and only emphasises the "righteousness of God".[29] Thus, GC-1999 not only gives pivotal emphasis to justification but also further requires assent to a traditional Protestant elaboration of the imputed righteousness of Christ as the *sine qua non* of soteriology.

GC-1999 acknowledges multiple models of atonement:

> the achieving of ransom, reconciliation, redemption, propitiation, and conquest of evil powers...[30]

At first sight this may seem a broad and inclusive recognition of the multiple metaphors of the New Testament. However, what is described in such a variety of terms, according to GC-1999, is not the atonement itself, but rather "this mighty substitutionary transaction".[31] Penal substitution is deemed the organising principle, the theological centre of gravity, around which the other models cluster as secondary descriptions. GC-1999 thus gives explicit and exclusive priority to penal substitution:

> Jesus paid our penalty in our place on his cross, satisfying the retributive demands of divine justice by shedding his blood in sacrifice and so making possible justification for all who trust in him...[32]

It is not merely the objective atonement, but penal substitution specifically that is described as an *essential element of the Gospel*. Penal substitution is thus not one model among many, nor even the primary model, but is taken to be synonymous with the atonement itself:

> We affirm that the atonement of Christ by which, in his obedience, he offered a perfect sacrifice, propitiating the Father by paying for our sins and satisfying divine justice on our behalf according to God's eternal plan, is an essential element of the Gospel.[33]

Consistent with this emphasis, propitiation is twice emphasised without any accompanying reference to expiation,[34] and substitution without any reference to representation.[35] In the companion statement of denial, the indispensability of penal

---

[28] GC-1999.
[29] Gundry, 2001.
[30] GC-1999.
[31] GC-1999.
[32] GC-1999.
[33] GC-1999.
[34] GC-1999.
[35] GC-1999.

substitution is made still more dogmatic, declaring any view of the atonement that rejects penal substitution to be incompatible with the Gospel.

> We deny that any view of the Atonement that rejects the substitutionary satisfaction of divine justice, accomplished vicariously for believers, is compatible with the teaching of the Gospel.[36]

Having asserted penal substitution to be the central meaning of the atonement, and therefore an essential, non-negotiable and core conviction of evangelical doctrine, GC-1999 allows no lassitude, no diversity:

> We deny that the doctrines of the Gospel can be rejected without harm. Denial of the Gospel brings spiritual ruin and exposes us to God's judgment.[37]

We noted an equivalent exclusivity in Chicago-78, where inerrancy was considered the essential and foundational conviction, which suggests that American conservatives make a habit of exclusivist assertions. (GC-1999 ironically falls foul of Chicago-78's strictures by preferring the term "infallible".[38]) In sum, penal substitution is not merely claimed as one among several biblical models of the atonement, or a distinctive historical emphasis of the evangelical tradition, but is deemed foundational to biblical interpretation, intrinsic to the gospel and prerequisite to salvation.

GC-1999 is narrowly calvinistic-exclusivist; it explicitly rejects alternative theologies, evangelical and non-evangelical alike, and shows no sympathies with Frei's "generous orthodoxy".[39] The statement omits any reference to spiritual gifts, and connects the empowering presence of the Spirit directly with conversion, precluding Pentecostal and some charismatic pneumatologies.

> ...all who have entrusted their lives to Jesus Christ are born again children of God (John 1:12), indwelt, empowered, and assured of their status and hope by the Holy Spirit...[40]

The anthropology is wholly negative, with no affirmation of any positive implications of the *imago dei*.[41] The sovereignty of God is affirmed in language that, while not specifically Calvinist, is plainly non-Arminian: "our faith...is itself the fruit of God's grace."[42] An expressly anti-Catholic soteriology is emphatic through repetition, not merely affirming justification by faith not works, but expressly denying Catholic teachings and leaving no room for inherent, infused or contributory works of righteousness.

---

[36] GC-1999.
[37] GC-1999.
[38] GC-1999.
[39] Frei, 1993.
[40] GC-1999.
[41] GC-1999.
[42] GC-1999.

We deny ...that the truth or authority of the Gospel rests on the authority of any particular church or human institution.[43]

We deny that any person can believe the biblical Gospel and at the same time reject the apostolic teaching of justification by faith alone in Christ alone.[44]

We deny that we are justified by the righteousness of Christ infused into us or by any righteousness that is thought to inhere within us.[45]

We deny that any works we perform at any stage of our existence add to the merit of Christ or earn for us any merit that contributes in any way to the ground of our justification...[46]

An expressly anti-liberal understanding of the divinity and bodily resurrection of Christ is presented as the necessary ground of salvation.

We deny that any view of Jesus Christ which reduces or rejects his full deity is Gospel faith or will avail to salvation.[47]

We deny that anyone who rejects the humanity of Christ, his incarnation, or his sinlessness, or who maintains that these truths are not essential to the Gospel, will be saved.[48]

We deny the validity of any so-called gospel that denies the historical reality of the bodily resurrection of Christ.[49]

Nor is there any obvious place for ecumenism, since the consequences of any departure from its formulations represents a "denial of the Gospel" and thus "brings spiritual ruin and exposes us to God's judgment".[50] While the actual nature of hell is not elaborated, the statement emphasises "eternal retributive judgment",[51] and is therefore inclined towards a literal understanding of the duration and nature of divine punishment. Unsurprisingly in this milieu, followers of other religions are expressly denied any grounds for hope.

The Bible offers no hope that sincere worshippers of other religions will be saved

---

[43] GC-1999.
[44] GC-1999.
[45] GC-1999.
[46] GC-1999.
[47] GC-1999.
[48] GC-1999.
[49] GC-1999.
[50] GC-1999.
[51] GC-1999.

without personal faith in Jesus Christ.[52]

Contrary to Lausanne-1974, GC-1999 fails to recognise any socio-political dimension intrinsic to the Gospel. The only references to such issues recognise first that Christians "are commanded to love each other despite differences of race, gender, privilege, and social, political, and economic background"[53] and second that the Gospel must be preached to all.[54] There is no suggestion that the consequence of love could be redistributive justice. All that is left of the societal dimension of Christian faith is philanthropic generosity - "acts of mercy and charity"[55] - stripped of broader and more radical socio-political dimensions. Nor is there any suggestion that the righteousness of God has implications for society as well as the church. The sole task to which GC-1999 commits its adherents is evangelism; the broader understanding of mission has all but disappeared. If the Church of England used to be the Tory party at prayer, American neo-conservative evangelicals are evidently the Republican Right at prayer.

The chasm between Nottingham-1977, where Packer was an increasingly disaffected participant, and GC-1999, where he was a member of the drafting team, is immense. And this is more than a difference of theological emphasis. While Nottingham-1977 allows for, indeed affirms, diversity of opinion among evangelicals, GC-1999 expressly disavows the legitimacy of any interpretation other than its own. According to GC-1999, to depart from it formulations is to depart from the Gospel, which means, logically, that it required some leading contributors to Nottingham-1977, as well as Arminians and Pentecostals, post-conservatives and open theists, no longer to be recognised as evangelicals, or even as authentic Christians. GC-1999 was conservatism's uncompromising riposte to the rising tide of open and postmodern evangelical theology.

This celebration of justification and penal substitution presents itself as a timeless and culture-free articulation of Gospel truth. Therefore the innovatory emphasis of Lausanne-1974, at least among evangelicals, upon cultural conditioning and the recognition that there is no such thing as truth in a culture-free form, is necessarily discounted. Engagement with the wider world of theology and diverse denominations, in other words Stott's cautiously open trajectory, is effectively precluded. Nor is there any obvious place for ecumenism, since the consequences of any departure from its formulations represents a "denial of the Gospel" and thus "brings spiritual ruin and exposes us to God's judgment".[56] GC-1999 is written as if the previous 30 or more years of constructive re-engagement by evangelicals had not happened. It is theology for the ghetto. If Lausanne-1974 presented itself as the "new face of evangelicalism", GC-1999 is the new face of the Right, a collaboration between calvinistic conservatism and neo-fundamentalism.

---

[52] GC-1999.
[53] GC-1999.
[54] GC-1999.
[55] GC-1999.
[56] GC-1999.

The contrast with EA-1846 is striking. The foundational basis that formalised evangelical identity affirmed "divine inspiration, authority and sufficiency" and emphasised crucicentricity with no exploration of penal substitution. EA-1846 affirmed the right of private judgment, expressly rejected (in its supplementary clauses) "the right authoritatively to define the limits of Christian brotherhood", and emphasised (in the accompanying General Resolutions) the need to "disclaim the thought, that those only who openly join this Society are sincere friends to the cause of Christian Union". Similarly, the 1996 "Practical Resolutions" affirmed:

> We recognise that not all who seek to know and serve Christ as Saviour and Lord, will wish to be members of the Alliance and that such persons are not, thereby, to be regarded as being out of Christian fellowship.

Here is an irenic, inclusive, non-judgmental approach, that affirms a broad framework of evangelical convictions while declining to elaborate contentious specifics, and rejects any suggestion that assent to specific evangelical formulations determines a boundary coterminous with Trinitarian orthodoxy.

The approach of GC-1999, mandating conformity to a systematic framework of elaborated and disputed specifics, could not be more different. From the perspective of GC-1999, EA-1846 fails to pass muster: it is sub-evangelical, a deficient account of the doctrinal assent necessary to qualify as legitimately, fully and uncompromisingly evangelical. If GC-1999 was correct in proposing such an elaborate soteriology as primary and non-negotiable doctrine, it stood as a damning indictment of the ecumenical breadth of the last 150 years of pan-evangelical bases of faith. However, from the perspective of EA-1846, GC-1999 replaces minimal biblical orthodoxy that sought maximal ecumenical unity with minimal inclusivity that promotes maximal, and indeed fundamentalising, conformity. Viewed from the older and broader evangelical tradition, GC-1999 represents a severe constriction of authentic pan-evangelicalism in favour of fundamentalism and neo-conservatism, a disputatious dismemberment of the evangelical coalition. It is over-dogmatic, sectarian, and uncompromisingly divisive.

The severity with which Chicago-1978 and GC-1999 delineate the boundaries of legitimate diversity, indeed essentially preclude diversity, has an obvious implication: if hard line conservatives really take their stand on what Chicago-1978 and GC-1999 unapologetically assert, they have positioned themselves as the sole legitimate expression of contemporary evangelicalism. The biblicist-crucicentric axis within pan-evangelicalism has begun to divide, probably irrevocably, against itself.

Chapter 11

Progressive Evangelicals: The Post-Conservative Emergence, 1996-2000

We have seen that from 1846 to 1981 there was a consistent trend in evangelical bases of faith, with the sole exception of the minimalist orthodoxy of 1912, towards increasing elaboration and increasing exclusivity. In particular, from the 1920s, fundamentalism appears to have had a magnetic influence upon evangelicalism, drawing each revision of a basis of faith rightwards. In the 1990s the emergent trend of Lausanne-1974 and Nottingham-1977 was more widely adopted, instilling a new willingness to reject the rightwards trend and develop post-fundamentalist frameworks of evangelical theology.

EA-1996

The National Assembly of Evangelicals in Bournemouth in 1996 was the climax to the 150th anniversary celebrations of the Evangelical Alliance. It was the final achievement of Calver's leadership, although by the time of the Assembly Calver was temporarily restricted by unstable blood pressure. By the end of the Assembly, Calver concluded that he needed to stand aside for Joel Edwards to take charge.[1]

Previously, Calver had avoided organising an Assembly, fearing any repetition of the divisive debacle of 1966. In the event, the Assembly went off quietly, perhaps too quietly since some complained that the event had been over-managed. The only hint of a storm came when Roy Clements (independent Baptist and doyen of the Right, who in the late 1990s came out as a practising homosexual, left his wife and church and became an advocate of gay rights) declared publicly that the Church of England should be disestablished. Unlike the 1960s, there was no corrective comment from the chair and the disputatious moment passed without public storm.

During the Assembly, a working group constructed the Bournemouth Declaration. While the event was deliberately designated at Calver's insistence "the national assembly of evangelicals", thereby indicating an intended inclusivity wider than the Evangelical Alliance, the concluding statement was designated the "Bournemouth Declaration of the Evangelical Alliance (UK)". This implicitly suggests either dissent from the right or a desire by the nascent post-Calver leadership of EA to reassert the public prominence of their organisation.

---

[1] Stated in personal interview.

The Declaration combined a series of theological affirmations with a proposed new agenda for evangelicals, the topics for which were derived from the seminar groups of the event. Each seminar was allotted a brief phrase that sought to encapsulate its insights. The Declaration broke significant ground both in theology and in tone. The document was split into three main sections, each of which combined a theological prologue with a series of action points: *Christ, Scripture and Unity*; *Church and Mission*; *God and Society*.

In *Christ, Scripture and Unity*, unity was given a prominence, by no means always evident in the evangelical tradition with its endemic fissiparous tendencies. This may reflect Calver's often repeated assertion that in times of weakness evangelicals unite, but in times of relative strength - which was how evangelicals perceived themselves by the mid-1990s, even though our analysis indicates their self-confidence was exaggerated and misplaced - they have a self-destructive tendency to fight among themselves. Three aspects of Christ's work are affirmed as central to Christian faith: "atoning death", "bodily resurrection" and "personal return". The phrasing is more succinct, less prescriptive than EA-1970 and UCCF-1981. The only subsequent reference to the atonement refers to "new life through the Cross". The objectivity of the atonement is thus affirmed but not defined.

The document is equally Christocentric concerning revelation. Christ is affirmed as "God's Word incarnate". Thus, "supreme authority is his". The Bible is then affirmed as "God's Word written", and is described as "definitive, normative and sufficient revelation". Just as the objectivity of the atonement is asserted without reference to penal substitution, the unique revelatory status of Scripture is asserted without reference to infallibility or inerrancy. This is in accordance with the EA bases, which represent the older and broader approach to divine inspiration. However, the document is more obviously neo-Barthian than EA-1970 in two ways. First, it affirms the priority of Christ as the Incarnate Word, rendering Scripture secondary. Second, the phrase "supreme authority", traditionally conferred by evangelicals upon the Bible is reserved for Christ himself. The understanding of revelation is thus orthodox but rigorously Christocentric, modifying conventional evangelical phraseology to avoid any charge of bibliolatry.[2]

On the basis of these affirmations of salvation and revelation, nuanced in such a way as to be recognisably evangelical but to the left of EA-1970, the Bournemouth Declaration took an unexpected turn. Given the sometimes (even often) deserved reputation of evangelicals for excessive dogmatism and consequent arrogance, the statement introduces a welcome note of failure and contrition, repenting "neglect of Scripture" and acknowledging "failure to maintain unity". This regretful and self-critical tone is reiterated in the conclusion, which more generally speaks of repentance for "our past failures". Here are indications of a new evangelicalism in

---

[2] Not that this approach satisfies every critic of evangelicalism. Barton (1993, 1997) argues that a neo-Barthian formula that affirms the primacy of the Word Incarnate and allocates a secondary authority to the Bible can still in practice co-exist with a quasi-fundamentalist conservatism.

the tradition of Lausanne, willing to acknowledge its own faults rather than merely berate the deficiencies of others.

Unity is affirmed as God's gift and intention for his people. The purpose of God, according to the Declaration, is that invisible oneness should find visible expression. While not anti-ecumenical, in the manner of many mid-twentieth century separatist formulations, the Declaration affirms a non-institutional centre of gravity for ecumenicity - "primarily through our shared commitment to God's Word, to each other and to his work."

The practical outcomes of the affirmation of unity implicitly recognise that pan-evangelicalism had become a broad coalition and reject the narrow conformity of fundamentalism, calling upon evangelicals to "affirm diversity" and to "treat one another with grace".

Two further statements recognise a lack of clarity within the evangelical tradition. First, the Declaration urges evangelicals to "work together with integrity" in order to "attempt to distinguish primary from secondary issues". Here is a double acknowledgment: first that this work had not previously been done, so that evangelical divisions may have occurred over what might have been considered secondary issues rather than non-negotiables; second, that this clarification should be *attempted*, rather than necessarily accomplished, which represents a realistic acknowledgment that one evangelical's incidental personal preference may be another's principled conviction upon which no compromise can be contemplated.

Second, evangelicals were invited to explore the extent to which "differing terminology can properly express the same truth". Here is a dramatic turn against propositionalism, acknowledging that "truth" finds a partial and provisional expression in any particular formulation. In part this represents an implicit repudiation of the mind-set behind the "inerrancy" debate, which attempted to enforce assent to a particular terminology as the decisive test of evangelical orthodoxy. However, the implications run much wider. If the suggested approach were accepted, and the Declaration goes no further than propose further consideration, several evangelical shibboleths are up for grabs: first, the very attempt to provide a once for all basis of faith, defining the boundaries of evangelical orthodoxy, is brought into question; second, the requirement of some organisations to sign their particular basis of faith in order to participate in their activities could be deemed unjustifiable, even arbitrary;[3] third, evangelical terminology is relativised, for language itself begins to be seen as intrinsically approximate, metaphorical, culture bound, subjective and allusive.[4] While hardly Derridean, this understanding of language as essentially metaphorical rejects the attempts of modernist conservatives to systematise evangelical theology with

---

[3] Notably, Douglas Johnson rejected Donald Coggan from further IVF involvement when the future Archbishop balked at the infallibilist clause - an emphasis which, as we have demonstrated, has never appeared in any EA basis of faith. Barclay, 1997; Barclay and Horn, 2002

[4] Derrida, 1974; Gadamer, 1975; Thiselton, 1980; Soskice, 1985; Rorty, 1989; Wittgenstein, 2001.

mathematical precision. It therefore marginalises to the footnotes of evangelical history the formulaic approaches of the Princetonians, recognising their contributions to be a dead-end, based on naïve , culture bound and discredited presuppositions, rather than a definitive and binding framework for future evangelical theology. This marks a new willingness to relativise verbal formulations of Christian faith.

The approach to mission is emphatically Trinitarian. The list of tasks is not so much a coherent agenda as an inchoate catalogue of varieties of activist engagement; the specific content is essentially arbitrary, being derived from the list of topics for the seminars at the Assembly, which had been drawn up by a working group over breakfast at a London hotel. The omission, therefore, of any reference to worship, preaching, relational evangelism and so on, does not entail a new policy or emphasis within pan-evangelicalism, but merely indicates these issues were not addressed in the seminars. What is significant is a persistent call to new and creative engagement. The agenda items are laboured and repetitive but indicate clear awareness of the need for the re-invention of mission and the re-imagining of the church. Once again, the Declaration is not offering solutions, nor defending yesterday's expressions of church as intrinsic to evangelical orthodoxy, but is rather calling for a new openness to the future and a new willingness to promote culturally specific experimentation, both consequent upon the priority of mission.

Despite the fact that the second section was entitled *Church and Mission*, the actual content focussed more narrowly upon evangelism. The wider issues of social action and justice were deferred to the final section entitled *God and Society*. This affirms an all-embracing mission agenda in the tradition of Lausanne-1974, seeking to be incarnational and transformational. Although there is the barest hint of ecological responsibility - "stewardship over all he has made" - this is not developed in the details, which focus upon human relations. Traditional issues of personal ethics - "the sanctity of human life", "responsible family living" - are conjoined with social justice and international issues - "peace and reconciliation", "justice and compassion". All forms of racism are repudiated, along with all other tendencies to "marginalise", and so evangelicals are called to work to "break down barriers of prejudice".

Just as the ecological dimension is omitted, which was surprising by the mid-1990s, so is sexism, apparently subsumed under the category of "prejudice" and "marginalisation". Whether an unfortunate oversight, or omitted because the Right wing was not yet convinced that sexism was as unacceptable as racism, in this regard evangelicals showed themselves to be politically inept and culturally out of step. Since by 2001,[5] there was still no woman among the staff directorate of the EA, the only woman on the senior team at Spring Harvest had responsibility for family ministry, and few women were asked to speak on the main platforms at evangelical events, the omission in 1996 of any explicit repudiation of sexism was no mere accident. Those evangelicals who affirm in principle gender equality in

---

[5] The first was eventually appointed in 2003.

work, marriage and ministry[6] are yet to address the issue of institutional sexism within their own organisations and events, and develop strategies that implement gender equality in practice.

The conclusion to the Bournemouth Declaration is characteristically activist and over-reaching. Delegates were invited to commit themselves to "pray and work together" and to "equip and mobilise Christians of all ages in pursuit of this agenda". The rhetoric ran away with the conclusion. The Declaration was being presented as more than it could be. The Evangelical Alliance was presuming for itself an anachronistically quasi-denominational role in a post-institutional era. An event was misconceived as a movement; a declaration was misdefined as an agenda.[7]

The Declaration certainly set the agenda for the EA internally, since it became the basis for the manifesto with which Joel Edwards habitually described the activities of the staff of EA until he developed "Movement for Change" as his long-term vision for pan-evangelicalism. However, there was little or no reference to the Declaration beyond the EA staff, among the affiliated denominations, member organisations or local churches.[8] The EA may have misunderstood its own Assembly, for this Declaration had no authority, no ownership, and no mandate as a decisive framework for subsequent evangelical initiatives. The evangelical coalition is far too diverse, fragmented and independent-minded to be shaped in the ways the Declaration proposed.

Nonetheless, the Declaration carried a greater significance theologically than was recognised at the time. It marked the closure of pre-Lausanne narrowness, with its adventurous embrace of a socio-political agenda. It also marked a decisive rejection of the fundamentalist undertow. EA-1996 proposed a theological agenda that would ask creative questions rather than be content with defending a previous generation's formulations of evangelicalism. Bournemouth failed to set a new agenda for evangelical action beyond the staff of the Evangelical Alliance, but it denotes a sea change in the evangelical consensus. Like Matthew Arnold's sea of faith ineluctably receding from Dover Beach,[9] English evangelical theology was showing evidence of

---

[6] According to a survey we have undertaken and hope to publish in due course, they appear to represent the substantial majority of British evangelicals today.

[7] The word "agenda" occurs in the subtitle, the introductory paragraph and the concluding statement.

[8] In conversation, Martyn Eden, then a senior staff member with EAUK, described the non-theological formulations of EA-1996 as a "quasi-political act", while Robert Amess, subsequently Chair of EA Council, described the wording as the result of "late night lobbying behind the scenes". Strikingly, the theological wording was not subject to such political negotiations, perhaps indicating the extent to which an a-theological pragmatism had overtaken popular evangelicalism during the dominance of the conversionist-activist axis.

[9]   The sea of faith
        Was once, too, at the full, and round earth's shore
        Lay like the folds of a bright girdle furl'd;
        But now I only hear

a tidal drift away from the conservative *idées reçues*. As the era of entrepreneurial identity waned, its pragmatism, critique of obdurate conservativism and promotion of culturally consonant experimentation all prepared the way, however unintentionally, for the progressive trajectories of the resurgent biblicist-crucicentric axis. A thoroughgoing theological reconstruction of evangelicalism, probably more radical than was apparent at the time, was endorsed at Calver's last major initiative, EA-1996.

London Bible College-1998

Derek Tidball returned to London Bible College as Principal in 1995, having previously been on staff from 1977-1985,[10] and in February 1998, London Bible College adopted a new "doctrinal basis". This was adapted from a new "Statement of Beliefs" agreed by Scripture Union International in Harare, Zimbabwe in 1985. LBC-1998/SU-1985 is corporate rather than individualistic, expressed in the repeated phrase "we believe". It has a liturgical rhythm and a doxological tone, reinforced by its versiform layout. If presented as prescriptive, it would be far too elaborate and verbose. Understood as doxological, it can be interpreted as permission giving, setting out a broad landscape of orthodoxy rather than pursuing the restrictive details of bases to its right. Significantly, in its prologue the very word "evangelical" is eschewed, preferring to identify more broadly with the "historic truths of Christian faith and conduct".

The basis begins with God, an approach first seen in IVF-1959 and EA-1970. But LBC-1998 is structured upon a highly developed Trinitarian schema, which gives shape to its first two thirds before it turns to the Scriptures, Church and Mission.

A positive anthropology is presented, alongside recognition of fall and judgment: humanity – employing gender inclusive language - is made in God's image, which confers "dignity and worth" upon all. Implicitly this points to the themes of justice and liberty addressed in the concluding section.

> Its melancholy, long, withdrawing roar,
> Retreating to the breath
> Of the night-wind down the vast edges drear
> And naked shingles of the world.
>
> from Dover Beach

Arnold's elegiac and wistful finality ignores the inevitability of the tide's return, which unintentionally subverts his metaphor.

[10] After leaving LBC, Tidball had been Senior Minister at Mutley Baptist in Plymouth, where Ian Coffey, a graduate of LBC, former staff worker for the EA and member of the Spring Harvest leadership team, now serves. During his time away from LBC, Tidball had been appointed chair of Mainstream, the evangelical and charismatic Baptist ginger group, President of the Baptist Union and then Secretary for Evangelism of the Baptist Union in succession to David Coffey, who became General Secretary. Derek Tidball was also a Vice President of the Evangelical Alliance and in 2004 became Chair of EA Council. Tidball's pedigree in English evangelicalism is impeccable.

Atonement is explored in four ways. First, in terms of justifying grace - "putting sinners right with himself when they place their trust in his Son." Then, in a threefold exploration of the cross: in terms of a representative (the word substitute is not used, but may be inferred) who secures expiation and propitiation ("redeeming... from the grip, guilt and punishment of sin"); in terms of the Second Adam, the head of the new humanity who overcomes death; and in terms of *Christus Victor*. The LBC version then appends, slightly disjointedly, a further dimension of Christology, to complete its paragraph on confessing Jesus Christ as Lord and God - "the Word who makes God known."

This approach to the atonement offers a middle path. While some traditional evangelicals have championed penal substitution as the pivotal, or even the sole adequate interpretation of the atonement, other theologians and moral philosophers have questioned the exegetical, systematic, ethical or missiological legitimacy of penal substitution as a way of exploring the atonement,[11] LBC-1998 offers penal substitution as one aspect within one of four models of the atonement. (The

---

[11] Vincent Taylor argued that "Penal substitution is a notion which modern Christianity has no option but to discard." (Taylor, 1940: 10). John Macquarrie dismissed penal substitution out of hand as self-evidently unreasonable and morally repugnant: "...an example of the kind of doctrine which, even if it could claim support from the Bible or the history of theology, would still have to be rejected because of the affront which it offers to reason and conscience." (1977: 315 - see also Lampe, 1962). Fiddes (1989) asserts but fails to demonstrate that penal substitution was located within Calvin's cultural context where justice was conceived retributively. For a subtle defence of the necessary objectivity of Christ as substitute, shifting the emphasis from models to metaphors of the atonement, and emphatically rejecting penal substitution, see Gunton (1988). For the new perspective on Paul, see Sanders 1977; Dunn, 1983, 1988a, 1998b, 1993, 1998; Wright 1991, 1996, 2002. For moderate evangelical defences of penal substitution that are critical of simplistic over-elaborations of the model and of crude polarisations between the Father and the Son, see Carey, 1986; Stott, 1989. For a progressive critique of penal substitution, see the St John's College, Nottingham symposium (Goldingay, 1995), to which Oak Hill College provided the uncompromising rebuttal of calvinistic conservatism (Peterson, 2001). Packer's 1973 Tyndale Lecture remains the most robust and unreconstructedly conservative evangelical defence of penal substitution, forcefully coherent in its own terms (Packer, 1974; see also Morris, 1955, 1983). Reformed evangelicals give no ground in defence of the penal theory, viewed as a *sine qua non* of soteriology – "the vital center of the atonement, the linchpin without which everything else loses its foundation" (Nicole in Hill and James, 2004: 451). Hill and James' contributors often have in their sights Green and Baker's (2000) exploration of the implications of multiple metaphors for evangelical atonement theology. As with publishing Carson but not Pinnock, IVP UK publish Hill and James but not Green and Baker, despite both being published by IVP USA. IVP UK appears to seek to sustain the mythic homogeneity of evangelical theology, coterminous with calvinistic conservatism. Chalke's repudiation of penal substitution as a form of divine child abuse (Chalke and Mann, 2003) resulted in the EA convening a day conference in Autumn 2004, followed by an academic conference jointly sponsored with LTS in Summer 2005. It is striking that this long-standing theological debate apparently only registered with EAUK as a result of a ghost-written populist book by a self-confessed non-academic personality preacher.

Abelardian, subjective model of the atonement is subsumed under the category of the Second Adam, and thus connected with the objectivity of the death of death in the bodily resurrection. Although in conservative evangelical theology, penal substitution and justification are treated as almost synonymous, LBC-1998 deftly separates justification as an over-arching soteriological category from the threefold models of atonement that follow.) LBC-1998 neither rejects nor absolutises penal substitution, but relativises it as one aspect among many within a broad soteriological understanding.[12]

On the Holy Spirit, LBC-1998 gives comprehensive coverage to the dimensions of the work of the Spirit often selectively treated in the previous evangelical bases Moreover it adds specific reference to spiritual fruit and gifts in a way that takes account of the charismatic movement while rejecting any mandatory conjunction of the baptism of the Spirit with the gift of tongues.

The dual authorship of the Scriptures and their full trustworthiness and supreme authority are affirmed, with no reference to infallibility or inerrancy. LBC-1998 then adds a further paragraph, not present in SU-1985, emphasising the importance of rightful interpretation. This represents evangelicals taking seriously biblical criticism and hermeneutics, affirming the importance of reason and scholarship.

Evangelism is emphasised by reference to the Great Commission, adhering closely to Matthew 28:19-20.[13] In the following paragraph, love of neighbours is the foundation for a resounding affirmation of social responsibility, requiring not only acts of compassion but also the active pursuit of socio-political righteousness: seeking reconciliation, proclaiming liberty, spreading Christ's justice. Here is not merely a call to practical kindness but the kernel of an evangelical liberation theology.

The concluding phrase is doxological - "until he comes again". Eschatology is freed from any secondary or speculative detail. There is nothing about the nature of Christ's coming, the nature of subsequent judgment, or the condition (eternal or non-eternal, literal or metaphorical) of the damned. Here is a discreet minimalism. More than that, the energy of eschatology is focussed in accordance with the New Testament, concentrating not upon speculative future prospects, but rather upon present priorities in the light of eternal hope. The impact of eschatology is not an otherworldly disengagement but rather a down-to-earth pursuit of justice and proclamation of the Good News.

Given the history of LBC, and the institution's previously recurrent difficulties in coming to terms with less conservative convictions, this represents a highly significant about face. The forced departures of some of its leading scholars trace the slow journey of disengagement of evangelicals from fundamentalistic

---

[12] Tidball's conclusion conserves yet re-contextualizes the conservative tradition: "I believe strongly the traditional evangelical theory is defensible and indispensable. But I also believe that the Bible's teaching about the Cross is much broader than that." *Baptist Times*, 30 August, 2001: 11.

[13] SU-1985 dropped the Matthean phrase "baptising them" presumably because of the delicate sensibilities of some paedobaptist supporters of their ecumenical organisation.

trajectories. In 1954, H.L. Ellison was obliged to resign after writing an article for *The Evangelical Quarterly* that was considered to espouse a Barthian view of the Bible. The minutes of the LBC Directors' meeting noted that complaints had been received from "members of the tutorial staff and by a number of friends, including Dr. Martyn Lloyd-Jones." [14] (Barth had been praised in the magazine of the Evangelical Alliance in 1930 and the organisation held a reception for him in London in 1937. This indicates a broad evangelical inclusivity at odds with Lloyd-Jones' obdurate exclusivity.) Ten years later, Ralph Martin wrote articles for *The Churchman* that praised Barth and Bonhoeffer. This provoked a storm of controversy that resulted in the board being told that he tended to "confuse the line between conservative and liberal views". [15] After Martin agreed to leave, he was told privately that he could remain on staff, teaching the New Testament but not doctrine. In 1976, Leslie Allen's commentary on Jonah argued that the book was in the form of a parable, even though there may be "a historical nucleus behind the story". [16] John Waite, a former LBC staff member, condemned Allen's approach in a review for *The Evangelical Times*. At this time, London Bible College was under assault from the Reformed Right, who set up the more conservative London Theological Seminary in 1977. At its opening, Lloyd-Jones denounced Bible colleges that allowed curricula to be shaped by "the liberal outlook", and repudiated examinations in the Old and New Testament as "almost blasphemous". [17] LBC was implicitly, but obviously, under his calvinistic cosh. Lloyd-Jones and his followers were charting a course into the separatist wilderness of an extreme and exclusive Reformed isolationism. Unlike Ellison and Martin, Allen was not obliged to leave, but he was moved into a safer post, teaching Hebrew, Aramaic and Judaism. It was further suggested that he might be more suited to university teaching, and he was asked to present a "balanced view" in his lectures and writings. [18] Although a public letter written by the Chairman of the Board to those who had complained about Allen, insisted that LBC "respects the integrity of its Faculty", [19] by normal university standards this attitude to academic liberty and integrity was repressive and coercive. However, by the turn of the century, Ellison, Martin and Allen's conclusions had become uncontentious among many moderate English evangelicals. The militant conservatism of their opponents, still championed by the successors to Lloyd-Jones, seems no longer capable of dominating the centre ground of contemporary evangelical discourse. As the evangelical tradition continues to evolve, just as it always has in theology and in practice, the distance between the mainstream majority and the militant right wing, whether designated

---

[14] Minutes of LBC Directors' meeting, 19 November 1954, quoted in Randall, 2000: 86.

[15] Minutes of LBC Governors' meeting, 29 July 1964, quoted in Randall, 2000: 128.

[16] Allen, 1976: 179. Perhaps surprisingly, the series editor for the *New International Commentary on the Old Testament* was R.K. Harrison, Barr's (1977) exemplar of reactionary conservatism.

[17] Randall, 2000: 206.

[18] Minutes of LBC Governors' meeting, 25 January 1980, quoted in Randall, 2000: 206.

[19] Randall, 2000: 207.

"fundamentalist", "ultra-conservative" or "uncompromisingly Reformed" is likely to become ever more of a chasm. LBC-1998 is a remarkable manifesto of open evangelicalism, arising from an institution non-evangelicals have traditionally considered a bastion of unyielding conservatism or even fundamentalism.

The SU statement was accompanied by an account of its "basic philosophy" that was subsequently developed into a framework of working principles[20] clarifying the organisation's approach to evangelism and teaching, Bible ministries, churches, equality and unity, volunteers and staff. Within a comprehensive account of priorities in each area, the following aspects are striking. First, there is an emphasis upon integrity: evangelists should "guard against calling for superficial responses"; biblical standards should apply to publicity, care for staff and volunteers and fund-raising that avoids "distorting the truth or using undue pressure". Second, there is an emphasis upon communication that is contemporary and culturally appropriate. Third, there is an emphasis upon promoting Bible reading that invites engagement with the "message of the whole Bible rather than...isolated passages". Hermeneutical issues are acknowledged in the express concern to interpret the text "in a way which enables people, in their contemporary situations, to hear for themselves the message of the Bible from its original context". Fourth there is an emphasis upon social justice - "The Gospel has inescapable social dimensions." This entails special responsibility for children who are "poor, deprived or exploited", and the need to treat everyone as of equal worth in God's sight. The document cites five kinds of discrimination that are expressly excluded - "race, colour, gender, language or social position". Fifth there is an emphasis upon mutual respect and an affirmation of legitimate diversity: expressing Christian commitment in "varied and creative ways"; handling controversial issues, "such as baptism, spiritual gifts and church order" so as to "promote harmony"; and seeking to establish indigenous leadership in each nation rather than fostering long-term dependence upon foreign leaders, since the Spirit "confers gifts of leadership on Christians of all nations without discrimination".

These enlightened working practices underline the sense of a new wind blowing through evangelicalism at the end of the twentieth century. A moderated evangelicalism, eschewing the remnants of the fundamentalist legacy, was endeavouring to articulate a contemporary orthopraxy, based upon integrity, respect for all and justice for the poor.

IVCF-2000

We turn now to the last, and in some ways the most remarkable pan-evangelical basis of faith of the twentieth century, agreed by the Board of Trustees of the

---

[20] Reproduced, but undated, on the SU international website - www.su-international.org. Accessed 2 August 2002. The "basic philosophy" was agreed in Madras, November 1980, developed from the statement agreed in Lausanne, 1967.

American equivalent to UCCF in October 2000.[21] Whereas the bases of the 1990s were fairly verbose, IVCF-2000 returns to the earlier succinct approach. It comprises 221 words, compared with 241 for EA-1970, 199 for UCCF-1974, and 311 for UCCF-1981. It therefore invites comparison with previous bases as an account of contemporary evangelical convictions. It follows precisely the clause order of EA-1970, but is consistently more positive in tone and to the left of EA-1970.

IVCF-2000 begins with an affirmation of a creedal community and ends with an expression of praise, presenting itself therefore as essentially doxological, as with EA-1996 and LBC-1998/SU-1985. The first clause affirms God as Creator and sums up the Trinity as "full of love and glory". Two emphases in EA-1970 are missing: sovereignty and judgment.

Clause 2, on the Bible, is shorter than EA-1970, without the details "supreme" and "in all matters of faith and conduct". IVCF-2000 is therefore less emphatic than EA-1970, let alone the infallible and inerrant bases.

Clause 3 introduces a positive anthropology - created in God's image - with a resultant emphasis upon the "value and dignity of all people", whereas EA-1970 conforms to the more conventional pattern of only emphasising sinfulness and guilt. "Value and dignity of all" has inevitable, if not explicit, implications in terms of racism, sexism and all other kinds of discriminatory prejudice. The phrase "justly subject to God's wrath" represents a softening from "subject to God's wrath and condemnation".

Clause 4 retains an emphasis upon penal substitution, which is the only acknowledged theory of the atonement. However, the clause is more Christological than soteriological.

Clause 5 retains emphasis upon justification solely by grace through faith, but makes the clause more positive, with divine grace more prominent.

Clause 6 on the Holy Spirit provides an equivalent emphasis to EA-1970, while avoiding technical diction. Unlike LBC-1998, there is no explicit reference to spiritual fruit and gifts.

Clause 7 provides a more coherent and complete account of the church than EA-1970. Where EA-1846 had emphasised ordained ministry and EA-1970 had reversed this emphasis, IVCF-2000 avoids any emphasis upon either clergy or laity, preferring instead to emphasise three key priorities for the local church, namely worship, witness and disciple-making.

---

[21] The Basis of Faith that Inter Varsity Christian Fellowship, USA used for over fifty years was adopted from the Nyack Missionary College in Nyack, New York, and listed the following five convictions:
  -The unique divine inspiration, entire trustworthiness and authority of the Bible;
  -The deity of our Lord Jesus Christ;
-The necessity and efficacy of the substitutionary death of Jesus Christ for the redemption of the world and the historic fact of his bodily resurrection;
  -The presence and power of the Holy Spirit in the work of regeneration;
  -The expectation of the personal return of our Lord Jesus Christ.

Clause 8 is also better balanced. The word "visible" is dropped, along with the cumbersome "expectation of". The connection between parousia and judgment is made explicit, but the last judgment is given a more positive cast by the clarification "with justice and mercy". This contrasts with "wrath and condemnation" in clause three of EA-1970. The phrase "eternal condemnation" insists upon the finality and inescapability of last judgment, but avoids any specifics concerning consequences for the condemned, in common with EA-1970 and the IVF/UCCF bases.

In contrast with UCCF-1980, IVCF-2000 makes no attempt to be exhaustive, preferring the simplicity of an outline of core convictions. Given that for the last 150 years the American contribution to pan-evangelical bases has been normatively conservative (the 1846 American clause, fundamentalism, WEF-1951, Chicago-1978, GC-1999) IVCF-2000 is exceptional. It is a revision to the left of EA-1970; it seeks to be sensitive to the perspectives of the unchurched and non-evangelicals,[22] consistently finds a positive emphasis - "love and glory", "value and dignity", "justice and mercy". In sum, it seeks to extricate progressive evangelicalism from neo-fundamentalism, refusing to be constrained by the preoccupations that had become intrinsic to the fundamentalist-influenced mid to late twentieth century pan-evangelical heritage.

EA-2005

On 17 February 2005 the Council of the Evangelical Alliance agreed to adopt a new basis of faith. Although it falls outside our period of primary investigation, it would be remiss not to consider its significance. Derek Tidball, appointed Chair of EA Council in 2004, commended it warmly: "It elegantly expresses the essentials of Evangelical faith, and defines clearly what underpins the Alliance's ministry and mission." [23] David Hilborn, EA's Head of Theology and co-ordinator of the revision process, observed: "I am delighted with the new Basis of Faith. It runs to roughly the same number of words as the previous version and maintains what was affirmed there, but manages more fully to reflect the witness of Scripture. The old version said nothing about the virgin birth, personal conversion, the ascension or the general resurrection. This covers all of those areas and says a good deal more about God's love and justice as well. It is expressed in clear and precise terms suited to the Alliance's ministry and mission in the 21st Century." [24]

Notwithstanding Hilborn's assertion, the law of increasing prolixity still applies. The new basis has 295 words, longer than every previous EA basis and longer than every version of the IVF-UCCF basis except UCCF-1981 (311 words). Hilborn's

---

[22] Bramadat (2000) explores this characteristic yet paradoxical evangelical combination of intentional accessibility with self-protecting distance.

[23] www.eauk.org/contentmanager/Content/press/media/files/basisoffaith.cfm. Accessed 9 September 2005.

[24] www.eauk.org/contentmanager/Content/press/media/files/basisoffaith.cfm. Accessed 9 September 2005.

declared intention was to increase the comprehensiveness of the EA basis, establishing greater parity with the conciliar creeds. This is in striking contrast to the pre-fundamentalist emphasis upon minimal evangelical distinctives to maximise inclusion. Comprehensiveness and the increased number of clarificatory clauses risks hardening new boundaries of exclusivity.

Although EA-2005 does provide a positive as well as negative anthropology, it is not doxological, does not mention anti-racism, fails to be explicitly anti-sexist, and fails explicitly to accept responsibility for the pursuit of social justice. On biblical inspiration the new basis is the equivalent of EA-1970, LBC-1998 and Nottingham-1977, but to the right of IVCF-2000, EA-1846, EA-1912 and EA-1996. On the atonement, EA-2005 is to the left of EA-1970 and UCCF-1981, but to the right of LBC-1998, EA-1846, EA-1912, EA-1996 and Nottingham-1977. EA-2005 therefore sustains the existing pattern of EA bases being more moderate than IVF/UCCF, but is to the right of previous EA bases, EA-1970 excepted.

EA-2005 exemplifies the pan-evangelical rejection of the fundamentalist undertow that we identified in mid-twentieth century bases. Nonetheless, while post-fundamentalist, EA-2005 fails to embrace or build upon the post-Lausanne trajectory of Nottingham-1977 and EA-1996. It also remains more rigorously exclusive than the pre-fundamentalist minimalism of EA-1846 and, above all, EA-1912. We conclude that EA-2005 represents a rather limited achievement: a superfluous comprehensiveness combines with a moderated conservatism that, while distanced from neo-conservative and fundamentalising tendencies, fails to recover the pre-fundamentalist pan-evangelical inclusivity or sustain the late twentieth century post-conservative trajectory. EA-2005 articulates the middle ground of the cautiously open evangelicals, too broad for the neo-conservatives yet too elaborated and prescriptive for the progressives. It remains to be seen whether this represents an enduring act of theological diplomacy or a transient compromise, an interstitial formulation within an ineluctably bifurcatory tradition.

New Directions

After Lausanne-1974 and particularly in the 1990s the rightward trend of mid-twentieth century bases was reversed, the fundamentalising tendencies were overturned, and a progressive consensus began to cohere: more subtly nuanced, irenic and affirmatory. The contrast is acute between GC-1999 and the progressive bases of the 1990s. Where GC-1999 present a negative anthropology, the reconstructionist bases all include a balancing, positive emphasis and an at least implicit emphasis upon anti-sexism and anti-racism. The obligation to pursue social justice is also explicit in EA-1996 and LBC-1998. These contemporary bases of faith are the theological progeny of Lausanne-1974. They provide a holistic understanding of the Gospel, extricated from the sectarian exclusivity and over-dogmatism that were central to the legacy of fundamentalism.

Table 38: Comparing key factors in bases of faith, 1970-2000

	Doxological	Anthropology	Anti-racist	Anti-sexist	Social justice
EA-1970	No	Negative	No mention	No mention	No mention
UCCF-1981	No	Negative	No mention	No mention	No mention
EA-1996	No	Positive & negative	Explicit	Implicit	Explicit
LBC-1998	Yes	Positive & negative	Implicit	Implicit	Explicit
IVCF-2000	Yes	Positive & negative	Implicit	Implicit	No mention
EA-2005	No	Positive & negative	No mention	Implicit	Implicit

We should not be surprised that the 1990s saw a doctrinal re-casting of evangelicalism. The history of evangelicalism leads us to expect such reconstruction in a newly emergent culture.[25] More remarkable is the locus: not among the self-styled radicals and pioneers of the evangelical coalition, but rather among august evangelical organisations. The venerables of the evangelical establishment were reconstructing pan-evangelicalism for postmodernity. Becoming reflexive in a transitioning culture, progressive evangelicals exemplified Habermas' paradigm of a dynamic tradition:

> Every continuation of a tradition is selective, and precisely this selectivity must pass
> through the filter of critique, of a self-conscious appropriation of history.[26]

The new trajectory of the 1990s bases, and their precursors in Lausanne-1974 and Nottingham-1977, represents a reformulation of a longstanding broad and inclusive evangelicalism. It marks the recovery of an older tradition of minimalist, biblical orthodoxy, stripped of the intervening accretions of secondary and often divisive convictions and extrapolations.[27]

The categories of bounded set and open set (progressive) evangelicalism can be delineated through a series of contrasts.[28] In terms of the focus of revelation,

---

[25] This evolutionary pattern confirms Noll's description of American evangelicalism as a form of "culturally adaptive biblical experimentalism" (Noll, 2001).

[26] Dews: 1992: 243.

[27] Murphy, 1996; Grenz, 2000. Contra Erickson, Helseth, Taylor, 2004.

[28] Hiebert, (1994, chapter 6) developed a missiological exploration of the mathematical

bounded set evangelicals emphasise propositions, doctrine and the systematic homogenisation of the Scriptures. Progressive evangelicals emphasise the person of Christ, narrative revelation, and diversity within unity in the Bible. The status of the Reformation tends to be absolutised by the bounded, relativised by the open. Concerning attitudes to culture and the wider theological community, the bounded are suspicious, the open dialogical. In their underlying concept of evangelicalism, the conservatives' bounded set emphasises exclusivity and guarding the boundaries. The progressives' open set emphasises inclusivity around a focus that is Trinitarian and Christocentric.

When Stott and Lloyd-Jones disputed the validity of mixed denominations, this was indicative of much broader tensions within the evangelical tradition between inclusivity and exclusivity, engagement and purity, minimal orthodoxy and maximal dogmatism. If Stott and Lloyd-Jones represented a polarisation inherent in pan-evangelicalism, the bifurcation that began to crystallise in the late twentieth century parallels their controversy on a much larger scale. The legacy of Stott is in mainstream British and international evangelicalism, although the tradition has continued to move beyond Stott's innate conservatism. The legacy of Lloyd-Jones is found in Reformed separatism and neo-fundamentalism. Where Stott and Lloyd-Jones' dispute was ecclesiological and resulted in irreconcilable differences, the inheritors of their legacy have now reached fundamental disagreement over a broader theological canvas: revelation, soteriology, social justice, the role of women and the interface between gospel and culture.

---

concept of bounded and fuzzy sets, developed from German mathematician Georg Cantor's work on well-formed set theory. Hiebert develops his analysis into four related categories: two with a well formed boundary, two with no sharply defined boundary; in each of these categories, one is an intrinsic set, formed on the basis of the "essential nature of the members themselves" and one is an extrinsic, or relational set. This results in four sets: bounded, centred, intrinsic fuzzy and extrinsic fuzzy. According to Hiebert, the bounded set represents the classical, separatist church, the intrinsic fuzzy set represents the classical, parish church, the extrinsic fuzzy set represents an inchoate collection of individualistic spiritual journeys without any communitarian coherence as a church, and the centred set represents the most effective missiological model, relationally open to all and yet conscious of its own centre. In bounded set thinking, the parameters, whether of the church or of evangelicalism, are well defined and readily identified. The insiders know confidently who is saved and who is sound. Fuzzy set thinking emphasises fluidity, uncertainty and provisionality. In church terms, fuzzy set thinking promotes inclusivity, a church with blurred edges that recognises and welcomes people on a journey into faith. Traditional evangelicalism clearly operated in terms of a bounded set of the elect, whereas it was the middle of the road Anglican church, serving the entire parish, that was more likely to express its mission in terms that can be represented as a fuzzy set. In practice, there may be little distinction between Hiebert's intrinsic fuzzy and centred sets as models of inclusive mission.

Table 39: Traditionalist and progressive evangelicals compared

	Bounded set	Open set
Focus of revelation	Propositions Systematic homogenisation of Scripture	Person of Christ Affirm diversity of biblical genres & theologies, & reclaims narrative in Scripture
Attitudes to Reformation	Tend to absolutise	Relativise
Attitudes to culture & wider theological community	Detached or oppositional "True" evangelicals coterminous with calvinistic conservatism	Dialogical Evangelicals a broad tradition within Trinitarian orthodoxy
Self-conception	Exclusive Guard the boundaries	Inclusive Affirm the centre

The resignation of Melvyn Tinker, Anglican leader of *Essentially Evangelical* from the EA Council in September 2001 on the grounds that EA had become too broad and inclusive was symptomatic of a new wave of assertive and self-confident exclusivism from the Reformed Right.[29] They are becoming increasingly separatist from moderate evangelicals[30] even though, as yet at least, more sabre-rattling than

---

[29] In an article in *The Churchman* Tinker (1992, republished in Tinker, 2001) repudiated evangelical Anglicans who had succumbed to secularization (Chris Sugden's politicized recasting of the Gospel), pluralism (James Jones' "confused thinking and careless exegesis" in wishing to affirm Christians who deny the bodily resurrection), relativism (N.T. Wright's emphasis upon the Bible's authority not as propositional truth but as a story of the community of faith in the light of which the living community can extemporize) and materialism (Wimber's power healing). The strictly Reformed and instinctively exclusivist evangelical has little time for the political activist, the ecumenist, the contemporary theologian or the charismatic. From this perspective the Evangelical Alliance is impossibly broad, inclusive and indiscriminate, actively including in its coalition various sectors the calvinistic-exclusivists would reject as less than evangelical.

[30] Contrast the progressive experimentalism of Middleton and Walsh (1984, 1995) and Grenz

separatist in terms of denominational affiliation. Just as the English Free Churches experienced a quasi-fundamentalistic separation through Lloyd-Jones in the 1960s, within the next ten years the Anglican Right are likely to agonise over whether to pursue a similar route, particularly if (or when) faced with women bishops and openly practising homosexual priests. The predictable consequence is that the more vocal and resolute second generation leaders of the new Right may ultimately secede,[31] while less intransigent advocates will ultimately find the status and security of the state church sufficiently endearing to mollify their exclusivist inclinations. Rather than immune to American fundamentalising tendencies, hard-line calvinistic-exclusivist Anglicans may be edging towards a similarly separatist route several decades later.

Mapping Biblicist-Crucicentric Divergence

We have charted the chronological development and divergence of three distinct phases of evangelical bases of faith: a traditional evangelical ecumenism, moving towards a minimalist biblical orthodoxy; an anti-liberal evangelical exclusivism, moving rightwards in an ever more elaborated conservatism; and a post-conservative evangelical openness, espousing biblical orthodoxy while ready to critique or even jettison the givens of the former consensus, inevitably provoking the reactive exclusivities of the neo-conservatives.

In the light of this chronological analysis, we can now codify the various bases of faith from left to right. To do so for every clause would be superfluous. Since the biblicist-crucicentric axis is dominant in evangelical bases of faith, we can focus upon the two storm-centres that preoccupy this axis: biblical inspiration and the atonement.

Classifying approaches to biblical inspiration we identify a clear gradation. Starting with the most conservative, the first statement asserts inerrancy and states

---

(2000) with Johnson and Fowler White (2001) and Erickson, Helseth and Taylor (2004), where the contributors repudiate post-conservatism and postmodernism and defend foundationalism, propositionalism and neo-conservative evangelicalism. The chasm is set unambiguously in the subtitle to this later collection of essays – "confronting evangelical accommodation in postmodern times." The extent of unconscious enlightenment and modernist accommodation is not addressed. Grenz's untimely death in 2005 at the age of fifty five severely weakened the theological gravitas of the American progressives.

[31] This prospect grew more likely after November 2005 when Richard Coekin of Dundonald Church, Wimbledon imported Bishop Martin Morrison from the Church of England in South Africa to conduct three ordinations (*The Times*, 4 November, 2005). Coekin's justification was that the Bishop of Southwark, Tom Butler, was too liberal on homosexuality. Butler had previously warned Coekin that he would lose his license to minister in Southwark if the ordinations went ahead. Coekin's church is a church plant from the non-parochial church of Emmanuel, Wimbledon, making him already semi-detached from normal parish ministry and the governance of the diocese. Coekin appears to have aspired to what can be termed "biblically principled ecclesiastical martyrdom". After the Bishop pressed his case but did not revoke Coekin's licence, both parties predictably claimed victory in the resultant stalemate.

that grave consequences follow from rejecting this conviction (consequences presumably suffered by Stott, as well as the countless contemporary evangelicals to his left). The second also affirms inerrancy, but without any dire warnings. Position three affirms infallibility. Position four speaks only of supreme authority, but retains relatively right wing status by asserting that the Bible is the means of grace by which God reveals himself in present experience which sounds like a polemical exclusivity in opposition to Christian mysticism, sacramentalism, existentialism and, perhaps most particularly since this formulation was composed in the 1960s, in resistance to the emerging experientialism of charismatic renewal. Position five uses the language of infallibility, but shifts the locus from the text to the Bible's function as a rule of faith and practice. Position six emphasises supreme authority without reference to infallibility. Position seven avoids the word "supreme", preferring the term "unique". Position eight affirms divine inspiration and authority with no additional adjectival reinforcers, neither negative (infallible, inerrant) nor positive (supreme, unique). Position nine affirms instead the supreme authority of Christ, describing Scripture as definitive, normative and sufficient revelation, but denoting its authority to be essentially secondary and derivative from the authority of the risen Christ.

Table 40: Accounts of biblical inspiration

1.   We affirm that canonical Scripture should always be interpreted on the basis that it is infallible and inerrant... However, we further deny that inerrancy can be rejected without grave consequences, both to the individual and to the Church.[32]

2.   God has revealed himself in the Bible, which consists of the Old and New Testament alone. Every word was inspired by God through human authors, so that the Bible as given is in its entirety the word of God, without error and fully reliable in fact and doctrine. The Bible alone speaks with final authority and is always sufficient for all matters of belief and practice.[33]

3.   The divine inspiration and infallibility of Holy Scripture, as originally given, and its supreme authority in all matters of faith and conduct.[34]

   Equivalent. The Holy Scriptures as originally given by God, divinely inspired, infallible, entirely trustworthy; and their supreme authority in all matters of faith and conduct.[35]

4.   Scripture is the supreme authority in all matters of faith and practice... It is also the means of grace through which God reveals himself in present experience.[36]

5.   We affirm the divine inspiration, truthfulness and authority of both Old and New Testament Scriptures in their entirety as the only written word of God,

---

[32] Chicago-1978.
[33] FIEC-1922.
[34] IVF/UCCF: *passim.*
[35] WEF-1951.
[36] Keele-1967.

without error in all that it affirms, and the only infallible rule of faith and practice.[37]

6.   The divine inspiration of the Holy Scripture and its consequent entire trustworthiness and supreme authority in all matters of faith and conduct.[38]

Equivalent. We believe that the Old and New Testament Scriptures are God-breathed since their writers spoke from God as they were moved by the Holy Spirit; hence, they are fully trustworthy in all that they affirm; and as the written Word of God they are our supreme authority for faith and conduct.[39]

Equivalent. In all matters of faith and conduct, the Bible is our supreme authority and guide, for Scripture was written for our instruction.[40]

Equivalent. The divine inspiration and supreme authority of the Old and New Testament Scriptures, which are the written Word of God - fully trustworthy for faith and conduct.[41]

7.   The unique divine inspiration, entire trustworthiness and authority of the Bible.[42]

8.   The divine inspiration, authority and sufficiency of the Holy Scriptures.[43]

9.   We confess the Lord Jesus Christ as God's Word incarnate; supreme authority is his. We recognise scripture as God's Word written, the definitive, normative and sufficient revelation of God's truth.[44]

When we consider approaches to the atonement, once again there is a clear gradation of emphasis. Position one emphasises penal substitution as fundamental and essential to the Gospel, using a similarly emphatic and exclusive formulation to that found in the most right wing statement on biblical inspiration. Position two emphasises penal substitution as the sole model of the atonement. Position three emphasises penal substitution as the central model of the atonement. Position four emphasises the broader concept of substitutionary sacrifice with no specific reference to penal substitution, which may be implicit but is certainly not presented as an explicit prerequisite of evangelical orthodoxy. Position five affirms multiple models of the atonement, declining to give any model priority, implicit or explicit. Position six affirms the objectivity of Christ's atoning death, while not referring to any specific models of the atonement. Position seven affirms multiple "biblical pictures" of the atonement, implicitly making them secondary to the event of the cross and resurrection in itself, and expressly acknowledging and legitimising differing evaluations of penal substitution among evangelicals. The fact that the wording avoids the specific term "penal substitution", which, as we have seen, some

---

[37] Lausanne-1974.
[38] EA-1970.
[39] LBC-1998.
[40] Nottingham-1977.
[41] EA-2005.
[42] IVCF-2000.
[43] EA-1846 and EA-1912.
[44] EA-1996.

had attempted to insert at the draft stage in this formulation is a tacit acknowledgment that while the developed theory of penal substitution remains the centre and pivot of the atonement for some traditional, reformed and calvinistic evangelicals, among others there has emerged a new unwillingness to affirm the legitimacy of any formulation more specific and developed than "Christ died in our place."

Table 41: Accounts of the atonement

1.   Jesus paid our penalty in our place on his cross, satisfying the retributive demands of divine justice by shedding his blood in sacrifice and so making possible justification for all who trust in him... We deny that any view of the Atonement that rejects the substitutionary satisfaction of divine justice, accomplished vicariously for believers, is compatible with the teaching of the Gospel.[45]

2.   Jesus Christ, fully human and fully divine, who lived as a perfect example, who assumed the judgment due sinners by dying in our place, and who was bodily raised from the dead and ascended as Savior and Lord.[46]

Equivalent. On the cross he died in the place of sinners, bearing God's punishment for their sin, redeeming them by his blood.[47]

3.   The atonement can be fully understood only when Christ is seen as bearing the penalty of our sins in our place. This is the deepest, though not the only, significance of the divine love demonstrated in the cross.[48]

4.   The substitutionary sacrifice of the incarnate Son of God as the sole and all-sufficient ground of redemption from the guilt and power of sin, and from its eternal consequences.[49]

Equivalent. Redemption from the guilt, penalty and power of sin only through the sacrificial death (as our Representative and Substitute) of Jesus Christ, the Incarnate Son of God.[50]

Equivalent. The salvation of lost and sinful men through the shed blood of the Lord Jesus Christ [51]

5.   The atoning sacrifice of Christ on the cross: dying in our place, paying the price of sin and defeating evil, so reconciling us with God.[52]

6.   We confess Jesus Christ as Lord and God, the eternal Son of the Father; as truly human, born of the virgin Mary; as Servant, sinless, full of grace and truth; as only Mediator and Saviour of the whole world, dying on the cross in our

---

[45] GC-1999.
[46] IVCF-2000.
[47] FIEC-1922.
[48] Keele-1967.
[49] EA-1970.
[50] IVF/UCCF: *passim.*
[51] WEF-1951.
[52] EA-2005.

place, representing us to God, redeeming us from the grip, guilt and punishment of sin; as the Second Adam, the head of a new humanity, living a life of perfect obedience, overcoming death and decay, rising from the dead with a glorious body, being taken up to be with the Father, one day returning personally in glory and judgement to bring eternal life to the redeemed and eternal death to the lost, to establish a new heaven and a new earth, the home of righteousness, where there will be no more evil, suffering or death; as Victor over Satan and all his forces, rescuing us from the dominions of darkness, and bringing us into his own kingdom; as the Word who makes God known.[53]

7.   The incarnation of the Son of God, His work of atonement for sinners of mankind...[54]

   Equivalent. ...the Lord Jesus Christ our God and Saviour who died for our sins and rose again[55]

   Equivalent. We honour Jesus Christ alone as Saviour and Lord. His atoning death, bodily resurrection and personal return are central to Christian faith.[56]

8.   ...we give different emphasis to the various biblical expressions of atonement. Some wish to see the truth that Christ died in our place as the central explanation of the cross, while others, who also give this truth a position of great importance, lay greater stress on the relative significance of other biblical pictures.[57]

Having delineated these clauses from Right to Left, we can categorise the bases themselves from most to least conservative. Identifying first the most conservative bases, we note that the two neo-conservative American statements, to which Packer contributed, are the most exclusive, producing tighter formulations than FIEC that ranks second in both categories. IVF/UCCF and WEF bases rank third most conservative on the Bible and fourth most conservative on the atonement, where they are joined by EA-1970. Keele-1967 is fourth most conservative on the Bible, third on the atonement, where it is more conservative than both IVF/UCCF and EA-1970. This confirms our previous observation that, in the 1960s, Stott's call to evangelical re-engagement with the wider church and mainstream theological scholarship arose from a highly conservative starting point.

The most unusual basis is IVCF-2000, which ranks third most moderate on biblical inspiration and yet second most conservative on the atonement. This may reflect the fact that, while evangelical debate concerning biblical inspiration is well-developed in the United States, where formulations of biblical inspiration more moderate than all these bases of faith have been developed on the radical left of the

---

[53] LBC-1998.
[54] EA-1846.
[55] EA-1912.
[56] EA-1996.
[57] Nottingham-1977.

evangelical tradition,[58] the concept of retributive justice remains far more culturally normative in the United States than in Western Europe, thus strengthening penal substitution's cultural correlatives. The European cultural consensus that opposes both the death penalty and retributive justice will inevitably influence European theologians' consideration of the relative significance or even the moral legitimacy of the model of penal substitution.

Nottingham-1977 is the most moderate formulation on the atonement. This confirms the extent to which Nottingham-1977 marked a sharp break with Keele-1967. Whereas the first NEAC was closely aligned with the IVF/UCCF school of conservatism, the second shifted dramatically to the left, much to Packer's disquiet. As we have argued, Stott inculcated a new engagement, both ecclesiological and theological, that took the next generation of evangelical Anglicans well beyond his own cautiously open conservatism. LBC-1998 and EA-1996 are among the most moderate, reflecting the reconfiguration of British evangelicalism in the 1990s, moving sharply away from the rightwards trend that had dominated from the 1920s through the 1980s.

More striking is the position of EA-1846 and EA-1912. Although the latter statement was much briefer, resulting in its routine dismissal among later conservatives, its formulations in these two areas at the heart of evangelical identity and controversy are identical with the founding basis of the Evangelical Alliance. Moreover, while on the atonement all three EA bases are slightly less moderate than Nottingham-1977, on the Bible these three EA bases are more moderate than any other formulation. The Evangelical Alliance has therefore consistently produced inclusive, broad-based formulations of moderate evangelical convictions. The only Evangelical Alliance bases that fail to rank among the most moderate in these two critical categories are the Stott revision of 1970, which, as we have demonstrated, is more accurately understood to be a slightly more moderate revision of IVF-1928, and also EA-2005.

Three conclusions arise from this analysis of the biblicist-crucicentric axis within contemporary evangelicalism. First, any attempt to characterise the entire evangelical movement as infallibilist and centred upon penal substitution proves in the light of the evident diversity among the bases of faith to be more of a caricature, or a misunderstanding of one trend within twentieth century evangelicalism, than a precise and historically justifiable conclusion. Second, the three evangelical eras we have been examining have had markedly different opponents: the primary mid-nineteenth century opponents were Popery and Puseyism; for the mid-twentieth century, it was liberalism; but in the post-liberal context of the late twentieth century, progressive and neo-conservative evangelicalism increasingly defined themselves over against one another. Each to the other has become the enemy within, to be disputed if not disowned. Third, the breadth of the coalition is coming

---

[58] See Murphy, 1996; Knight, 1997; Grenz, 2000, 2001. Gundry (1982) provided the first redactional commentary of a synoptic Gospel by a self-designated evangelical, though naturally he was not subsequently recognised as such by the inerrantists.

under growing strain, with an assertive, narrowing dogmatism on the Right and an increasingly rigorous questioning of conventional evangelical presuppositions on the Left.

Table 42: Comparing views on the Bible and the atonement

	Bible	Atonement
most conservative ▲	Chicago-1978	GC-1999
	FIEC	FIEC; IVCF-2000
	IVF/UCCF; WEF-1951	Keele-1967
	Keele-1967	IVF/UCCF; WEF-1951; EA-1970
	Lausanne-1974	EA-2005
	EA-1970; Nottingham-1977; LBC-1998; EA-2005	LBC-1998
	IVCF-2000	EA-1846; EA-1912; EA-1996
	EA-1846, EA-1912	Nottingham-1977
▼ **least conservative**	EA-1996	

In the light of our detailed examination of the major bases of faith, 1967-2000, we can trace in the late twentieth century three distinct groupings, within which can be found sub-types of evangelical. The Right comprise three categories: *the unreconstructed fundamentalists*, whose status as extreme or non-evangelicals remains contested;[59] *the neo-fundamentalists*, who claim to distance themselves from fundamentalism's overt anti-intellectualism, but employ a literalist hermeneutic and are stridently anti-evolutionist and anti-Catholic; and *the neo-conservatives*, notably Packer and Carson, who, while somewhat broader in their sympathies, are nonetheless uncompromisingly restrictive in the boundaries they set to authentic evangelicalism.

Then come the moderate mainstream, who have been disinclined to embrace the formula of "inerrancy" but are wary of the Left, lest their reconstructions entail an abandonment of what had previously been considered core convictions. The moderates comprise two sub-groups: *the moderate conservatives*, rooted in the earlier, inclusive tradition of minimal biblical orthodoxy to promote maximal ecumenical unity; and *the moderate, Lausanne-influenced mainstream*, particularly influenced by Stott.

On the Left are two types of progressives, first *the reconstructed evangelicals*,

---

[59] Barr, 1977; Marsden, 1991; Tidball, 1994; Knight, 1997; Dorrien, 1998; Harris, 1998.

who have become increasingly ascendant in the UK in recent years. If Packer represents the Right, although to the right of him are those who would counsel no dialogue with Roman Catholicism, and Stott represents the moderate conservatives, there is no single, dominant voice among the moderates, but they include many bishops and other leading churchmen appointed during the Primacy of George Carey, and several present and former principals of evangelical theological colleges, for example, John Goldingay, Graham Cray and Nigel Wright.[60] Finally, we identify *the radical evangelicals*, re-opening debates about the first principles of Christian theism while claiming to remain within the broad evangelical tradition, most notably Pinnock,[61] whose most enthusiastic British adherents, judging by their enthusiastic informal comments, are found among some leaders in the Arminian new church networks (Pioneer and Ichthus). It is more likely for Anglicans who have migrated to the evangelical Left to retain no more than a residual sense of 'roots in the evangelical tradition', while embracing a broader theology and understanding of the Church.

Here, then are six types of evangelical, even though some do not recognise every other type as authentically evangelical: neo-fundamentalists, neo-conservatives, moderate conservatives, Lausanne mainstream, reconstructed evangelicals and radical evangelicals. The fundamentalists are the marginal grouping to the Right. To the Left are those previously known as evangelicals, migrating into a broader churchmanship and theology, without necessarily being identified self-consciously as post-evangelical, following Tomlinson.[62] Some interviewees further suggested the possible emergence of hyper-entrepreneurials, for whom the title "evangelical" appears to represent the Free Church equivalent of the Liberian flag of convenience, whose activism is relentless, but who show scant regard for biblicism, crucicentrism and even conversionism; if such really do exist, their standing as authentic exponents of the evangelical tradition appears doubtful.

From its inception, EA has sought to function as a coalition of all types of evangelical. Its own bases accord with the more moderate positions, but in pursuit of inclusiveness it has worked to embrace the more conservative. There are two related reasons why this broad coalition may have become, by the end of this period of major transitions 1967-2000, all but untenable. From the Right, the neo-conservatives have always tended to be wary of the breadth of the Evangelical Alliance, some from within its membership, some from without. But now the Right

---

[60] My own reading of Nigel Wright (1996) places him in the reconstructed category, since he is less iconoclastic than Pinnock, but is unambiguously progressive. For North American reconstructed evangelicals, see the literature survey in the introduction.

[61] Pinnock et al, 1994; Pinnock, 2001. Compare Erickson, 1997, 1998; Gray, 2000, Erickson, Helseth and Taylor, 2004.

[62] Tomlinson's sub-type will probably prove to be a transitional reaction against evangelical modernity that results in rapid re-absorption into the liberal or post-liberal mainstream, since post-evangelicals define themselves negatively and seem unlikely to develop a sustainable and distinct theological agenda. Nonetheless, those operating within a postmodern milieu may more readily resonate with Tomlinson than Calver or Lloyd-Jones, Stott or Packer.

is affirming inerrancy and penal substitution with newly assertive exclusivity, claiming that both should be considered intrinsic and prerequisite to authentic evangelicalism. From the Left, the progressive evangelical emphasis upon a multiple metaphor understanding of the atonement and a neo-Barthian approach to biblical inspiration stand in marked contrast. We conclude that, as the Right becomes more hard-line, it will tolerate less diversity and become more impatient of the Left, particularly since some progressives are likely to dismantle and repudiate rather than reconstruct a recognisably evangelical theology. At the same time, the progressive evangelical Left is likely to find it ever more difficult not to lose patience with what it considers the increasingly obscurantist and sectarian over-dogmatism of the Right. Like American fundamentalists and neo-evangelicals, the Right and Left of English pan-evangelicalism may ultimately prove mutually incompatible.[63] Progressives and neo-conservatives both function within the broad parameters of the pre-fundamentalist evangelical tradition, and so may yet have enough in common to remain in loose coalition. Nonetheless, the evangelical tradition is more than enduringly diverse, for we have demonstrated its evolution in two distinct directions. When bifurcatory energy is found in both wings, the centre may not hold.

In Kuhn's terms, this bifurcation represents a paradigm shift with the inevitable result of mutual misunderstanding, because of the circular defence of each paradigm in any debate about paradigm choice.

> To the extent, as significant as it is incomplete, that two scientific schools disagree about what is a problem and what a solution, they will inevitably talk through each other when debating the relative merits of their respective paradigms... each paradigm will be shown to satisfy more or less the criteria that it dictates for itself, and to fall short of a few of those dictated by its opponent.[64]

---

[63] Ammerman (1990) traces the neo-fundamentalist takeover of the Southern Baptists and the subsequent departure of the moderate evangelicals, including Ammerman herself. The abortive campaigns of the original fundamentalists to gain control of existing denominations makes this late twentieth naïve century success the more surprising. Ammerman concludes that the moderates were politically and denominationally loyal and woke up too late to fundamentalist reorientation of their already conservative denomination. Timothy George (1992) provides a quite different perspective that fails to recognize the evangelical convictions of some who were alienated by the fundamentalist take-over: "For only the second time in this century, a major American denomination veering from its historical, evangelical roots has changed its trajectory." Reisinger and Allen's pro-fundamentalist contribution to the Southern Baptist debate explicitly claimed, as did Warfield, that exclusivist neo-calvinism is the only legitimate expression of authentic evangelicalism: "The choice is between the deep-rooted, God-centred theology of evangelical Calvinism and the man-centred, unstable theology of the other perspectives present in the convention." (Reisinger and Allen, 2000: 12). Packer's extraordinary claims that John Wesley was a confused Calvinist and C.S. Lewis an inconsistent Calvinist, exhibit the same monopolising pretensions (cited in Walls and Dongell, 2004: 153-4).

[64] Kuhn, 1962: 110.

Evangelicals' propensity for missiological pragmatism leads to cognitive bargaining with the prevailing popular culture.[65] With the post-enlightenment cultural shift, the two evangelical sectors engage in cognitive bargaining, conscious or instinctual, with two mutually exclusive presuppositional frameworks: the enlightenment, typically in terms of common sense rationalism through the filter of Old Princeton;[66] and postmodernity, usually in terms of critical realism.[67]

In Gadamer's terms,[68] neo-conservatism entails a premature fusion of horizons in which the essential otherness of the past – including the Bible – is denied and the present cultural context as a discrete horizon is not taken sufficiently seriously. Ironically, a Christian tradition that emphasises the missiological priority, by emphatically rejecting the postmodern context in favour of an enclave of enlightenment rationalism, diminishes its own capacity to engage in sustainable, culturally consonant mission.[69]

MacIntyre defined a living tradition as "an historically extended, socially embodied argument and an argument precisely in part about the goods which constitute that tradition." [70] Post-conservatism can lay claim to functioning as a living tradition, in dialogue with the enduring past and the changing present, particularly where post-conservatives rediscover the broad ecumenical and patristic heritage of Trinitarian orthodoxy as well as engaging with the post modern context, both cultural and philosophical.[71] In MacIntyre's terms, "conservative antiquarianism" by failing to function reflexively as a "not-yet completed narrative", represents a tradition that is no longer open to the future but has ossified.[72] Post-conservatism represents a continuation of "an historically extended, socially embodied argument",[73] that is an open-ended formulation of the evangelical tradition, "sustained and advanced by its own internal arguments and conflicts".[74] However, post-conservatism should presently be considered "interstitial and transitory",[75] for it encompasses those who seek to retain and reinterpret the evangelical tradition without the legacy of rationalistic calvinistic-exclusivism, but also those for whom the rejection of the (often unconscious) enlightenment

---

[65] Hunter, 1983.

[66] Knight, 1997; Harris, 1998.

[67] Wright, 1992; Grenz, 2000; McGrath, 2002.

[68] Gadamer, 1975; Thiselton, 1980.

[69] Bosch (1991) provided a seminal contemporary missiology, although his conflation of postmodern and ecumenical paradigms is too convenient to be persuasive. He underestimates the alien otherness of post-Christian postmodernity and the precariousness of present ecumenical endeavours. Murray (2004) similarly conflates too easily the cultural context of "post-Christendom" with an idealised anabaptist paradigm.

[70] MacIntyre, 1985: 222.

[71] Webber, 1999; Williams, 1999; Oden, 2003; Abraham, 2003.

[72] MacIntyre, 1985: 223.

[73] MacIntyre, 1985: 222.

[74] MacIntyre, 1985: 260.

[75] Bell's epithet for post-industrial society (1976: ix) is highly apposite.

foundationalism of traditional evangelical theology has produced an at-least-provisional post-evangelicalism, whether explicit or implicit.[76]

Just as in the macrocosm of American Protestantism Roof and McKinney identified "the collapse of the middle" [77] and Wuthnow identified a "religious realignment" [78] either side of a "great divide" between Liberals and Conservatives, we have found in the microcosm of evangelical bases of faith, 1967-2000 a deepening polarisation. The development of mutually exclusive trajectories within the biblicist-crucicentric axis of contemporary evangelicalism clearly indicates that partnership between progressive and neo-conservative evangelicals may prove untenable and unsustainable. Irreconcilable and increasingly explicit differences within the biblicist-crucicentric axis may lead the twentieth century pan-evangelical coalition towards a twenty-first century divorce.

---

[76] As one interviewee observed: "I cannot agree with the neo-conservatives and that makes me an open evangelical, but I have more in common with the conservatives than the far left of open evangelicalism, for whom evangelicalism is little more than a cover for neo-liberalism."
[77] Roof and McKinney, 1987.
[78] Wuthnow, 1988.

CONCLUSION

Conflictual Identities: The Dynamics and Trajectories of Evangelical Convictions

In the light of our analysis of the twin axes of pan-evangelicalism, conversionist-activist and biblicist-crucicentric, we now draw together the implications of these reconstructions and trajectories in evangelical identity.[1] This concluding synthesis needs to take full account of the historical developments, theological diversity and sociological perspectives we have examined in this study, reflecting the new integration, identified by Callum Brown, of history, religious studies and sociology in the examination of Christianity in the context of contemporary secularization.[2] What has become clear is that our focal period of investigation, 1966-2001, represents an era of successive and tumultuous upheavals within pan-evangelicalism. For the biblicist-crucicentric axis, the primary narrative runs between the two Evangelical Assemblies of 1966 and 1996, tracing the journey from the demise of the conservative hegemony to the emergence of the progressives. Beyond 1996 the bifurcatory pressures became more pronounced, as evidenced in GC-1999 and IVCF-2000, and also in the increasingly contentious debate between rival and even mutually exclusive schools of evangelical theologians.[3] For the conversionist-activist axis, the narrative is focussed upon the impact of Calver, appointed to EA in 1982, and runs through to 2001, by which time EA and SH had plateaued or declined, the 1990s initiatives in evangelism and church planting had indulged vision inflation, and *Alpha* had come to dominate the conversionist-activist axis, at least for a season. Before Calver's era, the entrepreneurial activists had begun to emerge into new prominence with the Festival of Light in 1971, which, we have argued, represents the quickening of an evangelical reaction against both the ethical revolution of the 1960s and the pan-evangelical disarray following the disruption of 1966-7.

We have built upon Bebbington's quadrilateral and Marsden's concept of conflictual priorities within pan-evangelicalism[4] to propose and test the model of two competing axes, the conversionist-activist and biblicist-crucicentric. Our study of the evolution of English pan-evangelicalism demonstrates that the theoretical model of twin axes can be constructively applied to Bebbington's quadrilateral to

---

[1] For a diagrammatic representation of this analysis, see Appendix 3.

[2] During a day conference at New College, Edinburgh, 15 April 2005.

[3] Pinnock et al, 1994; Carson, 1996; Murphy, 1996; Wright N.G, 1996; Erickson, 1997, 1998; Knight, 1997; Dorrien, 1998; Harris, 1998; Barnett, 2000; Gray, 2000; Grenz, 2000, 2003; Olson, Wilson and Grenz, 2000; Grenz and Franke, 2001; Johnson and Fowler White, 2001; Pinnock, 2001; Tinker, 2001; Wright N.T., 2001; Erickson, Helseth and Taylor, 2004.

[4] Marsden, 1984.

provide a more precisely modulated and dynamic account of the tensions and rivalries inherent within the evangelical tradition. The conversionist-activist axis predominant among the pragmatic entrepreneurs typically functions in dialectical tension with the biblicist-crucicentric axis predominant among the more theologically oriented. Within biblicist-crucicentrism we traced the bifurcation between neo-conservatives and progressives, with the cautiously open conservatives as the intermediate sector. We further refuted the claim, made both by the neo-conservatives and some non-evangelicals, that infallibility / inerrancy and penal substitution represent the *sine qua non* of evangelical theology. We found such emphases to be novel, transient and contested within the broad and evolving pan-evangelical tradition. We conclude that Bebbington's quadrilateral is best conceived not as a static commonality but rather as a confluence of priorities in tension, sometimes dynamic, sometimes conflictual. We have therefore reconceptualised Bebbington's quadrilateral to demonstrate within pan-evangelicalism an inherent bipolarity between the twin axes, conversionist-activist and biblicist-crucicentric.

David Martin argued that the convertive aspirations of the evangelical tradition lead ineluctably to a subcultural lifestyle, since, "In practice, one cannot convert everybody."[5] He identified a paradox within evangelicalism:[6] on the one hand, evangelicals create and sustain "institutional and conceptual boundaries", while other Christian subcultures are more readily absorbed into the cultural mainstream and are dissipated into embodiments of the virtues of a secularized citizenry; on the other hand, evangelicalism's emphasis upon convertive piety, what Martin calls "heartwork", can serve to minimalise religious ritual and institutions, thus making the subcultural boundaries more fragile. Indeed, Smith and Bramadat's studies of evangelical missiology,[7] accommodating to the prevailing culture while seeking to rearticulate their convertive convictions, heighten the paradox. The subcultural conviction about the need for conversion in the majority culture obliges the participants to experiments in acculturation that have the unintended impact of making the subcultural boundaries porous and this, almost inevitably, tends to bring the more traditional aspects of subcultural identity into question.

In this study we have identified in particular the temporarily successful reinvention of the pan-evangelical subculture by the entrepreneurials, following the fragmentation of conservative evangelical identity. This was an era in which pan-evangelicals were jettisoning their former subcultural capital and no longer holding to the details of their former restrictive and absolutist lifestyle – for example regarding birth control and popular entertainment, notably the cinema and theatre; no longer wedded to ossifying formality in worship and preaching; adhering in rapidly diminishing numbers to the traditional evangelical spirituality of the "quiet time"; no longer buying the same magazines or books, but decentralising their purchasing power into a plethora of sub-subcultures. In this context of diminishing

---

[5] Martin, 2005: 5.

[6] Martin, 2005: 6.

[7] Smith, 1998, 2000; Bramadat, 2000.

subcultural capital,[8] and in the face of growing secularization, the entrepreneurials developed a narrative of imminent success, evidently beguiling for participants, at least in the short-term, even if, as we have demonstrated, ultimately quixotic, even fictive. While the wholly sectarian forms of calvinistic conservatism became more rigorously isolated, the increased stridency of the broadly entrepreneurial pan-evangelical subculture in the 1990s, in the context of what we have designated as at least the possibility of late-onset decline, may have been symptomatic of the subculture's capital breaking down, making it increasingly difficult to sustain the social construction of subcultural realities.[9] This study has identified two successive failed experiments in pan-evangelical identity. The conservative hegemony was destined to fragment faced with an excess of mutually exclusive certainties. The entrepreneurial mobilisation proffered certain success in the face of ineluctable secularizing trends, and was therefore doomed to the illusions of vision inflation.

When examining the connectedness between the Protestant ethic and the spirit of capitalism, Weber identified the law of unintended consequences.

> We shall thus have to admit that the cultural consequences of the Reformation were to a great extent...unforeseen and even unwished-for results of the labours of the reformers. They were often far removed from or even in contradiction to all that they themselves thought to attain.[10]

The law of unintended consequences can be readily applied to this period of successive evangelical reconstructions. We have argued that the conservative hegemony prepared the way for the entrepreneurial era. The latter may have enjoyed a period of dominance without this accidental preparation, given the alternating prominence of the twin axes of evangelical identity and consequent upon the cultural transitions in an era that increasingly preferred entrepreneurialism, pragmatism, experientialism and detraditionalization. Nonetheless, the conservative fragmentation opened the door, unintentionally, to the conversionist-activists, by creating a vacuum at the heart of pan-evangelicalism.

The entrepreneurs reconstructed subcultural identity, but their novel emphases were volatile and transitory. Pragmatic contemporaneity can only provide transient subcultural capital in a rapidly changing culture: yesterday's up-to-the-minute song or Bible week is tomorrow's has-been. A narrative of irresistible growth and advance will inevitably fall into disrepute when the ostensibly assured success is not delivered: the hype of the mid to late 1990s could be no more than a stop-gap deferral of disappointment, disillusion and disarray. Culturally consonant emphases upon autonomy[11] necessarily dissipate collective identity and subvert conventional

---

[8] Thornton, 1995; Gelder and Thornton, 1997.
[9] Berger and Luckmann, 1967.
[10] Weber, 1958: 90.
[11] This emphasis upon autonomy built, as we have argued, upon the individualism inherent in the classical evangelical emphasis upon personal salvation, the Cartesian emphasis upon the individual thinking subject, and the Lockean-Protestant emphasis upon private judgment, all

and conformist inclinations to ethical and doctrinal dogmatism.[12] Cognitive and ethical bargaining[13] in missiological pursuit of cultural relevance erodes residual conservatism.

In their turn, the entrepreneurs opened the door unintentionally for the reassertion of the biblicist-crucicentric axis. Once again, we note that the resurgence may have happened without this preparation, but the theological transitions were undoubtedly facilitated and precipitated by both the emphases and the increasingly evident deficiencies of the entrepreneurial axis. The progressives turned away from the conservative hegemony as an enlightenment construct and from the entrepreneurial boom as a period of late-modern cultural captivity. However, they were undoubtedly assisted by the entrepreneurs' pragmatic relativising of the conservatives' cognitive and ethical absolutism, which had, albeit indirectly, already partly exposed and discredited the conservatives' rationalistic and epistemic enlightenment dependency. At the same time, the neo-conservatives were reacting against both the entrepreneurs' pragmatic activism that had supplanted their predecessors' hegemony and the progressives, whom they considered increasingly captive to mainline theology, political correctness or postmodernity. While the progressives can reasonably claim to be heirs to maximal inclusivity of 1846, the neo-conservatives are the heirs to early fundamentalism, which was not innately anti-intellectual,[14] but rather sought to provide a coherent intellectual framework, pre- and anti-critical, that built unawares upon enlightenment presuppositions.[15]

The rivalry between the axes and their alternating prominence should not conceal the fact that they are two sides of the one tradition. The conservatives and progressives continue to aspire to conversionist-activism, even though their conceptions of appropriate motivations and methods were entirely different and both were inclined to distance themselves from entrepreneurialism. Even so, the entrepreneurs continued to employ bases of faith to legitimate their subcultural identity, although their pragmatic priorities served to diminish the importance of their biblicist-crucicentric convictions.

Weber identified four sub-groups within ascetic Protestantism: Calvinism, Pietism, Anglo-American Methodism and the Baptist sects.[16] J.D. Hunter recast this quartet in his examination of evangelicalism - described erroneously as "a

---

three of which became conflated with the post-1960s emphasis of the autonomous consumer of late modernity.

[12] Compare Smith, 1998, 2000.

[13] Hunter, 1983, 1987; Smith, 1998, 2000.

[14] Contra Packer (1958), Stott (Edwards and Stott, 1988: 90-91) and Calver (Calver, Coffey, Meadows, 1993).

[15] For neo-evangelicalism's dependence upon Princeton, see Barr 1977, Knight 1997, Dorrien 1998, Harris 1998, Grenz 2000, Webber 2002. Compare Barr, 1984; Marsden, 1984, 1987, 1991; Balmer, 1989; Marty, Appleby et al, 1991, 1993, 1993, 1994, 1995; Murphy, 1996; Percy, 1996, 2002; Coleman, 2000; Bruce, 2001; Partridge, 2001.

[16] Weber, 1958: 95-154.

religiocultural phenomenon unique to North America"[17] - as four major traditions: Baptist, Holiness-Pentecostal, Anabaptist and Reformational-Confessional.[18] *Baptist* signifies an emphasis upon individual salvation, personal choice, subjective faith, and congregationalism. (Hunter noted that the cultural flavour and theological emphases of the Baptist tradition were currently dominant in the United States.[19]) *Holiness* emphasises personal piety and the Holy Spirit. *Anabaptist* emphasises social activism and communitarianism and, according to Hunter, tends to be less experiential. *Reformed* emphasises rational faith and its formal expression. It is in this fourth dimension of evangelicalism that coalescence between pre-critical, pre-Barthian Calvinist theology and enlightenment assumptions finds its fullest flowering. To suggest that the entire Reformed-evangelical tradition is an enlightenment construct is an over-simplification. Nonetheless, this prominent strand of evangelicalism tends to emphasise propositional truth, systematic theology and the primacy of reason in terms concomitant with enlightenment presuppositions.[20] The conceptual transitions entailed in moving to a post-

---

[17] Hunter, 1983: 7.

[18] Hunter, 1983: 7-9, 1987: 4.

[19] Hunter, 1983:8. Finke and Stark (1992) trace American Protestant history through three very different eras: the colonial establishment (Congregationalist, Presbyterian and Episcopalian); their numerical supplanting by the upstart sects (Methodist and Baptist) 1776-1850; the Methodist decline into churchly respectability and the subsequent Baptist dominance, 1850-1990.

[20] We previously quoted Warfield's assertion that "...Evangelicalism stands or falls with Calvinism,...every proof of Evangelicalism is proof of Calvinism." The word "proof" indicates his rationalist construct. Warfield also described the Reformation as "from the theological point of view, an Augustinian revival." (Warfield, 1970: 8-9, 269). Warfield gave explicit sanction to calvinistic hegemony:

I think it important to insist here that Calvinism is not a specific variety of theistic thought, religious experience, evangelical faith, but the perfect expression of these things. The difference between it and other forms of theism, religion, evangelicalism, is a difference not of kind but of degree. There are not many kinds of theism, religion, evangelicalism, each with its own special characteristics, among which men are at liberty to choose, as may suit their individual tastes. There is but one kind of theism, religion, evangelicalism, and if there are several constructions laying claim to these names they differ from one another, not as correlative species of a more inclusive genus, but only as more or less good or bad specimens of the same thing differ from one another.

Calvinism comes forward simply as pure theism, religion, evangelicalism, as over against less pure theism, religion, evangelicalism. It does not take its position then by the side of other types of these things; it takes its place over them, as what they too ought to be. It has no difficulty thus, in recognizing the theistic character of all truly theistic thought, the religious note in all really religious manifestations, the evangelical quality of all actual evangelical faith. It refuses to be set antagonistically over against these where they really exist in any degree. It claims them in every instance of their emergence as its own, and seeks only to give them their due place in thought and life. Whoever believes in God, whoever recognizes his dependence on God, whoever hears in his heart the echo of the *Soli Deo gloria* of the evangelical profession—by whatever name he may call himself; by whatever logical puzzles

enlightenment cultural context are particularly conflicted for this strand of evangelicalism. It is also the sector most inclined to attempt to corner the market and claim a monopoly of authentic evangelical convictions. From Warfield to Lloyd-Jones and beyond, calvinistic-exclusivism is a recurrent theme.[21]

The Weber-Hunter approach has significant advantages over that of Dorrien,[22] who identified four evangelical traditions in chronological sequence: classical (Lutheran, Reformed and Anglican), pietist (early dissent and Wesleyan), early to mid-twentieth century fundamentalist and now the emergent progressives. Weber and Hunter dissociate more precisely the anabaptist, holiness and conversionist sectors that are conflated by Dorrien within pietism, and recognise the continuing interaction of divergent sectors within the chronological development.

In the UK, Hunter's formulation of these four traditions can be recast as Conversionist (Hunter's Baptist), Holiness (Hunter's Methodist), Reformed (Hunter's Reformational-Confessional) and Anabaptist (*idem*). In left-right theological – and socio-political - sequence they can then be re-ordered as Anabaptist, Holiness, Conversionist and Reformed. The conversionist-activist axis predominates among the Anabaptists, Holiness and Conversionist traditions, and the biblicist-crucicentric among the Reformed. Pentecostalism, the dominant twentieth century expression of the Holiness tradition, tends to be closest to the calvinistic-exclusivists in its theological conservatism.[23] However, rationalistic fundamentalism has always balked at Pentecostals' emphatic expressivism and expansive supernaturalism. Although the intellectual prominence of Anglican evangelicalism tends to conceal the impact of Weber's quartet in the UK context, all four emphases may nonetheless be found in creative tension among English evangelicals, not only in the Free Churches, but also within the various streams of evangelical Anglicans and Anglican evangelicals.

This approach provides a comprehensive and succinct identification of the broad contours and distinctive landscape of the evangelical tradition, denoting the enduring and irresolvable differences between the various schools of evangelicals.

---

his understanding may be confused—Calvinism recognizes such as its own, and as only requiring to give full validity to those fundamental principles which underlie and give its body to all true religion to become explicitly a Calvinist.
Warfield, 1970: 308

From this perspective, taking enlightenment assumptions as self-evident, any variance from pre-critical calvinistic rationalism is a dilution of doctrinal purity and evangelical authenticity. A positive transition to postmodern theological constructs is inconceivable. This rationalist exclusivism is an enlightenment-constrained dead-end. Indeed, Warfield was remarkably close to David Hume's scepticism when he asserted that not a single miracle had occurred since the death of the last apostle (Warfield, 1918:21). In their understanding of the present, Warfield and Hume both inhabited a similarly closed universe, one sceptical, the other dispensational.

[21] Carson, 1996; Murray, 2000; Erickson, Helseth et al, 2004.

[22] Dorrien, 1998: 4-7.

[23] Kay, 2000.

Weber-Hunter's four traditions can plausibly be recast as conflictual emphases, generating new expressions of the evangelical tradition in their mutual friction. These rivalries and incompatibilities indicate tendencies that are fissiparous yet evolutionary. Contrary to the claims of the exclusivist tendency that denounces rivals and claims monopolistic and exclusive rights as sole arbiter of evangelical legitimacy, the long-term capacity for sustainability and reconfiguration within the evangelical tradition resides not in any supposedly monolithic homogeneity and conformity, but rather in conflictual heterogeneity. Evangelicalism is a tradition through which the fault lines of contradictory emphases proliferate and yet this diversity produces not only a proneness to fragmentation, but also a perdurable capacity for experiments in self-reconstruction.

Building on Weber-Hunter's four traditions, in the light of our study of English pan-evangelicalism, we can construct an historical taxonomy of evangelical traditions and trajectories. Nineteenth century revivalism and the Keswick movement both represent periods of coalescence between the holiness and conversionist traditions, as does twentieth century charismatic experientialism. By the end of the twentieth century, the long-standing sectors within the evangelical tradition had evolved into seven micro-paradigms[24] - social activism, post conservatism, charismatic experientialism, pentecostal expressivism, conventional conversionism, calvinistic conservatism, and calvinistic-exclusivism. (Around the margins are three further sectors we have identified, related but distinct from the pan-evangelical continuum: the fundamentalists, post-evangelicals and hyper-entrepreneurials.) These seven sectors can be grouped into three meso-paradigms – progressives, cautiously open conservatives and exclusivists. These need, of course, to be conceived as a continuum rather than a tripolarity.

Our final, additional level of necessary complexity is to locate the interrelationship between this continuum within the sub-traditions of evangelicalism and the twin axes we have identified and examined. Paradoxically, the biblicist-crucicentric axis is predominant both on the Left and on the Centre-Right to Right of the tradition, inevitably with substantively different modulations. In the Centre to Centre-Left the conversionist-activist axis predominates. The complex internal dynamics of pan-evangelicalism demonstrate the difficulties of sustaining coalition and priority negotiation between the sub-traditions. Their various paradigms, depending on which axis predominates and according to their enlightenment or postmodern orientation, may often, as Kuhn argued concerning scientific paradigms,[25] render the various sectors alienated from one another and mutually uncomprehending.

The evangelical tradition has always been far more protean and diverse than the more zealous advocates of various evangelical certainties have been prepared to acknowledge. The broad and evolving evangelical coalition is a complex matrix of

---

[24] Kung applied Kuhn's paradigm theory to Christian theology and proposed the need for macro, meso and micro paradigms (1989: 21). See also Bosch, 1991: 181-189.

[25] Kuhn, 1962.

strands in tension. We have examined three profound reconstructions of English evangelicalism in the period 1966-2000, establishing three successive loci of pan-evangelical identity: the fissile conservative hegemony; the entrepreneurial boom and bust; and the emergent post-conservative experiments, paralleled on the Right by resurgent fundamentalising tendencies. Since enlightenment-oriented neo-conservatives and postmodern-oriented progressives operate within mutually exclusive paradigms, we conclude that the evangelical tradition appears to be in the process of bifurcation. It is even possible that both sectors may ultimately prefer to avoid the title evangelical, from the Right as diluted by accommodation, both progressive and entrepreneurial, from the Left as tainted with the negativities of fundamentalism and the absurdities of vision inflation. We further conclude that at the end of the period herein studied, pan-evangelical identity appeared severely weakened, with no grouping well-placed to generate new subcultural capital and thus reconstruct pan-evangelical identity: the neo-conservatives are too exclusivist, the activists too implausible, and the progressives too alienated from the excesses of the two previously dominant sectors.

The progressives' readiness to critique the evangelical tradition may result in an impatient dismissal of the undelivered promises of naïve entrepreneurialism and the tentative re-engagement of the cautiously open conservatives with the breadth of church, theology and culture. At the same time, the unreconstructed conservatives will inevitably consider the progressives compromised in their reformulations of the theological tradition. Unreflexive entrepreneurs may similarly consider progressives half-hearted or merely cynical when they remain unconvinced by the grandiose expectations of the latest entrepreneurial initiatives.

The pivotal sector in this diversification is the moderate conservatives. They are united with the Right by their instinctive conservatism and resistance to compromise. At the same time, their commitment to the conversionist-activist axis instils a continuing willingness to engage with church and society, wider theology and culture. (In the 1980s-1990s, some staff members within UCCF, according to interviews, appeared to have typified this ambivalent middle ground, more conservative than the current evangelical consensus, and yet greatly influenced by Stott and thus far resisting any further absorption into the narrow neo-conservatism of Chicago-1978 and GC-1999, yet coming under increasing pressure from the Right.[26]) The moderate conservatives, inhabiting the cautiously open middle ground, are likely to determine the fate of the evangelical coalition, as they decide whether their future is more with the neo-conservatives or the progressives. If, as I suspect, the cautiously open will ultimately prefer to align more closely with the neo-conservatives, it is the progressives who are more likely to evolve away from pan-evangelicalism, not so much repudiating their roots in the evangelical tradition, but alienated by the intensifying fundamentalising tendencies of the Right.

Our analysis finds the evangelical tradition repeatedly reconfigured, often unconsciously, by the majority culture they wish to influence and from which they

---

[26] Indicated to me in conversation by senior staff.

seek a measure of protective isolation. They emerge as dogged optimists and resiliently pragmatic opportunists among the Christians traditions, innovating with an evolutionary energy that belies their image of die-hard conservatism, diverse in their theologies and responses to the wider church and postmodernity. They have the demonstrated capacity to achieve more than the prescriptive formulations of the secularization thesis had anticipated, yet considerably less than their own rhetoric, particularly among the entrepreneurials, has habitually promised.

We have identified the disruptive implications of a theological pluralism grounded in mutually exclusive certainties that undermine any claims to pan-evangelical homogeneity. The common conviction of unreconstructed conservatism and enthusiastic entrepreneurialism is that the other is evangelicalism's Achilles' heel. However, we have argued that they are in equal need of rigorous and self-critical reformulation to secure any prospect of broader credibility within, let alone beyond the evangelical constituency. Evangelicalism could be self-marginalised by an absorption into neo-fundamentalism, or self-deluded by hyper-entrepreneurial vision inflation. Neither unreconstructed conservatism nor the extravagantly optimistic and highly pragmatic entrepreneurialism that supplanted it as the dominant form of English evangelicalism 1980-2000 has the plausibility to construct and sustain a new hegemony within the evangelical tradition in the early twenty-first century. The twin axes of pan-evangelicalism – conversionist-activist and biblicist-crucicentric – have both been diminished by excessive and assertive certainties.

The numerical collapse of alternative traditions, Protestant and Catholic,[27] means that any post-secular Christian future will inevitably and perhaps increasingly be shaped by the evangelicals. A successful deviant religion is energized by the voluntarism of convertive piety notwithstanding the absence of a sympathetic societal sacred canopy.[28] There still adheres to evangelicalism something of the sectarian energy of the early Baptists, Wesleyans and Pentecostals, and even the proselytizing resilience of the first Christians who, in facing an empire both hostile and indifferent, transitioned rapidly from a Jewish sect to the most effective cult of the late Roman Empire.[29] If European secularization should prove terminal, as Bruce argued,[30] evangelicals can now be expected to face late-onset decline, followed by full participation in the death of Christian Europe.[31] However, if European secularization proves to be self-limiting, as Stark concluded,[32] although more likely

---

[27] The decline in Catholic churchmanship during the decade to 1998 was 48%, compared with 11% for liberal and 19% for broad church (Brierley: 1998, 1999, 2000, 2001). The comparative decline for evangelicals was 3%. The evangelicals are therefore not immune to decline, but are either declining at an entirely different long-term rate or facing late-onset decline. Either way, at least in the short to medium term, their relative numerical strength will almost certainly continue to increase.

[28] Berger, 1967; Stark and Bainbridge, 1985; Cox, 1996; Martin, 2002.

[29] Stark, 1997.

[30] Bruce, 1995, 2002.

[31] Brown, 2001.

[32] Stark and Bainbridge, 1985, 1987.

to result in an enduring spiritual residue than a spiritual revolution,[33] the futures of evangelicalism depend on which sectors of the evangelical tradition survive and prosper through the internecine battles of reconstruction currently in ferment.

Frei aspired to the emergence of a generous orthodoxy[34] to which he believed evangelicals could make a significant contribution. If progressive evangelicals can combine an irenic and inclusive embrace of broad and generous Trinitarian orthodoxy with a robust retention of urgency and creativity in mission - that is a postmodern integration of the biblicist-crucicentric with the conversionist-activist - they may yet make a highly constructive contribution to the future, perhaps even the survival, of the European church. Three factors in the continuing evolution of pan-evangelicalism seem inevitable: entrepreneurs will continue to promise extravagant and imminent results; neo-conservatives will remain obdurately exclusivist, with overt or implicit fundamentalising tendencies; and the twin axes of pan-evangelicalism, biblicist-crucicentric and conversionist-activist, will continue to produce alternative and often conflictual formulations of evangelical convictions, priorities and subcultural identity.

---

[33] Heelas, Woodhead et al, 2005.

[34] Frei, 1993: 208. Lindbeck was similarly irenic: "If the sort of research program represented by postliberalism has a real future as a communal enterprise of the church, it's more likely to be carried on by evangelicals than by anyone else." (Phillips and Ockholm, 1996: 253).

APPENDICES

Appendix 1 - The Semi-Structured Interviews

1) Evangelical Alliance

What were the key factors in growth in the late twentieth century?
Why did EA membership plateau in early 1990s?
How significant was EA-1996?
What are the strengths and weaknesses of EA, historically and at present?

2) Spring Harvest

How and why did it begin?
What are its key ingredients, strengths and weaknesses?
Why has it been so successful?
How do you explain the combination of new church and parachurch speakers with delegates mainly from the historic denominations?
How do you assess the Calver-Meadows partnership? - contributions and phases.
Were the 1990s different? Had it become the new evangelical establishment? How did it function as the biggest event when it was no longer growing?
How do you view the leadership transition and future prospects?
To what extent and in what ways has SH changed the face of British pan-evangelicalism?
Why did SH come to be seen as a threat by some in the late 1990s?

3) Magazines

Why have subscription levels to evangelical magazines declined since the early 80s?

4) Morale and Vision

How do you see changing morale and opportunities in 1980s, 1990s, 2000s?
Has pan-evangelicalism served women well?

5) Other Observations

Do you want to add any other comments on evangelicals in this period?

Appendix 2 - Progressive Faith

Although some post-conservatives will doubt the value of any basis of faith other than the conciliar creeds, we have demonstrated that pan-evangelicalism has exhibited a sustained and distinctive predilection for new-minted bases. In the light of the trajectories previously identified, we offer the following as a succinct, post-conservative reformulation of the pre-fundamentalist evangelical tradition within the broader context of a generous and inclusive Trinitarian orthodoxy.

Generous Orthodoxy - *a progressive affirmation*
We believe in:

The only true God, the almighty Creator of the cosmos - full of love and glory - existing eternally in three persons, Father, Son, and Holy Spirit.

The supreme authority of the Lord Jesus Christ as God's Word incarnate; the unique divine inspiration, trustworthiness and authority of the Bible; and the right and duty of private judgment in the interpretation of the Scriptures.

The value, dignity and equality of all people, irrespective of gender, ethnicity or age, made in God's image to live in love and goodness, but alienated from God and one another through self-centred living.

The full divinity and humanity of Christ, his sinless life, atoning death, bodily resurrection, ascension into heaven, and victorious reign.

Justification by God's grace alone for all who repent and put their faith in Christ.

The transforming presence of the Holy Spirit, who draws women and men into the Trinity's communion of love.

The unity of all believers in Christ; manifest in worshipping and witnessing churches, called to make disciples and proclaim worldwide God's Kingdom of forgiveness and reconciliation, freedom and justice, care for creation and eternal salvation.

Christ's final judgment of all people, with mercy and justice, and his welcome for all he redeems into eternal glory.

To the God of eternal love be praise forever.

Appendix 3 - Evangelical Traditions in Twentieth Century Transitions

Fundamentalists

Formative Evangelical traditions			
Anabaptist	Holiness	Conversionist	Reformed

Methodism / Revivalism C18th-19th
Evangelical Alliance mid C19th
Keswick late C19th
IVF/UCCF early C20th

Mid C20th variants			
Social activism	Pentecostal expressivism	Conventional conversionism	Calvinistic conservatism

Late C20th developments

Charismatic experientialism (from 1960s)
Engaged Evangelicals – Lausanne (from mid-1970s)
Entrepreneurial Evangelicals – Calverism (from 1980s)

Late C20th / Early C21st:- 7 sectors						
Post-conservatism	Social activism	Charismatic experientialism	Pentecostal expressivism	Conventional conversionism	Calvinistic conservatism	Calvinistic exclusivism

The Evangelical Spectrum:- 3 orientations		
Progressives	Cautiously open Conservatives	Exclusivists
biblicist-crucicentric	*conversionist-activist*	*biblicist-crucicentric*

Former Evangelicals

Bibliography

Abraham, William J. (1981). *The Divine Inspiration of Scripture*. Oxford, Oxford University Press.

Abraham, William J. (1984). *The Coming Great Revival: Recovering the Full Evangelical Tradition*. San Francisco, Harper & Row.

Abraham, William J. (1989). *The Logic of Evangelism*. Grand Rapids, Mich., Eerdmans.

Abraham, William J. (1998). *Canon and Criterion in Christian Theology: From the Fathers to Feminism*. Oxford, Oxford University Press.

Abraham, William J. (2003). *The Logic of Renewal*. London, SPCK.

ACUTE (1998). *Faith, Hope and Homosexuality*. Carlisle, Paternoster.

Adey, L. (1988). *Hymns and the Christian Myth*. Vancouver, University of Colombia Press.

Adler, Patricia A and Peter Adler (1994). Observational Techniques. *Handbook of Qualitative Research*. N. Denzin and Y. S. Lincon, Eds. Newbury Park, Sage: 377-392.

Adorno, Theodor W. and J. M. Bernstein (1991). *The Culture Industry: Selected Essays on Mass Culture*. London, Routledge.

Agar, M (1980). *The Professional Stranger*. New York, Academic Press.

Alliance of Confessing Evangelicals (1996). "The Cambridge Declaration". 20 April, 1996. www.alliancenet.org/intro/CamDec.html

Allen, Leslie C. (1976). *The Books of Joel, Obadiah, Jonah, and Micah*. Grand Rapids, Mich., Eerdmans.

Alter, Robert (1981). *The Art of Biblical Narrative*. New York, Basic Books.

Alter, Robert (1985). *The Art of Biblical Poetry*. Edinburgh, T & T Clark.

Ammerman, Nancy Tatom (1990). *Baptist Battles: Social Change and Religious Conflict in the Southern Baptist Convention*. New Brunswick, Rutgers University Press.

Ammerman, Nancy Tatom, Jackson W. Carroll, et al., Eds. (1998). *Studying Congregations*. Nashville, Abingdon Press.

Anderson, Allan (2004). *An Introduction to Pentecostalism - Global Charismatic Christianity*. Cambridge, Cambridge University Press.

Anderson, Ray S. (2001). *The Shape of Practical Theology - Empowering Ministry with Theological Praxis*. Downers Grove, Ill., IVP.

Anselm (ET 1998). *The Major Works*. Oxford, Oxford University Press.

Armstrong, Karen (2000). *The Battle for God: Fundamentalism in Judaism, Christianity and Islam*. London, Harper Collins.

Arnold, David O, Ed. (1970). *The Sociology of Subcultures*. Berkeley, Glendessary Press.

Arrington, Robert L and Mark Addis, Eds. (2001). *Wittgenstein and Philosophy of Religion*. London, New York, Routledge.

Arweck, Elisabeth and Martin D Stringer, Eds. (2002). *Theorizing Faith: The Insider / Outsider Problem in the Study of Ritual*. Birmingham, University of Birmingham Press.

Avis, Paul, Ed. (2003). *Public Faith - the State of Religious Belief and Practice in Britain*. London, SPCK.

Balleine, G. R. (1908). *A History of the Evangelical Party in the Church of England*. London, Longmans, Green.

Balmer, Randall Herbert (1989). *Mine Eyes Have Seen the Glory: A Journey into the Evangelical Subculture in America*. New York, Oxford, Oxford University Press.

Barclay, Oliver R. (1997). *Evangelicalism in Britain 1935-1995: A Personal Sketch.* Leicester, IVP.

Barclay, Oliver R. and Robert M. Horn (2002). *From Cambridge to the World: 125 Years of Student Witness.* Leicester, IVP.

Barna, G (2002). "American Faith Is Diverse - as Shown among Five Faith-Based Segments," http://www.barna.org/FlexPage.aspx?Page=BarnaUpdate&BarnaUpdateID=105

Barnett, P. (2000). Tom Wright and the New Perspective. www.anglicanmediasydney.asn.au/pwb/ntwright_perspective.htm

Barr, James (1961). *The Semantics of Biblical Language.* Oxford, Oxford University Press.

Barr, James (1977). *Fundamentalism.* London, SCM.

Barr, James (1984). *Escaping from Fundamentalism.* London, SCM.

Barr, James (2004). *The Concept of Biblical Theology.* London, SCM.

Barrett, David, Kurian George, et al., Eds. (1982, 2001). *The World Christian Encyclopedia.* Oxford, New York, Oxford University Press.

Barrett, David and Todd Johnson (2001). *World Christian Trends.* Pasadena, William Carey Library.

Barth, Karl (1963). *Evangelical Theology: An Introduction.* London, Weidenfeld & Nicolson.

Barthes, Roland (1977). *Image, Music, Text.* London, Fontana.

Bartholomew, Craig, Colin Greene, et al. (2000). *Renewing Biblical Interpretation.* Carlisle, Paternoster.

Bartholomew, Craig, Robin Parry, et al., Eds. (2003). *The Futures of Evangelicalism.* Leicester, IVP.

Barton, John (1993). *People of the Book? The Authority of the Bible in Christianity.* London, SPCK.

Barton, John (1997). *The Spirit and the Letter: Studies in the Biblical Canon.* London, SPCK.

Baudrillard, Jean (2001). *Selected Writings.* Oxford, Polity.

Bauman, Zygmunt (1991). *Modernity and Ambivalence.* Cambridge, Polity.

Bauman, Zygmunt (1997). *Postmodernity and Its Discontents.* Cambridge, Polity.

Bauman, Zygmunt (2000). *Liquid Modernity.* Cambridge, Polity.

Bax, Josephine (1986). *The Good Wine: Spiritual Renewal in the Church of England.* London, Church House Publishing.

Beasley-Murray, Paul (1992). *Radical Believers: The Baptist Way of Being the Church.* Didcot, Oxon, Baptist Union of Great Britain.

Beasley-Murray, Paul and Alan Wilkinson (1981). *Turning the Tide: An Assessment of Baptist Church Growth in England.* London, Bible Society.

Bebbington, D. W. (1989). *Evangelicalism in Modern Britain: A History from the 1730s to the 1980s.* London, Unwin Hyman.

Bebbington, D. W. (1994). Evangelicalism in Its Settings: The British and American Movements since 1940. *Evangelicalism: Comparative Studies of Popular Protestantism in North America, the British Isles and Beyond.* M. A. Noll, D. W. Bebbington and G. A. Rawlyk, Eds. Oxford, Oxford University Press: 365-388.

Bebbington, D. W. (2005). *The Dominance of Evangelicalism: The Age of Spurgeon and Moody.* Leicester, IVP.

Beckham, William (1995). *The Second Reformation.* Houston, Touch Publications.

Begbie, Jeremy, Ed. (2002). *Sounding the Depths: Theology through the Arts.* London, SCM.

Bell, Daniel (1976). *The Coming of Post-Industrial Society.* New York, Basic Books.

Bellah, Robert Neelly, Richard Madsen, et al. (1996). *Habits of the Heart: Individualism and Commitment in American Life.* Berkeley, University of California Press.

Benjamin, Walter (1968). *Illuminations*. New York, Harcourt Brace & World.
Bennett, Andy and Keith Kahn-Harris, Eds. (2004). *After Subculture*. London, Palgrave Macmillan.
Berger, Peter L. (1961). *The Noise of Solemn Assemblies: Christian Commitment and the Religious Establishment in America*. Garden City, N.Y, Doubleday.
Berger, Peter L. (1967). *The Sacred Canopy: Elements of a Sociological Theory of Religion*. Garden City, N.Y, Doubleday.
Berger, Peter L. (1970). *A Rumour of Angels: Modern Society and the Rediscovery of the Supernatural*. London, Allen Lane.
Berger, Peter L. (1979). *The Heretical Imperative: Contemporary Possibilities of Religious Affirmation*. New York, Doubleday.
Berger, Peter L., Ed. (1999). *The Desecularization of the World: Resurgent Religion and World Politics*. Washington, D.C., Grand Rapids, Mich., Ethics and Public Policy Center.
Berger, Peter L. and Thomas Luckmann (1966). *The Social Construction of Reality: A Treatise in the Sociology of Knowledge*. New York, Doubleday.
Bhabha, Homi K (1994). *The Location of Culture*. London, New York, Routledge.
Bibby, Reginald (1987). *Fragmented Gods: The Poverty and Potential of Religion in Canada*. Toronto, Irwin.
Bibby, Reginald and Martin Brinkerhoff (1973). "The Circulation of the Saints: A Study of People Who Join Conservative Churches." *Journal for the Scientific Study of Religion* 112: 273-285.
Bibby, Reginald and Martin Brinkerhoff (1974). "When Proselytizing Fails: An Organizational Analysis." *Sociological* Analysis 35: 189-200.
Bibby, Reginald and Martin Brinkerhoff (1983). "Circulation of the Saints Revisited: A Longitudinal Look at Conservative Church Growth." *Journal for the Scientific Study of Religion* 22: 253-262.
Blamires, Harry (1963). *The Christian Mind*. London, SPCK.
Blamires, Harry (2001). *The Post-Christian Mind*. London, SPCK.
Bloesch, Donald G. (1983). *The Future of Evangelical Christianity: A Call for Unity Amid Diversity*. Garden City, N.Y., Doubleday.
Bloesch, Donald G. (1984). *Crumbling Foundations*. Grand Rapids, Mich., Zondervan.
Bonhoeffer, Dietrich (ET 1971). *Letters and Papers from Prison*. London, SCM.
Booker, M and M Ireland (2003). *Evangelism - Which Way Now?* London, Church House Publishing.
Bosch, David Jacobus (1991). *Transforming Mission: Paradigm Shifts in Theology of Mission*. Maryknoll, N.Y, Orbis Books.
Bosso, Christopher J (1999a). The Color of Money: Environmental Groups and the Pathologies of Fund Raising. *Interest Group Politics*. A. J. Cigler and B. A. Loomis. Washington, Congressional Quarterly Press.
Bosso, Christopher J (1999b). "Review of the Protest Business? Moblizing Campaign Groups by Grant Jordan and William Maloney." *American Political Science Review* 93: 467.
Bourdieu, P (ET 1984). *Distinction: A Social Critique of the Judgment of Taste*. Cambridge, Harvard University Press.
Brady, S. and H. Rowdon, Eds. (1996). *For Such a Time as This: Perspectives on Evangelicalism, Past Present and Future*. Milton Keynes, Scripture Union.
Bramadat, Paul (2000). *The Church on the World's Turf: An Evangelical Christian Group at a Secular University*. New York, Oxford, Oxford University Press.
Brencher, John (2002). *Martyn Lloyd-Jones (1899-1981) and Twentieth-Century*

Evangelicalism. Carlisle, Paternoster.

Brierley, Peter W. (1991a). *'Christian' England: What the 1989 English Church Census Reveals*. London, MARC Europe.

Brierley, Peter W. (1991b). *Prospects for the Nineties: All England: Trends and Tables from the English Church Census, with Denominations and Churchmanships*. London, MARC Europe.

Brierley, Peter W. (1998). *Religion in Britain 1900-2000*. London, Christian Research.

Brierley, Peter W. (2000). *The Tide Is Running Out: What the English Church Attendance Survey Reveals*. London, Christian Research.

Brierley, Peter W., Ed. (2001). *Religious Trends 3*. London, Christian Research.

Brierley, Peter W. (2003). *Turning the Tide*. London, Christian Research.

Brierley, Peter W. (2006) *Pulling out of the Nosedive: A Contemporary Picture of Churchgoing - What the 2005 English Church Census Reveals*. London, Christian Research.

Brierley, Peter W. (2006) *Religious Trends 6*. London, Christian Research.

Brierley, Peter W., Deborah Davies, et al., Eds. (1998). *Religious Trends 1*. London, Christian Research; Carlisle, Paternoster.

Brierley, Peter W. and Georgina Sanger, Eds. (1999). *Religious Trends 2*. London, Christian Research; London, Harper Collins.

Brown, Callum G. (2001). *The Death of Christian Britain: Understanding Secularisation 1800-2000*. London, Routledge.

Brown, Callum G. (2006). *Religion and Society in Twentieth-Century Britain*. London, Longman.

Brown, Dale (1978). *Understanding Pietism*. Grand Rapids, Mich., Eerdmans.

Brown, Ford K. (1961). *Fathers of the Victorians: The Age of Wilberforce*. Cambridge, Cambridge University Press.

Brown, T. (1853). *Proceedings of the General Assembly of the Free Church of Scotland, Held in Edinburgh, May 1843*. Edinburgh, John Greig & Son.

Brown, T. (1892). *Annals of the Disruption, with Extracts from the Narratives of Ministers Who Left the Scottish Establishment in 1843*. Edinburgh, MacNiven & Wallace.

Browning, Don S. (1991). *A Fundamental Practical Theology - Descriptive and Strategic Proposals*. Minneapolis, Augsburg Fortress.

Bruce, Steve (1989). *God Save Ulster*. Oxford, Oxford University Press.

Bruce, Steve (1995). *Religion in Modern Britain*. Oxford, Oxford University Press.

Bruce, Steve (1996). *Religion in the Modern World: From Cathedrals to Cults*. Oxford, Oxford University Press.

Bruce, Steve (1999). *Choice and Religion*. Oxford, Oxford University Press.

Bruce, Steve (2001). *Fundamentalism*. Malden, Mass., Polity.

Bruce, Steve (2002). *God Is Dead: Secularization in the West*. Oxford, Blackwell.

Brueggemann, Walter (1997). *Theology of the Old Testament*. Minneapolis, Augsburg Fortress.

Brummer, Vincent (2005). *Atonement, Christology and the Trinity*. Aldershot, Ashgate.

Bruyn, Severyn (1966). *The Human Perspective in Sociology: The Methodology of Participant Observation*. Englewood Cliffs, Prentice Hall.

Bstan-dzin-rgya-mtsho, Dalai Lama XIV (1999). *The Dalai Lama's Book of Wisdom*. London, Harper Collins.

Buber, Martin (ET 1958, new edition 2000). *I and Thou*. New York, Scribner.

Bunyan, John (1955). *Grace Abounding to the Chief of Sinners*. London, SCM Press.

Cahoone, Lawrence, Ed. (1996). *From Modernism to Postmodernism*. Oxford, Blackwell.

Caird, George B. (1980). *The Language and Imagery of the Bible*. London, Duckworth.

Calver, Clive (1987). *Where Truth and Justice Meet*. London, Hodder & Stoughton.

Calver, Clive (1992). "The Jerusalem Paper" – 28 November 1992. Unpublished. London, Evangelical Alliance.

Calver, Clive (1999). "Postmodernism: An Evangelical Blind Spot?" October 1999. Evangelical Missions Quarterly. www.wheaton.edu/bgc/EMIS/1999/postmodern2.htm

Calver, Clive, Ian Coffey, et al. (1993). *Who Do Evangelicals Think They Are?* London, Evangelical Alliance.

Calver, Clive, Derek Copley, et al., Eds. (1984). *A Guide to Evangelism*. Basingstoke, Marshall, Morgan & Scott.

Calver, Clive and R. Warner (1996). *Together We Stand*. London, Hodder & Stoughton.

Cameron, Helen, Philip Richter, et al., Eds. (2005). *Studying Local Churches*. London, SCM.

Cameron, Nigel M de S., Ed. (1992). *Universalism and the Doctrine of Hell: Papers Presented at the Fourth Edinburgh Conference in Christian Dogmatics, 1991*. Carlisle, Paternoster; Grand Rapids, Mich., Baker Book House.

Campbell, Ted A. (1991). *The Religion of the Heart*. Columbia, University of South Carolina Press.

Capon, John (1977). *Evangelicals Tomorrow: The National Evangelical Anglican Congress 1977*. Glasgow, Collins.

Carey, George (1977). *I Believe in Man*. London, Hodder & Stoughton.

Carey, George (1986). *The Gate of Glory*. London, Hodder & Stoughton.

Carnell, Edward John (1959). *The Case for Orthodox Theology*. Philadelphia, Westminster Press.

Carson, Donald A. (1978). *The Sermon on the Mount: An Evangelical Exposition of Matthew 5-7*. Grand Rapids, Mich, Baker.

Carson, Donald A., Ed. (1984). *Biblical Interpretation and the Church: Text and Context*. Exeter, Paternoster.

Carson, Donald A. (1986). *From Triumphalism to Maturity: A New Exposition of 2 Corinthians 10-13*. Leicester, IVP.

Carson, Donald A. (1996). *The Gagging of God: Christianity Confronts Pluralism*. Leicester, IVP.

Carson, Donald A. (undated). "Domesticating the Gospel: a Review of *Renewing the Center* by Stanley J. Grenz", www.modernreformation.org/monthly/grenzreview.html

Carson, Donald A. and John D. Woodbridge (1983). *Scripture and Truth*. Leicester, IVP.

Carson, Donald A. and John D. Woodbridge, Eds. (1986). *Hermeneutics, Authority and Canon*. Leicester, IVP.

Carter, Grayson (2001). *Anglican Evangelicals: Protestant Secessions from the Via Media, C. 1800-1850*. Oxford, Oxford University Press.

Cartledge, Mark J (2003). *Practical Theology - Charismatic and Empirical Perspectives*. Carlisle, Paternoster.

Casanova, Josâe (1994). *Public Religions in the Modern World*. Chicago, London, University of Chicago Press.

Catherwood, C (1984). *Five Evangelical Leaders*. London, Hodder & Stoughton.

Chadwick, Owen (1966). *The Victorian Church: Volume 1, 1829-1859*. Oxford, New York, A & C Black.

Chadwick, Owen (1970). *The Victorian Church: Volume 2, 1860-1901*. Oxford, New York, A & C Black.

Chadwick, Owen (1975). *The Secularization of the European Mind in the Nineteenth Century: The Gifford Lectures in the University of Edinburgh for 1973-4*. Cambridge, Cambridge University Press.

Chalke, Steve and Alan Mann (2003). *The Lost Message of Jesus*. London, Grand Rapids, Mich., Zondervan.

Cheney, David (2004). Fragmented Cultures and Subcultures. *After Subculture*. A. Bennett and K. Kahn-Harris, Eds. London, Palgrave Macmillan.

Childs, Brevard (1979). *Introduction to the Old Testament as Scripture*. Philadelphia, Fortress.

Childs, Brevard (1985). *The New Testament as Canon: An Introduction*. Waco, Word Publishing.

Chung, Sung Wook, Ed. (2003). *Alister E. McGrath & Evangelical Theology*. Carlisle, Paternoster.

Church of England (2000). *Statistics: A Tool for Mission*. London, Church House Publishing.

Clapp, Rodney (1996). *A Peculiar People: The Church as Culture in a Post-Christian Society*. Downers Grove, Ill., IVP.

Coates, Gerald (1991). *An Intelligent Fire*. Eastbourne, Kingsway.

Cohen, Albert K. (1955). *Delinquent Boys: The Culture of the Gang*. Glencoe, Ill., The Free Press.

Cohen, Norman J, Ed. (1990). *The Fundamentalist Phenomenon: A View from within; a Response from Without*. Starkoff Institute Studies in Ethics and Contemporary Moral Problems. Grand Rapids, Mich., Eerdmans.

Coleman, Simon (2000). *The Globalisation of Charismatic Christianity: Spreading the Gospel of Prosperity*. Cambridge, Cambridge University Press.

Collins, Peter (2002). Connecting Anthropology and Quakerism: Transcending the Insider / Outsider Dichotomy. *Theorizing Faith - the Insider / Outsider Problem in the Study of Ritual*. E. Arweck and M. D. Stringer, Eds. Birmingham, University of Birmingham Press: 77-96.

Collins, Raymond (1983). Fundamentalism. *A New Dictionary of Christian Theology*. A. Richardson and J. Bowden, Eds. London, SCM: 223.

Colson, Charles W. and Michael Scott Horton, Eds. (1992). *Power Religion: The Selling Out of the Evangelical Church?* Chicago, Moody.

Cowan, Steven, Ed. (2000). *Five Views on Apologetics*. Grand Rapids, Mich., Zondervan.

Cox, Harvey (1996). *Fire from Heaven*. London, Cassell.

Cox, Jeffrey (1982). *The Churches in a Secular Society: Lambeth 1870-1930*. Oxford, Oxford University Press.

Cray, Graham (1992). "From Here to Where? The Culture of the Nineties." *Board of Mission Occasional Papers* 3.

Cray, Graham, Ed. (2004). *Mission-Shaped Church*. London, Church House Publishing.

Croft, Steven, Rob Frost, et al. (2005). *Evangelism in a Spiritual Age*. London, Church House Publishing.

Crossan, John D. (1991). *The Historical Jesus: The Life of a Mediterranean Jewish Peasant*. San Francisco, HarperSanFrancisco.

Crossan, John D. (1998). *The Birth of Christianity*. New York, Harper Collins.

Crouch, Colin (1999). *Social Change in Western Europe*. Oxford, Oxford University Press.

Cupitt, Don (1980). *Taking Leave of God*. London, SCM.

Currie, Robert, Alan Gilbert, et al. (1977). *Churches and Churchgoers: Patterns of Church Growth in the British Isles since 1700*. Cambridge, Cambridge University Press.

Dallimore, Arnold (1970). *George Whitefield: The Life and Times of the Great Evangelist of the Eighteenth-Century Revival (Vol 1)*. London, Banner of Truth.

Dallimore, Arnold (1980). *George Whitefield: The Life and Times of the Great Evangelist of the Eighteenth-Century Revival (Vol 2)*. Edinburgh, Banner of Truth.

Dallimore, Arnold (1984). *Spurgeon*. Edinburgh, Banner of Truth.

Darwin, Charles (1958 [1859]). *The Origin of Species*. New York, Mentor.

Davie, Grace (1994). *Religion in Britain since 1945: Believing without Belonging*. Oxford, Blackwell.

Davie, Grace (2000). *Religion in Modern Europe: A Memory Mutates*. Oxford, Oxford University Press.

Davie, Grace (2002). *Europe: The Exceptional Case*. London, Darton, Longman & Todd.

Davie, Grace (2007). *The Sociology of Religion*. London, Sage.

Davie, Grace, Paul Heelas, et al., Eds. (2003). *Predicting Religion*. Aldershot, Ashgate Publishing.

Davies, Ron (1992). *I Will Pour out My Spirit: A History and Theology of Revivals and Evangelical Awakenings*. Tunbridge Wells, Monarch.

Dayton, Donald W. (1987). *Theological Roots of Pentecostalism*. Metuchen, Scarecrow Press.

Dayton, Donald W. and Robert K. Johnston, Eds. (1991). *The Variety of American Evangelicalism*. Downers Grove, Ill., IVP.

Denzin, Norman K. (1970). *The Research Act in Sociology: A Theoretical Introduction to Sociological Methods*. London, Butterworths.

Denzin, Norman K. (1989). *Interpretive Interactionism*. Newbury Park, Sage.

Derrida, Jacques (1974). *Of Grammatology*. Baltimore, John Hopkins University Press.

Derrida, Jacques and Gil Anidjar (2002). *Acts of Religion*. New York, London, Routledge.

Dews, Peter, Ed. (1992). *Autonomy and Solidarity: Interviews with Jurgen Habermas*. London, Verso.

Dillon, Michelle, Ed. (2003). *Handbook to the Sociology of Religion*. Cambridge, Cambridge University Press.

Dobbelaere, K (1981). "Secularization: A Multi-Dimensional Concept." *Current Sociology* 29 (2): 1-213.

Donovan, Vincent J. (1982). *Christianity Rediscovered: An Epistle from the Masai*. London, SCM.

Dorrien, Gary J. (1998). *The Remaking of Evangelical Theology*. Louisville, Ky., Westminster John Knox Press.

Drane, John W. (2000). *Cultural Change and Biblical Faith: The Future of the Church: Biblical and Missiological Essays for the New Century*. Carlisle, Paternoster.

Drane, John W. (2000). *The McDonaldization of the Church: Spirituality, Creativity, and the Future of the Church*. London, Darton, Longman & Todd.

Dudley-Smith, Timothy (1999). *John Stott: The Making of a Leader*. Leicester, IVP.

Dudley-Smith, Timothy (2001). *John Stott: A Global Ministry*. Downers Grove, Ill., IVP.

Duffy, Eamon (1992). *The Stripping of the Altars: Traditional Religion in England C.1400-C.1580*. New Haven, London, Yale University Press.

Dulles, Avery (1976). *Models of the Church*. Dublin, Gill & Macmillan.

Dulles, Avery (1983). *Models of Revelation*. Dublin, Gill & Macmillan.

Dunn, James D. G. (1970). *Baptism in the Holy Spirit*. London, SCM.

Dunn, James D. G. (1975). *Jesus and the Spirit*. London, SCM.

Dunn, James D. G. (1977). *Unity and Diversity in the New Testament: An Inquiry into the Character of Earliest Christianity*. London, SCM.

Dunn, James D. G. (1987). *The Living Word*. London, SCM.

Dunn, James D. G. (1988). *Romans 1-8*. Dallas, Word Books.

Dunn, James D. G. (1988). *Romans 9-16*. Dallas, Word Books.

Dunn, James D. G. (1993). *Christian Liberty: A New Testament Perspective*. Carlisle, Paternoster.

Dunn, James D. G. (1998). *The Theology of Paul the Apostle*. Edinburgh, T & T Clark.

Dunn, James D. G. and Alan M. Suggate (1993). *The Justice of God: A Fresh Look at the Old Doctrine of Justification by Faith*. Carlisle, Paternoster.

Dunn, James Douglas Grant (1983). "The New Perspective on Paul." *BJRL* 65 (1983): 95-122.

Durkheim, Emile (1912, ET 2001). *The Elementary Forms of Religious Life*. Oxford, New York, Oxford University Press.

Dyrness, William A. (1982). *Christian Apologetics in a World Community*. Downers Grove, Ill., IVP.

Dyrness, William A. (2001). *Visual Faith: Art, Theology, and Worship in Dialogue*. Grand Rapids, Mich., Baker.

Earwicker, John and David Spriggs (1994). The 1994 Evangelistic Projects - a Review for the Council of the Evangelical Alliance. Unpublished. London, Evangelical Alliance.

Edwards, Brian H. (1990). *Revival! A People Saturated with God*. Durham, Evangelical Press.

Edwards, David L. (1987). *The Futures of Christianity*. London, Hodder & Stoughton.

Edwards, David L. (2002). *The Church That Could Be*. London, SPCK.

Edwards, David L. and John R. W. Stott (1988). *Essentials*. London, Hodder & Stoughton.

Eliot, George (1855). "Evangelical Teaching: Dr Cumming." *Westminster Review* 8.

Elwell, Walter A. (1984). *Evangelical Dictionary of Theology*. Grand Rapids, Mich; Carlisle, Baker; Paternoster.

Emerson, Michael and Christian Smith (2000). *Divided by Faith*. New York, Oxford University Press.

Erickson, Millard J. (1997). *The Evangelical Left: Encountering Postconservative Evangelical Theology*. Grand Rapids, Mich., Baker.

Erickson, Millard J. (1998). *Postmodernizing the Faith: Evangelical Responses to the Challenge of Postmodernism*. Grand Rapids, Mich., Baker.

Erickson, Millard J., Paul Kloss Helseth, et al., Eds. (2004). *Reclaiming the Center: Confronting Evangelical Accommodation in Postmodern Times*. Wheaton, Crossway.

Erikson, K T (1967). "A Comment on Disguised Observation in Sociology." *Social Problems* 14: 366-373.

Escott, Phillip and Alison Gelder (2002). *Church Life Profile 2001 - Denominational Results for the Baptist Union*. New Malden, London, Churches Information for Mission.

Evangelical Alliance (1845). *Conference on Christian Union: Being a Narrative of the Proceedings of the Meetings Held in Liverpool, October 1845*. London, Evangelical Alliance.

Evangelical Alliance (1847). *Report of the Proceedings of the Conference Held at Freemasons' Hall, London, from August nineteenth to September second Inclusive, 1846*. London, Partridge & Oakley.

Evangelical Alliance (1968). *On the Other Side*. London, Scripture Union.

Evangelical Alliance and EMA (1998). The Inaugural Annual Report of the EA/EMA Commission on Strategic Evangelism in the UK. Unpublished report. London, Evangelical Alliance and Evangelical Missionary Alliance.

Evans, Craig A (2000). *Mark 8:27-16:20*. Waco, Nelson Word.

Evans, E (1969). *The Welsh Revival of 1904*. Bridgend, Evangelical Press of Wales.

Fackre, G (1984). "Evangelical, Evangelicalism". *A New Dictionary of Christian Theology*. A. Richardson and J. Bowden, Eds. London, SCM.

Farrar, F. W. (1868). "The Attitude of the Clergy Towards Science." *Contemporary Review* 9.

Fenn, Richard, Ed. (2001). *Sociology of Religion*. The Blackwell Companion. Oxford, Blackwell.

Festinger, Leon (1957). *A Theory of Cognitive Dissonance*. Stanford (Calif.), Stanford University Press.

Festinger, Leon, Henry W. Riecken, et al. (1964). *When Prophecy Fails: A Social and Psychological Study of a Modern Group That Predicted the Destruction of the World*. New York; London, Harper & Row.

Feuerbach, Ludwig (1989). *The Essence of Christianity*. New York, Prometheus Books.

Feyerabend, Paul (1988). *Against Method*. London, Verso.

Fiddes, Paul S. (1988). *The Creative Suffering of God*. Oxford, Clarendon Press.

Fiddes, Paul S. (1989). *Past Event and Present Salvation: The Christian Idea of Atonement*. London, Darton Longman & Todd.

Fiddes, Paul S. (2000). *Participating in God*. Oxford, Darton, Longman & Todd.

Fielder, Geraint D. (1988). *Lord of the Years: Sixty Years of Student Witness: The Story of the Inter-Varsity Fellowship, Universities and Colleges Christian Fellowship, 1928-1988*. Leicester, IVP.

Finke, Roger and Rodney Stark (1992). *The Churching of America, 1776-1990: Winners and Losers in Our Religious Economy*. New Brunswick, N.J, Rutgers University Press.

Finney, Charles G. (1835). *Lectures on Revivals of Religion*. New York, Leavitt Lord; Boston, Crocker & Brewster.

Finney, John (1992). *Finding Faith Today*. Swindon, Bible Society.

Finney, John (2000). *Fading Splendour? A New Model of Renewal*. London, Darton, Longman & Todd.

Fischer, Claude (1975). "Towards a Subcultural Theory of Urbanism." *American Journal of Sociology* 80: 1319-1341.

Fish, Stanley (1980). *Is There a Text in This Class?* Cambridge, Harvard University Press.

Flanagan, Kieran (1992). "Sociology and Milbank's City of God." *New Blackfriars* vol 73, no 861, June 1992: 333-414.

Flannery, Austin, Ed. (1975, 1981). *Vatican Council II: The Conciliar and Post Conciliar Documents*. New York, Costello Publishing.

Florovsky, George (1972). *Bible, Church, Tradition: An Eastern Orthodox View*. Belmont, Nordland.

Fogel, Robert William (2000). *The Fourth Great Awakening and the Future of Egalitarianism*. Chicago, University of Chicago Press.

Forster, Chris (1995). *Planting for a Harvest: A Report on the Spiritual State of England*. Unpublished report. London, Challenge 2000.

Foster, Richard J. (1998). *Streams of Living Water - Celebrating the Great Traditions of Christian Faith*. San Francisco, Harper Collins.

Foucault, Michel (1984). *The Foucault Reader*. New York, Pantheon Books.

Fowler, James W. (1981). *Stages of Faith*. New York, Harper Collins.

Fowler, Linda L. and Ronald G. Shaiko (1987). "The Grass Roots Connection: Environmental Activists and Senate Roll Calls." *American Journal of Political Science* 31: 484-510.

France, R.T. (2002). *The Gospel of Mark*. Grand Rapids, Mich., Eerdmans.

France, R.T. and A.E. McGrath, Eds. (1993). *Evangelical Anglicans: Their Role and Influence in the Church Today*. London, SPCK.

Frei, Hans W. (1974). *The Eclipse of Biblical Narrative - a Study in Eighteenth and Nineteenth Century Hermeneutics*. New Haven, London, Yale University Press.

Frei, Hans W., George Hunsinger, et al. (1993). *Theology and Narrative - Selected Essays*. New York, Oxford, Oxford University Press.

Frost, Rob (2002). *Essence*. Warwick, CPAS; Eastbourne, Kingsway.

Frye, Northrop (1982). *The Great Code: The Bible and Literature*. London, Routledge & Kegan Paul.

Gadamer, Hans-Georg (1976). *Philosophical Hermeneutics*. Berkeley, University of California Press.

Gadamer, Hans-Georg (ET 1975). *Truth and Method*. London, Sheed & Ward.

Gallup Jr, G.H. (1996). *Religion in America*. Princeton, The Princeton Religious Research Centre.

Gallup Jr, G.H. and T. Jones (2000). *The Next American Spirituality*. Colorado Springs, Cook Communications.

Gallup Jr, G.H. and D.M. Lindsay (1999). *Surveying the Religious Landscape*. Harrisburg, Morehouse.

Gee, Peter and John Fulton, Eds. (1991). *Religion and Power, Decline and Growth: Sociological Analyses of Religion in Britain, Poland and the Americas*. London, British Sociological Association, Sociology of Religion Study Group.

Geertz, Clifford (1973). *The Interpretation of Cultures*. New York, Basic Books.

Gelder, Ken and Sarah Thornton, Eds. (1997). *The Subcultures Reader*. London, Routledge.

George, Timothy (1992). The Southern Baptist Wars. 9 March, 1992. *Christianity Today*.

George, Timothy (2000). "The Gospel Statement Revisited." 7 February, 2000. *Christianity Today*.

Gerth, H. H. and C. Wright Mill, Eds. (1948, new edition 1991). *From Max Weber*. London, New York, Routledge.

Gibbs, Eddie (1981). *I Believe in Church Growth*. London, Hodder & Stoughton.

Gibson, Alan F., Ed. (1992). *The Church and Its Unity*. Leicester, IVP.

Giddens, Anthony (1991). *Modernity and Self-Identity - Self and Society in the Late Modern Age*. Cambridge, Polity.

Giddens, Anthony (2006 (5th edition)). *Sociology*. Cambridge, Polity.

Gilbert, Alan D. (1980). *The Making of Post-Christian Britain - a History of the Secularization of Modern Society*. London, Longman.

Gill, Robin (1993). *The Myth of the Empty Church*. London, SPCK.

Gill, Robin (1995). *A Textbook of Christian Ethics*. London, T & T Clark.

Gill, Robin (1996). *Theology and Sociology*. London, Cassell.

Gill, Robin (1999). *Churchgoing and Christian Ethics*. Cambridge, Cambridge University Press.

Gill, Robin (2001). The Future of Religious Participation and Belief in Britain and Beyond. *The Blackwell Companion to Sociology of Religion*. R. Fenn. Oxford, Blackwell: 279-291.

Gill, Robin (2002). *Changing Worlds*. Edinburgh, T & T Clark.

Gill, Robin (2003). *The "Empty Church" Revisited*. Aldershot, Ashgate.

Gillquist, Peter (1992). *Becoming Orthodox*. Ben Lomand, Conciliar Press.

Goffman, Erving (1956). *The Presentation of Self in Everyday Life*. Edinburgh, University of Edinburgh Social Sciences Research Centre.

Gold, R L (1958). "Roles in Sociological Field Observation." *Social Forces* 36: 217-223.

Goldingay, John (1987). *Theological Diversity and the Authority of the Old Testament*. Grand Rapids, Mich., Eerdmans.

Goldingay, John (1994). *Models for Scripture*. Grand Rapids, Mich,, Eerdmans; Carlisle, Paternoster.

Goldingay, John, Ed. (1995). *Atonement Today*. London, SPCK.

Goldingay, John (1995). *Models for Interpretation of Scripture*. Grand Rapids, Mich., Eerdmans; Carlisle, Paternoster.

Gordon, James M. (1991). *Evangelical Spirituality*. London, SPCK.

Gordon, Milton, M (1947). "The Concept of the Sub-Culture and Its Application." *Social Forces* 26: 40-42.

Gospel Celebration (1999). "Gospel Celebration, Special Supplement." 14 June, 1999. *Christianity Today*.

Graham, Billy (1997). *Just as I Am: The Autobiography of Billy Graham*. London, Harper Collins.

Graham, Elaine L (2002). *Transforming Practice: Pastoral Theology in an Age of Uncertainty*. Eugene, Wipf and Stock.

Graham, Elaine L, Heather Walton, et al., Eds. (2005). *Theological Reflection: Methods*. London, SCM.

Gray, T and C Sinkinson, Eds. (2000). *Reconstructing Theology: A Critical Assessment of the Theology of Clark Pinnock*. Carlisle, Paternoster.

Green, Joel B and Mark D Baker (2000). *Recovering the Scandal of the Cross: Atonement in New Testament and Contemporary Contexts*. Downers Grove, Ill., IVP.

Green, Michael (1975). *I Believe in the Holy Spirit*. London, Hodder & Stoughton.

Green, Michael (1981). *I Believe in Satan's Downfall*. London, Hodder & Stoughton.

Grenz, Stanley (1993). *Revisioning Evangelical Theology*. Downers Grove, Ill., IVP.

Grenz, Stanley (1994). *Theology for the Community of God*. Carlisle, Paternoster.

Grenz, Stanley (1996). *A Primer on Postmodernism*. Grand Rapids, Mich., Eerdmans.

Grenz, Stanley (2000). *Renewing the Center: Evangelical Theology in a Post-Theological Era*. Grand Rapids, Mich., Baker.

Grenz, Stanley (2003). "Toward an Undomesticated Gospel: A Response to D. A. Carson." *Perspectives in Religious Studies* 30: 455-461.

Grenz, Stanley and John R. Franke (2001). *Beyond Foundationalism: Shaping Theology in a Postmodern Context*. Louisville, Ky., Westminster John Knox Press.

Grudem, Wayne A. (1994). *Systematic Theology: An Introduction to Biblical Doctrine*. Leicester, IVP.

Guelich, Robert A (1989). *Mark 1-8:26*. Waco, Tex., Nelson Word.

Guest, Matthew (2002). 'Alternative Worship': Challenging the Boundaries of the Christian Faith. *Theorizing Faith - the Insider / Outsider Problem in the Study of Religion*. E. Arweck and M. D. Stringer, Eds. Birmingham, University of Birmingham Press: 35-56.

Guest, Matthew, Karin Tusting, et al., Eds. (2004). *Congregational Studies in the UK*. Aldershot, Ashgate.

Guinness, Os (1995). *Fit Bodies, Fat Minds: Why Evangelicals Don't Think and What to Do About It*. London, Hodder and Stoughton.

Gundry, Robert Horton (1982). *Matthew: A Commentary on His Literary and Theological Art*. Grand Rapids, Mich., Eerdmans.

Gundry, Robert Horton (2001). "Why I Didn't Endorse 'The Gospel of Jesus Christ: An Evangelical Celebration', Even Though I Wasn't Asked To." February, 2001. *Christianity Today*.

Gunton, Colin E. (1988). *The Actuality of Atonement*. Edinburgh, T & T Clark.
Gunton, Colin E. (1991, 1997, 2003). *The Promise of Trinitarian Theology*. Edinburgh, T. & T. Clark.
Gunton, Colin E. (1993). *The One, the Three and the Many: God, Creation and the Culture of Modernity*. Cambridge, Cambridge University Press.
Gunton, Colin E. (2001). *Becoming and Being: The Doctrine of God in Charles Hartshorne and Karl Barth*. London, SCM.
Hall, Stuart, David Held, et al., Eds. (1992). *Modernity and Its Futures*. Cambridge, Polity.
Halman, Loek, Ed. (2001). *The European Values Study: A Third Wave*. Tilburg, Tilburg.
Halman, Loek and Ole Riis (2002). *Religion in Secularizing Society: The Europeans' Religion at the End of the twentieth Century*. Leiden; Boston, Brill
Hamilton, Malcolm B. (1995). *The Sociology of Religion: Theoretical and Comparative Perspectives*. London, New York, Routledge.
Hammond, Phillip E. (1992). *Religion and Personal Autonomy: The Third Disestablishment in America*. Columbia, University of South Carolina.
Harries, Richard (2002). *God Outside the Box*. London, SPCK.
Harris, Harriet Anne (1998). *Fundamentalism and Evangelicals*. Oxford, Clarendon.
Harvey, David (1990). *The Condition of Postmodernity: An Enquiry into the Origins of Cultural Change*. Oxford, Blackwell.
Hastings, Adrian (2001). *A History of English Christianity 1920-2000*. London, SCM.
Hatch, N. O. (1989). *The Democratization of American Christianity*. New Haven, Yale University Press.
Hauerwas, Stanley (2001). *The Hauerwas Reader*. Durham, London, Duke University Press.
Hebdige, D (1979). *Subculture: The Meaning of Style*. London, Methuen.
Heelas, Paul, David Martin, et al., Eds. (1998). *Religion, Modernity, and Postmodernity*. Oxford, Blackwell.
Heelas, Paul, Linda Woodhead, et al., Eds. (2005). *The Spiritual Revolution - Why Religion Is Giving Way to Spirituality*. Oxford, Blackwell.
Henry, Carl F. H. (1976-82, 6 vols). *God, Revelation, and Authority*. Waco, Tex., Word Books.
Henry, Carl F. H. (1976). "Reaction and Realignment". Vol. 20, Issue 20, *Christianity Today*.
Herberg, Will (1955). *Protestant, Catholic, Jew: An Essay in American Religious Sociology*. Garden City, N.Y., Doubleday.
Hervieux-Léger, Danielle (1986). *Vers Un Nouveau Christianisme?* Paris, Cerf.
Hervieux-Léger, Danielle (1999). *Le Pèlerin Et Le Converti. La Religion En Mouvement*. Paris, Flammarion.
Hick, John, Ed. (1964). *Faith and Philosophers*. London, Macmillan.
Hicks, Peter (1998). *Evangelicals & Truth: A Creative Proposal for a Postmodern Age*. Leicester, IVP.
Hiebert, P.G. (1994). *Anthropological Reflections on Missiological Issues*. Grand Rapids, Mich., Baker.
Hilborn, David (1997). *Picking up the Pieces: Can Evangelicals Adapt to Contemporary Culture?* London, Hodder & Stoughton.
Hilborn, David, Ed. (2000). *The Nature of Hell*. Carlisle, Paternoster.
Hilborn, David, Ed. (2001). *"Toronto" in Perspective*. Carlisle, Paternoster.
Hilborn, David, Ed. (2004). *Movement for Change*. Carlisle, Paternoster.
Hill, Charles E and Frank A James, Eds. (2004). *The Glory of the Atonement - Biblical, Theological and Practical Perspectives*. Downers Grove, Ill., IVP.

Hill, Charles E. (2001). "N.T. Wright on Justification", vol.3, number 22, 2001. IIIM Magazine Online. www.thirdmill.org/files/english/html/NT.h.Hill.Wright.html.

Hirsch, E. D. (1967). *Validity in Interpretation*. Yale, Yale University Press.

Hirsch, E. D. (1976). *The Aims of Interpretation*. Chicago, University of Chicago Press.

Hobsbawn, Eric and Terence Ranger, Eds. (1983). *The Invention of Tradition*. Cambridge, Cambridge University Press.

Hocken, Peter (1997 (1986)). *Streams of Renewal*. Carlisle, Paternoster.

Hodder, Edwin (1887). *The Life and Work of the Seventh Earl of Shaftesbury, K.G.* London, Cassell.

Hopewell, James F. (1987). *Congregation - Stories and Structures*. Philadelphia, Fortress Press.

Hopler, T. (1981). *A World of Difference*. Downers Grove, Ill., IVP.

Houston, J. M. (1980). *I Believe in the Creator*. London, Hodder & Stoughton.

Howard, Anthony (2005). *Basil Hume: The Monk Cardinal*. London, Headline.

Hufford, David J (1995). "The Scholarly Voice and the Personal Voice: Reflexivity in Belief Studies." *Western Folklore* 54: 57-76.

Hughes, R.K. (1995). *Are Evangelicals Born Again?* Wheaton, Ill., Crossway.

Hume, Basil (1979). *Searching for God*. London, Hodder & Stoughton.

Hume, David (1993). *Dialogues Concerning Natural Religion and the Natural History of Religion*. Oxford, Oxford University Press.

Hume, David (1999 (1748)). *An Enquiry Concerning Human Understanding*. Oxford, Oxford University Press.

Hunt, Stephen (2001). *Anyone for Alpha? Evangelism in a Post-Christian Society*. London, Darton, Longman & Todd.

Hunt, Stephen (2004). *The Alpha Enterprise*. Aldershot, Ashgate.

Hunter, James Davison (1983). *American Evangelicalism: Conservative Religion and the Quandary of Modernity*. New Brunswick, Rutgers University Press.

Hunter, James Davison (1987). *Evangelicalism: The Coming Generation*. Chicago, Ill.; London, University of Chicago Press.

Hunter, James Davison (1990). Fundamentalism in Its Global Contours. *The Fundamentalist Phenomenon: A View from within; a Response from Without*. N. J. Cohen, Ed. Grand Rapids, Mich., Eerdmans: 56-72.

Hunter, James Davison (1991). *Culture Wars: The Struggle to Define America*. New York, Basic Books.

Hybels, Lynne and Bill (1995). *Rediscovering Church: The Story and Vision of Willow Creek*. Grand Rapids, Mich., Zondervan.

Hylson-Smith, K (1988). *Evangelicals in the Church of England 1734-1984*. Edinburgh, T & T Clark.

Irwin, John (1970). Notes on the Present Status of the Concept Subculture. *The Sociology of Subcultures*. David O. Arnold, Ed. Berkeley, Glendessary Press: 164-170.

Israel, Jonathan Irvine (2001). *Radical Enlightenment: Philosophy and the Making of Modernity 1650-1750*. Oxford, Oxford University Press.

Jackson, Bob (2002). *Hope for the Church*. London, Church House Publishing.

James, John Angel (1834). *The Anxious Inquirer after Salvation Directed and Encouraged*. London, Religious Tract Society.

James, John Angel (1834, third edition 1861). *The Principles of Dissent, and the Duties of Dissenters*. London, Hamilton, Adams and Co.

Jamieson, Alan (2002). *A Churchless Faith: Faith Journeys Beyond the Churches*. London,

SPCK.

Jeffrey, David Lyle, Ed. (1987). *English Spirituality in the Age of Wesley.* Grand Rapids, Mich., Eerdmans.

Jenkins, Henry (1992). *Textual Poachers.* London, Routledge.

Jenkins, Philip (2002). *The Next Christendom: The Coming of Global Christianity.* New York, Oxford, Oxford University Press.

Jinkins, Michael (1999). *The Church Faces Death: Ecclesiology in a Post-Modern Context.* New York, Oxford, Oxford University Press.

Johnson, Benton (1963). "On Church and Sect." *American Sociological Review* 28: 539-549.

Johnson, Gary and R Fowler White, Eds. (2001). *Whatever Happened to the Reformation?* Phillipsburg, Presbyterian & Reformed.

Johnston, A (1978). *The Battle for World Evangelism.* Wheaton, Ill., Tyndale House.

Jungel, Eberhard (2001). *Justification: The Heart of the Christian Faith: A Theological Study with an Ecumenical Purpose.* Edinburgh, New York, T & T Clark.

Kant, Immanuel (ET 1929). *Critique of Pure Reason.* Basingstoke, Palgrave Macmillan.

Kant, Immanuel (ET 1997). *Critique of Practical Reason.* Cambridge, Cambridge University Press.

Kant, Immanuel (ET 1998). *Religion within the Boundaries of Mere Reason.* Cambridge, Cambridge University Press.

Kay, William K. (2000). *Pentecostals in Britain.* Carlisle, Paternoster.

Kay, William K. and Anne E. Dyer, Eds. (2004). *Pentecostal and Charismatic Studies.* London, SCM.

Kelley, Dean M. (1972). *Why Conservative Churches Are Growing: A Study in Sociology of Religion.* New York, Harper & Row.

Kermode, Frank (1979). *The Genesis of Secrecy: On the Interpretation of Narrative.* Cambridge, Mass, Harvard University Press.

Kermode, Frank (1990). *Poetry, Narrative, History.* Oxford, Blackwell.

Kessler, J. B. A. (1968). *A Study of the Evangelical Alliance in Great Britain.* Goes, Netherlands, Oosterbaan & Le Cointre.

Kirk, J. Andrew (1999). *What Is Mission? Theological Explorations.* London, Darton, Longman & Todd.

Knight, Henry H. (1997). *A Future for Truth.* Nashville, Abingdon Press.

Kraft, Charles H. (1979). *Christianity in Culture: A Study in Dynamic Biblical Theologizing in Cross-Cultural Perspective.* Maryknoll, N.Y., Orbis Books.

Kraft, Charles H. (1998). *I Give You Authority.* Crowborough, Monarch.

Kuhn, Thomas (1962). *The Structure of Scientific Revolutions.* Chicago, University of Chicago Press.

Kung, Hans (ET 1989). *Paradigm Change in Theology.* New York, Crossroad.

Kung, Hans and Jurgen Moltmann, Eds. (1992). *Fundamentalism as an Ecumenical Challenge.* Concilium; 1992/3. London, SCM.

Lambert, Yves (2000). Religion in Modernity as a New Axial Age. *The Secularization Debate.* W. Swatos and D. Olson. Oxford, Rowman & Littlefield: 95-125.

Lampe, Geoffrey (1962). The Atonement: Law and Love. *Soundings.* A. R. Vidler. Cambridge, Cambridge University Press: 173-191.

Lane, Anthony N. S. (2002). *Justification by Faith in Catholic-Protestant Dialogue.* London, New York, T & T Clark.

Lausanne Committee for World Evangelization (1982). *Evangelism and Social Responsibility: An Evangelical Commitment.* Exeter, Paternoster.

Lewis, Donald M., Ed. (2004). *Christianity Reborn: The Global Expansion of Evangelicalism in the Twentieth Century.* Studies in the History of Christian Missions. Grand Rapids, Mich., Eerdmans.

Lewis, Sinclair (1927). *Elmer Gantry.* London, Jonathan Cape.

Lincoln, Bruce (1996). "Theses on Method." *Method & Theory in the Study of Religion* 8/3: 225-227.

Lindbeck, George A. (1984). *The Nature of Doctrine: Religion and Theology in a Postliberal Age.* Philadelphia, Westminster Press.

Lindbeck, George A. and James Joseph Buckley (2002). *The Church in a Postliberal Age.* London, SCM.

Lindsell, Harold (1976). *The Battle for the Bible.* Grand Rapids, Mich., Zondervan.

Lindsell, Harold (1979). *The Bible in the Balance.* Grand Rapids, Mich., Zondervan.

Lindsey, Hal and Carole C. Carlson (1971). *The Late Great Planet Earth.* London, Lakeland.

Lints, Richard (1993). *The Fabric of Theology: A Prolegomenon to Evangelical Theology.* Grand Rapids, Mich., Eerdmans.

Lloyd-Jones, David Martyn (1989). *Knowing the Times: Addresses Delivered on Various Occasions, 1942-1977.* Edinburgh, Banner of Truth.

Lloyd-Jones, David Martyn (1991). *Unity in Truth.* Darlington, Evangelical Press.

Locke, John (1870 [1689-1693]). *Four Letters on Toleration.* London, Alexander Murray.

Lovelace, Richard F. (1979). *Dynamics of Spiritual Life: An Evangelical Theology of Renewal.* Exeter, Paternoster.

Lundin, Roger, Clarence Walhout, et al. (1999). *The Promise of Hermeneutics.* Grand Rapids, Mich., Eerdmans.

Lyotard, Jean Francois (1979, 1984). *The Postmodern Condition: A Report on Knowledge.* Manchester, Manchester University Press.

Machin, G.I.T. (1998). *Churches and Social Issues in Twentieth Century Britain.* Oxford, Oxford University Press.

MacIntyre, Alasdair (1964). Is Understanding Religion Compatible with Believing? *Faith and Philosophers.* J. Hick. London, Macmillan.

MacIntyre, Alasdair (1984, 1985). *After Virtue.* Notre Dame, University of Notre Dame Press.

MacIntyre, Alasdair (1988). *Whose Justice? Which Rationality?* London, Duckworth.

MacLaren, Duncan (2003). Precarious Visions - a Sociological Critique of European Scenarios of Desecularization. Unpublished PhD thesis. *King's College, London University.*

MacLaren, Duncan (2004). *Mission Implausible - Restoring Credibility to the Church.* Carlisle, Paternoster.

Macquarrie, John (1966, 1977). *Principles of Christian Theology.* London, SCM.

Mallone, George (1984). *Those Controversial Gifts: Prophecy Dreams Visions Tongues Interpretation Healing.* London, Hodder & Stoughton.

Mann, H (1853). *Census of Great Britain, 1851: Religious Worship, England and Wales. Reports and Tables. Presented to Both Houses of Parliament by Command of Her Majesty.* London, Eyre & Spottiswoode for Her Majesty's Stationery Office.

Mannheim, Karl (1936). *Ideology and Utopia.* London, Routledge & Kegan Paul.

Manwaring, Randle (1985). *From Controversy to Co-Existence: Evangelicals in the Church of England, 1914-1980.* Cambridge, Cambridge University Press.

Marsden, George M. (1980). *Fundamentalism and American Culture: The Shaping of Twentieth Century Evangelicalism, 1870-1925.* New York, Oxford University Press.

Marsden, George M. (1984). *Evangelicalism and Modern America.* Grand Rapids, Mich,

Eerdmans.

Marsden, George M. (1987). *Reforming Fundamentalism: Fuller Seminary and the New Evangelicalism.* Grand Rapids, Mich., Eerdmans.

Marsden, George M. (1990, 2001 second edition). *Religion and American Culture.* San Diego; London, Harcourt Brace Jovanovich.

Marsden, George M. (1991). *Understanding Fundamentalism and Evangelicalism.* Grand Rapids, Mich, Eerdmans.

Marsden, George M. and Bradley J. Longfield (1992). *The Secularization of the Academy.* New York, Oxford, Oxford University Press.

Marshall, I. Howard (1977). *I Believe in the Historical Jesus.* London, Hodder & Stoughton.

Marshall, I. Howard (1982). *Biblical Inspiration.* London, Hodder & Stoughton.

Martin, Bernice (1998). From Pre- to Post-Modernity in Latin America: The Case of Pentecostalism. *Religion, Modernity and Postmodernity.* P. Heelas, D. Martin and P. Morris, Eds. Oxford, Blackwell: 102-146.

Martin, David (1978). *The Dilemmas of Contemporary Religion.* Oxford, Blackwell.

Martin, David (1978). *A General Theory of Secularization.* Oxford, Blackwell.

Martin, David (2002). *Pentecostalism: The World Their Parish.* Oxford, Blackwell.

Martin, David (2005). *On Secularization: Towards a Revised General Theory.* Aldershot, Ashgate.

Marty, Martin E. (1992). What Is Fundamentalism? Theological Perspectives. *Fundamentalism as an Ecumenical Challenge.* H. Kung and J. Moltmann. London, SCM: 3-13.

Marty, Martin E., R. Scott Appleby, Eds. (1991). *Fundamentalisms Observed.* Chicago, London, University of Chicago Press.

Marty, Martin E., R. Scott Appleby, Eds. (1993). *Fundamentalisms and Society: Reclaiming the Sciences, the Family and Education.* Chicago, London, University of Chicago Press.

Marty, Martin E., R. Scott Appleby, Eds. (1993). *Fundamentalisms and the State: Remaking Polities, Economies and Militance.* Chicago, London, University of Chicago Press.

Marty, Martin E., R. Scott Appleby, Eds. (1995). *Fundamentalisms Comprehended.* Chicago, London, University of Chicago Press.

Marty, Martin E., R. Scott Appleby, Eds. (1994). *Accounting for Fundamentalisms: The Dynamic Character of Movements.* Chicago, London, University of Chicago Press.

Marx, Karl and Friedrich Engels (1992 [1848, ET 1888]). *The Communist Manifesto.* Oxford, Oxford University Press.

Maurice, F. D. (1853, 4th edition 1881). *Theological Essays.* London, MacMillan and Co.

McBain, Douglas (1997). *Fire over the Waters: Renewal among Baptists and Others from the 1960s to the 1990s.* London, Darton, Longman & Todd.

McCutcheon, Russell T, Ed. (1999). *The Insider / Outsider Problem in the Study of Religion.* London, New York, Cassell.

McFague, Sallie (1975). *Speaking in Parables: A Study in Metaphor and Theology.* London, SCM.

McGavran, Donald Anderson (1970). *Understanding Church Growth.* Grand Rapids, Mich., Eerdmans.

McGrath, Alister E. (1994). *Evangelicalism and the Future of Christianity.* London, Hodder & Stoughton.

McGrath, Alister E. (1994). *The Making of Modern German Christology, 1750-1990.* Leicester, IVP.

McGrath, Alister E. (1996). *A Passion for Truth: The Intellectual Coherence of*

Evangelicalism. Leicester, IVP.

McGrath, Alister E. (1997). *To Know and Serve God: A Life of James I. Packer*. London, Hodder & Stoughton.

McGrath, Alister E. (2001). *A Scientific Theology Volume 1: Nature*. Edinburgh, T & T Clark.

McGrath, Alister E. (2002). *A Scientific Theology Volume 2: Reality*. Edinburgh, T & T Clark.

McGrath, Alister E. (2003). *A Scientific Theology Volume 3: Theory*. London, T & T Clark.

McGrath, Alister E. (2004). *The Science of God*. London, T & T Clark.

McIntire, C.T. (1984). Fundamentalism. *Evangelical Dictionary of Theology*. W. A. Elwell, Ed. Grand Rapids, Mich; Carlisle, Baker; Paternoster: 435.

McLaren, Brian (2004). *A Generous Orthodoxy*. Grand Rapids, Mich., Zondervan.

Merenlahti, Petri (2002). *Poetics for the Gospels?* London, T & T Clark.

Meyers, Kenneth (1992). A Better Way: Proclamation Instead of Protest. *Power Religion: The Selling out of the Evangelical Church*. C. Colson and M. Horton, Eds. Chicago, Moody Press.

Middleton, J. Richard and Brian J. Walsh (1995). *Truth Is Stranger Than It Used to Be: Biblical Faith in a Postmodern Age*. London, SPCK.

Milbank, John (1990). *Theology and Social Theory: Beyond Secular Reason*. Oxford, Blackwell.

Milbank, John, Catherine Pickstock, et al. (1998). *Radical Orthodoxy: A New Theology*. London, Routledge.

Mill, John Stuart (1974 [1859]). *On Liberty*. London, Penguin.

Milne, Bruce (1982). *Know the Truth: A Handbook of Christian Belief*. Leicester, IVP.

Moltmann, Jurgen (1977). *The Church in the Power of the Spirit: A Contribution to Messianic Ecclesiology*. London, SCM.

Moltmann, Jurgen and Margaret Kohl (1992). *The Spirit of Life: A Universal Affirmation*. London, SCM.

Monk, Ray (1991). *Ludwig Wittgenstein: The Duty of Genius*. London, Random House.

Montefiore, Hugh, Ed. (1992). *The Gospel and Contemporary Culture*. London, Mowbray.

Montgomery, J (2001). "It Is a Dawn Strategy If." www.dawnministries.org

Moore, James R, Ed. (1988). *Religon in Victorian Britain, Vol 3 Sources*. Manchester, Manchester University Press.

Morris, J. N. (1992). *Religion and Urban Change: Croydon, 1840-1914*. Woodbridge, Suffolk; Rochester, N.Y., Boydell Press for The Royal Historical Society; Boydell & Brewer.

Morris, Leon (1955). *The Cross in the New Testament*. London, Tyndale Press.

Morris, Leon (1976). *I Believe in Revelation*. London, Hodder & Stoughton.

Morris, Leon (1983). *The Atonement: Its Meaning and Significance*. Leicester, IVP.

Morrison, Ken (1995). *Marx, Durkheim, Weber*. London, Sage.

Muggleton, David and Rupert Weinzierl, Eds. (2003). *The Post-Subcultures Reader*. Oxford, New York, Berg.

Murphy, Nancey (1994). Textual Relativism, Philosophy of Language and the Baptist Vision. *Theology without Foundations*. S. Hauerwas, N. Murphy and M. Nation. Nashville, Abingdon Press: 245-270.

Murphy, Nancey (1996). *Beyond Liberalism and Fundamentalism: How Modern and Postmodern Philosophy Set the Theological Agenda*. Valley Forge, Pa., Trinity Press International.

Murray, Iain H. (1982). *David Martyn Lloyd-Jones: The First Forty Years 1899-1939.* Edinburgh, Banner of Truth.

Murray, Iain H. (1990). *David Martyn Lloyd-Jones: The Fight of Faith 1939-1981.* Edinburgh, Banner of Truth.

Murray, Iain H. (1994). *Revival and Revivalism: The Making and Marring of American Evangelicalism, 1750-1858.* Edinburgh, Banner of Truth.

Murray, Iain H. (2000). *Evangelicalism Divided.* Edinburgh, Banner of Truth.

Murray, Stuart (1998). *Church Planting: Laying Foundations.* Carlisle, Paternoster.

Murray, Stuart (2004). *Post-Christendom.* Carlisle, Paternoster.

Neighbour, Ralph W. (1990). *Where Do We Go from Here?* Houston, Touch Publications.

Neuhaus Richard, John (1986). *The Naked Public Square.* Grand Rapids, Mich., Eerdmans.

Neuhaus, Richard John and Paul Johnson, Eds. (1986). *Unsecular America: Essays.* Grand Rapids, Mich., Eerdmans Publishing.

Newbigin, Lesslie and Churches World Council of (1989). *The Gospel in a Pluralist Society.* Grand Rapids, Mich. Eerdmans; Geneva, WCC Publications.

Newman, Carey C., Ed. (1999). *Jesus and the Restoration of Israel: A Critical Assessment of N.T. Wright's Jesus and the Victory of God.* Downers Grove, Ill. IVP; Carlisle, Paternoster.

Newman, John Henry (1956 [1864]). *Apologia Pro Vita Sua.* Boston, Riverside.

Nicholas, Thomas (1860). *Dr Davidson's Removal from the Professorship of Biblical Literature in the Lancashire Independent College, Manchester, on Account of Alleged Error in Doctrine: A Statement of Facts, with Documents, Together with Remarks and Criticisms.* London, Williams & Norgate.

Nicholls, Mike (1992). *C. H. Spurgeon: The Pastor Evangelist.* Didcot, Baptist Historical Society.

Nicole, Roger (2004). Postcript on Penal Substitution. *The Glory of the Atonement.* C. E. Hill and F. A. James, Eds. Downers Grove, Ill., IVP.

Niebuhr, H. Richard (1929). *The Social Sources of Denominationalism.* New York, Henry Holt.

Niebuhr, Helmut Richard (1952). *Christ and Culture.* London, Faber & Faber.

Noll, Mark A. (1994). *The Scandal of the Evangelical Mind.* Grand Rapids, Mich. Eerdmans; Leicester, IVP.

Noll, Mark A. (2000). *American Evangelical Christianity: An Introduction.* Oxford, Malden, Mass., Blackwell.

Noll, Mark A. (2004). *The Rise of Evangelicalism.* Leicester, IVP.

Noll, Mark A., D. W. Bebbington, et al., Eds. (1994). *Evangelicalism: Comparative Studies of Popular Protestantism in North America, the British Isles, and Beyond, 1700-1990.* New York, Oxford, Oxford University Press.

O'Connell Killen, Patricia and John de Beer (2004). *The Art of Theological Reflection.* New York, Crossroad.

O'Donovan, Oliver (1996). *The Desire of the Nations.* Cambridge, Cambridge University Press.

Oden, Thomas (1990). *Agenda for Theology.* Grand Rapids, Mich., Zondervan.

Oden, Thomas (2003). *The Rebirth of Orthodoxy.* San Francisco, Harper Collins.

Olson, Roger (1995). "Postconservative Evangelicals Greet the Postmodern Age." *Christian Century* May 3, 1995: 480-483.

Olson, Roger (2000). Reforming Evangelical Theology. *Evangelical Futures: A Conversation on Theological Method.* G. Stackhouse John, Eds. Grand Rapids, Mich. Baker; Leicester,

IVP: 201-207.

Olson, Roger, Jonathan Wilson, et al. (2000). The Word Made Fresh: A Call for a Renewal of the Evangelical Spirit. www.home.apu.edu/~ctrf/fellowship/archives/wordmadefresh.html.

Osborn, Lawrence and Andrew Walker (1997). *Harmful Religion: An Exploration of Religious Abuse*. London, SPCK.

Otto, Rudolf (ET 1923). *The Idea of the Holy*. Oxford, Oxford University Press.

Packer, James I. (1958). *"Fundamentalism" and the Word of God*. London, IVF.

Packer, James I. (1973). *Knowing God*. London, Hodder & Stoughton.

Packer, James I. (1979). *God Has Spoken: Revelation and the Bible*. London, Hodder & Stoughton.

Packer, James I. (1989). *Laid-Back Religion? A Penetrating Look at Christianity Today*. Leicester, IVP.

Packer, James I. and Alister E. ed McGrath (1999). *The J.I. Packer Collection*. Leicester, IVP.

Packer, James I. (1962). "Questions About Inter-Varsity Fellowship." *Break Through* 11: 13-19.

Packer, James I. (1974). "What Did the Cross Achieve." *Tyndale* Bulletin 25: 3-45.

Packer, James I. (1978). *The Evangelical Anglican Identity Problem*. Oxford, Latimer House.

Padilla, C. R, Ed. (1976). *The New Face of Evangelicalism: An International Symposium on the Lausanne Covenant*. London, Hodder & Stoughton.

Parry, Robin (2005). *Worshipping Trinity*. Carlisle, Paternoster.

Partridge, Christopher H., Ed. (2001). *Fundamentalisms*. Carlisle, Paternoster.

Penning, James M. and Corwin E. Smidt (2002). *Evangelicalism: The Next Generation*. Grand Rapids, Mich., Baker.

Percy, Martyn (1996). *Words, Wonders and Power: Understanding Contemporary Christian Fundamentalism and Revivalism*. London, SPCK.

Percy, Martyn (1997). "Sweet Rapture: Subliminal Eroticism in Contemporary Charismatic Worship." *Theology and Sexuality* 6: 71-106.

Percy, Martyn (1998). "Join the Dots Christianity: Assessing Alpha." *Reviews in Religion and Theology* May, 1998.

Percy, Martyn (2003). Mind the Gap: Generational Change and Its Implications for Mission. *Public Faith? The State of Religious Belief and Practice in Britain*. P. Avis, Ed. London, SPCK.

Percy, Martyn (2005). *Engaging with Contemporary Culture: Christianity, Theology and the Concrete Church*. Aldershot, Ashgate.

Percy, Martyn and Ian Jones, Eds. (2002). *Fundamentalism, Church and Society*. London, SPCK.

Percy, Martyn, Andrew Walker, et al. (2001). *Restoring the Image: Essays on Religion and Society in Honour of David Martin*. Sheffield, Sheffield Academic Press.

Perriman, Andrew, Ed. (2003). *Faith, Health and Prosperity: A Report on "Word of Faith" and "Positive Confession" Theologies*. Carlisle, Paternoster.

Peskett, Howard and Vinoth Ramachandra (2003). *The Message of Mission*. Leicester, IVP.

Peterson, David, Ed. (2001). *Where Wrath and Mercy Meet*. Carlisle, Paternoster.

Peterson, Robert A. and Michael D. Williams (2004). *Why I Am Not Am Arminian*. Downers Grove, Ill., IVP.

Phillips, J.B. (1984). *The Price of Success*. London, Hodder & Stoughton.

Phillips, Timothy and Dennis Ockholm, Eds. (1996). *The Nature of Confession: Evangelicals and Postliberals in Conversation*. Downers Grove, Ill., IVP.

Pinnock, Clark H. (1985). *The Scripture Principle*. London, Hodder & Stoughton.
Pinnock, Clark H. (1990). Defining American Fundamentalism: A Response. *The Fundamentalist Phenomenon: A View from within; a Response from Without*. N. J. Cohen, Ed. Grand Rapids, Mich., Eerdmans: 38-55.
Pinnock, Clark H. (1996). *Flame of Love: A Theology of the Holy Spirit*. Downers Grove, Ill., IVP.
Pinnock, Clark H. (2001). *Most Moved Mover: A Theology of God's Openness*. Carlisle, Paternoster.
Pinnock, Clark H., R Rice, et al. (1994). *The Openness of God: A Biblical Challenge to the Traditional Understanding of God*. Downers Grove, Ill., IVP.
Plantinga, Alvin and Nicholas Wolterstorff, Eds. (1983). *Faith and Rationality: Reason and Belief in God*. Notre Dame, Ind., University of Notre Dame Press.
Pointer, Roy (1984). *How Do Churches Grow?* Basingstoke, Marshall, Morgan & Scott.
Pollock, J. C. (1978). *Wilberforce*. Berkhampstead, Lion Publishing.
Popper, Karl R. (1989). *Conjectures and Refutations: The Growth of Scientific Knowledge*. London, Routledge.
Porterfield, Amanda (2001). *The Transformation of American Religion*. Oxford, New York, Oxford University Press.
Postman, Neil (1985). *Amusing Ourselves to Death*. London, Methuen.
Price, Charles W. and Ian M. Randall (2000). *Transforming Keswick*. Carlisle, Paternoster.
Pullman, Philip (1995). *Northern Lights*. London, Scholastic.
Pullman, Philip (1997). *The Subtle Knife*. London, Scholastic.
Pullman, Philip (2000). *The Amber Spyglass*. London, Scholastic.
Putnam, Robert D. (2000). *Bowling Alone: The Collapse and Revival of American Community*. New York, Simon & Schuster.
Puttick, Elizabeth (1997). *Women in New Religions: In Search of Community, Sexuality and Spiritual Power*. London, Macmillan.
Pytches, David (1990). *Some Said It Thundered*. London, Hodder & Stoughton.
Quebedeux, R (1974). *The Young Evangelicals: Revolution in Orthodoxy*. New York, Harper & Row.
Ramm, Bernard L. (1973). *The Evangelical Heritage*. Grand Rapids, Mich., Baker.
Ramm, Bernard L. (1983). *After Fundamentalism: The Future of Evangelical Theology*. San Francisco, Harper & Row.
Randall, Ian M. (1999). *Evangelical Experiences: A Study in the Spirituality of English Evangelicalism 1918-1939*. Carlisle, Paternoster.
Randall, Ian M. (2000). *Educating Evangelicalism: The Origins, Development and Impact of London Bible College*. Carlisle, Paternoster.
Randall, Ian M. and David Hilborn (2001). *One Body in Christ: The History and Significance of the Evangelical Alliance*. Carlisle, Paternoster.
Raschke, Carl (2004). *The Next Reformation: Why Evangelicals Must Embrace Postmodernity*. Grand Rapids, Mich., Baker.
Reid, Gavin (1969). *The Gagging of God: The Failure of the Church to Communicate in the Television Age*. London, Hodder & Stoughton.
Reisinger, Ernest C and D Matthew Allen (2000). *A Quiet Revolution: A Chronicle of Beginnings of Reformation in the Southern Baptist Convention*. Cape Coral, Founders.
Rennie, Ian S (1994). Fundamentalism and the Varieties of North Atlantic Evangelicalism. *Evangelicalism: Comparative Studies of Popular Protestantism in North America, the British Isles, and Beyond, 1700-1990*. M. A. Noll, D. W. Bebbington and G. A. Rawlyk,

Eds. New York, Oxford, Oxford University Press: 333-350.

Richardson, Alan and John Bowden, Eds. (1984). *A New Dictionary of Christian Theology.* London, SCM.

Ricoeur, Paul (ET 1970). *Freud and Philosophy.* New Haven, Yale University Press.

Ricoeur, Paul (ET 1977). *The Rule of Metaphor.* London, New York, Routledge.

Ritzer, George (1993). *The McDonaldization of Society: An Investigation into the Changing Character of Contemporary Social Life.* Thousand Oaks; London, Pine Forge.

Ritzer, George (1998). *The McDonaldization Thesis: Explorations and Extensions.* London, Sage.

Robbins, Thomas (1988). *Cults, Converts and Charisma.* London, Sage.

Robinson, John A. T. (1963). *Honest to God.* London, SCM.

Robson, Colin (2002). *Real World Research.* Oxford, Blackwell.

Roof, Wade Clark (1999). *Spiritual Marketplace.* Princeton, Princeton University Press.

Roof, Wade Clark and William McKinney (1987). *American Mainline Religion: Its Changing Shape and Future.* New Brunswick, Rutgers University Press.

Rorty, Richard (1989). *Contingency, Irony, and Solidarity.* Cambridge, Cambridge University Press.

Rorty, Richard (1991). *Objectivity, Relativism and Truth.* Cambridge, Cambridge University Press.

Rorty, Richard (1999). *Philosophy and Social Hope.* London, Penguin.

Rouse, R and S Neill (1954). *A History of the Ecumenical Movement.* London, SPCK.

Sacks, Jonathan (2003). *The Dignity of Difference: How to Avoid the Clash of Civilisations.* London, Continuum.

Sacks, Jonathan (2005). *To Heal a Fractured World: The Ethics of Responsibility.* London, Continuum.

Sadgrove, M and N.T. Wright (1977). Jesus Christ the Only Saviour in *Obeying Christ in a Changing World.* J. R. W. Stott, Ed. London, Collins.

Samuel, Vinay and Chris Sugden (1999). *Mission as Transformation: A Theology of the Whole Gospel.* Oxford, Regnum.

Sanders, E. P. (1977). *Paul and Palestinian Judaism: A Comparison of Patterns of Religion.* London, SCM.

Saroglou, Vassilis (2006). "Religious *Bricolage* as a Psychological Reality: Limits, Structures and Dynamics." *Social Compass* 53(1): 109-115.

Saunders, Teddy and Hugh Sansom (1992). *David Watson: A Biography.* London, Hodder & Stoughton.

Saussure, Ferdinand de (1966). *Course in General Linguistics.* New York, McGraw Hill.

Saward, Michael (1987). *The Anglican Church Today: Evangelicals on the Move.* Oxford, Mowbray.

Schaeffer, Francis A. (1948). "Should the Christian Tolerate the World Council? Or Is Liberalism Dead?" *Christian Beacon* (29 July 1948): 4-5.

Schaeffer, Francis A. (1968). *The God Who Is There: Speaking Historic Christianity into the Twentieth Century.* London, Hodder & Stoughton.

Schaeffer, Francis A. (1984). *The Great Evangelical Disaster.* Westchester, Ill., Crossway Books.

Schleiermacher, Friedrich (ET 1988 [1799]). *On Religion - Speeches to Its Cultured Despisers.* Cambridge, Cambridge University Press.

Schleiermacher, Friedrich (ET 1998 [1838]). *Hermeneutics and Criticism and Other Writings.* Cambridge, Cambridge University Press.

Schluter, Michael, Ed. (2000). *Christianity in a Changing World: Biblical Insight on Contemporary Issues*. London, Marshall Pickering.

Schreiter, Robert J. (1985). *Constructing Local Theologies*. Maryknoll, Orbis.

Schwarz, Christian A. (1996). *Natural Church Development*. Moggerhanger, BCGA.

Scotland, Nigel (1995, second edition 2000). *Charismatics and the New Millennium*. Guildford, Eagle.

Scripture Union (1995). Council Report and Accounts. Unpublished report. London, Scripture Union.

Scripture Union International Council (1985). Aims, Beliefs and Basic Philosophy of Scripture Union. London, Scripture Union.

Sheppard, D (1983). *Bias to the Poor*. London, Hodder & Stoughton.

Sider, Ronald J. (1987). *Rich Christians in an Age of Hunger*. London, Hodder & Stoughton.

Silvoso, Ed (1994). *That None Should Perish: How to Reach Entire Cities for Christ through Prayer Evangelism*. Ventura, Regal Books.

Sjoberg, Gideon (1960). *The Preindustrial City, Past and Present*. Glencoe, Ill, Free Press.

Smail, Thomas A. (1975). *Reflected Glory*. Grand Rapids, Mich., Eerdmans.

Smail, Thomas A. (1980). *The Forgotten Father*. Grand Rapids, Mich., Eerdmans.

Smail, Thomas A. (1988). *The Giving Gift*. London, Hodder.

Smail, Thomas A., Andrew Walker, et al. (1995). *Charismatic Renewal: The Search for a Theology*. London, SPCK.

Smith, Christian (1998). *American Evangelicals: Embattled and Thriving*. Chicago, University of Chicago Press.

Smith, Christian (2000). *Christian America? What Evangelicals Really Want*. Berkeley, London, University of California Press.

Smith, Christian and Linda Lundquist Denton (2005). *Soul Searching: The Religious and Spiritual Lives of American Teenagers*. New York, Oxford University Press.

Smith, David (1998). *Transforming the World? The Social Impact of British Evangelicalism*. Carlisle, Paternoster.

Soskice, Janet M. (1985). *Metaphor and Religious Language*. Oxford, Oxford University Press.

Spinoza, Benedictus De (ET 1951 (1670)). *A Theologico-Political Treatise and a Political Treatise*. New York, Dover.

Spradley, James P. (1980). *Participant Observation*. New York, Holt, Rinehart & Winston.

Spring Harvest (2001). *Worship Today*. Uckfield, Spring Harvest.

Stackhouse, Ian (2004). *The Gospel-Driven Church*. Carlisle, Paternoster.

Stackhouse, John G., Ed. (2000). *Evangelical Futures: A Conversation on Theological Method*. Grand Rapids, Mich. Baker; Leicester, IVP.

Stackhouse, John G. (2002). *Evangelical Landscapes*. Grand Rapids, Mich., Baker.

Stark, Rodney (1997). *The Rise of Christianity*. San Francisco, Harper Collins.

Stark, Rodney and William S. Bainbridge (1985). *The Future of Religion: Secularization, Revival, and Cult Formation*. Berkeley, London, University of California Press.

Stark, Rodney and William S. Bainbridge (1987). *A Theory of Religion*. New York, Peter Lang.

Stark, Rodney and Roger Finke (2000). *Acts of Faith: Explaining the Human Side of Religion*. Berkeley, London, University of California Press.

Storrar, William F and Andrew R Morton, Eds. (2004). *Public Theology for the 21st Century*. London, T & T Clark.

Stott, John R. W. (1975). *Walk in His Shoes*. Leicester, IVP.

Stott, John R. W. (1992). *The Contemporary Christian: Applying God's Word to Today's World*. Downers Grove, Ill., IVP.

Stott, John R. W. and Robert B. Coote, Eds. (1981). *Down to Earth: Studies in Christianity and Culture - the Papers of the Lausanne Consultation on Gospel and Culture*. London, Hodder & Stoughton.

Stott, John R. W. (1975, 1986). *Christian Mission in the Modern World*. London, Eastbourne, Falcon, Kingsway.

Stott, John R. W. (1977). *What Is an Evangelical?* London, CPAS.

Stott, John R. W. (1970). *Christ the Controversialist: A Study in Some Essentials of Evangelical Religion*. London, Tyndale.

Stott, John R. W., Ed. (1977). *Obeying Christ in a Changing World*. London, Collins.

Stott, John R. W. (1982). *I Believe in Preaching*. London, Hodder & Stoughton.

Stott, John R. W. (1984 second edition 1990). *Issues Facing Christians Today*. London, Collins/Marshall Pickering.

Stott, John R. W. (1989). *The Cross of Christ*. Leicester, IVP.

Stott, John R. W. (1999). *Evangelical Truth: A Personal Plea for Unity*. Leicester, IVP.

Stott, John R. W. (1999). *New Issues Facing Christians Today*. London, Marshall Pickering.

Stott, John R. W. and David L. Edwards (1988). *Essentials: A Liberal-Evangelical Dialogue*. London, Hodder & Stoughton.

Stout, Harry S (1991). *The Divine Dramatist: George Whitefield and the Rise of Modern Evangelicalism*. Grand Rapids, Mich., Eerdmans.

Strauss, A and J Corbin (1990). *Basics of Qualitative Research: Grounded Theory Procedures and Techniques*. Newbury Park, Sage.

Swatos, William and Daniel Olson, Eds. (2000). *The Secularization Debate*. Lanham, Maryland, Rowman & Littlefield.

Swinburne, Richard (1979, 2004). *The Existence of God*. Oxford, New York, Oxford University Press.

Synan, Vinson (1971, 1997). *The Holiness-Pentecostal Tradition*. Grand Rapids, Mich., Eerdmans.

Tamney, Joseph B. (2002). *The Resilience of Conservative Religion: The Case of Popular, Conservative Protestant Congregations*. Cambridge, Cambridge University Press.

Tanner, Kenneth and Christopher A. Hall, Eds. (2002). *Ancient and Postmodern Christianity*. Downers Grove, Ill., IVP.

Taylor, Mark C. (1984). *Erring: A Postmodern a/Theology*. Chicago, Chicago University Press.

Taylor, Vincent (1940). *The Atonement in New Testament Teaching*. London, Epworth.

Thiselton, Anthony C. (1977). Understanding God's Word Today. *Obeying Christ in a Changing World*. John R. W. Stott, Ed. London, Collins.

Thiselton, Anthony C. (1980). *The Two Horizons: New Testament Hermeneutics and Philosophical Description with Special Reference to Heidegger, Bultmann, Gadamer, and Wittgenstein*. Exeter, Paternoster.

Thiselton, Anthony C. (1992). *New Horizons in Hermeneutics*. London, Harper Collins.

Thiselton, Anthony C. (1995). *Interpreting God and the Postmodern Self: On Meaning, Manipulation and Promise*. Edinburgh, T & T Clark.

Thiselton, Anthony C. (2002). *A Concise Encyclopedia of the Philosophy of Religion*. Oxford, Oneworld.

Thomas, Geoff (2000). Essentially Evangelical, January 2000. Banner of Truth Magazine. www.banneroftruth.co.uk/articles/2000/01/essentially_evangelical.htm

Thomas, Keith (1971). *Religion and the Decline of Magic: Studies in Popular Beliefs in Sixteenth and Seventeenth Century England*. London, Weidenfeld and Nicolson.

Thornton, Sarah (1995). *Club Cultures: Music, Media and Subcultural Capital*. Cambridge, Polity.

Tice, Rico and Barry Cooper (2002). *Christianity Explored*. Carlisle, Paternoster.

Tidball, Derek (1994). *Who Are the Evangelicals? Tracing the Roots of the Modern Movements*. London, Marshall Pickering.

Tidball, Derek (2001). *The Message of the Cross: Wisdom Unsearchable, Love Indestructible*. Leicester, IVP.

Tinker, Melvin (1992). "Battle for the Mind." *Churchman* 106.

Tinker, Melvin (2001). *Evangelical Concerns*. Fearn, Christian Focus.

Tomlin, Graham (2002). *The Provocative Church*. London, SPCK.

Tomlinson, Dave (1995). *The Post-Evangelical*. London, Triangle.

Torrance, Thomas (1969). *Theological Science*. Oxford, Oxford University Press.

Troeltsch, Ernst (1992 [1911]). *The Social Teaching of the Christian Churches*. Louisville, Ky., Westminster/John Knox Press.

Turner, Max (1996). *The Holy Spirit and Spiritual Gifts*. Carlisle, Paternoster.

Vanhoozer, Kevin J. (1998). *Is There a Meaning in This Text? The Bible, the Reader, and the Morality of Literary Knowledge*. Leicester, IVP.

Vanhoozer, Kevin J. (2000). The Voice and the Actor. *Evangelical Futures: A Conversation on Theological Method*. John G. Stackhouse, Ed. Grand Rapids, Mich., Baker; Leicester, IVP.

Vanhoozer, Kevin J. (2002). *First Theology: God, Scripture and Hermeneutics*. Downers Grove, Ill., Leicester, IVP.

Vanhoozer, Kevin J., Ed. (2003). *The Cambridge Companion to Postmodern Theology*. Cambridge, Cambridge University Press.

Veith, Gene Edward (1994). *Postmodern Times: A Christian Guide to Contemporary Thought and Culture*. Wheaton, Ill., Crossway.

Virgo, Terry (1985). *Restoration in the Church*. Eastbourne, Kingsway.

Virgo, Terry (1996). *A People Prepared*. Eastbourne, Kingsway.

Virgo, Terry (2001). *No Well Worn Paths*. Eastbourne, Kingsway.

Voas, David (2005). *The Gender Gap in Religiosity: Evidence from European Surveys*. Paper presented at the Religion and Gender Conference (11-13 April, 2005) of the Sociology of Religion Study Group within the British Association of Sociology, University of Lancaster.

Volf, Miroslav (1996). *Exclusion and Embrace: A Theological Exploration of Identity, Otherness, and Reconciliation*. Nashville, Abingdon Press.

Wagner, Peter C. (1984). *Leading Your Church to Growth*. Ventura, Regal.

Wagner, Peter C. (1987). *Strategies for Church Growth*. Ventura, Regal.

Wagner, Peter C. (1990). *Church Planting for a Greater Harvest*. Ventura, Regal.

Wagner, Peter C. (1997). *Your Spiritual Gifts Can Help Your Church Grow*. Ventura, Regal.

Wagner, Peter C., Ed. (1998). *The New Apostolic Churches*. Ventura, Regal.

Wagner, Peter C. (2002). *Spheres of Authority*. Colorado Springs, Wagner Publishing.

Wagner, Peter C. and F. Douglas Pennoyer, Eds. (1990). *Wrestling with Dark Angels*. Ventura, Regal.

Walker, Andrew (1989, [1985]). *Restoring the Kingdom: The Radical Christianity of the House Church Movement*. London, Hodder & Stoughton.

Walker, Andrew (1987). *Enemy Territory: The Christian Struggle for the Modern World*.

London, Hodder & Stoughton.

Walker, Andrew (1988). *Different Gospels*. London, Hodder & Stoughton.

Walker, Andrew (1996). *Telling the Story: Gospel, Mission and Culture*. London, SPCK.

Walker, Andrew (2002). Crossing the Restorationist Rubicon: From House Church to New Church. *Fundamentalism, Church and Society*. M. Percy and I. Jones, Eds. London, SPCK: 53-65.

Walker, Andrew and Kristin Aune, Eds. (2003). *On Revival*. Carlisle, Paternoster.

Wallace, Anthony F.C. (1966). *Religion: An Anthropological View*. New York, Random House.

Wallis, Arthur (1981). *The Radical Christian*. Eastbourne, Kingsway.

Wallis, Jim (1981). *The Call to Conversion*. Tring, Lion.

Wallis, Roy (1976). *The Road to Total Freedom: A Sociological Analysis of Scientology*. London, Heinemann Educational.

Wallis, Roy (1981). Yesterday's Children: Cultural and Structural Change in a New Religious Movement. *The Social Impact of New Religious Movements*. B. R. Wilson, Ed. New York, Edwin Mellen.

Wallis, Roy (1984). *Elementary Forms of the New Religious Life*. London, Routledge, Kegan Paul.

Walls, Andrew F. (2002). *The Cross-Cultural Process in Christian History*. Edinburgh, T & T Clark.

Walls, Jerry L and Joseph R Dongell (2004). *Why I Am Not a Calvinist*. Downers Grove, Ill., IVP.

Walsh, Brian J. and J. Richard Middleton (1984). *The Transforming Vision: Shaping a Christian World View*. Downers Grove, Ill., IVP.

Ward, Pete (1998). "Alpha - the McDonaldization of Religion." *Anvil* 15(4): 279-86.

Ward, Pete (2002). *Liquid Church*. Carlisle, Paternoster.

Ward, Pete (2005). *Selling Worship*. Carlisle, Paternoster.

Warfield, Bejamin B. (1918). *Counterfeit Miracles*. Phillipsburg, Presbyterian and Reformed,

Warfield, Bejamin B. (1970). *Selected Shorter Writings*. Phillipsburg, Presbyterian and Reformed, web edition, www.oaksoft.org.

Warner, Rob (1999 [1994]). *21st Century Church*. London, Hodder & Stoughton; Eastbourne, Kingsway.

Warner, Rob (2003). Ecstatic Spirituality and Entrepreneurial Revivalism. *On Revival: A Critical Examination*. A. Walker and K. Aune, Eds. Carlisle, 2003: 221-238

Warner, Rob (2006). "Pluralism and Voluntarism in the English Religious Economy." *Journal of Contemporary Religion* 21(3): 389-404

Warner, Rob (2008). "The Evangelical Matrix: Mapping Diversity and Trajectories in Theology and Social Policy." *Evangelical Quarterly*.

Warren, Max (1944). *What Is an Evangelical? An Enquiry*. London, Church Book Room.

Warren, Max (1976) *I Believe in the Great Commission*. London, Hodder & Stoughton.

Warren, Rick (1996). *The Purpose Driven Church*. Grand Rapids, Mich., Zondervan.

Warren, Rick (2003). *Daily Inspiration for the Purpose Driven Life: Scriptural Reflections from the 40 Days of Purpose*. Grand Rapids, Mich., Zondervan.

Warren, Rick (2003). *The Purpose Driven Life*. Grand Rapids, Mich., Zondervan.

Watson, David C. K. (1976). *I Believe in Evangelism*. London, Hodder & Stoughton.

Watson, David C. K. (1978). *I Believe in the Church*. London, Hodder & Stoughton.

Watt, David Harrington (1991). *A Transforming Faith: Explorations of Twentieth-Century American Evangelicalism*. New Brunswick, N.J, Rutgers University Press.

Webber, Robert (1985). *Evangelicals on the Canterbury Trail: Why Evangelicals Are Attracted to the Liturgical Church.* Waco, Word Books.

Webber, Robert (1999). *Ancient-Future Faith: Rethinking Evangelicalism for a Postmodern World.* Grand Rapids, Mich., Baker.

Webber, Robert (2002). *The Younger Evangelicals: Facing the Challenges of the New World.* Grand Rapids, Mich., Baker.

Weber, Max (ET 1948, new edition 1991). Bureacracy. *From Max Weber.* H. H. Gerth and C. Wright Mill, Eds. London, New York, Routledge: 196-244.

Weber, Max (ET 1948, new edition 1991). The Meaning of Discipline. *From Max Weber.* H. H. Gerth and C. Wright Mill, Eds. London, New York, Routledge: 253-264.

Weber, Max (ET 1948, new edition 1991). The Protestant Sects and the Spirit of Capitalism. *From Max Weber.* H. H. Gerth and C. Wright Mill, Eds. London, New York, Routledge: 302-322.

Weber, Max (ET 1948, new edition 1991). Religious Rejections of the World and Their Directions. *From Max Weber.* H. H. Gerth and C. Wright Mill, Eds. London, New York, Routledge: 323-362.

Weber, Max (ET 1948, new edition 1991). The Sociology of Charismatic Authority. *From Max Weber.* H. H. Gerth and C. Wright Mill, Eds. London, New York, Routledge: 245-252.

Weber, Max (ET 1958). *The Protestant Ethic and the Spirit of Capitalism.* New York, Scribner's.

Wells, David F. (1984). *The Person of Christ: A Biblical and Historical Analysis of the Incarnation.* Westchester, Ill; London, Crossway; Marshall Morgan & Scott.

Wells, David F. (1993). *No Place for Truth, or, Whatever Happened to Evangelical Theology?* Grand Rapids, Mich., Eerdmans.

Wells, David F. (1994). *God in the Wasteland: The Reality of Truth in a World of Fading Dreams.* Grand Rapids, Mich, Eerdmans.

Wells, David F. (1994). On Being Evangelical. *Evangelicalism: Comparative Studies of Popular Protestantism in North America, the British Isles, and Beyond, 1700-1990.* M. A. Noll, D. W. Bebbington and G. A. Rawlyk, Eds. New York, Oxford, Oxford University Press: 389-410.

Wells, David F. (1998). *Losing Our Virtue: Why the Church Must Recover Its Moral Vision.* Leicester, IVP.

Wells, David F. and John D. Woodbridge (1975). *The Evangelicals: What They Believe, Who They Are, Where They Are Changing.* Nashville, Abingdon Press.

Whitefield, George (1960). *George Whitefield's Journals.* London, Banner of Truth.

Whyte, William Foote (1955). *Street Corner Society: The Social Structure of an Italian Slum.* Chicago, London, University of Chicago Press.

Williams, D. H. (1999). *Retrieving the Tradition and Renewing Evangelicalism.* Grand Rapids, Mich., Eerdmans.

Williams, Eric (1944). *Capitalism and Slavery.* Chapel Hill, University of North Carolina Press.

Williams, Rowan (1987). *Arius: Heresy and Tradition.* London, Darton, Longman & Todd.

Williams, Rowan (1992). "Saving Time: Thoughts on Practice, Patience and Vision." *New Blackfriars* 73, no 861, June 1992: 319-326.

Williams, Rowan (2000). *On Christian Theology.* Oxford, Blackwell.

Wilson, A. N. (1999). *God's Funeral.* London, John Murray.

Wilson, Bryan R (1982). *Religion in Sociological Perspective.* Oxford, Oxford University

Press.

Wilson, Bryan R. (1966). *Religion in Secular Society: A Sociological Comment*. London, C.A. Watts.

Wilson, Bryan R. (1970). *Religious Sects: A Sociological Study*. London, Weidenfeld & Nicolson.

Wilson, Bryan R., Ed. (1981). *The Social Impact of New Religious Movements*. New York, Edwin Mellen.

Wimber, John and Kevin Springer (1985). *Power Evangelism: Signs and Wonders Today*. London, Hodder & Stoughton.

Wimber, John and Kevin Springer (1987). *Power Healing*. London, Hodder & Stoughton.

Wittgenstein, Ludwig (1974). *Tractatus Logico-Philosophicus*. London, New York, Routledge.

Wittgenstein, Ludwig (2001). *Philosophical Investigations*. Oxford, Blackwell.

Wolffe, John (1994). *God and Greater Britain - Religious and National Life in Britain and Ireland, 1843-1945*. London, Routledge.

Wolffe, John (1995). *Evangelical Faith and Public Zeal: Evangelicals and Society in Britain, 1780-1980*. London, SPCK.

Wolfgang, Marvin E and Franco Ferracuti (1970). Subculture of Violence: An Integrated Conceptualization. *The Sociology of Subcultures*. David O. Arnold, Ed. Berkeley, Glendessary Press: 135-149.

Woodhead, Linda, Ed. (2001). *Peter Berger and the Study of Religion*. London, Routledge.

Woodhead, Linda and Paul Heelas, Eds. (2000). *Religion in Modern Times*. Religion and Modernity. Oxford, Blackwell.

Woodward, James and Stephen Pattison, Eds. (2000). *The Blackwell Reader in Pastoral and Practical Theology*. Oxford, Blackwell.

World Council of Churches (1982). *Baptism, Eucharist and Ministry*. Geneva, World Council of Churches.

World Council of Churches (1986-1988). *Churches Respond to Baptism, Eucharist and Ministry (6 Vols)*. Geneva, World Council of Churches.

Wright, N. T. (1991). *The Climax of the Covenant: Christ and the Law in Pauline Theology*. Edinburgh, T & T Clark; Minneapolis, Fortress.

Wright, N. T. (1992). *The New Testament and the People of God*. London, SPCK.

Wright, N. T. (1996). *Jesus and the Victory of God*. London, SPCK.

Wright, N. T. (2001). The Shape of Justification. www.angelfire.com/mi2/paulpage/Shape.html

Wright, N. T. (2002). The Letter to the Romans. *The New Interpreter's Bible, Volume X*. Nashville, Abingdon Press.

Wright, N. T. (2003). *The Resurrection of the Son of God*. London, SPCK.

Wright, Nigel G. (1989). *The Fair Face of Evil*. London, Marshall Pickering.

Wright, Nigel G. (1991). *Challenge to Change*. Eastbourne, Kingsway.

Wright, Nigel G. (1996). *The Radical Evangelical*. London, SPCK.

Wright, Nigel G. (2000). *Disavowing Constantine: Mission, Church and the Social Order in the Theologies of John Howard Yoder and Jurgen Moltmann*. Carlisle, Paternoster.

Wuthnow, Robert (1988). *The Restructuring of American Religion*. Princeton, Princeton University Press.

Wuthnow, Robert (1992). *Rediscovering the Sacred: Perspectives on Religion in Contemporary Society*. Grand Rapids, Mich., Eerdmans.

Wuthnow, Robert (1998). *After Heaven: Spirituality in America since the 1950s*. Berkeley and Los Angeles, University of California Press.

Yeats, Charles, Ed. (1995). *Has Keele Failed? Reform in the Church of England.* London, Hodder & Stoughton.

Yinger, J Milton (1960). "Contraculture and Subculture." *American Sociological Review* 25: 625-635.

Young, Lawrence A, Ed. (1997). *Rational Choice Theory and Religion.* New York, London, Routledge.

Zizioulas, John (1985). *Being as Communion: Studies in Personhood and the Church.* Crestwood, N.Y, St Vladimir's Seminary Press.

General Index

Abraham, William, 4, 9, 26, 28, 106, 232, 250

activism, 16-17, 19, 25, 53, 55, 62-3, 81, 100, 108, 165, 230, 238, 240, 248

ACUTE, 62, 250

All Soul's, Langham Place, 133

Allen, Leslie, 215, 250

Alpha, 21, 74, 8-8, 90-1, 93, 115-37, 144, 234, 262, 268, 274

American Evangelical Theological Society, 9

Ammerman, Nancy, 1, 28, 141, 151, 231, 250

Anabaptist, 238-9, 248

Anglican Right, 223

Anglican, Anglicanism, 1, 3, 30, 39-40, 44-5, 48-53, 56-7, 60-1, 67, 71-3, 79, 88-9, 107, 112, 115, 129, 133, 135, 139, 144, 149-50, 153, 162, 174-81, 191-3, 205, 207, 221-3, 228, 230, 239, 250-1, 254-5, 259, 262, 264, 268, 270, 277

anthropology, negative, 154, 219

anthropology, positive, 167, 212, 217

anti-liberal, 204, 223

Arnold, Matthew, 211

Assemblies of God, 21, 49, 52, 160

atonement, 6, 9, 13, 154, 157, 160, 162, 164-6, 169, 174, 183, 185, 189, 190, 200, 202-3, 208, 213, 217, 219, 223, 225-9, 231, 253, 258, 260-1, 263, 266-7, 272

penal substitution, 6, 9, 13, 17, 34, 149, 154-5, 157, 160, 162, 166, 169, 174, 180, 189-90, 201-3, 205-6, 208, 213, 217, 225-6, 228, 231, 235

Augustine, 16, 17

Bainbridge, William, 22, 27, 32, 41, 75, 137, 140, 172, 242, 271

Baptist, 1, 4, 21, 31, 48-50, 52-3, 67, 71, 73, 79, 91, 107, 112, 117, 151-3, 177, 179, 207, 212, 214, 231, 237-9, 242, 250-1, 257, 259, 265-7, 269

Baptist Union of Great Britain and Northern Ireland, 21, 48, 52, 79, 116-7, 151, 177, 212, 251, 257

Barclay, Oliver, 17, 94, 110, 171, 180, 209, 251

Barnett, Paul, 12-13, 234, 251

Barrr, James, 8, 28, 65, 79, 139, 168, 215, 229, 237, 251

Barth, Karl, 8, 12, 17, 215, 251, 261

Barton, John, 208, 251

Bash camps, 122, 131

Bebbington, David, 1, 2, 8, 16-20, 28-9, 34, 41, 65, 81, 97, 113, 143-4, 152, 199, 234, 251, 267, 269, 275

BEC, 40, 138, 160, 165-7, 171, 172

Bell, Daniel, 232, 251

Bellah, Robert, 27, 69, 139, 144, 251

Berger, Peter, 22, 24-5, 27, 33-4, 41, 67, 81, 98, 142, 242, 252, 276

Bibby, Reginald, 27-8, 141, 143, 252

Bible

biblical criticism, 26, 196, 214

inerrancy, 6, 7, 9, 149, 153, 155, 157, 160, 166, 171, 174, 187, 189, 191-9, 203, 208-9, 214, 217, 223-4, 229, 231, 235

infallibility, 6, 9, 34, 149, 153, 155, 158-60, 163-4, 166, 171,

Studies in Evangelical History and Thought
(All titles uniform with this volume)
Dates in bold are of projected publication

Andrew Atherstone
Oxford's Protestant Spy
The Controversial Career of Charles Golightly
Charles Golightly (1807–85) was a notorious Protestant polemicist. His life was dedicated to resisting the spread of ritualism and liberalism within the Church of England and the University of Oxford. For half a century he led many memorable campaigns, such as building a martyr's memorial and attempting to close a theological college. John Henry Newman, Samuel Wilberforce and Benjamin Jowett were among his adversaries. This is the first study of Golightly's controversial career.
2006 / 1-84227-364-7 / approx. 324pp

Clyde Binfield
Victorian Nonconformity in Eastern England
Studies of Victorian religion and society often concentrate on cities, suburbs, and industrialisation. This study provides a contrast. Victorian Eastern England—Essex, Suffolk, Norfolk, Cambridgeshire, and Huntingdonshire—was rural, traditional, relatively unchanging. That is nonetheless a caricature which discounts the industry in Norwich and Ipswich (as well as in Haverhill, Stowmarket and Leiston) and ignores the impact of London on Essex, of railways throughout the region, and of an ancient but changing university (Cambridge) on the county town which housed it. It also entirely ignores the political implications of such changes in a region noted for the variety of its religious Dissent since the seventeenth century. This book explores Victorian Eastern England and its Nonconformity. It brings to a wider readership a pioneering thesis which has made a major contribution to a fresh evolution of English religion and society.
2006 / 1-84227-216-0 / approx. 274pp

John Brencher
Martyn Lloyd-Jones (1899–1981) and Twentieth-Century Evangelicalism
This study critically demonstrates the significance of the life and ministry of Martyn Lloyd-Jones for post-war British evangelicalism and demonstrates that his preaching was his greatest influence on twentieth-century Christianity. The factors which shaped his view of the church are examined, as is the way his reformed evangelicalism led to a separatist ecclesiology which divided evangelicals.
2002 / 1-84227-051-6 / xvi + 268pp

Jonathan D. Burnham
A Story of Conflict
The Controversial Relationship between Benjamin Wills Newton and
John Nelson Darby
Burnham explores the controversial relationship between the two principal
leaders of the early Brethren movement. In many ways Newton and Darby were
products of their times, and this study of their relationship provides insight not
only into the dynamics of early Brethrenism, but also into the progress of
nineteenth-century English and Irish evangelicalism.
2004 / 1-84227-191-1 / xxiv + 268pp

Grayson Carter
Anglican Evangelicals
Protestant Secessions from the Via Media, c.1800–1850
This study examines, within a chronological framework, the major themes and
personalities which influenced the outbreak of a number of Evangelical clerical
and lay secessions from the Church of England and Ireland during the first half
of the nineteenth century. Though the number of secessions was relatively
small between a hundred and two hundred of the 'Gospel' clergy abandoned
the Church during this period—their influence was considerable, especially in
highlighting in embarrassing fashion the tensions between the evangelical
conversionist imperative and the principles of a national religious establishment.
Moreover, through much of this period there remained, just beneath the surface,
the potential threat of a large Evangelical disruption similar to that which
occurred in Scotland in 1843. Consequently, these secessions provoked great
consternation within the Church and within Evangelicalism itself, they
contributed to the outbreak of millennial speculation following the
'constitutional revolution' of 1828–32, they led to the formation of several new
denominations, and they sparked off a major Church–State crisis over the legal
right of a clergyman to secede and begin a new ministry within Protestant
Dissent.
2007 / 1-84227-401-5 / xvi + 470pp

J.N. Ian Dickson
Beyond Religious Discourse
Sermons, Preaching and Evangelical Protestants in Nineteenth-Century
Irish Society
Drawing extensively on primary sources, this pioneer work in modern religious history explores the training of preachers, the construction of sermons and how Irish evangelicalism and the wider movement in Great Britain and the United States shaped the preaching event. Evangelical preaching and politics, sectarianism, denominations, education, class, social reform, gender, and revival are examined to advance the argument that evangelical sermons and preaching went significantly beyond religious discourse. The result is a book for those with interests in Irish history, culture and belief, popular religion and society, evangelicalism, preaching and communication.
2005 / 1-84227-217-9 / approx. 324pp

Neil T.R. Dickson
Brethren in Scotland 1838–2000
A Social Study of an Evangelical Movement
The Brethren were remarkably pervasive throughout Scottish society. This study of the Open Brethren in Scotland places them in their social context and examines their growth, development and relationship to society.
2003 / 1-84227-113-X / xxviii + 510pp

Crawford Gribben and Timothy C.F. Stunt (eds)
Prisoners of Hope?
Aspects of Evangelical Millennialism in Britain and Ireland, 1800–1880
This volume of essays offers a comprehensive account of the impact of evangelical millennialism in nineteenth-century Britain and Ireland.
2004 / 1-84227-224-1 / xiv + 208pp

Khim Harris
Evangelicals and Education
Evangelical Anglicans and Middle-Class Education in
Nineteenth-Century England
This ground breaking study investigates the history of English public schools founded by nineteenth-century Evangelicals. It documents the rise of middle-class education and Evangelical societies such as the influential Church Association, and includes a useful biographical survey of prominent Evangelicals of the period.
2004 / 1-84227-250-0 / xviii + 422pp

July 2005

Mark Hopkins
Nonconformity's Romantic Generation
Evangelical and Liberal Theologies in Victorian England
A study of the theological development of key leaders of the Baptist and
Congregational denominations at their period of greatest influence, including
C.H. Spurgeon and R.W. Dale, and of the controversies in which those among
them who embraced and rejected the liberal transformation of their evangelical
heritage opposed each other.
2004 / 1-84227-150-4 / xvi + 284pp

Don Horrocks
Laws of the Spiritual Order
*Innovation and Reconstruction in the Soteriology of Thomas Erskine
of Linlathen*
Don Horrocks argues that Thomas Erskine's unique historical and theological
significance as a soteriological innovator has been neglected. This timely
reassessment reveals Erskine as a creative, radical theologian of central and
enduring importance in Scottish nineteenth-century theology, perhaps equivalent
in significance to that of S.T. Coleridge in England.
2004 / 1-84227-192-X / xx + 362pp

Kenneth S. Jeffrey
When the Lord Walked the Land
The 1858–62 Revival in the North East of Scotland
Previous studies of revivals have tended to approach religious movements from
either a broad, national or a strictly local level. This study of the multifaceted
nature of the 1859 revival as it appeared in three distinct social contexts within a
single region reveals the heterogeneous nature of simultaneous religious
movements in the same vicinity.
2002 / 1-84227-057-5 / xxiv + 304pp

John Kenneth Lander
Itinerant Temples
Tent Methodism, 1814–1832
Tent preaching began in 1814 and the Tent Methodist sect resulted from
disputes with Bristol Wesleyan Methodists in 1820. The movement spread to
parts of Gloucestershire, Wiltshire, London and Liverpool, among other places.
Its demise started in 1826 after which one leader returned to the Wesleyans and
others became ministers in the Congregational and Baptist denominations.
2003 / 1-84227-151-2 / xx + 268pp

Donald M. Lewis
Lighten Their Darkness
The Evangelical Mission to Working-Class London, 1828–1860
This is a comprehensive and compelling study of the Church and the complexities of nineteenth-century London. Challenging our understanding of the culture in working London at this time, Lewis presents a well-structured and illustrated work that contributes substantially to the study of evangelicalism and mission in nineteenth-century Britain.
2001 / 1-84227-074-5 / xviii + 372pp

Herbert McGonigle
'Sufficient Saving Grace'
John Wesley's Evangelical Arminianism
A thorough investigation of the theological roots of John Wesley's evangelical Arminianism and how these convictions were hammered out in controversies on predestination, limited atonement and the perseverance of the saints.
2001 / 1-84227-045-1 / xvi + 350pp

Lisa S. Nolland
A Victorian Feminist Christian
Josephine Butler, the Prostitutes and God
Josephine Butler was an unlikely candidate for taking up the cause of prostitutes, as she did, with a fierce and self-disregarding passion. This book explores the particular mix of perspectives and experiences that came together to envision and empower her remarkable achievements. It highlights the vital role of her spirituality and the tragic loss of her daughter.
2004 / 1-84227-225-X / xxiv + 328pp

Don J. Payne
The Theology of the Christian Life in J.I. Packer's Thought
Theological Anthropology, Theological Method, and the Doctrine of Sanctification
J.I. Packer has wielded widespread influence on evangelicalism for more than three decades. This study pursues a nuanced understanding of Packer's theology of sanctification by tracing the development of his thought, showing how he reflects a particular version of Reformed theology, and examining the unique influence of theological anthropology and theological method on this area of his theology.
2005 / 1-84227-397-3 / *approx. 374pp*

Ian M. Randall
Evangelical Experiences
A Study in the Spirituality of English Evangelicalism 1918–1939
This book makes a detailed historical examination of evangelical spirituality
between the First and Second World Wars. It shows how patterns of devotion
led to tensions and divisions. In a wide-ranging study, Anglican, Wesleyan,
Reformed and Pentecostal-charismatic spiritualities are analysed.
1999 / 0-85364-919-7 / xii + 310pp

Ian M. Randall
Spirituality and Social Change
The Contribution of F.B. Meyer (1847–1929)
This is a fresh appraisal of F.B. Meyer (1847–1929), a leading Free Church
minister. Having been deeply affected by holiness spirituality, Meyer became
the Keswick Convention's foremost international speaker. He combined
spirituality with effective evangelism and socio-political activity. This study
shows Meyer's significant contribution to spiritual renewal and social change.
2003 / 1-84227-195-4 / xx + 184pp

James Robinson
Pentecostal Origins
Early Pentecostalism in Ireland in the Context of the British Isles
Harvey Cox describes Pentecostalism as 'the fascinating spiritual child of our
time' that has the potential, at the global scale, to contribute to the 'reshaping of
religion in the twenty-first century'. This study grounds such sentiments by
examining at the local scale the origin, development and nature of
Pentecostalism in Ireland in its first twenty years. Illustrative, in a paradigmatic
way, of how Pentecostalism became established within one region of the British
Isles, it sets the story within the wider context of formative influences emanating
from America, Europe and, in particular, other parts of the British Isles. As a
synoptic regional study in Pentecostal history it is the first survey of its kind.
2005 / 1-84227-329-1 / xxviii + 378pp

Geoffrey Robson
Dark Satanic Mills?
Religion and Irreligion in Birmingham and the Black Country
This book analyses and interprets the nature and extent of popular Christian
belief and practice in Birmingham and the Black Country during the first half of
the nineteenth century, with particular reference to the impact of cholera
epidemics and evangelism on church extension programmes.
2002 / 1-84227-102-4 / xiv + 294pp

July 2005

Roger Shuff
Searching for the True Church
Brethren and Evangelicals in Mid-Twentieth-Century England
Roger Shuff holds that the influence of the Brethren movement on wider
evangelical life in England in the twentieth century is often underrated. This
book records and accounts for the fact that Brethren reached the peak of their
strength at the time when evangelicalism was at it lowest ebb, immediately
before World War II. However, the movement then moved into persistent
decline as evangelicalism regained ground in the post war period.
Accompanying this downward trend has been a sharp accentuation of the
contrast between Brethren congregations who engage constructively with the
non-Brethren scene and, at the other end of the spectrum, the isolationist group
commonly referred to as 'Exclusive Brethren'.
2005 / 1-84227-254-3 / xviii+ 296pp

James H.S. Steven
Worship in the Spirit
Charismatic Worship in the Church of England
This book explores the nature and function of worship in six Church of England
churches influenced by the Charismatic Movement, focusing on congregational
singing and public prayer ministry. The theological adequacy of such ritual is
discussed in relation to pneumatological and christological understandings in
Christian worship.
2002 / 1-84227-103-2 / xvi + 238pp

Peter K. Stevenson
God in Our Nature
The Incarnational Theology of John McLeod Campbell
This radical reassessment of Campbell's thought arises from a comprehensive
study of his preaching and theology. Previous accounts have overlooked both his
sermons and his Christology. This study examines the distinctive Christology
evident in his sermons and shows that it sheds new light on Campbell's much
debated views about atonement.
2004 / 1-84227-218-7 / xxiv + 458pp

Kenneth J. Stewart
Restoring the Reformation
British Evangelicalism and the Réveil at Geneva 1816–1849
Restoring the Reformation traces British missionary initiative in post-Revolutionary Francophone Europe from the genesis of the London Missionary Society, the visits of Robert Haldane and Henry Drummond, and the founding of the Continental Society. While British Evangelicals aimed at the reviving of a foreign Protestant cause of momentous legend, they received unforeseen reciprocating emphases from the Continent which forced self-reflection on Evangelicalism's own relationship to the Reformation.
2006 / 1-84227-392-2 / approx. 190pp

Martin Wellings
Evangelicals Embattled
Responses of Evangelicals in the Church of England to Ritualism, Darwinism and Theological Liberalism 1890–1930
In the closing years of the nineteenth century and the first decades of the twentieth century Anglican Evangelicals faced a series of challenges. In responding to Anglo-Catholicism, liberal theology, Darwinism and biblical criticism, the unity and identity of the Evangelical school were severely tested.
2003 / 1-84227-049-4 / xviii + 352pp

James Whisenant
A Fragile Unity
Anti-Ritualism and the Division of Anglican Evangelicalism in the Nineteenth Century
This book deals with the ritualist controversy (approximately 1850–1900) from the perspective of its evangelical participants and considers the divisive effects it had on the party.
2003 / 1-84227-105-9 / xvi + 530pp

Haddon Willmer
Evangelicalism 1785–1835: An Essay (1962) and Reflections (2004)
Awarded the Hulsean Prize in the University of Cambridge in 1962, this interpretation of a classic period of English Evangelicalism, by a young church historian, is now supplemented by reflections on Evangelicalism from the vantage point of a retired Professor of Theology.
2006 / 1-84227-219-5 / approx. 350pp

Linda Wilson
Constrained by Zeal
Female Spirituality amongst Nonconformists 1825–1875
Constrained by Zeal investigates the neglected area of Nonconformist female spirituality. Against the background of separate spheres, it analyses the experience of women from four denominations, and argues that the churches provided a 'third sphere' in which they could find opportunities for participation.

2000 / 0-85364-972-3 / xvi + 294pp

Paternoster
9 Holdom Avenue,
Bletchley,
Milton Keynes MK1 1QR,
United Kingdom
Web: www.authenticmedia.co.uk/paternoster

July 2005